COPPER SCROLL STUDIES

edited by

GEORGE J. BROOKE
and
PHILIP R. DAVIES

T & T CLARK INTERNATIONAL
A Continuum imprint
LONDON • NEW YORK

To Joan Allegro, with gratitude

Published by T&T Clark International
A Continuum imprint
The Tower Building, 11 York Road, London SE1 7NX
15 East 26th Street, Suite 1703, New York, NY 10010

www.tandtclark.com

First published 2002 in the JSPS series
This edition published 2004

British Library Cataloguing-in-Publication Data
A catalogue record for this book is available from the British Library

ISBN 0567084566 (paperback)

Typeset by Sheffield Academic Press
Printed on acid-free paper in Great Britain by Antony Rowe Ltd, Chippenham

CONTENTS

Part III
INTERPRETING THE COPPER SCROLL

List of Figures

List of Tables

Acknowledgments

The Manchester–Sheffield Centre for Dead Sea Scrolls Research was launched in 1994 and since then has been involved in various research projects such as the preparation and publication of *The Allegro Qumran Collection* (edited by George J. Brooke with the collaboration of Helen K. Bond; Leiden: Brill and IDC, 1996) of photographic images as an official supplement to *The Dead Sea Scrolls on Microfiche* (edited by Emanuel Tov with the collaboration of Stephen J. Pfann; Leiden: Brill and IDC, 1993). The International Symposium on the Copper Scroll was conceived by us as a conference at which the focus would be on just one problematic scroll. The aims and purposes of the symposium thus resembled those of the International Symposium on the Temple Scroll which was held in Manchester in 1987 to mark the tenth anniversary of the publication of 11QT[a] (see George J. Brooke [ed.], *Temple Scroll Studies: Papers Presented at the International Symposium on the Temple Scroll, Manchester, December 1987* [JSPSup, 7; Sheffield: JSOT Press, 1989]).

Mounting an international meeting of scholars like this requires financial subsidy. We are very grateful to the following for their financial assistance: the Anglo-Israel Archaeological Society and the Foreign Ministry, Government of Israel (for sponsoring Hanan Eshel's contribution); Bodycote International plc (Mr J.C. Dwek, Director); the Department of Religions and Theology, University of Manchester; the Faculty of Arts Research Fund, University of Manchester; the Manfred and Anne Lehmann Foundation, New York (for sponsoring Israel Knohl's contribution); Sheffield Academic Press; the University of Manchester Institute of Science and Technology; and the University of Manchester Research Support Fund. Dr Manfred Lehmann was unable to attend the symposium but his innovative article, 'Identification of the Copper Scroll Based on its Technical Terms', *Revue de Qumrân* 17.1 (1964), pp. 97-105, was distributed at his suggestion to all participants.

The symposium came shortly after fresh restoration work on the Copper Scroll had been completed in France. We are grateful to Electricité de

France for permission to publish images which accompany the article by Régis Bertholon, Noël Lacoudre and Jorge Vasquez. Before the restoration work was begun, more detailed photographic analysis of the Scroll had been undertaken by West Semitic Research and we are grateful to Bruce and Ken Zuckerman for permission to publish the images which accompany the article by Marilyn Lundberg and Bruce Zuckerman. We are also grateful to Elsevier Science for permission to republish the short article by Professor W. Johnson and to E. Crowley of Windsor, Ontario, Canada, for translating the article by Émile Puech.

George J. Brooke, Manchester
Philip R. Davies, Sheffield

Abbreviations

AASOR	Annual of the American Schools of Oriental Research
AB	Anchor Bible
ABD	David Noel Freedman (ed.), *The Anchor Bible Dictionary* (New York: Doubleday, 1992)
ADAJ	*Annual of the Department of Antiquities of Jordan*
AHL	Academy of the Hebrew Language
ARN	*Abot de Rabbi Nathan*
ATD	Das Alte Testament Deutsch
BA	*Biblical Archaeologist*
BARev	*Biblical Archaeology Review*
BASOR	*Bulletin of the American Schools of Oriental Research*
BDB	Francis Brown, S.R. Driver and Charles A. Briggs, *A Hebrew and English Lexicon of the Old Testament* (Oxford: Clarendon Press, 1907)
BETL	Bibliotheca ephemeridum theologicarum lovaniensium
BHS	*Biblia hebraica stuttgartensia*
Bib	*Biblica*
BibOr	Biblica et orientalia
BJRL	*Bulletin of the John Rylands University Library of Manchester*
BJS	Brown Judaic Studies
BR	*Bible Review*
BZ	*Biblische Zeitschrift*
BZAW	Beihefte zur *ZAW*
CAD	Ignace I. Gelb *et al.* (eds.), *The Assyrian Dictionary of the Oriental Institute of the University of Chicago* (Chicago: Oriental Institute, 1964–)
CII	*Corpus inscriptionum iudaicarum*
CIL	*Corpus inscriptionum latinarum*
CIS	*Corpus inscriptionum semiticarum*
CNRS	Centre National de la Recherche Scientifique
DBSup	*Dictionnaire de la Bible, Supplément*
DJD(J)	Discoveries in the Judaean Desert (of Jordan)
DSD	*Dead Sea Discoveries*
DSS	Dead Sea Scrolls
EBAF	Ecole Biblique et Archéologique Française (Jerusalem)
EBH	Early Biblical Hebrew

EDF	Electricité de France
EncJud	*Encyclopaedia Judaica*
ETL	*Ephemerides theologicae lovanienses*
GKC	*Gesenius' Hebrew Grammar* (ed. E. Kautzsch, revised and trans. A.E. Cowley; Oxford: Clarendon Press, 1910)
HALAT	Ludwig Koehler *et al.* (eds.), *Hebräisches und aramäisches Lexikon zum Alten Testament* (5 vols.; Leiden: E.J. Brill, 1967–95)
HSM	Harvard Semitic Monographs
HTR	*Harvard Theological Review*
ICC	International Critical Commentary
IEJ	*Israel Exploration Journal*
JAOS	*Journal of the American Oriental Society*
JBL	*Journal of Biblical Literature*
JJS	*Journal of Jewish Studies*
JNES	*Journal of Near Eastern Studies*
JQR	*Jewish Quarterly Review*
JSJ	*Journal for the Study of Judaism in the Persian, Hellenistic and Roman Period*
JSOT	*Journal for the Study of the Old Testament*
JSOTSup	*Journal for the Study of the Old Testament*, Supplement Series
JSPSup	*Journal for the Study of the Pseudepigrapha*, Supplement Series
JTS	*Journal of Theological Studies*
KB	Ludwig Koehler and Walter Baumgartner (eds.), *Lexicon in Veteris Testamenti libros* (Leiden: E.J. Brill, 1953)
KhQ	Khirbet Qumran
LA	*Liber Annuus*
LBH	Late Biblical Hebrew
LQ	*Lutheran Quarterly*
MGWJ	*Monatsschrift für Geschichte und Wissenschaft des Judentums*
NEA	*Near Eastern Archaeology*
NTOA	Novum Testamentum et orbis antiquus
OLZ	*Orientalistische Literaturzeitung*
OTL	Old Testament Library
PAM	Palestine Archaeological Museum (Photograph Number)
PEQ	*Palestine Exploration Quarterly*
RB	*Revue biblique*
RevQ	*Revue de Qumran*
RHR	*Revue de l'histoire des religions*
SBT	Studies in Biblical Theology
STDJ	Studies on the Texts of the Desert of Judah
TLG	Thesaurus Linguae Graecae
TLZ	*Theologische Literaturzeitung*
UMIST	University of Manchester Institute of Science and Technology

VT	*Vetus Testamentum*
VTSup	*Vetus Testamentum*, Supplements
WBC	Word Biblical Commentary
WSRP	West Semitic Research Project
ZAW	*Zeitschrift für die alttestamentliche Wissenschaft*
ZDPV	*Zeitschrift des deutschen Palästina-Vereins*

References in the scrolls are given in the following ways: (1) where separate columns are readily identifiable, the reference to column and line number is given in standard Arabic numerals (3Q15 1.3 = Copper Scroll column 1, line 3); (2) where the manuscript evidence is more fragmentary, the fragment number is given in Arabic numerals introduced by the abbreviation frag(s)., the column number (where appropriate) in small roman numerals introduced by the abbreviation col(s)., and the line number in Arabic numerals.

LIST OF CONTRIBUTORS

MEIR BAR-ILAN
Jewish History Department, Bar-Ilan University, Israel

RÉGIS BERTHOLON
Conservation and Restoration Section, University of Paris

GEORGE J. BROOKE
University of Manchester, England

PHILIP R. DAVIES
Department of Biblical Studies, University of Sheffield, England

JOHN F. ELWOLDE
Faculty of Oriental Studies, University of Oxford, England

HANAN ESHEL
Bar-Ilan University, Israel

RUTH FIDLER
University of Haifa, Israel

STEPHEN GORANSON
Duke University, North Carolina, USA

WILLIAM JOHNSON
St Austell, Cornwall, England

ISRAEL KNOHL
Hebrew University of Jerusalem, Israel

NOËL LACOUDRE
Laboratoire Valectra, Electricité de France, GDL, Saint-Denis, France

ARMIN LANGE
University of North Carolina, Chapel Hill, USA

JUDAH LEFKOVITS
Flushing, New York, USA

JOHN LÜBBE
University of South Africa, Pretoria, South Africa

MARILYN LUNDBERG
West Semitic Research, California, USA

PIOTR MUCHOWSKI
Adam Mickiewicz University, Poznań, Poland

STEPHEN J. PFANN
University of the Holy Land, Jerusalem, Israel

ÉMILE PUECH
École Biblique et Archéologique Française, Jerusalem and CNRS, Paris, France

LAWRENCE H. SCHIFFMAN
New York University, New York, USA

BRENDA LESLEY SEGAL
Yardley, Pennsylvania, USA

BARBARA THIERING
Mosman, New South Wales, Australia

LIKA TOV
Jerusalem, Israel

JORGE VASQUEZ
Artefact *Conservation préventive et restauration*, Paris, France

MICHAEL O. WISE
Northwestern College, Minnesota, USA

AL WOLTERS
Redeemer University College, Ontario, Canada

BRUCE ZUCKERMAN
University of Southern California and West Semitic Research, California, USA

Introduction

George J. Brooke

This volume contains 22 papers, most of which were presented at the International Symposium on the Copper Scroll that was held at the University of Manchester Institute of Science and Technology (UMIST) in September 1996. The Symposium brought together most of the world's scholars who have been working closely on the Copper Scroll in recent years and was a very enjoyable occasion. The sessions of the Symposium were held in the main building of UMIST close to where Professor H. Wright Baker and his team had worked on the scroll over 40 years before. This set of essays is fortunate to include a personal recollection of Professor Wright Baker by William Johnson, one of his students who later succeeded him in his university post. I learnt quite by chance that William Johnson had written a short study on the basis of his personal connection with Professor Wright Baker and since his essay has appeared in print in a place where few, if any, Dead Sea Scrolls scholars are likely to look, it seemed doubly suitable that it should be revised slightly and included in this volume.

The Symposium had a banquet at which the guests of honour were Mrs Joan Allegro and her son Mark. The recent publication of all of John Allegro's photographs of the Copper Scroll[1] meant that it was particularly appropriate for Joan Allegro to be present, and this collection of studies is affectionately dedicated to her as a mark of the gratitude owed to her by a generation of Dead Sea Scrolls scholars and their publishers who have found her consistently helpful in answering queries about photographs and other matters. A small book on the Copper Scroll by Al Wolters was specially published in time for the Symposium and its centrepiece, most suitably, is a set of eight previously unpublished colour photographs of the

1. George J. Brooke (ed.), *The Allegro Qumran Collection* (with the collaboration of Helen K. Bond; Leiden: E.J. Brill; IDC, 1996).

Copper Scroll from the Allegro collection.[2] Allegro's unofficial edition of the Copper Scroll is well known;[3] though his work was much less detailed than that of J.T. Milik's *editio princeps*,[4] it is interesting to note that several of the contributors to this volume prefer his readings of some of the scroll's problematic passages. Philip Davies's contribution sets Allegro's reputation with regard to the Copper Scroll in a broader context.[5]

The papers in this book are arranged in three broad categories. In the first group are studies concerned with the opening, restoration and reading of the Copper Scroll. In addition to the essays mentioned above on Wright Baker by Johnson and on Allegro by Davies, the other three studies in this section concern technical matters. Alongside the Allegro photographs recently published in their entirety, the Copper Scroll has been intensively scrutinized twice in recent years. In 1988 the Zuckerman brothers photographed the whole scroll in Amman to provide, among other things, a set of images that could be used by Professor P. Kyle McCarter[6] in the preparation of his edition of the scroll for the Princeton Seminary project under the general editorship of J.H. Charlesworth.[7] Marilyn Lundberg and Bruce Zuckerman describe some aspects of the significance of this photo-

2. Al Wolters, *The Copper Scroll: Overview, Text and Translation* (with a Foreword by George J. Brooke; Qumran Literature, Hebrew–English Edition, 1; Sheffield: Sheffield Academic Press, 1996).

3. John M. Allegro, *The Treasure of the Copper Scroll: The Opening and Decipherment of the Most Mysterious of the Dead Sea Scrolls, a Unique Inventory of Buried Treasure* (London: Routledge & Kegan Paul, 1960); a second revised edition was published in paperback without the transliteration of the Hebrew text (Garden City, NY: Doubleday, 1964).

4. J.T. Milik, 'Le rouleau de cuivre provenant de la grotte 3Q (3Q15): Commentaire et Texte', in M. Baillet, J.T. Milik and R. de Vaux, *Les 'petites grottes' de Qumrân* (DJDJ III; Oxford: Clarendon Press, 1962), pp. 211-302.

5. On the topic of Allegro's reputation, see also his study '*Notes en marge*: Reflections on the Publication of DJDJ 5', in H.-J. Fabry, A. Lange and H. Lichtenberger (eds.), *Qumranstudien: Vorträge und Beiträge der Teilnehmer des Qumranseminars auf dem internationalen Treffen der Society of Biblical Literature, Münster, 25.-26. Juli 1993* (Schriften des Institutum Judaicum Delitzschianum, 4; Göttingen: Vandenhoeck & Ruprecht, 1996), pp. 103-109.

6. Professor McCarter was prevented by illness from attending the Manchester Symposium.

7. James H. Charlesworth (ed.), *The Dead Sea Scrolls: Hebrew, Aramaic, and Greek Texts with English Translations* (Princeton Theological Seminary Dead Sea Scrolls Project; Tübingen: Mohr Siebeck; Louisville, KY: Westminster/John Knox Press, 1994–). The edition of the Copper Scroll is scheduled to appear in volume 9.

graphic work, and this book contains some examples of the images taken then.

Even more significantly, in the early 1990s the research wing of Electricité de France (EDF), the French electricity company, was entrusted by the Jordanian Department of Antiquities with the conservation and restoration of the Copper Scroll, and this volume contains two important studies related to that work. The first by Régis Bertholon, Noël Lacoudre and Jorge Vasquez, members of the scientific team who undertook the complex work, is a description of what was involved, both in understanding what had taken place in Manchester in the 1950s and in working on the fragile remains of the scroll in the 1990s. It was pleasing to hear them confirm that cutting the scroll into segments had been the only option and that the work done by Wright Baker had been as skilful as anyone could have been in the 1950s. Several images are included that illustrate their essay. The second study related to the recent French work of conservation is by Émile Puech, who worked alongside the scientific team as the project's epigraphist; his essay contains the principal conclusions concerning his view of how the Copper Scroll should be read in light of EDF's new work of restoration and conservation.[8]

The second part of this book contains archaeological and linguistic studies. These essays are concerned with matters of detail, smaller pieces of the jigsaw that make up how this enigmatic document should be best understood. Most of these studies consider the language of the scroll, which has many problematic features. John Lübbe discusses linguistic issues in general and urges interpreters of the language of the Copper Scroll to work within a much more subtle and varied model of how languages work than has commonly been the case; his essay can be taken as providing the beginnings of a valid framework for the analysis of the language of the scroll. John Elwolde considers the linguistic affiliation of the scroll's language and its lexicography; although much of the evidence which he discusses can be contested, he argues that the language of the Copper Scroll can be placed on a suitable trajectory in the first century CE. While much of Elwolde's comparative evidence is from Hebrew texts later than the Copper Scroll, Lawrence Schiffman compares and contrasts the architectural vocabulary of the scroll with that of the Temple Scroll:

8. As Puech's essay notes, his complete new edition of the Copper Scroll is to be published as 'Le Rouleau de Cuivre de la grotte 3 de Qumrân (3Q15)' in the volume prepared by EDF for the NTOA Series archaeologica (Göttingen: Vandenhoeck & Ruprecht; Fribourg: Presse Universitaire, forthcoming).

although some shared terms are obviously in common use, the comparison reveals once again in a striking way the biblicizing tendency of the Temple Scroll and that it predates the Copper Scroll. Armin Lange analyses the meaning of דמע in the Copper Scroll and some other literature; he argues that it should be understood at a more general level of definition than is generally the case and concludes that in the Copper Scroll the term should be translated as 'valuables' or 'treasure'. Judah Lefkovits looks at the abbreviation ככ and challenges the widely accepted view that it is short for ככרין; although some later scribes may have misunderstood the abbreviation in the way that many modern scholars have done, Lefkovits proposes instead that it is most likely an abbreviation of כסף כרשין, referring to the Persian Karsh of ten shekels.[9]

From an archaeological perspective Hanan Eshel considers the aqueducts that are referred to in the scroll and proposes several positive identifications where treasure may have been buried. Giving such appropriate attention to remains on the ground drives home the point that the contents of the scroll are very unlikely to be a matter of fiction. In a comprehensive way Stephen Pfann reviews the information on the so-called tithe jars, the כלי דמע of the Copper Scroll, in search of information about the various kinds of jar that have been found at Qumran; he argues neatly that few, if any, of the distinctive jars found there would have been produced with the intention that they should one day hold scrolls.

The third section of this book contains essays that are concerned with the broader interpretation and understanding of the Copper Scroll. An overview of the many unanswered riddles of the Copper Scroll has recently been provided by Al Wolters.[10] He has noted that the Copper Scroll's chief characteristics concern the material it is written on, its script, its orthography, its subject matter, its language, its literary structure and the Greek letters, and that the major interpretative issues for the scroll can be grouped under three main headings: the dating of the scroll, the authenticity of its treasure, and its relation to the rest of the scrolls found at or near Qumran. Many of these topics are treated in detail in this section of the book and

9. See also his recent book, *The Copper Scroll—3Q15: A Reevaluation: A New Reading, Translation and Commentary* (STDJ, 25; Leiden: E.J. Brill, 2000), pp. 471-88.

10. Wolters, *Copper Scroll*, pp. 9-18; this is the text of an article on the Copper Scroll that has subsequently also been published in L.H. Schiffman and J.C. VanderKam (eds.), *Encyclopedia of the Dead Sea Scrolls* (New York: Oxford University Press, 2000), pp. 144-48.

Piotr Muchowski's essay highlights just how, over the 40 or more years of its study, the answers to one or more of these issues have produced a very wide range of theories about the scroll.

Three essays consider how the scroll might have been written, how it might have been put together as a document. Meir Bar-Ilan proposes that the character of the text as a list is determined in large measure by the order of the hiding of the various caches of treasure. Ruth Fidler proposes alternatively that the order of the geographical locations may be used more as clues to literary structure and the religious outlook behind it than as a list of precisely how the treasure was placed in the various hiding places.[11] Al Wolters outlines and refines his theory on how a consistent pattern underlies each entry in the inventory. He has identified seven types of material: place, specification, command, distance, treasure, comment and, in a few cases, some Greek letters. Although no entry in the list contains all seven types, everything in the list is classifiable under one of the seven categories. Appreciating that there is no structural variation from this list of types allows for the settling of various disputed questions of interpretation; in his contribution Wolters provides several examples of how such disputes might best be settled.

Knowing that suitable interpretations also depend on how individual letters are read, Al Wolters also considers the scroll's palaeography and comments in detail on the apparent confusion in several places between *beth* and *mem*, between *he* and *ḥeth*, and between *waw* and *daleth* or *resh*. He argues that editors should not accept an unusual form of a letter unless there are one or more parallels in the immediately surrounding context. He intriguingly explains some of the readings in his own edition of the scroll on the basis of that methodological principle. His palaeographical comments are complemented by a brief note by Lika Tov. Many scholars, including Wolters, have noted that the scroll was probably written by more than one engraver. While working closely on the Copper Scroll in preparation for her collograph, which was commissioned for the Symposium,[12] Lika Tov came to the conclusion that the scroll was probably written by

11. A similar approach was taken by Philip S. Alexander in his informal presentation at the Symposium.

12. A reproduction of this artistic interpretation of the Copper Scroll forms the frontispiece of this book. The original belongs to the University of Manchester as a legacy of the Symposium. It was on display to the public during the 1997–98 Exhibition *Treasures from the Dead Sea: The Copper Scroll after 2000 Years* held at the Manchester Museum to mark the 50th anniversary of the discovery of Qumran Cave 1.

a very large variety of hands, more than previously suggested, and more than the four identified by David Wilmot;[13] her observations will need to be considered in future studies of the scroll's inscriptions.

Several studies have things to say about possible historical settings for the scroll. In addition to comments in some of the essays already mentioned, notably that by Émile Puech, Stephen Goranson considers the possible trans-Jordanian hints in the scroll and remains firm in his conviction that the treasure is to be linked with the Essenes as money accumulating for the future restored and purified temple. In a different vein, through an analysis of *Miqṣat Ma'aśē ha-Torah* (MMT), Israel Knohl suggests that an alliance between the Boethus priests of Jerusalem and the Essenes of Qumran explains both how the Copper Scroll itself came to be in Cave 3 and also how some of the Jerusalem Temple's treasure came to be buried at locations close to Qumran. Barbara Thiering wonders whether the treasure described in the scroll might be a reflection of Herod's bank account; Thiering also makes some very specific suggestions as to where the money was hidden. The Symposium was also fortunate to have Hartmut Stegemann present an informal summary of his view that the treasure in the scroll is indeed that from the Jerusalem Temple and represents for the most part the private accounts of wealthy individuals; it has nothing to do with Qumran or its occupants. Stegemann bases his conclusion in part on the observation that none of the items mentioned in the Copper Scroll are visible on the famous relief on the Arch of Titus, which might imply that they were indeed secreted away successfully before the Romans sacked the Temple in 70 CE. Although the Romans did indeed find some valuables, Stegemann surmises that most of the deposits were recovered by their owners after the end of the Jewish War.[14]

A set of important proposals for the understanding of the scroll were made by the late David Wilmot as he prepared his doctoral dissertation on the scroll at the University of Chicago. Michael Wise summarizes Wilmot's key conclusions and comments on them: the Copper Scroll was written by four scribes, it uses economic terminology that distinguishes between bullion and coin, its makers were associated with the treasurers of the Jerusalem Temple, and generically it is best understood as a summarizing inventory list.

13. See the comments on the contribution by Michael Wise below.

14. See H. Stegemann, *The Library of Qumran: On the Essenes, Qumran, John the Baptist, and Jesus* (Leiden: E.J. Brill; Grand Rapids, MI: Eerdmans, 1998), pp. 72-74.

In a short contribution, Brenda Lesley Segal highlights why the Copper Scroll can claim to be the most intriguing of all the Dead Sea Scrolls and she shows how it grips the imagination not only of those who would wish to find lost treasure from 2000 years ago in the wilderness, but also of many learned scholars; in fact, for Segal an imaginative study of the scholarly fascination with the scroll would be almost as rewarding as the study of the scroll itself.

The Symposium ended with a plenary session at which Israel Knohl, Émile Puech and Al Wolters, the principal speakers, interacted with the other participants. It was considered appropriate at the end of the session that there should be some attempt to see whether a consensus of opinion about the Copper Scroll was emerging in the opinions of those present. It was agreed that there was some slight confusion in the various descriptions of the discovery of the two rolls so that caution needed to be exercised in determining whether or not the scroll should be linked in some way with the other manuscript deposits in Cave 3. The opening of the scroll in Manchester was commended; the cutting of the scroll had caused very minimal loss of text. The restoration and conservation work by EDF was enthusiastically welcomed, though it was acknowledged that many matters would remain debatable, since although there could now be some greater measure of legibility, what precisely should be read was often open to a variety of opinion.

There was some general discussion of why the text had been written on copper. The majority view stressed that this was probably done to increase the longevity of the scroll, since its contents were so materially significant. Perhaps the material also had some purity status that might have been significant. Although the surviving sheets seem to have holes by which they could have been fastened to a supporting plaque, it was generally agreed that this text would never have been put on public display on a wall: why hide treasures and then declare openly where they all are?

Exactly how the scroll was actually engraved remained an open question. Although it could have been inscribed by a single scribe, it is more likely that several scribes worked on it and that they could have been illiterate, merely copying as faithfully as they could from a written exemplar. Perhaps this was done to retain as much secrecy as possible concerning the contents of the document. Such a means of production would help explain the poor formation of many of the letters and the resulting confusion for modern scholars in trying to decipher precisely what was written.

It was agreed that the text of the Copper Scroll should be understood generically as a list. Even though there could still be some debate about how the list was composed, this view of its genre made it very unlikely that it was a work of fiction. Most of those present at the Symposium were convinced that the treasures referred to in this text were real and the majority opinion was that in some way this wealth should be connected with the Jerusalem Temple, even if sympathetic members of the Qumran community or the wider Essene movement were involved in assisting some elements of the Jerusalem priesthood. A strong minority view, held by some leading experts, preferred to see the treasure as exclusively associated with Qumran and its inhabitants, not least because of the place of discovery, the location of several of the places mentioned in the scroll, and the possibility that over time such a community could have accumulated large amounts of money. Whether associated with Jerusalem or Qumran, nearly all the participants in the Symposium preferred to date the scroll to the middle of the first century CE; several maintained the view that it should be linked with the political and military events of 66–74 CE.

Given the majority opinion that the treasures in the Copper Scroll are real, would it be a good idea to launch further expeditions to search for the gold and silver and other matters? Most of those present at the Symposium considered that it was very unlikely that anything would be found today; not only were most of the locations in the scroll too general and vague, but more significantly it is also likely that any treasure was recovered in antiquity, either by the Romans or by the survivors among those who had originally hidden the deposits.

The Symposium on the Copper Scroll was followed towards the end of 1997 and at the start of 1998 by an exhibition on the Dead Sea Scrolls at the Manchester Museum. The newly restored Copper Scroll was the principal exhibit on display together with a copy of its new facsimiles. The exhibition was opened by HRH Princess Sarvath El Hassan, then the Crown Princess of the Hashemite Kingdom of Jordan, and was visited by nearly 40,000 people, including HE the Ambassador of Israel. Work on this volume began after the Exhibition had been dismantled, but it has taken much longer to bring to fruition than was originally expected. Sincere apologies are due both to the contributors, who have eagerly awaited their work in print, and to our intended readership. In the meantime the contributions have not lost their freshness, because little work on the Copper Scroll has been published, apart from the revised form of Judah Lefkovits's large dissertation on the scroll.[15]

We hope that the variety of opinion represented in the studies published in this volume will stimulate further research on the enigmatic Copper Scroll.[16] May further work on this fascinating scroll be undertaken in as cordial a manner as was evident at the Manchester Symposium.

15. See n. 9 above; even the conclusions of that dissertation were known when the Symposium was held, because of its preliminary publication in two volumes: Ann Arbor, MI: University Microfilms International, 1993 (No. 9411113).

16. The Symposium itself stimulated some more popular reflections on the scroll, such as Rolf Rolfsen, 'Den gåtefulle Kobberrullen', UKE-Adressa (5 October 1996), pp. 16-17; George J. Brooke, *Treasures from the Dead Sea: The Copper Scroll after 2000 Years—A Guide to the Story of the Copper Scroll and the Treasures from the Dead Sea* (Manchester: Manchester Museum, 1997); R. Feather, *The Copper Scroll Decoded: One Man's Search for the Fabulous Treasures of Ancient Egypt* (London: Thorsons, 1999).

Part I

Opening, Restoring and Reading the Copper Scroll

1

The Conservation and Restoration of the Copper Scroll from Qumran

Régis Bertholon, Noël Lacoudre and Jorge Vasquez

Introduction

The 23 cylindrical segments of the Copper Scroll are the result of the cutting up of the two rolls of sheets of copper discovered in 1952 in a cave near the Dead Sea. So that the text on these sheets of copper could be read, all involved had to resign themselves to the inevitability of the rolls being cut. After nearly 2000 years, the metal of these rolls was completely oxidized.

Remarkable work of consolidation was undertaken in 1955 and 1956 in the laboratory in Manchester both before and after each roll was submitted to the thin blade of the saw. Then about 40 years passed during which the materials used in consolidating the scroll aged and successive handling of the segments resulted in new breaks that were 'repaired' with products that were sometimes less than adequate. With some sense of urgency a highly skilled assessment of the state of the document became necessary. Then the work of conservation began, using methods that recent research had put at our disposal. This involved removing surface adhesives and putting back together and consolidating the fragmented segments with more stable materials that were often less obtrusive. At the request of the Hashemite Kingdom of Jordan and thanks to the coordination of the Institut Français d'Archéologie du Proche-Orient and of the École Biblique et Archéologique Française, Electricité de France (EDF), in the form of its technological and scientific wing, offered its help in undertaking this ambitious programme.

The work was done between 1994 and 1996 at the Laboratoire EDF–Valectra, which is at the heart of EDF's Groupe des Laboratoires de l'Exploitation du Parc Nucléaire. There, experts with competence in the behaviour of metals could lend their support: metallurgists with their electron microscopes, X-ray diffractometers and analysis by fluorescence; chemists for the microanalysis of all kinds of treating solutions; and those who would assess the non-destructive X-ray images, which had never been attempted before on the segments of this text whose copper had totally disappeared.

It was possible not only to establish for each of the 23 segments, recto and verso, an extremely detailed 'status report', but also to contribute some unpublished information concerning both the engraved text and the inner structure of the material of which the Copper Scroll is constituted. Supported by the technical expertise of the laboratories of EDF's Direction des Études et Recherches, other work was undertaken at the same time, such as the digital treatment of the radiography images at Saint-Denis. These analyses enabled us to give the fragmentary document an appearance close to that of the original and to restore its inscribed text with the greatest possible feasibility.

All the important moves in the restoration process were presented step by step to the competent authorities of the Jordanian Department of Antiquities, who also gave their agreement to the solution for the final support of these precious shells. In a similar way, the reassembly of certain fragments was achieved with the endorsement of Émile Puech (CNRS—Centre national de la recherche scientifique), the epigraphist responsible for the new reading of the manuscript.

Forty Years of Conservation and Handling of This Unique Document

The status reports have enabled us to redress the balance sheet after 40 years of conservation and to determine the causes of various damage that has occurred since the treatment of 1955–56 (Table 1.1; Fig. 1.1). This damage is tied up with the aging of the products used, with the continuous handling of the scroll, and with the conditions under which it was stored and presented. This has provided an opportunity for learning about the consequences of the choice of treatment in 1955–56, notably with respect to the interventions made for consolidation, and for evaluating the behaviour of resins, some of which are still used today.

At the time of each status report it was important to document and conserve a faithful image of the segments before any intervention. Numerous photographs have been taken in conjunction with the observation of the segments and the analysis of the materials. Each segment has likewise been subjected to radiography from several angles which has allowed us to form a complete radiographic covering of the scroll before any intervention.

Table 1.1. *Summary of treatments of the Qumran Copper Scroll before 1992*

1955–56: Treatment in the laboratory in Manchester (Baker 1956, Baillet *et al.* 1962)
For each of the 23 segments:

- mechanical cleaning of dust and concretions from the outer surface;
- mounting on a steel axle and sealing with plaster;
- removal of traces of cellulose resin by washing with acetone;
- consolidation with an epoxy resin lightly diluted in toluene (Araldite 102/ hardening Araldite 951), heating to 40°C;
- gluing of the fragments with cellulose nitrate (Durofix);
- gluing of strips of reinforcement of methyl polymetacryl (perspex) by cellulose nitrate (Durofix) and reinforcement with a layer of epoxy resin (Araldite);
- cutting by circular saw at high speed;
- cleaning with a nylon brush;
- mechanical cleaning of the products of corrosion from the inner surface;
- consolidation of the surface with a solution of methyl polymetacryl (Perspex) in chloroform;
- photographs;
- construction of a support for the Amman Museum.

1977: Technical appraisal (Oddy 1977)

Undated: Pinpoint regluing of fragments, placing reinforcements of green linen.

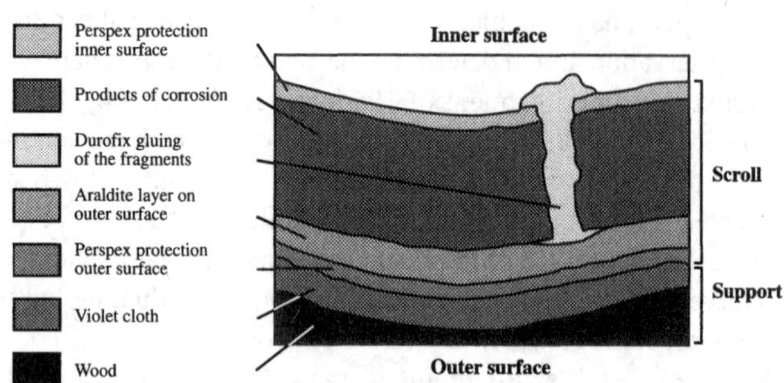

Fig. 1.1. *Transverse cut of a segment with its support after the treatment of 1955 and at the time of its storage at Amman Museum*

The principal ascertainable changes are:

- the fragmentation of the majority of the segments;
- non-adjoining gluings, either in the wrong places or simply unaesthetically;
- the presence of blue-green efflorescence, possibly indicating active corrosion;
- the peeling of the layer of Araldite from the consolidation of the outer surface;
- the relative insolubility of the perspex film of the consolidation of the inner surface;
- the adhesion of violet fabric from the support of the segments and the presence of brown traces on the outer surface of the segments.

Except for the peeling of the layer of Araldite, all the changes had already been noticed by A. Oddy[1] at the time of an earlier status report in 1977, about 22 years after the original treatment (Oddy 1977).

The diagnoses completed in 1977 and 1994 have come to practically the same conclusions:

- The great fragility of the segments was the cause of the fragmentation observed since 1956. This fragility had not inhibited the handling of the segments. The peeling of the layer of Araldite was not implicated here because the fragmentation was taking place without any differentiation in areas of both adherence and of peeling; however, the solidity of the layer of Araldite appeared insufficient.
- Although some non-adjoining gluings or those in the wrong place date from the treatment of 1955–56, numerous others are undoubtedly the result of later interventions that are undocumented but were intended to remedy accidents from the handling of the segments. The yellowing, which was due to the aging of the Durofix glue based on cellulose nitrate used in 1955, was responsible for the unaesthetic appearance of the gluings. However, the mechanical grip of the glues was good and the solubility of the Durofix seemed unchanged.
- The analysis of the blue-green efflorescence, done in 1994, indicated that it was principally a question of copper hydroxychlor-

1. We thank Andrew Oddy for kindly communicating the result of his assessment to us.

ides (atacamite and paratacamite). The efflorescence was localized on fractures, in fissures and at places where the cleaning of 1955 had made a layer of brown-coloured corrosion appear. Rather than being an active corrosion brought about by a rapid transformation of the metal, which in fact does not exist any longer in the entirely oxidized segments, it seemed to us that it was a question only of the transformation of the copper chlorides (nantokite) into copper hydrochlorides. This transformation could have been generated by mechanical constraints, particularly at the heart of cracks, which had facilitated the cracks' propagation (Bertholon 1995a).

- The changes in the resins used in 1955 were probably due to the combined action of light and humidity. The solubility of the film of perspex (methyl polymetacrylate, PMMA) was noticeably different according to whether it was acting as a protecting film on the inscribed (and exposed) inner surface or on the outer surface (cf. Fig. 1.1). The latter remained soluble in solvents of PMMA (Horie 1992) at the same time as the protecting film on the inner surface had become soluble in acetone only with difficulty. The detachments visible on the two surfaces no longer presented the same features: whitening of the accumulation of resins present in the hollows and lack of suppleness for the inner surface, but tearing on the outer surface. In both cases the film of perspex no longer seemed to play any role in protecting or consolidating the surface.

There was another very important element in the status report. The examination conducted in 1955 had concluded that the original surface (the surface of the segments at the time of their abandonment, which is nearest to the inscribed surface) should be located near a brown layer, still actually very visible and composed of a layer of red copper oxide (cuprite): 'a distinctive film of dark-brown colour covers what is now the base material' (Baker 1956). In spite of this remark, the cleaning of 1955 had not intended to eliminate the products of corrosion situated above this layer but to remove various accretions and some products of corrosion just at the green layer of hydroxilated copper, that is, well above the original surface. The deep imprint of the inscriptions meant that the document was very legible without cleaning down to the original surface.

The examination and analysis done in 1994 through the spectrometry of the florescence of X-rays coupled with observation through scanning with an electron-microscope enabled us to establish that the original surface was situated at the heart of the layer of cuprite at the interface of a brown-to-black layer and the upper cuprite layer. This ability to locate the original surface rests, among other things, on the presence of inclusions composed of silica or calcium coming from the buried layer situated just above the original surface and of certain elements of the original alloy of tin, belonging to the layer situated just below the original surface. This seems to corroborate the observations made in 1955.

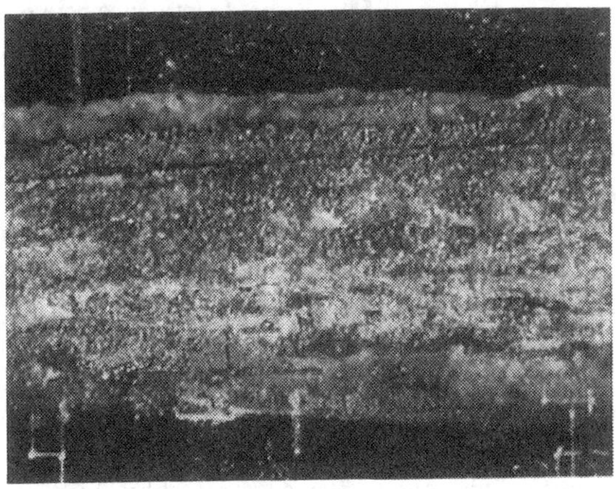

Fig. 1.2. *Stratigraphy of the layers of corrosion in the Copper Scroll after a transverse cut of a segment*

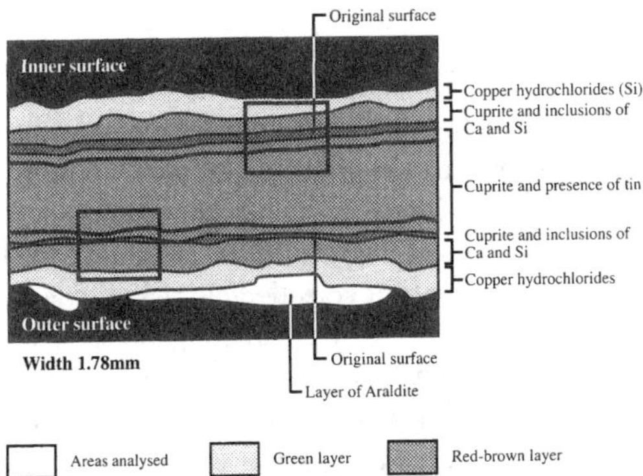

Fig. 1.3. *Transverse cut of a segment indicating the stratigraphy of the layers of corrosion visible on Fig. 1.2*

Objectives of the 1994 Conservation and Restoration

Diagnosis had shown that the intrinsic fragility of the scroll was the principal cause of its deterioration, together with it having been handled numerous times. It was important to give the scroll adequate cohesiveness and mechanical resistance sufficient to allow its conservation for the long term.

The consolidation of the scroll itself had to be compatible with the treatments already given in 1955 so as not to introduce heterogeneity into the cohesiveness and chemical behaviour of the materials applied on the segments. At the same time it was essential to use very stable materials so as to prevent for as long as possible the expiry of any new and always very delicate intervention. As far as possible, in any intervention it was also important to provide for some reversibility.

These objectives have been pursued through taking care to intervene as minimally as possible so as not to jeopardize the future of the document, but to allow for its natural aging, and that of the strengthening products too. Also, to enable the manipulation of the segments without danger, given the necessities of the study, an important part of the consolidation was brought about through the construction of individual supports and a customized packing case.

The objectives of the conservation and restoration of the segments also involved the readability of the inscription (after remounting and cleaning). With the same care taken not to jeopardize the future of the document through too much intervention, its cleaning was deliberately limited.

Interventions for Conservation and Restoration in 1994–1995

The improvement of the mechanical holding of the segments necessitated the redoing of the consolidation of 1955. The partial removal of the layer of Araldite led to heterogeneity in the mechanical resistance of the segments and so was a source of fragmentation. To remove the layer entirely appeared to put the segments at considerable risk. It was possible to re-establish a certain homogeneity by completing the layer with something similar, a layer of Araldite AY103/ hardener HY956 of a type very close to that used in 1955 and which ages in a similar way (Down 1984, 1986). To enable reversibility, this new layer is isolated by a film of Paraloïd B72, which involves some difference in adhesion but does not change the rigidity of the layer (Fig. 1.4).

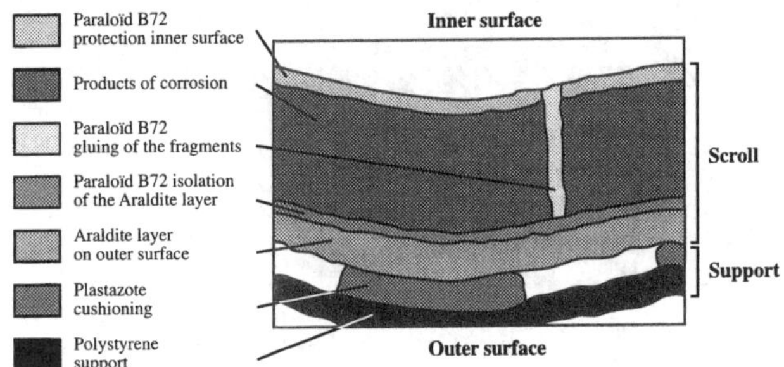

Fig. 1.4. *Transverse cut of a segment after the treatment of 1994*

This redoing of the consolidation was completed by the important work of the support of the segments. The characteristics of this support are the following:

- support of the whole surface of each segment by a rigid base of heat-formed polystyrene;
- intermediary cushioning between the segment and the base with a foam of polyethylene-reticulated Plastazote, to relieve the effects of shocks and vibrations;
- the fixing of each segment and the conceiving of the base to allow usual holding and manipulation of the segment by its base;
- the removable fixing of the segment by Plexiglas screwed hooks that allow for the holding of the segment itself in exceptional circumstances (e.g. for the study of the reverse);
- the use of long-term stable materials (polyethylene, polystyrene, acrylics);
- the presentation of the different segments at the same height in a Plexiglas box conceived to that effect;
- the making of a cushioned case for transportation (see Fig. 1.5).

The individual bases allowed for the handling of each segment in good conditions of safety, thus facilitating the study of the document.

The gluing together was redone with Paraloïd B72 so as to permit reversibility and to improve aging (Koob 1986).

It was decided not to proceed with cleaning down to the original surface but to limit this to certain areas that still had deposits of dirt or where further study was needed because the detail of certain letters was hidden. Because of the depth of the inscription, this minimal intervention for cleaning was entirely compatible with presenting the document as legible; however, certain details relating to the preparation of the document (such

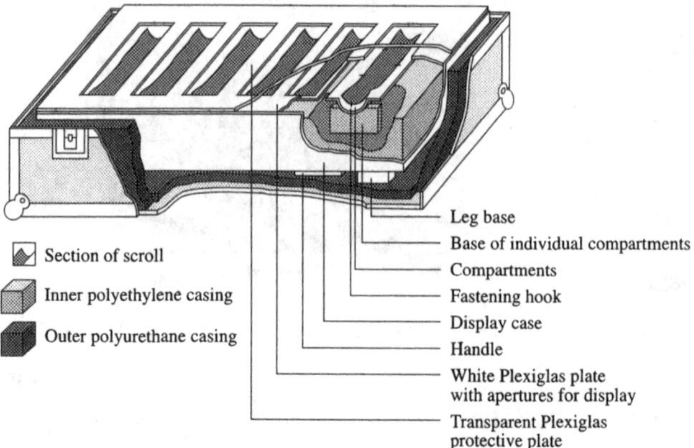

Fig. 1.5. *View of the transportation case containing the presentation box within which are placed the segments, each on its individual base*

as engraved lines) are not always visible on the surface of the products of corrosion. Various criteria were taken into account when deciding on cleaning being limited to certain areas:

- the minimization of the risks inherent in every cleaning technique (mechanical, chemical, or both) on the delicate sheets, which are deeply mineralized;
- the possibility of recovering hidden information (such as engraved lines) thanks to the exploitation of the X-ray images and their treatment;
- a refusal to modify the 'image' of the scroll, that is, a concern to conserve its appearance as familiar to the interested public and to retain its representative antiquity.

The complete list of interventions for conservation and restoration is presented in Table 1.2. The photographs of segments after treatment show only faint changes to the general appearance of the scroll.

Minimal intervention for conservation and restoration always allows for the better safeguarding of the integrity of a document. Such intervention has been undertaken on the Copper Scroll from Qumran because the technical means available at present offer other possibilities for the improvement of the legibility of the document. Conjointly the treatment of the digitized X-ray images and the flat reproduction of the scroll by galvanoplasty based on the casts of the segments were achieved.

Table 1.2. *Treatment of the Qumran Copper Scroll completed in 1994*

- Survey of the data of the cutting of 1955.
- Partial elimination of the 1955 materials of consolidation: elimination of the perspex films from the inner and outer surfaces and dismantling of the Durofix gluings by immersion in acetonitric, pinpoint mechanical elimination of the layer of Araldite, removal of the small plates of supporting Plexiglas.
- Pinpoint mechanical cleaning of the calcareous accretions masking certain characters.
- Stabilization of the corrosion by immersion in a partial vacuum in benzotriazol at 3 per cent in ethanol.
- Gluing of the fragments with Paraloïd B72 at 60 per cent in xylene.
- Insulation, consolidation, protection: insulation of the gluings and of the outer surface by Paraloïd B72 at 20 per cent in acetone, lining on the outer surface by a film of Araldite, protection of the inner surface and of the layer of Araldite on the external surface by a film of Paraloïd B72 at 5 per cent in acetone.
- Continuation of the data of the cutting of 1955 on each segment.
- Support:
  - the taking of a plaster imprint of each segment which allowed the making of a counter-image imprinted in plaster;
  - the making of shells through the heat treatment of sheets of polystyrene on the counter-images;
  - adjustment of each segment on its shell through cushioning with a polyethylene foam (Plastazote);
  - fixing of the segments on their shells.
- Presentation, storage and transport: the making of presentation and storage boxes in Plexiglas, the making of cases for transportation with a cushion of polyethylene foam.

Applying the X-rays and Digitized Images to the Epigraphy of the Copper Scroll

The X-rays of the segments enable an easier reading of the scroll and reveal certain inscriptions that have been difficult to see because of the roughness of the surface due to disturbances brought about by corrosion. They have also contributed to the elaboration of the status report by making apparent the cracks and various superimpositions of fragments that have been difficult to ascertain by visual examination. The digitization of the rolls of copper was undertaken in order to make a new and more feasible copy of the text; until now this has been a very intricate task because of the scroll's deformities and the uneven relief of the surface of the segments. On the basis of the radiography of the segments, the engineers of the Direction des Études et Recherches of EDF have been able to digitalize the inscriptions as the curves and deformities were made flat and as the displaced fragments were readjusted with the help of Émile Puech (École Biblique). Thus, thanks to the assembly of different images by computer, a new vision of this document has been obtained that will lead to its renewed epigraphic study.

Moulding and Reproduction by Galvanoplasty

Each of the 23 segments was moulded with a stretchable silicone. The negatives obtained in this way were flattened and put alongside one another to enable, for each of the three riveted sheets, the making of a positive in plaster that would constitute a faithful flat replica (with a variation in measurement of less than 2 per cent, that is, a character of 5 mm is reproduced with a length of 4.98 mm).

The new mould then makes a second negative obtainable in silicon, which now reflects the totality of the sheet. A positive in copper is then made by galvanoplasty (the deposit of metal by electrolysis), after the silicone sheet has been rendered conductible through the application of a fine layer of graphite. The facsimile in copper obtained for each of the three sheets of the document allows a new reading of the document inasmuch as it is a close representation of its original state.

Conclusion

The work of conservation and restoration of the Copper Scroll from Qumran undertaken by the Valectra laboratory was conducted simultaneously in several different directions:

- (Re)restoration compatible with the work done in Manchester in 1955 and minimal intervention for cleaning so as not to change fundamentally the appearance of this unique object of the world's heritage: it is the only Dead Sea scroll on copper.
- Creation of individual supports for each segment, intended to facilitate their handling by researchers and conservators, and the construction of boxes for presentation and for transport in order to minimize risk of further deterioration resulting from human handling.

- Creation and digitalization of X-ray images, and the making of galvanoplasty moulds that offer henceforth new presentations of the text that might satisfy the requirements of the epigraphists. The different reproductions are complementary: the revelation by the X-rays of movements of the scribe in the metal, the evocation of the complete document on the basis of the connecting of the digitized images and the faithfulness of the model in the smallest detail to the mould of the inscribed surface of each segment. The digitized X-ray images are capable of being broadcast widely within the scientific community. The copper replicas made through galvanoplasty also offer opportunities for museums and for the education of the general public because this document now appears in a state close to that of the original.

This discreet (re)restoration guided by the principles of reversibility and of minimal intervention will enable, we hope, the improvement of the scroll's conservation and presentation for the long term. Let us recall that the (re)restoration of this unique document was made possible thanks to pertinent choices being made concerning the treatment and the quality of materials used in 1955; these had good aging properties. We hope that our work reduces the chance that the scroll will need further restoration soon, and we also hope that any future restorers will come to their task facilitated by the choices we have made today.

BIBLIOGRAPHY

Baillet, M., J.T. Milik and R. de Vaux

1962 *Les 'petites grottes' de Qumrân* (DJDJ III; Oxford: Clarendon Press, 1962).

Baker, H. Wright

1956 'Notes on the Opening of the "Bronze" Scrolls from Qumran', *BJRL* 39: 45-56.

Bertholon, R.

1995a *Rouleau de cuivre 3Q15 de Qumrân: Rapport d'expertise technique et projet de conservation-restauration*, internal report of Electricité de France, No. D5711/RB94.2003/BTO.

1995b 'De nouvelles approches de la lecture du rouleau de cuivre de Qumrân: re-restauration minimale, radiographie X et traitement d'image, moulage et galvanoplastie', in R. Bertholon *et al.*, *Restauration, dé-restauration, re-restauration: Colloque sur la conservation restauration des biens culturels* (Paris: Association des restaurateurs d'art et d'archéologie): 295-306.

1998 'Corrosion du rouleau de cuivre de Qumrân et localisation de la surface originelle', in R. Bertholon, L. Robbiola and N. Lacoudre (eds.), *Metal 98* (London: James and James): 125-35.

2001 'Characterisation and Location of Original Surface of Corroded Metallic Archaeological Objects', *Surface Engineering* 17.3: 241-45.

Down, J.L.

1984 'The Yellowing of Epoxy Resin Adhesives: Report on Natural Dark Aging', *Studies in Conservation* 29: 63-76.

1986 'The Yellowing of Epoxy Resin Adhesives: Report on High-intensity Light Aging', *Studies in Conservation* 31: 159-70.

Horie, C.V.

1992 *Materials for Conservation, Organic Consolidants, Adhesives and Coatings* (Oxford: Butterworth, 1992).

Koob, S.P.

1986 'The Use of Paraloid B72 as an Adhesive: Its Application for Archeological Ceramics and Other Materials', *Studies in Conservation* 31: 7-14.

Oddy, W.A.

1977 *Report on the Scientific Examination of the Copper Scroll from Qumran in the Archaeological Museum, Amman* (unpublished report kindly communicated by the author).

2

John Allegro and the Copper Scroll

Philip R. Davies

Although the Copper Scroll was opened in Manchester in 1956, it was not until 1960 that John Allegro published his account, including a transcription of the text and a translation, entitled *The Treasure of the Copper Scroll: The Opening and Decipherment of the Most Mysterious of the DEAD SEA SCROLLS, a Unique Inventory of Buried Treasure.*[1] The dedication reads: 'By gracious permission this book is dedicated with the author's profound admiration and respect to His Majesty King Hussein of Jordan.'

Behind the publication of this book lies a fascinating story, to which I shall come presently. Some of it is revealed in the first edition of the book. Naturally, there is an account here of the discovery of these two copper rolls in Cave 3, and Allegro's impatience at the slow pace of events. These rolls were lying in Jerusalem, on display to the public, 'unread and unreadable' as he says (p. 19) without any move towards opening them up. It was through Allegro's persistence, both in Manchester and Jerusalem, that in the end the Jordanian authorities agreed to let the rolls come, one at a time, to England to be cut open in the Manchester College of Technology by a specially constructed contraption created by Professor H. Wright Baker.

One of the reasons why John Allegro was so anxious to open these rolls was his belief that they were a list of buried treasures. This had been the view of Professor K.G. Kuhn from Göttingen, who had managed, on a visit to Jerusalem, to decipher some of the words from the outside. It would not be unfair to say that John Allegro always had a fascination for the sensational, and tried harder than anyone to generate public interest in the scrolls. He was a tireless public speaker and prolific writer on them, in

1. London: Routledge & Kegan Paul, 1960.

striking contrast to his fellow editors. In this case, of course, he was fully justified, for that is indeed what the Copper Scroll turned out to be.

The second roll arrived in Manchester in 1956 and Allegro quickly deciphered and translated it, though now he faced some personal and political difficulties which the first edition of his book does not mention, and which I will come to presently.

A second edition, completely revised, of *The Treasure of the Copper Scroll*, was published in 1964.[2] Here, however, the transcription contained in the original edition was left out; only the translation is presented. What we have instead is a much more racy, personal, popular account of the scroll and its discovery and opening, and the reader might think that the transcription was omitted simply for the reason that a more popular readership would not find it useful. That is not necessarily the case, however, because by now two other transcriptions had been published in the official edition, one by the editor Józef Milik and the other by H. Wright Baker. Presumably the latter had been done in Manchester, with or without Allegro's knowledge or consent.

But this second edition of Allegro's book also contains more of the story. The fourth chapter carries the account of the decipherment forward. The 'reasonably complete, though still very tentative translation of the second part of the scroll' that he had made in February 1956 was sent to Jerusalem, 'but never acknowledged', because 'by this time a most strange atmosphere of secrecy and even churlishness had enveloped our work' (p. 29). The reason for this is then given. Already by this time a bit of a rift had begun to emerge between Allegro and his colleagues on the team of editors who were responsible for the publication of the scrolls. This was because of his view, which he had already hinted at in earlier books, that the scrolls showed many aspects of Christianity to have been anticipated in the Qumran scrolls. But—and this is not mentioned—there was also friction between Allegro and Professor Rowley, his departmental head in Manchester. While the Copper Scroll was still in Manchester, Allegro gave a series of radio broadcasts on the BBC's Northern service (not a national broadcast) in which he suggested, among other things, that the religious leader mentioned in the scrolls may have been crucified, as Jesus was. On learning of this broadcast, his colleagues in Jerusalem published a letter to *The Times* refuting his claims. Although these ideas of Allegro's had nothing directly to do with the publication of the Copper Scroll,

2. J.M. Allegro, *The Treasure of the Copper Scroll* (Garden City, NY: Doubleday, 2nd rev. edn, 1964).

Allegro suddenly felt that he was being shut off and his hands tied. Control of the affair was being taken over, and especially control over press and media coverage. The last straw was when the official press release disclosing the contents of the Copper Scroll was issued; the treasure list that it contained was said to be legendary, unreal. And to add to this, Allegro's own part in the revealing of the contents was unacknowledged.

The preparation of the official edition of the Copper Scroll was entrusted not to Allegro, but to another member of the editorial team, Józef Milik, who had been present when the scroll was actually discovered. Allegro does not seem to have minded this, though he tells us he was surprised when, in 1957, on a visit to Amman where the Copper Scroll was displayed, he discovered that the details of the scroll's contents were being kept secret from even the Director of Antiquities. He must have suspected that his own zest for publicity and perhaps even his views on the significance of the scrolls had prompted de Vaux to assign the Copper Scroll to what seemed a safer pair of hands.

Imagine how someone like John Allegro would have felt about the contents of what he regarded as a genuine treasure list being withheld. He agreed not to publish his own views on this text until Milik's official edition had appeared, but as Milik's translation failed to appear, he became ever more impatient. He was, however, allowed to study the document in Amman, and make further notes. He claims, in fact (p. 35), that the Director of Antiquities gave him permission to publish his translation. If the claim is true, it suggests that there was a certain lack of full communication and understanding between the editorial team based in Jerusalem and the Department of Antiquities in Amman. This indeed may have been the case, as we shall see.

In the end, Milik published the contents of the Copper Scroll first in an article in *Revue Biblique*.[3] Then in 1960 Allegro published his book *The Treasure of the Copper Scroll*. Milik's 'official' edition did not come out until 1962, as volume III in the series Discoveries in the Judean Desert of Jordan (DJDJ), together with other texts from the so-called 'Minor Caves'. In Milik's edition the view was again expressed that the treasure list was fictitious, a view that, indeed, remained standard until fairly recently, though Allegro's second edition makes a sustained case for the treasure having belonged to the Jerusalem temple. Allegro was also convinced that

3. J.T. Milik, 'Le rouleau de cuivre de Qumrân (3Q15): Traduction et commentaire topographique', *RB* 66 (1959), pp. 321-57.

the hiding places mentioned were real and lay in the Judaean Desert, and indeed, this motivated an expedition he led to the area in 1959–60. But Allegro also identifies some of the places with sites in Jerusalem, including the Temple area itself. His own view was that the Temple treasures were carried from Jerusalem during the war that broke out with Rome in 66 CE, by members of the Zealot movement who then had control of the sanctuary. It was Zealots who took the treasures to the Judaean desert and, perhaps, also occupied Qumran for a brief period. To the Temple treasures they may have added, he believed, the booty from raids on Qumran and other similar places in the Dead Sea valley.

This view, in fact, that the Copper Scroll records real treasure probably from the Jerusalem temple, is the one that the majority of experts now seem to favour, at least according to a straw poll taken at the 1996 conference in Manchester. But my topic is not the Copper Scroll itself, nor its treasure. There is another treasure, to which I have kindly been given access by Joan Allegro, namely copies of letters written by and to John Allegro. These enable the story I have just given to be filled out in more detail, and they confirm most of what Allegro says in the second edition of *The Treasure of the Copper Scroll.*

The sequence of letters on the Copper Scroll opens towards the end of May 1955, when John Allegro is busy writing and telephoning various people in Manchester, including the Carborundum Company Ltd of Trafford Park. The supervising engineer there, a Mr Scholes, points out that his firm does not have the necessary equipment, but suggests that the use of a 'thin slitting wheel' would be the best method. Simultaneously, however, Allegro was writing to Professor Thompson of the University of Manchester and then to the Principal of the College of Technology, Dr Bowden, enclosing photographs of the rolls. The reaction of Professor Thompson was, as Allegro saw it, 'lukewarm', and his proposal involved the use of chemicals to soften the copper before prising the rolls open. Allegro may have been right to reject this method, but the decision not to have the rolls opened at the university endeared Allegro even less to Professor Rowley, the head of his department. At all events, by June 1955 John Allegro was in Jerusalem and had managed to get permission from the Jordanian Department of Antiquities for the first of the rolls to come to the College of Technology, carried personally by the Director of Antiquities, Lankester Harding. The strictest secrecy was being insisted upon, and even the other members of the scroll's editing team were unaware of what was happening.

The cutting machine, as is well known, was designed and operated by Professor H. Wright Baker, and if anyone is interested, Allegro gives a detailed description of the device. By 1 October 1955 the first cut had been made by Wright Baker on his own. It took ten minutes, with another ten minutes to lift off the freed section. But in two of a series of regular letters to Lankester Harding,[4] reporting on the proceedings, Allegro characteristically suggested (more than once) that the cutting and reading of the scroll should be done with the press, television 'and all the rest' in attendance, thus raising money for more scrolls purchases. (At that time, purchase of the Cave 4 scroll fragments in the possession of the Beduin was a priority.) As it is, he was careful to take lots of pictures, and some cine film of the operation. Allegro was always taking pictures; and he must already have had in mind at this time the possibility of a television programme in the near future.

By 5 October 1955 the first roll was done, to the satisfaction of all, including the Jordanian embassy official who had been delegated to keep an eye on this valuable antiquity. It was soon being read, and before having deciphered even more than three columns, an excited Allegro wrote to Harding,[5] 'These copper scrolls are red hot... Next time your [*sic*] down at Qumran, take a spade and dig like mad by the airhole of the iron smelting furnace...there should be nine of something there.' It is clear that Allegro's first guess was that the treasures are hidden at Qumran itself.

But he now realized something else, and changed his mind about publicity. He wrote, 'Naturally, this increases enormously the need for absolute security. One whisper that there's real treasure awaiting the digger at Qumran, and the Bedu would be down there in a flash and turn the whole joint upside down.' He added, 'Nothing will leak here.' But he did expect that a treasure hunt would be organized in Jordan by the authorities.

The reply from Harding to this news[6] already indicated the secrecy that would be needed: the Jordanian Ambassador was to be told that the contents appeared to be 'a list of goods of some kind belonging to the monastery'. Nevertheless, he took the precaution of writing, 'I shall deny ever having heard from you if they [any members of the Jordanian government] accuse me of hiding things in the future.'

4. Dated 1.10.55 and 5.10.55.
5. Letter to Harding 14.10.55.
6. Dated 19.10.55.

As for the treasure—which he also took at this point to be real—Harding did not think there was likely to be much left by then. But Allegro's reply was characteristically more enthusiastic: 'I think you are being somewhat unduly pessimistic over the chances of finding the swag still there.' But despite his ever-growing excitement, he promised to keep the inquisitive press out of the story for the time being. That must have been for him quite an exercise of willpower. But over the Copper Scroll, it must be said, Allegro did behave with a good deal of restraint, at least publicly. In any event, his instructions from Amman were to keep entirely quiet about the contents of this scroll[7] and to wait for the arrival of the second roll.

There are, unfortunately, no documents directly indicating the point of view of the Jordanian government, but they clearly felt that something was going on of which they ought to know. Hence, 'Awni Dajani, an archaeologist employed in the Department of Antiquities, arrived on 15 November 1955 in Manchester—at the Ambassador's request and without Harding's knowledge—to inspect the work done, including the cutting machine and photographs, together with a written report. He also asked for a translation of the contents of the first roll. Allegro, by his own account, persuaded him that the translation was not ready, and showed him the transcription instead.

But while Allegro was making every effort to keep the contents of the Copper Scroll from becoming public, he was privately lobbying both Harding and de Vaux to organize excavations for the treasure in the Qumran vicinity, being convinced that something would turn up, and indeed that once the discoveries were made, a general Beduin invasion was inevitable. Neither of these two men seems to have been very keen on the idea or prepared to confront the consequences. Still lobbying, Allegro sent the transcription, translation and notes of roll 1 to Harding towards the end of November.

In the middle of this bout of correspondence with Harding and de Vaux, Allegro dropped a bombshell. He had been assigned to work on texts of biblical interpretation from Cave 4, including a commentary on the book of Nahum. He now told de Vaux[8] that this text stated that the leader of the Qumran sect, called the 'teacher of righteousness', had been crucified by Gentiles and was expected to rise again. He reminded de Vaux that he

7. Letter from Harding 30.10.55.
8. Letter of 2.12.55.

intended to publish this text in the American *Journal of Biblical Literature* (for which he had some time earlier received permission from de Vaux).

De Vaux replied immediately.[9] First, he had by then seen Allegro's transcription and translation of the first part of the Copper Scroll, but was not convinced the treasures were hidden at Qumran or nearby. And as for the reading in the Nahum commentary, well, the advice was: do not hurry to publish; make sure of the reading first. If you come to Jerusalem in the spring, we can talk about it then.

All this time, Allegro's frustration was being fuelled by the political wrangles in Amman that were delaying the dispatch of the second and larger copper roll. But it finally and suddenly arrived in England on 3 January 1956 and was deposited in Wright Baker's bank along with the first. By 11 January Wright Baker had begun to slice it open.

Just at this moment, however, came a dramatic turn of events. Allegro had no desire to wait to spread his idea about the crucifixion of the Qumran leader. He mentioned this in a series of three BBC broadcasts a few days earlier, which were reported widely, including in the *New York Times* (5 February) and in *Time* magazine (6 February). These radio talks were the crossing of a Rubicon, intentionally or otherwise, and it cast a long and deep shadow over Allegro's future fate both in Jerusalem and in Manchester. It had an immediate effect on his dealings with colleagues in Jordan and Manchester. De Vaux immediately wrote a letter accusing Allegro of having 'disregarded the conventions that govern the work of our team'; later, that 'you have seriously contravened the proper scientific method to which we want our editing work to conform'. The letter contains much else in the same tone. The interpretation that Allegro offers is rejected, says de Vaux, by his fellow editors, who have also looked at the manuscript (which remained, of course, in the Palestine Archaeological Museum in Jerusalem). A public renunciation had, with the agreement of Lankester Harding, been sent to the British and American press.

Allegro was in fact already suspected of leaking ideas based on the Copper Scroll, in contravention of the agreed line. In an earlier letter to de Vaux[10] he had denied hotly that he had said anything based on data in the Copper Scroll. Instead, his idea that the leader of the Qumran sect had been crucified was determined by his interpretation of the Nahum commentary he was editing. Yet, as his letter makes clear, he *had* said publicly that this idea was *confirmed*, and the 'confirmation', as the letter explains,

9. Letter of 11.12.55.
10. Letter of 9.2.56.

came from the first column of the Copper Scroll, where Allegro had translated a phrase as 'in the sepulchre of the Son of Sleep, the Crucified (or Hanged)'. This place, thought Allegro, was at or near Qumran.

But as yet unaware of the reactions in Jerusalem to all this, he wrote, on the very same day that de Vaux wrote his angry letter, raising again the question of the secrecy over the opening of the Copper Scroll. Those institutions that had contributed towards the project, including the College of Technology and the British Council (who paid for the Copper Scroll to be brought from Jordan) had been getting on his conscience. So he asked again[11] whether something should not be said to the Great British public of what was going on in their midst. Then came the suggestion of showing his film of the opening of the scroll, in a short 5–10 minute television feature.

One can see the inner struggle: here is an instinctive communicator, always in touch with the public, always with the popular edge, forced to maintain, and for reasons of politics in a far-off land, one of the most sensational events of the century: the opening of a 2000-year-old treasure list. But his pleas met with a frosty silence. A dispassionate observer can perhaps see both sides of the matter (and indeed so could Allegro), but my own sympathies are with Allegro here, as they should be, since it is on account of his enthusiasm and thanks to his instinct for publicity that 50 years on we can see the Copper Scroll actually being cut open, even though the television documentary he wanted made was never undertaken.

But already a dramatic change of attitude towards Allegro had taken place in Jordan. For the cutting of the second roll, he was not allowed to be present. His transcriptions and translations were duly made and sent within a week, but no mention was made of his part in the entire enterprise. His confidant Lankester Harding did not communicate; Dr Wright Baker was under the impression (and said so) that Allegro had been discredited by his colleagues in Jerusalem. He had become a *persona non grata*.

Shortly after sending his first letter of rebuke, de Vaux sent another in reply to Allegro's protestations. He wanted to see the text of the radio broadcast; he challenged the claim that Allegro's interpretation of a crucifixion is 'certain'. It seems, nevertheless, a more amicable communication, making the positive suggestion that Allegro's texts, translation and interpretation of the Cave 4 manuscripts assigned to him should be

11. Letter of 11.2.56 to Lankester Harding.

published quickly, with two of his editorial colleagues giving their own views in a subsequent issue of the same journal.

Allegro's reply expressed astonishment at the fuss, and he protested that he had not got all his material ready: too much haste would not be good. He enclosed the requested scripts, then assured de Vaux that he was not campaigning against the church. This was an interesting theme, for he repeated it in a letter the next day to his friend and fellow editor John Strugnell, with whom he had long been on close terms. Neither Strugnell nor de Vaux had made this accusation. Yet another letter went to Claus-Hunno Hunzinger, another erstwhile editor from Germany, in which the same point is repeated; and one wonders whether the idea came from within Allegro himself rather than anyone else. How far, if at all, it is true, could be the topic of another lecture.

Opposition to Allegro was not only from Jerusalem, however. In his own department, Professor Rowley was making clear his own dislike of Allegro's views and his reputation. This is occasionally reported back to Allegro, for example, by another fellow editor of his, Frank Cross, in a letter at this time that seemed fairly cordial.[12]

But meantime the text of Allegro's radio talks had reached de Vaux, and he found in them everything that Allegro claimed was media invention. Another letter followed,[13] advising Allegro of a letter sent to the London *Times* refuting his interpretations and signed by most of his fellow editors: de Vaux, Milik, Skehan, Starcky and Strugnell. This appeared on 16 March 1956, and as far as Allegro was concerned it was the last straw. It concluded: 'It is our conviction that either he [Allegro] has misread the texts or he has built up a chain of conjectures which the materials do not support.' Before the letter even appeared, Allegro wrote back to de Vaux, saying, 'I only hope for your sake that the editor of *The Times* is so completely mystified that he returns it to you. Otherwise, I fear that you are all going to look rather silly, if nothing worse.'[14] Then on the day it appeared he wrote to the editor of *The Times*. This concluded, 'I presume the real core of my colleagues' objections is in the inferences which have been drawn by others from this hypothetical reconstruction of events with similar occurrences recorded in the Christian gospels…' He wrote on the same day to de Vaux again, accusing him and others of defaming his competence and making a reference to 'ecclesiastical honour'.

12. Letter of 27.2.56.
13. Letter of 4.3.56.
14. Letter of 7.6.56.

The feud went on. I have perhaps dwelt too long on it, for it was not a dispute about the Copper Scroll. Nevertheless, it partly explains the chilly atmosphere in which the opening of the second copper roll took place. It demonstrates a breakdown of trust between Allegro and his colleagues, and against this background must be seen the subsequent history of publication of the Copper Scroll.

As I mentioned earlier, it had been agreed that the definitive edition was to be entrusted to Józef Milik. On 20 April 1956, de Vaux rather coolly thanked Allegro for his work on the text, but said,

> You were responsible for being present at the opening, and making transcriptions in case an accident should happen. You have done this, and we thank you. But...the provisional translation that you have sent and your general interpretation of the document do not seem accurate to us.

In addition, Allegro's own book, *The Dead Sea Scrolls: A Reappraisal*,[15] originally published in 1956, had to go into its second edition (1958) with no mention of the Copper Scroll. As he characteristically noted in one of his letters, 'It would sell another million if I could.'[16] Meanwhile the authorities in Jordan were saying as little as possible about the Copper Scroll, except that it is a collection of 'traditions of buried treasure';[17] none of the place names can be identified and it probably has nothing to do with the rest of the Qumran scrolls.

It was not long before Allegro was thinking about a 'popular treasure book' in collaboration with the American biblical scholar David Noel Freedman.[18] He needed clearance from de Vaux, but of course assumed that the Milik volume would appear first. However, he heard from Cross that Milik, at the insistence of de Vaux and Harding, was not being urged to publish the text until the whole of the next volume of DJDJ was ready to go. Cross offered two reasons: one was that the DJDJ volume was about the campaign of exploration of the cliffs by the archaeological team, from which the Copper Scroll was the only really important outcome; and the other reason was that, in his own words, 'no one wants all our antiquities sites dug into confusion'. In late July de Vaux told Allegro that the Milik edition would not appear for another two years. This quickly became three or five years. In December 1956 Allegro wrote to Milik, asking to see the

15. London: Penguin Books.
16. Letter to Hunzinger of 23.4.56.
17. This is how Lankester Harding phrased it in his letter of 28.5.56.
18. Letter to Cross of 16.7.56.

facsimile and photographs again 'to refresh my memory on certain points' and Milik promised to lend him his copy during a forthcoming visit to England.

Some years later, there is a strange letter of 14 September 1959 from Allegro to Cross. His collaborator on the *Treasure of the Copper Scroll* book, David Noel Freedman, had telephoned him about a request from Cross (who was a close colleague of Freedman's) to him to postpone publication because Milik's volume was not yet ready. He also said that some hint of dire consequences was mentioned. So he invited Cross to deliver the message to him personally. Cross's reply (five weeks later)[19] denied bearing any such message for Allegro and any kind of threat; he admitted there was some delay in DJDJ III, and expressed his disapproval of publication ahead of 'official editions'.

Whom to believe? Was John Allegro succumbing to a persecution complex? Or were his colleagues being disingenuous in their protestations of friendship and denials of intrigue? Or both? These are questions that can be pondered endlessly. In the end, we can never be sure of our interpretations.

The story I have told has a rather unhappy ending. The man who did so much to associate Manchester with the Dead Sea Scrolls was told in February 1957 that his appointment was not to be renewed beyond another year. In fact, this outcome was avoided, and Allegro remained as a lecturer at Manchester University until his resignation in 1970. In the meantime his conviction that there were still scrolls and treasures to be found by the Dead Sea prompted him to organize several expeditions to the area, and to set up a 'Dead Sea Scrolls Fund' for the purpose of such exploration.[20]

In 1968 Allegro's volume of edited manuscripts from Cave 4 (DJDJ V) was published, with the cooperation of his Manchester colleague Arnold Anderson; this too met with a cool reception from some of his editorial colleagues.[21] His disillusionment with conventional biblical scholarship and his love of Semitic philology, both strongly developed during the

19. Letter of 21.10.59.

20. Explorations took place in 1959, 1962 and 1963 (see his *Search in the Desert* [London: W.H. Allen, 1965]); the Fund was in existence from 1962 to 1970.

21. See my 'Notes en marge: "Reflections on the Publication of DJDJ 5" ', in H.-J. Fabry, Armin Lange and Hermann Lichtenberger (eds.), *Qumranstudien* (Schriften des Institutum Judaicum Delitzschianum, 4; Göttingen: Vandenhoeck & Ruprecht, 1996), pp. 103-109.

1950s, and especially during the period I have described, led him during the 1960s towards his notorious attack on the former by means of the latter in his *The Sacred Mushroom and the Cross* and its companion, *The End of a Road*, both in 1970.[22]

He had proved himself to be a difficult character to deal with in some ways: excitable, impetuous, maybe a little slippery. But it would be difficult to say that he was the villain of this story. Whatever his motives, and whatever the quality of his transcriptions and interpretations compared with those of others, he remained firmly on the side of the populace and their right to know about the scrolls. At any rate, his correspondence enables us to see behind the public face of academic research and publication to the clash of personality and temperament, the pressures of politics and the pull of the media that those of us following the path of Qumran scholarship have come to know (and love?) so well.

22. J. Allegro, *The Sacred Mushroom and the Cross* (London: Hodder & Stoughton, 1970); *idem, The End of a Road* (London: McGibbon & Kee, 1970). For his later reflections on the impact of the Dead Sea Scrolls on Christianity (in the light of his 'mushroom' thesis) see *The Dead Sea Scrolls and the Christian Myth* (Newton Abbot: Westbridge Books, 1979).

3

Professor Henry Wright Baker: The Copper Scroll and his Career*

William Johnson

Introduction

During a visit to the UK—mainly to study modern impact engineering at the University of Manchester Institute of Science and Technology (UMIST) by an expert in the subject from the Mechanical Engineering Department in Haifa, Israel—at one point a general discussion took off on a different topic of mutual interest, namely the Dead Sea Scrolls. It was surprising to find how little the younger generation present at the *ad hoc* discussion knew of the first events surrounding the subject. Reflecting on this lack of acquaintanceship led older members to observe that there are indeed reports of new findings of scrolls of the same age as those first found in the same region, but few which recapitulate the history of the opening of the original scrolls. This topic itself relates to the history of early Judaism and early Christianity, and to the politics of the time, including the Roman occupation of the area at the time of Hillel and Jesus. The emergence of any new knowledge about the beliefs and writings of the religious sects in the centuries either side of the birth of Jesus almost always causes friction and controversy between scholars about, among other things, the origins of Christianity. In reporting new discoveries, however, there is seldom mention of the practical techniques developed early on to facilitate the opening of scrolls without causing damage, so that they can be easily read.

* This article is a version, slightly revised by the editors, of my article entitled 'Letter to the Editor: Professor Henry Wright Baker: The Dead Sea Scrolls and his Centenary', which first appeared in the *Journal of Materials Processing Technology* 94 (1999), pp. 66-72. It is reprinted here with permission from Elsevier Science. I wish to thank Dr Chris Leach for stimulating discussion on the first part of this paper; I am also very grateful to my wife, Heather, for typing the first published form of this paper.

The task of cutting the first roll of the Copper Scroll was a very important one, not only because it was one that had not been previously carried out, but also because it was being performed on artefacts that are unique and irreplaceable. Had the task failed, those who carried it out would have had to shoulder the opprobrium entailed. The opening of the Copper Scroll not only required technical excellence but courage as well. Strangely, the work was not carried out 'on site' or in neighbouring laboratories but well away, in Manchester, England—once the world centre of manufacturing and machine-tool development! To recall what led to the series of practical events that resulted is a primary purpose of this short paper.

The man of courage and technical competence at the centre of this sterling effort was Professor Henry Wright Baker and here I describe his work in successfully unrolling the metal scrolls, and thus facilitating their reading by scholars. Since the centenary of Professor Baker's birth was passed only recently, I also take the opportunity to recite other notable features of his life's work.

The Opening of the Copper Scroll

The 11-page paper entitled 'Notes on the Opening of the "Bronze" Scrolls from Qumran' was the subject of a lecture by Professor Baker in the John Rylands Library, Manchester, in March 1956. He wrote:

> It was entirely through a chance conversation in a local train that the writer was asked, as an engineer, if it was possible to cut pieces from old and brittle bronze, and gave his opinion that the cutting itself should present no special difficulty if fragmentation were prevented by the application to the exposed surfaces of one of the modern adhesives, which should form a tough and resilient backing having considerable powers of penetrating the interstices of the corroded material.[1]

Some weeks after the conversation, Professor Baker tells us that the Director of Antiquities from Jordan placed the scroll on his desk in Manchester. The task of cutting each roll took only a few days after months of preparation. Principally, the tools he used were a dentist's drill and a small circular saw (normally used for splitting pen nibs). The two rolls of the Copper Scroll were said to be more fragile than thin glass. Stiffening of the rolls for the purpose of cutting them was achieved by

1. 'Notes on the Opening of the "Bronze" Scrolls from Qumran', *BJRL* 39 (1956), pp. 45-56 (46-47).

using aircraft glue. A vacuum cleaner was used to suck up the dust created during the cutting.

It was on 14 March 1952 that two rolled-up beaten copper strips were found in a cave in the foothills near Qumran to the north-west of the Dead Sea. Attempts to open the strips were prevented because they had become extremely brittle and soon crumbled at the edges, even with the application of the smallest of forces. The rolls were originally described as bronze, but they appeared at some stage 'to have formed a single plaque of soft copper-based metal, about 8 feet long and 11 inches wide, built from three pieces of the same size riveted together at the ends, the thickness of the metal being three or four times that of a post card (0.03 in.–0.04 in.)'.[2] The sheets would have been lettered in square Hebrew while they were resting on a soft base, such as wood. The whole riveted scroll had been rolled up some 2000 years ago. The process of rolling had caused one set of rivets to fail, so that one roll contained two pieces and the other the third. Both sides of the broken joint were visible on the outsides of the rolls. The task of unrolling was beset not only with the products of decomposition but also with the adhesion of foreign material.

In December 1953 John M. Allegro had joined the international team set up to edit the scrolls. A graduate of the University of Manchester and subsequently appointed as an assistant lecturer there, Allegro was instrumental in having the Copper Scroll rolls sent to Manchester for cutting. The two rolls had lain in the Palestine Archaeological Museum for months, awaiting a method of opening them without causing damage. The Johns Hopkins University, Baltimore, USA, studied the problem and though it made progress in the matter of reconstituting corroded material, under a Dr Corwin, reluctantly advised that they could not restore the flexibility of the copper. It was concluded that the rolls would have to be cut into strips to render them readable. Allegro tells us that in the spring of 1955 he suggested allowing them to be taken to his city of residence in the UK, where he felt sure, he said, the required technical work could be done while he himself would be near at hand and be available to advise and watch over the cutting.[3] In short, permission was obtained to do this and in July, the first roll was delivered to the Manchester College of

2. Baker, 'Notes', p. 45.

3. Allegro tells his version of the story in *The Dead Sea Scrolls* (Harmondsworth: Penguin Books, 1956), pp. 181-84. The full collation of the two accounts by Wright Baker and Allegro is evidently a little wanting, as is the matter of assistance rendered by technicians.

Technology and in particular put in the hands of Professor Baker of the Department of Mechanical Engineering.

Full technical details of the cutting and handling of the Copper Scroll are given in Wright Baker's lecture published in the *Bulletin of the John Rylands Library* and in his subsequent contribution to the publication of the principal edition of the scroll.[4]

When I last talked to Professor Baker about the Copper Scroll in the summer of 1960, he told me that he had, by then, given about 130 lectures on it. He possessed a physical or relief map—perhaps 2.5 sq. ft—of the country around the Qumran caves. His lecture was enormously successful everywhere, and he was a great favourite, especially on church lecture circuits.

It is remarkable that an achievement, so notable for its method of technical approach (and which allowed so large an amount of knowledge to be unfolded by scholars) and the courage it required, should have attracted so little attention and rewarding recognition by any of the state, university, church or professional bodies.

Henry Wright Baker: His Life and Achievements

Henry Wright Baker was born in November 1893 near Birmingham but brought up in the dark North of England, attending well-known Liverpool College. He told that it took him more than one attempt to matriculate, but he graduated from Owen's College, Manchester University in 1915, in the middle of World War I. He was a member of a Quaker family and hence served in France in a non-combatant role with the Friends' War Victims Relief Committee for four and a half years and 'spending a lot of time on motor transport'. Demobilized, he returned to Owen's to 'rub up' his engineering, but was soon appointed to a part-time assistantship, becoming a full-time assistant lecturer the following year, a lecturer in 1923 and being promoted to senior lecturer as from September 1939—being throughout a member of Professor A.H. Gibson's department, a man distinguished for his work in hydraulics. However, Wright Baker was appointed to the Chair at 'the Tech'[5] from that same date. The achieve-

4. 'Notes on the Opening of the Copper Scrolls from Qumrân', in M. Baillet, J.T. Milik and R. de Vaux, *Les 'petites grottes' de Qumrân* (DJDJ III; Oxford: Clarendon Press, 1962), pp. 203-10.

5. 'The Tech' was the familiar name of the Manchester College of Technology, which is now UMIST.

ments of Professor Baker by then included the award to him of a Thomas Hawksley Premium by the Institution of Mechanical Engineers and in 1938 of the T. Bernard Hall prize.

He had published nine papers on internal combustion engines and directed the research of a number of postgraduate students. At some stage he studied the elasticity of small beams. He was in charge of all the testing of materials and internal combustion engines in the departmental laboratories for external bodies. For his researches on piston temperatures in internal combustion engines he was awarded his University's DSc degree.

He asserted that his first job in the Chair was to clear away inherited 'gigantic' machinery and to replace it with war-surplus equipment which he was able to obtain from the German materials lists controlled by the Ministry of Supply.

In his post at the College of Technology he was mainly responsible for full-time degree and part-time day and evening Higher National and Ordinary National Certificate students; success with the HNC students qualified men for membership of the Institution of Mechanical Engineers. However, in 1940 no students graduated, in 1941 there was one male graduate, in 1942 three, and in 1943 five, of which I was one and so formed one-fifth of the year's graduate output! The war years saw a large rate of growth of graduates; in 1944 the number jumping to about 18 and into the 40s in 1945. The latter increases were due to the introduction of state bursaries, aiming to produce men better trained for the army (for the Corps of Royal Electrical and Mechanical Engineers) and for research in government research establishments.

An endeavour of Professor Baker was to start, in 1952, a *Bulletin of Mechanical Engineering Education* with (now Professor) Dr K.L. Johnson as its first editor. This small publication has now been available for more than 45 years, but, alas, its circulation is still fewer than about 300; despite the efforts of the *Bulletin* Board chairman and editor, it has never attained what could be claimed to be true world status or worldwide circulation. Further, many of the articles published over the years failed to demonstrate a clear teaching element.

For some years after Dr K.L. Johnson left for Cambridge, the editorship was in the hands of Dr John Parker and Dr J.H. Lamble. In the mid-1960s, Pergamon Press was persuaded to take on the publication of this journal and indeed its size and length grew to match that of other regular Pergamon journals. Unfortunately, after some years it was seen to have failed to interest a sufficiently large number of teachers and was rejected by

Robert Maxwell for not being able to make a profit of at least 20 per cent. The aim of the *Bulletin*—teaching—was noble, but its history truly underlines the fact that advancement in academia does not lie there. Subsequently, the *Bulletin* was offered to the Institution of Mechanical Engineers for it to take over. For some of us, this seemed the *Bulletin*'s natural home as a regular professional organ dedicated to technical training. It could have been a journal committed to supporting and pointing the way for the training of mechanical engineers (of all grades, professional or not)—a publication devoted to discussing course content, examinations, teaching methods and standards, and so on. The Institution turned down the invitation, thus proving that it had little time and little imagination for dealing with the essential material of education. Today the *Bulletin* appears at about the same size and with the same frequency as it had initially, but it does not fill the bright role teachers had hoped for or by fulfilling the aims that Professor Baker desired.

In the 1950s Professor Baker started a 'Clearing House' for checking admission qualifications and for placing mainly grammar school boys in the technical faculties of British universities. It was an innovative and unofficial service that Professor Baker willingly took on.[6] The situation today is that the role of a 'Clearing House' has been superseded by a national office, working for would-be students in any subject. Whether UCAS (Universities and Colleges Admissions Service) derives entirely from Professor Baker's initial work, I cannot say.

It was claimed by Professor Baker that he developed a degree course with a bias towards Production Engineering. He meant by this, of course, the study of the physical processes of manufacture and not such subjects as were to be found in a Department of Industrial Administration—the study of planning, progressing, time and motion, commercial law, economics, labour relations and works organizational structure, and so on. Indeed, the latter kind of subjects seemed sometimes to incur his displeasure. He started a sub-department of Machine Tool Design in the 1950s, claiming it to be the first of its kind in the UK. (In fact, he was following a well-established German specialism.) The department was fortunate in having recruited Dr (later Professor) Frank Koenigsberger to its staff in the late 1940s. He and his family were refugees from Germany. This sub-department received continuous extra support for development well into the 1960s. Soon after my own appointment succeeding Professor

6. I had from him, incidentally, a letter in which he nicely indicates the origin of the practice.

Baker in September 1960, I decided to arrange the department in three divisions: myself leading the Applied Mechanics Division, Dr Koenigsberger was promoted from reader to professor of Machine Tool Engineering, while Dr Rowland Benson, reader in Mechanical Engineering at Liverpool University, became a professor (and director) of the Division of Thermo- and Fluid-mechanics.

It is possible to make out a departmental bias towards the study of manufacturing engineering even from the year of the department's inception in 1897 with the appointment of Professor John Nicholson. He visited the USA and Canada and saw there a divergence towards research work in metal-cutting theory and machine design. Typical of the former was the measurement of cutting forces and the development of tool life equations, as originally established by F.W. Taylor.[7] Manchester Tech., by virtue of Professor Baker's early initiative, had for several years the only MSc course in Machine Tool Engineering in any conventional university. Through the 1960s and 1970s the department developed very successfully research in metal cutting and later metal forming. It was one of Professor Baker's undergraduates, Professor F.W. Travis, who went on to establish and himself become the editor of the now *Journal of Materials Processing Technology*—probably the prime international engineering journal of its field today.

Professor Baker edited two volumes of *Modern Workshop Technology*, with theory, in 1948 that subsequently ran into several more editions. His principal interest was, however, in thermodynamics, and it is by Inchley's *The Theory of Heat Engines* (London: Longmans, Green, 1913) that he is most widely known. William Inchley had produced his book in 1913 but was killed in action in World War I in December 1915. Dr A. Morley with others revised the first edition and, as a tribute to their colleague, republished it in 1920, again in 1928 and at intervals until October 1936. Further revision was seen as necessary and the need for a fourth edition was met by Professor Baker in 1938. *The Technology of Heat*, an adaptation of the former book, appeared in 1966. Contributions to internal combustion engine science, through scientific work, can be found in footnotes of the second volume of D.R. Pye's *Internal Combustion Engines*.[8]

7. There is a very well-known equation, complicated variants of which are still found, between tool life (T) and cutting tool speed (V), as $VT^n = a$, constant, and n being an empirically determined constant for a given material and circumstances.

8. D.R. Pye, *Internal Combustion Engines* (London: Oxford University Press, 1934), pp. 79, 82.

Professor Baker was a member of the Institution of Mechanical Engineers, of the Institution of Automobile Engineers and President of the Manchester Association of Engineers, 1952–53. He was a member of the General Board of the National Physical Laboratory in 1951 and his department came to possess excellent metrology equipment, such that it was accepted as a National Testing Centre for the North of England—testimony to his constant effort to enlarge and upgrade his department's laboratories. CIRP, the International College for Research in Production, was established by the French in about 1953, and until retirement Professor Baker, a founder member, remained a staunch supporter of its activities.

Professor Wright Baker 'coined' his own double-barrelled name to distinguish himself from Professor John Baker of Cambridge, who had been appointed to that Engineering Department in 1943. Wright Baker was a well-made man of fine appearance and, if seen in his laboratory coat, immediately inspired great faith in his competence for tackling any mechanical engineering problem with his own large hands. He looked 'every inch a professor', when displaying his gold watch and chain on a brown waistcoat. His lecturing style and written hand were not the most prepossessing and, strangely, he was not a stickler for discipline in classes. His personality has been variously described but most people found him friendly and engaging, vigorous and communicative but always with firmly held views that he was not backward in expressing. He was a Quaker and, one suspects, little swayed by titles. For ten years he was a resident senior tutor at Dalton Hall, a fine student residence, and sometime Vice Chairman. Professor Baker was a noted lecturer to extra-mural classes at the Summer School for teachers in technical institutions.

His wife, Kathleen M. Drew DSc (1928), was a distinguished senior lecturer in the Department of Botany at Owen's College. They had two children, their son becoming a fine veterinary surgeon. When not professionally active, Professor Baker made some of his own furniture in an attic workshop, indulged himself with wide-angled photography and was open to discussion of music, stereophonic sound, gardening and able to execute, he said, 'his own bit of modern sculpture'.

After retiring—his wife predeceased him—he was appointed by UNESCO and the Indian government to be Chief Advisor on the setting up of the Central Mechanical Engineering Laboratory at Durgapur, about 100 miles from Calcutta, which he visited for a few months each year in the period 1960–64. Professor Henry Wright Baker died on 1 May 1969.

4

When Images Meet: The Potential of Photographic and Computer Imaging Technology for the Study of the Copper Scroll*

Marilyn J. Lundberg and Bruce Zuckerman

The last decade has witnessed an explosion in the use of photography, computer imaging and other advanced technologies for the study of ancient manuscripts and inscriptions. These approaches to epigraphy and paleography represent a major departure from the standard procedures used in virtually every epigraphic and philological study of a manuscript or inscription for the past two hundred years. These established procedures have usually involved studying the original text or squeeze by eye, producing a hand drawing of the text also by eye and from there a transcription/ transliteration and translation with supporting commentary. Within the last hundred or so years photographs have often accompanied publications, but rarely have epigraphers thought of these images as the primary data upon which their readings are based. Rather, the primary data tends to be presented as either hand drawings or even transliterations based upon the best epigraphic judgment of the researcher. Epigraphers wanting to do new editions or wanting to check uncertain readings have usually had only one recourse: to go back to the original inscriptions. And even then they have had to rely on their own 'eye-witness' testimony to back any differences they would propose from their predecessors' readings. This has made epigraphy a somewhat doubtful science, since the level of subjectivity is inevitably high and the ability to arbitrate among various interpretations is invariably low. Besides, there are other unfortunate results that come of

* This article was originally written in 1996 and reflects current technology at the time. Technology has, of course, changed radically since that date, and many advances have been made in the computer techniques used by the West Semitic Research Project.

this state of affairs. For one thing, the more a given inscription is examined, the more it is subjected to the risk of damage and deterioration. On the other hand, because so few students have opportunity of seeing a text clearly, they can go through an entire course of study in 'epigraphy' without examining anything more than a printed transcription and drawing in a textbook.

In the past such has been the case with the Copper Scroll. John Allegro's edition of the scroll provides hand drawings, transcriptions and translations, with an occasional photograph as illustration.[1] The edition by J.T. Milik provides hand drawings and composite photographs of the various columns, but the photographs in many places are unclear and difficult to use.[2] Until 1988 the only other photographic resource was the negatives of those composite photographs in the Palestine Archaeological Museum (PAM) collection, themselves apparently taken from prints.

In 1988 a new series of photographs of the Copper Scroll was taken in Amman, Jordan, by Bruce and Kenneth Zuckerman of the West Semitic Research Project (WSRP) of the University of Southern California, in cooperation with the Princeton Theological Seminary as part of a project to publish a new edition of the scroll under the joint sponsorship of the Department of Antiquities, Jordan (Ghazi Bisheh and Fawzi Zayadine), the West Semitic Research Project (Bruce Zuckerman), Princeton Theological Seminary (James Charlesworth), and Johns Hopkins University (P.K. McCarter).

Photographing the scroll presented unique challenges—especially in terms of lighting—since each segment is curved, requiring very precise light placement for the interior of a partial cylinder. In addition, the letters are sometimes only lightly incised, the surface is often corroded and some pieces have broken off.

In order to get the best photographic results, the Zuckermans constructed a 'cradle' in the shape of a half cylinder, lined in black, in which the segments were remounted and could be easily rotated. Each segment was photographed with large format (4 ins. × 5 ins.) film as color transparencies and black-and-white negatives in three or four different rotations, usually left, center and right, and two lighting directions, from the top and from the bottom. So that each area of a cut would be optimally represented in

1. J.M. Allegro, *The Treasure of the Copper Scroll* (London: Routledge & Kegan Paul, 1960), e.g., pp. 25, 26.

2. M. Baillet, J.T. Milik and R. de Vaux, *Les 'petites grottes' de Qumrân* (DJDJ III; Oxford: Clarendon Press, 1962), e.g., pls. XLIX, LI.

at least one photograph, approximately seven photographs were taken of each cut at bracketed exposures. Lighting was done with two strobe flashes, both having snoot reflectors. A 'snoot' consists essentially of an open-ended cylinder about 6 ins. long through which the light generated from an electronic strobe is converted into a narrow column of light. Since this light column is so narrow, it is possible to send it in at an extremely low angle relative to the surface being illuminated; hence the shadows created can often throw even the most subtle indentations into startling relief. Because this light covers only a limited amount of area, the snoots were stacked diagonally so that each light covered approximately half the scroll section with an area of overlap in the middle.

The new photographs have been made available to the editors of the new edition and other interested researchers, usually in the form of color prints or black-and-white transparencies. In our experience, the use of both color and black-and-white is important, since each type of film can give different kinds of information. In general, we prefer to use transparencies with a light box for study purposes, since transparencies yield a far greater dynamic range from light to dark than a paper print and therefore possess a greater degree of subtlety.

The WSRP photographs, while a great improvement over what was previously available, also have certain limitations. First, the Zuckermans did not have the opportunity to do detailed photographs of the scroll, particularly of the problem areas. It is possible to make photographic enlargements of these areas from the existing transparencies and negatives, but the process is time consuming, and at some point, even starting from high-resolution, large format film, there will be a loss of resolution that inhibits epigraphic analysis. Second, the photographs were taken 36 years after the discovery of the scroll, after a certain amount of deterioration had occurred. Third, scholarly access is still difficult, since there are 148 different photographs in the series, including shots of the back, and reproducing the whole series is both expensive and time consuming. Fourth, study is somewhat awkward since one needs to work with a minimum of six photographs for every cut.

Because it is difficult, if not impossible, to reclaim with new photographs the way the scroll looked nearly 50 years ago, interest in early photographs of the Copper Scroll has remained high throughout the years, although none of them have been available for study; indeed, little was known about their whereabouts until fairly recently. In an early version of the Introduction to *The Dead Sea Scrolls Catalogue*, Dr Stephen Reed had noted that a number of photographs taken by Mr Ashton and J. Starcky were in existence, but the location of those photographs was unknown to him, and, indeed, remains unknown to the present time.

In late 1993 West Semitic Research, through George Brooke, became aware of a set of early photographs belonging to the estate of John Allegro and held by the University of Manchester. Dr Brooke told us that publication of a microfiche edition of those photographs was going to be done by E.J. Brill. We suggested that West Semitic Research produce the prints for the microfiche edition, and, at the same time, make copies of selected negatives as use copies to be held by WSR for an agreed-upon period, while right of distribution would remain at the discretion of Joan Allegro. An agreement was eventually entered into with Mrs Allegro and the Manchester Museum, and in the spring of 1995 Dr Brooke flew out to Los Angeles with the Allegro collection, leaving it with us for reproduction and archiving.

The Allegro collection consists of approximately 1450 images. Most of these are 2.25 ins. square black-and-white negatives, but some are 35 mm color or black-and-white transparencies. The collection includes not only Copper Scroll photographs, but three other sets as well: (1) archeological photographs taken at Qumran and other sites in the Judean desert; (2) historical photographs of many of the people involved in the finding and editing of the Dead Sea Scrolls (including Allegro); and (3) various Dead Sea Scrolls (DSS) documents other than the Copper Scroll, including pictures of various editors piecing together DSS manuscripts.

The Copper Scroll photographs themselves document several steps in the unrolling process: (1) the unopened scrolls; (2) the cutting process done by Henry Wright Baker; (3) the cleaning process, done primarily by Rosalind Baker; (4) the layout of the scrolls in specially built 'cradles'; and (5) the individual segments taken at various angles and rotations. The last category includes two sets: shots of the segments laid out in their holders, and shots of the segments held by hand in sunlight.

The photographs in the latter two categories seem to have been done using the same basic principles as those used by the Zuckermans in Jordan in 1988, albeit in a somewhat less sophisticated and technical manner. Those principles involve the rotation of the partial-cylinder cuts and the use of different light angles to obtain the optimal readings for each part of the cut.

In addition to documentation of the opening process, itself a fascinating record, the early photographs supply valuable information about the condition of the scroll when it was first cut. In several key areas early photographs show intact areas that have since cracked or broken. While we have not ourselves done a detailed examination of all the photographs, it may also prove to be the case that there are areas of dispute that can be clarified by these early pictures, or readings near the edges that can be reclaimed. The publication of the microfiche edition has added a valuable resource to the study of the scroll and is one solution to the problem of access.

The Allegro microfiche project and others like it—such as E.J. Brill's microfiche edition of the Dead Sea Scrolls photographs,[3] efforts by the Ancient Biblical Manuscript Center to collect photographs and microfilms of biblical documents, the new images provided by Electricité de France (EDF) and the West Semitic Research Project's numerous photographic projects—are the result of a growing awareness that photographs, once taken only for inventory or documentation purposes, themselves can be a valuable resource for study. Indeed, many early PAM and Shrine of the Book photographs of the Dead Sea Scrolls now provide the only source for many subsequently lost or damaged texts.

Along with this growing appreciation of photographs, there has in the last decade been an increasing interest in the use of computer imaging in the study of ancient texts, of which the Oxford University Project, the Ugaritic Tablets Digital Edition,[4] sponsored by a consortium of scholars and universities, and the work done by EDF, are only three examples.

The West Semitic Research Project has been exploring the uses of computer imaging for the past decade and a half, but it is only recently that the price of equipment has come down and the memory capacity of soft media has been expanded to the point where the high-resolution scans necessary for detailed study have become practical to the scholar of ancient texts. The availability of equipment and memory has made it possible for us to set up an imaging laboratory, the Ancient Manuscript Digitization and Distribution Project (AMDDP), in Leavey Library at the University of Southern California. There we have been applying computer techniques to the study of a number of texts, including the Copper Scroll, in an effort to demonstrate the potential of the technology for detailed examination

3. Timothy H. Lim in consultation with Philip S. Alexander (eds.), *The Dead Sea Scrolls: Electronic Reference Library*, I (London: Oxford University Press; Leiden: E.J. Brill, 1996).

4. For an example of the work made possible by the project, see Theodore J. Lewis, 'The Disappearance of the Goddess Anat: The 1995 West Semitic Research Project on Ugaritic Epigraphy', *BA* 59 (1996), pp. 115-21.

and decipherment of ancient inscriptions. The following images[5] will show a number of ways in which computers can be of value for the study of the Copper Scroll photographs and by implication for other ancient documents and inscriptions.

(1) The simplest procedures, using an imaging program such as Adobe Photoshop, involve enhancing the quality of a scanned image with tools that adjust such things as brightness, color balance, contrast and sharpness (Fig. 4.1). Many of these same techniques can be done with standard dark-room equipment, but the process is much more difficult, haphazard and time consuming. On the computer, even enlarging becomes a relatively quick and simple matter when all one has to do is click on the image. What is especially important is the precision of manipulation for digital images. One can work with an exactitude that was simply impossible previously.

(2) Fitting fragments together, or restoring broken edges, can be done on the computer, without having to handle the original, fragile, pieces. When the Zuckermans photographed Cut 10 of the Copper Scroll, several of the pieces from the lower right were not attached to the main part of the cut, but kept in a separate box. An attempt was made to fit the pieces to the cut by hand, but the joins were only approximate. Using imaging tools the pieces can be 'cut out' (Fig. 4.2) and moved with greater precision to their original places (Fig. 4.3). Comparison with an early photograph of the intact cut can be used to verify placement (Fig. 4.4). This procedure becomes especially important when broken pieces have deteriorated over time or have simply been lost or destroyed. One can then search the older images for these 'missing links' and proceed to put them back in place with other images. We have demonstrated this procedure with fragments of 1QDan^{b} in a recent publication.[6]

(3) The curved surface of the Copper Scroll cuts makes it impossible to view any one photograph and read the whole cut with any degree of accuracy. The editors of the DJDJ III volume realized this and attempted

5. The original images shown at the International Symposium were 35 mm color transparencies, backed up on computer by high-resolution color images. The black-and-white prints necessary for this publication do not reflect the quality of the original images. Should readers desire to see the original images they can contact West Semitic Research, 12 Empty Saddle Road, Rolling Hills Estates, CA 90274, USA.

6. Marilyn Lundberg and Bruce Zuckerman, 'New Aramaic Fragments from Qumran Cave One', *The Comprehensive Aramaic Lexicon Newsletter* 12 (Autumn, 1996), pp. 1-5.

Fig. 4.1. *3Q15 Copper Scroll, Cut 15* [7]

Fig. 4.2. *3Q15 Copper Scroll, Cut 10, lower right*

Fig. 4.3. *3Q15 Copper Scroll, Cut 10, lower right, restored*

Fig. 4.4. *3Q15 Copper Scroll, Cut 10*
(Photograph by John Allegro, courtesy Joan Allegro)

7. Unless otherwise stated, the figures in this chapter were photographed by Bruce and Kenneth Zuckerman in collaboration with the Princeton Theological Seminary. Courtesy Department of Antiquities, Amman. Imaging by Marilyn Lundberg.

to build composite photographs, apparently by cutting up prints and rephotographing the prints in their composite form. Computer imaging enables such composites to be built with a great deal more precision so that a 'flattened' cut can be displayed on screen, written onto film and published (Fig. 4.5[a]-[d]). Here the flattest areas from four rotations of Cut 15, col. 8 have been selected and moved to create a simulation of the section before it was rolled (cf. Fig. 4.1). The same can be done with separate cuts to complete whole columns of text (Fig. 4.6). In this case, composites were made of Cuts 5 and 6 (col. 2) and then joined together to create an entire column. The joins between cuts, of course, are more visible, due to the deterioration over time of the edges of the cuts.

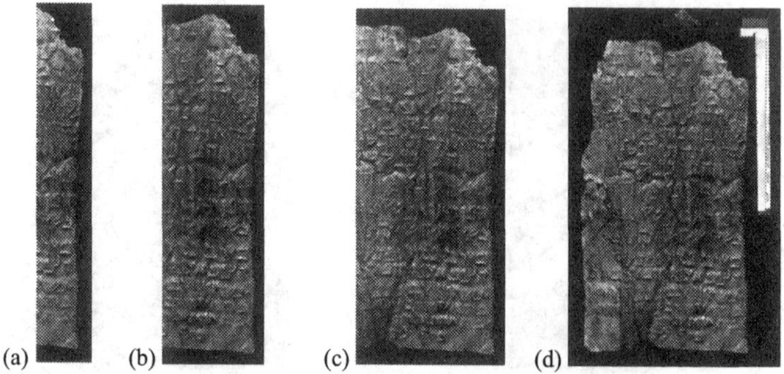

Fig. 4.5. *3Q15 Copper Scroll, Cut 15: (a) far right; (b) right ½ flattened; (c) right ¾ flattened; (d) flattened*

Fig. 4.6. *3Q15 Copper Scroll, Cuts 5 and 6*

(4) The convention of drawing becomes easier on a computer screen because computer programs such as Adobe Photoshop offer powerful tools that can turn any trained epigrapher into a superior graphic artist. A series of points can be placed along a given letter (Fig. 4.7). The computer joins, or draws, between the points, which can be precisely adjusted at high magnification. One need not be very good at drawing to produce precision drawing accurate to a scale of microns. In addition, the ability to draw right on the text allows for a very high degree of accuracy (Fig. 4.8).

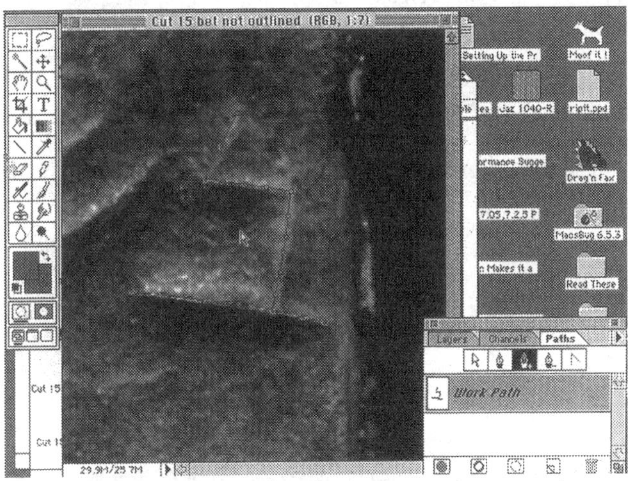

Fig. 4.7. *3Q15 Copper Scroll, Cut 15 detail, showing the use of 'Paths' in Adobe Photoshop to electronically outline the letter* beth

Fig. 4.8. *3Q15 Copper Scroll, Cut 15 detail, showing an electronic drawing superimposed on an image of the Copper Scroll*

(5) It has been noted that some of the letters on the Copper Scroll are difficult to distinguish from one another: *beth* and *mem, beth* and *kaph, yod* and *waw, he* and *ḥeth.* This lack of distinction is the basis for many of the disputed readings of the text. Using the computer to build a script chart allows a much more precise comparison of letter shapes, and, it is hoped, clarification in a number of questioned readings. The example included here, while not technically a script chart, shows sample letters from all sides of the Incirli Inscription, a Phoenician Inscription from the eighth century BCE, that have been cloned and lifted to a separate file in the same manner that a script chart could be built (Fig. 4.9).

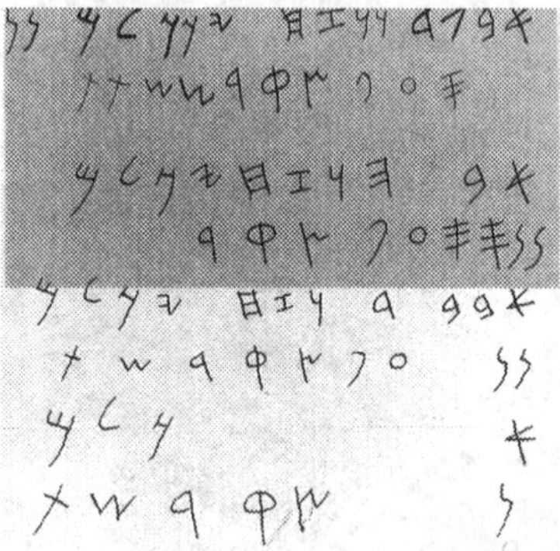

Fig. 4.9. *Incirli Inscription script*
(Imaging by Marilyn Lundberg and Bruce Zuckerman)

(6) It is also possible to clone clear letters and use them to clarify less certain letters, or attempt reconstruction where one letter is broken or only partially visible. We did this successfully with fragments of 1QDan[b]. We had identified parts of the letter *lamedh* in a new fragment we photographed in 1995 and in the large fragment of the text photographed by John Trever in 1949. We decided to reconstruct the whole letter using the scribe's own handwriting as a template. We found another whole *lamedh* in the main fragment, drew it using computer imaging tools, copied it and dragged it down to the partial letter, where we made the cloned letter semi-opaque and used it as a guide to draw the reconstructed letter (Figs. 4.10 and 4.11). We have also used cloned letters extensively in the Incirli Inscription. On that text many of the letters are worn and unclear. Using this technique we can try different letters out to see which fits, or which is the most probable fit. Similar techniques seem ideal for the Copper Scroll.

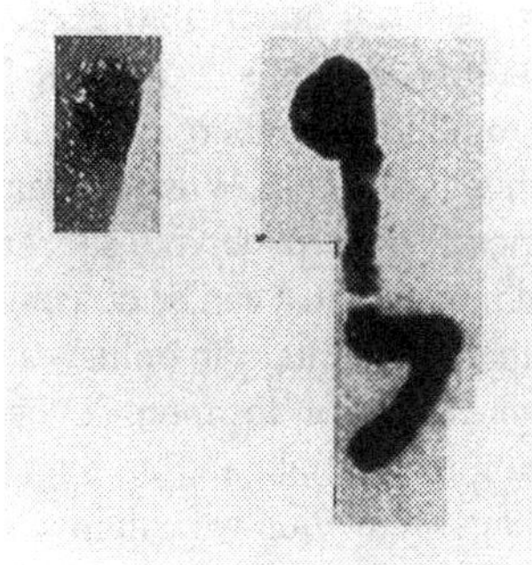

Fig. 4.10. *1QDan*[b]
(Imaging by Marilyn Lundberg and Bruce Zuckerman)

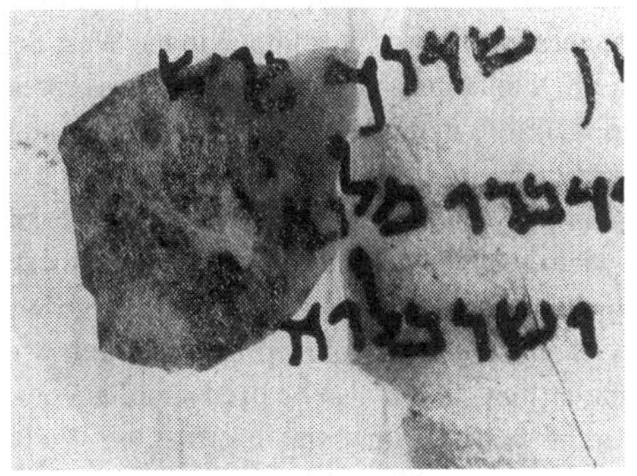

Fig. 4.11. *1QDan*[b] *detail*
(Imaging by Marilyn Lundberg and Bruce Zuckerman. Photographs by John Trever, Marilyn Lundberg and Bruce Zuckerman)

The combination of the early Allegro photographs, the high-resolution West Semitic Research Project photographs, computer imaging and the images produced by EDF provides a powerful array of tools for future study of the Copper Scroll and other ancient texts.

First, high-resolution computer imaging can allow close, detailed study of images of the original text. Computers allow nearly instantaneous enlargement of problem areas and simultaneous examination of those areas in several different photographs.

Second, the use of high-quality, high-resolution photographs and high-resolution scanning can have the effect of democratizing study, making distribution quicker and less expensive and giving access to many more students and scholars than can either view the original text or obtain photographic reproductions. With this in mind the WSRP has applied for and received a grant from the Annenberg Center for Communications at the University of Southern California. With the grant we are in the process of building a dual-purpose World Wide Web site, one with low-resolution images for educational purposes that can be downloaded from the Internet and a second section that will include an online catalogue of images that can be obtained in high-resolution form on CD or other media, since at this time high-resolution images take far too long to download from the Internet. To meet that latter limitation we will investigate ways of sending high-resolution images over the Internet in the future.[8]

Third, the publication of the Allegro archive allows access to the earliest images of the Copper Scroll, allowing retrieval of information on areas of the scroll that have since deteriorated. Availability of these photographs through the Manchester Museum, in addition to the West Semitic Research photographs and EDF pictures, means that each cut is represented by multiple images and therefore multiple rotation and lighting angles that can be checked for clarification of disputed readings.

Fourth, the multiple images of each cut can be more easily manipulated and compared when scanned at high resolution, sized to a common scale, and brought up onto a computer screen. Pictures old and new can be studied side-by-side and even combined in a way that was never before possible. Computer images can also be used simultaneously with photographic transparencies to optimize the information. We have found this combination of techniques to be indispensable in the decipherment of the Incirli Inscription. One might be tempted to consider computers as a replacement for conventional photography, but in our experience this is simply not the case. Computer imaging allows for ease of manipulation and study in many ways, but good photographic images contain information that computers cannot reproduce—a certain three-dimensional quality that is invaluable in the study of inscriptions in hard media. While on soft-media Dead Sea Scrolls this is less crucial, for an incised inscription like the Copper Scroll, the subtlety of the photographic image should be used to match the power of the digital image.

8. Since the article was written, WRSP has established the website: http://www.usc.edu.dept/LAS/wsrp, and has begun developing InscriptiFact, a database of high-resolution images for distribution over the Internet. For further details, write to the address given in n. 5. High-resolution digital images of the Copper Scroll are currently available on CD-ROM.

Our remarks on the images included here are by no means intended to be an exhaustive course in photography and computer imaging, but rather are meant to convey just a hint of the possibilities available as, more and more, technology is made available for scholars and researchers of the Copper Scroll, and other ancient texts of all scripts and languages.

5

Some Results of a New Examination of the Copper Scroll (3Q15)

Émile Puech

Introduction

Right after the discovery of the Copper Scroll by archaeologists in Cave 3, on 20 March 1952, a first rapid examination established that it had to do with 'a Hebrew non-biblical text, divided into short paragraphs with numerical signs and abbreviations', in short, 'a sort of catalogue'.[1] After studying the scrolls in the Rockefeller Museum in Jerusalem, September–October 1953, Professor K.-G. Kuhn expressed the hypothesis that they contained a description of the places where the riches of the Qumran community had been hidden.[2] However, this could only remain a hypothesis while the unrolling of the scrolls was awaited; the unrolling would allow for the study of the text in its entirety. Since the corroded state of the copper made their unrolling impossible, the College of Technology of the University of Manchester, which had become interested in cutting them open, gave the delicate task to Professor H. Wright Baker, who successfully completed the task between July 1955 and January 1956. The 23 strips were returned to Jordan in April 1956 and the editing of the text was entrusted to J.T. Milik, who thus had at his disposal the originals, the photographs and the copy prepared under the direction of Wright Baker.[3] Milik rapidly prepared a provisional translation that was the basis for press

1. Cf. R. de Vaux, 'Introduction', in M. Baillet, J.T. Milik and R. de Vaux, *Les 'petites grottes' de Qumrân* (DJDJ III; Oxford, Clarendon Press, 1962) (cited hereafter as DJDJ III), p. 201.

2. K.-G. Kuhn, 'Les rouleaux de cuivre de Qumrân', *RB* 61 (1954), pp. 193-205.

3. Cf. H.W. Baker, 'Notes on the Opening of the Copper Scrolls from Qumrân', DJDJ III, pp. 207-10: it is pointed out that this was a copy made by a person who did not know Hebrew.

releases on 1 June 1956, in Jordan, England, USA and France,[4] and then a translation and a topographical commentary, which was published in 1959.[5] The diplomatic edition, delivered to the volume's editor in September 1959, was published by Oxford's Clarendon Press in 1962.[6] Meanwhile J.M. Allegro, who had been able to study the scroll and the photographs at Manchester as early as 1955–56, published his own unofficial edition in London in 1960.[7]

In the first decade after its discovery this text intrigued scholars, but then for the most part it was forgotten in research; a renewal of interest in the scroll was resumed only after B. Pixner's study was published in 1983.[8] Numerous detailed studies have been dedicated to it since and several re-editions are in preparation. One of these, by P.K. McCarter, in the Princeton series edited by J.H. Charlesworth, has benefited from new photographs by the Zuckerman brothers taken during the winter of 1988–89 at Amman, which were the basis for the studies by McCarter in 1992 and 1994.[9] For his part, A. Wolters, who has prepared his own edition and translation, speaks of having studied the scroll at length in Amman in June 1991.[10]

4. Cf. 'Communiqué de R. de Vaux à la séance du 1er juin', *Comptes rendus de l'Académie des inscriptions et belles lettres* (1956), pp. 224-25.

5. J.T. Milik, 'Le rouleau de cuivre de Qumrân (3Q15): Traduction et commentaire topographique', *RB* 66 (1959), pp. 321-57.

6. Cf. DJDJ III, pp. 211-302, 314-17, with a palaeographic note by F.M. Cross, pp. 217-21.

7. J.M. Allegro, *The Treasure of the Copper Scroll* (London: Routledge & Kegan Paul, 1960).

8. B. Pixner, 'Unravelling the Copper Scroll Code: A Study on the Topography of 3Q15', *RevQ* 11 (1983), pp. 323-65.

9. P.K. McCarter, 'The Mysterious Copper Scroll: Clues to Hidden Temple Treasure', *BR* 8.4 (1992), pp. 34-41, 63-64, with a French translation 'Le mystère du *Rouleau de cuivre*', in H. Shanks (ed.), *L'aventure des manuscrits de la mer Morte* (Paris: Editions du Seuil, 1996); P.K. McCarter, 'The Copper Scroll Treasure as an Accumulation of Religious Offerings', in M.O. Wise, N. Golb, J.J. Collins and D. Pardee (eds.), *Methods of Investigation of the Dead Sea Scrolls and the Khirbet Qumran Site: Present Realities and Future Prospects* (Annals of the New York Academy of Sciences, 722; New York: The New York Academy of Sciences, 1994), pp. 133-48.

10. Cf. A. Wolters, 'Literary Analysis and the Copper Scroll', in Z.J. Kapera (ed.), *Intertestamental Essays in Honour of Jósef Tadeusz Milik* (Qumranica mogilanensia, 6; Krakow: Enigma Press, 1992), pp. 239-52; *idem*, 'History and the Copper Scroll', in Wise *et al.* (eds.), *Methods of Investigation*, pp. 285-98 (292), where he makes reference to two other studies to appear, 'Cultic Terminology in the Copper Scroll'

The scroll was then entrusted to Electricité de France (EDF) for scientific restoration and conservation; first of all, excellent X-ray images were made and from now on these alone should serve as a starting point for the decipherment of the delicate and controversial points of the preserved text. M. Albouy of the Direction Générale-Mécénat technologique et scientifique (EDF), in full agreement with J.T. Milik, the official editor and author of the *editio princeps* of the scroll, very much wanted to associate me with his project of collating the text, which, together with the work of restoration and conservation, became one of the goals of EDF's research. A new edition had been long awaited by the scholarly community. I had all the time needed to study the X-ray images in the laboratories of EDF during several stays in Paris between 1994 and 1996. In order to see this enterprise through to a successful conclusion and discover the exact dimension of the scroll when flat, which was no longer possible with the original, but was important for the configuration of the gaps or other matters, it was proposed that a cast should be prepared which would be an exact replica of the scroll. This project was skilfully carried out by the experts at EDF–Valectra between 1994 and 1996.

For a rigorous palaeographic study of the text, we were thus able to have at our disposal threefold documentation: (1) the X-ray images of the sections taken from different angles, taking into account the curvature of the metal, which especially distorted the letters on either side of the central axis; (2) photographs of the flattened replica and of the galvanoplasty itself, as well as (3) a re-examination of the original in 1996.[11] The two series of images had to be studied jointly so as to be sure of the exact configuration of the original and of the carving of the letters on the engraving;[12] it must be remembered that the process of etching cannot have the

(forthcoming in vol. 2 of the Milik Festschrift) and 'Textual Notes on the Copper Scroll'. See also his new edition and translation, A. Wolters, *The Copper Scroll: Overview, Text and Translation* (Sheffield: Sheffield Academic Press, 1996).

11. See my re-edition of the text 'Le Rouleau de Cuivre de la grotte 3 de Qumrân (3Q15)' to appear in the volume prepared by EDF Mécénat technologique et scientifique for the NTOA Series archaeologica (Göttingen: Vandenhoeck & Ruprecht; Fribourg: Presse Universitaire, forthcoming) from which the main points of this paper have been extracted.

12. It definitely involves engraving with a mallet, which alone can explain the impact of the tool, the alignment of marks and the reduplication of certain impressions, not an incision or a simple line made with the help of a stylus. There is nothing comparable with the incisions well known in other respects on delicate sheets or strips of gold, silver, bronze or lead.

same precision and homogeneity as writing in ink by an experienced scribe. Anyone a little familiar with this matter quite quickly becomes aware that the writing underwent change as the etching of the columns proceeded, as if the attention of the copyist petered out or his time was short and he had to hurry to finish. The mistakes and carelessness become more and more frequent as we approach the end: there are jumbles, a number of cursive letters, segmenting, haplographies, and so on.

In our edition we have made a new graphic mock-up of the 12 columns in which we tried to be as faithful as possible to the mind of the engraver. This mock-up has benefited from having the cast as a replica that is identical to the original except for the joins between the sections. The photographs taken before each step of the original cutting, to which we have not had access, might make it possible to add some vertical strokes that have disappeared under the teeth of the saw and so, in some rare cases still under discussion, verify the presence or absence of a *waw* or *yod*, which can be of some importance (e.g. col. 12.8: *kl* or *kly byt* …; col. 1.10 *hšb'* or *hšbw'*…). The copy in the *editio princeps* is essentially that which was prepared through the good offices of the laboratory in Manchester, whose draughtsmen did not know Hebrew, but that copy was read and corrected by Milik, who collated it with the original in Amman in 1959.[13] It does not represent a tracing of the original, the editor warns us; to have that, a flat impression would have had to be used, but at that time this was not possible since there were no sufficiently tested means for dealing with the originals, which were so oxidized and fragile.

Milik recalls that a number of small fragments were already broken off the first scroll (cols. 1-8) at the time of the discovery and that other generally tiny and uninscribed pieces fell off when it was cut into strips. In May 1956 he attempted to join to the scroll most of those which contained complete letters or parts of letters, and made transcriptions of

13. Cf. Milik, DJDJ III, pp. 211-12: 'J'ai essayé de rémédier aux inexactitudes qui en sont la conséquence: ajoutant des traits omis et supprimant des traces qui n'appartiennent pas aux lettres ou chiffres; corrigeant les tracés; retouchant les signes—si c'était possible—de façon à rétablir les proportions et l'inclinaison réelles des traits composant les lettres et les chiffres. Le résultat…ne représente pas un décalque matériel de l'original; il nous paraît néanmoins d'une fidélité suffisante pour garantir l'exactitude de l'aspect formel de l'écriture et, sauf mention contraire… l'exactitude foncière de la transcription proposée… Une photographie meilleure et plus exacte, et ainsi un fac-similé plus fidèle, pourraient être obtenus à partir d'un estampage à plat. Mais on avait des raisons de craindre que les moyens actuellement connus (papier, plâtre, pliatex) n'abîment sérieusement les rouleaux du cuivre oxydé.'

them, though he left them aside without sticking them back together. It is regrettable that Milik did not report the exact position of these detached inscribed fragments, since some suggestions about readings depend on their positioning.[14]

Subsequent studies have relied on the *editio princeps*, of course, but also on Allegro's, which was far from satisfactory in many ways.[15] Although most authors were critical of the defects of the photographic documentation available, as far as I have been able to determine, none of them, editor(s) included, were curious enough to make the most of all the documentation published in 1962 in the *editio princeps*. Nonetheless, that documentation has surprises in store that even the latest techniques in clarifying matters cannot make up for, since these cannot deal with more than what is preserved.

Decipherment

For a start, here are some results that were accessible to any decipherer of the scroll right from the moment of its publication in 1962.[16]

Column 10.16-17

The lower right angle of column 10 has disappeared, perhaps at the time of the cutting of the copper strips 17-18 or shortly before. Every author has stumbled over the beginnings of these lines. But the photograph of the scroll before the cutting shows all the inscribed part of the bottom of this column preserved (DJDJ III, pl. XLIII.3): on the back *hšqt* can be read without hesitation. Milik noted: 'entre *qoph* et *taw*, et peut-être entre *šin* et *qoph*, traces incertaines de traits verticaux qui représentaient un *yod* ou un *waw*'.[17] As a matter of fact, the reproductions of the front of the scroll leave room for doubt, but not those of the back.

14. Milik, DJDJ III, p. 212: 'Entre temps, ils se sont égarés et je n'ai pas pu les retrouver au printemps de 1959.'

15. Allegro (*Treasure of the Copper Scroll*) obviously did not take into account either in his copy or in his readings the small fragments still extant. Many of his readings are far from being credible palaeographically (see below) and the author published no reproductions to support his transcription, which is what one has the right to expect of an edition.

16. Even as early as 1954 with regard to col. 10.16-17, see W.L. Reed, 'The Qumran Caves Expedition of March 1952', *BASOR* 135 (1954), pp. 8-13 (10).

17. Milik, DJDJ III, p. 295: 'between *qoph* and *taw*, and perhaps between *shin* and *qoph*, uncertain marks of vertical strokes which might represent a *yod* or a *waw*'.

The place name at the start of the line (10.17; item 51)[18] is missing in the scroll. Milik noted: 'Du *nom du monument* rectangulaire qui doit être tout près du Tombeau de Ṣadoq ne subsiste que la dernière lettre'[19] and he adds:

> je considère maintenant [ ]*h* comme le pronom se rapportant à Siloé ... avec le *'yn* féminin sous-entendu, et je restitue *[bbrkt]h* '[dans] sa [piscine]', à savoir celle de Siloé, différente de la source elle-même et des installations balnéaires qui s'y trouvaient. On peut songer encore à *[b' syḥ]h*, même sens avec moins de vraisemblance à mon avis. Il s'agirait par conséquent de la Birket el-Hamra de nos jours... On traduira donc: '[Dans] le [réservoir] de (Siloé), à (chacun de) ses (quatre) angles, un vase d'aromates...'[20]

This reading has been followed by García Martínez and Beyer who reads *[wbbrkt]h*.[21]

In fact the photograph taken before the cutting gives the name of the place preserved in its entirety and in a very readable state: *bgnt ṣdwq b'rb't // mqṣw'wt zhb kly dm' btkn 'ṣlm* (DJDJ III, pl. XLIII.3). The remnants preserved from the original are therefore not those of a *he* but of a *qoph*. This is indeed a structure that is part of Zadok's Tomb (not part of a pool), a structure attested again in 11.5-6, *m'rb / ngd gnt ṣdwq*... and interpreted there perfectly by Milik. It is not a matter of a garden, but of an important part of a tomb. This funerary sense is not attested in

18. In my edition the numbering of the items (sections) differs to a small extent from that of Milik.

19. Milik, DJDJ III, p. 271: 'Only the last letter remains of the name of the rectangular monument which should be right next to the Tomb of Zadok.'

20. Milik, DJDJ III, pp. 301-302 (addendum): 'I now consider *[ ]h* as the pronoun referring to Shiloah...with the *'yn* feminine understood, and I restore *[bbrkt]h* "[in] its [pool]", namely, that of Shiloah, different from the spring itself and from the bathing installations that were built there'. We can think as well of *[b'syḥ]h*, which has the same meaning, but is less likely in my opinion. It would appear consequently to be the present-day Birket el-Hamra. The phrase might then be translated: '[In] the [reservoir] of (Shiloah) at (each of) its (four) corners, a vase of spices...' The editor finds confirmation in the use of *mqṣw'wt* in 11.1, exactly like a *mqṣ'* of another *birkeh* in the catalogue (2.13).

21. F. García Martínez, '3QCopper Scroll (3Q15)', in *idem*, *The Dead Sea Scrolls Translated* (Leiden: E.J. Brill, 1994), pp. 461-63; K. Beyer, '3Q15: Die Kupferrolle (kurz vor 70 n. Chr.)', in *idem*, *Die aramäischen Texte vom Toten Meer samt den Inschriften aus Palästina, dem Testament Levis aus der Kairoer Genisa, der Fastenrolle und den alten talmudischen Zitaten, Ergänzungsband* (Göttingen: Vandenhoeck & Ruprecht, 1994), pp. 224-33.

Mishnaic Hebrew *gnh* or Judaeo-Aramaic *gnt'*, but is present in Nabataean in *gnt smk'*, 'banquet courtyard', which was in front of the entrance of the tomb and when needed served as a triclinium (*CIS* II.350). In Mishnaic Hebrew this sense is met under the form *gt* whose minimal dimensions are 6 square cubits (*m. B. Bat.* 6.8; *t. Ohol.* 15.7).[22] The meaning of the word *gnt* seems to fit perfectly the structures in front of the entrance of the tomb of Jason in Jerusalem,[23] or of some other tomb in the holy city. This reading by itself does not justify Milik's correction of *mqṣw'wt zhb* to *mqṣw'wtyhm*, and an examination of the original in fact stands against it.[24]

Column 8.1-8

The last parts of the lines of the first half of this column have caused problems in the published edition as well as in readings and translations. Some fragments are no longer in place at the end of line 2, a strip of copper has gone missing with the upper rivets, and the left part is somewhat creased. The recent treatment was unable to touch these wrongly glued joints, so as not to risk damaging the whole section. Only the false join at the beginning of line 2 could be restored by putting back together the small fragment bearing the *aleph* and the top of the *lamedh*. So the reading *'wṣr* is certain, with perhaps the traces of the top of the *he* of a definite article (there is enough room for the article in the line).[25] The photograph of pl. XLIII.1 makes it possible for me to be certain about the reading of the *taw* of *byt* as entirely preserved; thus the phrase *byt [h?]'wṣr*, probably with the article, allows on the one hand for the elimination of the inexplicable *byt 'ḥṣr*, 'Bet Ḥaṣor', of the *editio princeps*, and of *byr 'ḥṣr* of Wolters. On the other hand, the same plate helps in the decipherment of line 2. At the end of the line, in place of the impossible *'ḥzr*, 'Ḥazor', of the edition, identified with Baal Ḥaṣor–Mount Azor to the north of Bethel,[26] *'ḥw/y (/z)h* should be read, apparently without another letter after it; therefore *'ḥyh*, 'Aḥiyah', comparable with *mtyh*, 'Matthiyah', in 2.5, should be read, which is much preferable to *'ḥzh,* 'property, domain', while keeping in mind that sometimes the *zayin* in this hand-

22. Cf. Milik, DJDJ III, p. 246 n. 83, but the application to Jn 19.41 seems improbable.

23. Cf. L.Y. Rahmani, 'Jason's Tomb', *IEJ* 17 (1967), pp. 61-100.

24. Milik, DJDJ III, p. 302 (addendum). The original no longer supports Allegro's reading (*Treasure of the Copper Scroll*, pp. 52-53): *mqṣw'wtyh bkly*.

25. In this regard, the transcriptions of the edition (DJDJ III, pl. LXII) and Allegro (*Treasure of the Copper Scroll*, p. 46) are incorrect and have some strange forms.

26. Cf. Milik, DJDJ III, pp. 292-93, 267 (23), and 228-29 (4b, 13c).

writing can be rendered as *waw/yod*, though it is engraved in the normal way five letters earlier and below in *mzrḥ*. As a result, the readings *šmyd h'twn* (an Aramaism) of Allegro,[27] followed by Lurie, or of *'ḥwd* (Wolters), or *'hwd* (Beyer) have no graphic support.

At the end of 8.3, Milik hesitantly read *'l tbs* (?), 'Ne te (les) *approprie* pas!' ('Do not appropriate [them]!')[28] The readings *'l hklyn*, 'in amongst the jars' (Allegro), and *'l tkl*, 'Eltukal' (Beyer), are also wrong, having no graphic support, as are *w'lt ks[p]*, and 'a bar of sil[ver]' (Wolters) and *'l tmr* (Muchowski).[29] However, once again pl. XLIII.1 makes it possible to read the end of the line correctly. *'l tdqm* should be read, with the downstroke of the *qoph* which intersects with another letter in 8.4 and a part of the *mem* which is faintly preserved: 'Do not damage them!' This reading is confirmed by the new negatives and the cast with the exception of the *mem*, which is difficult to make out. The prohibition is perfectly understandable in the case of books that must not be damaged.

The same plate seems to confirm the reading of the edition in line 4, *btk ḥrh*, which can be interpreted in many ways, but it excludes *btk hdr* of Allegro, 'in the middle of the Circle-on-the-Stone, buried at seventeen cubits', and of Wolters, which seems to be an unrealistic proposal.

At the end of 8.8, the edition read *hqdrwh*, 'ha-Kidro(n)', but pl. XLIII.1 does not support the reading of a partially engraved *he* as the final letter of the word, since the original edge of the sheet is preserved at this place, but rather that of a final *nun* that is quite short because of the rivet and perhaps has its top visible on the left. The orthography *hqdrwn* is what would be expected.

Examination of the engravings at the end of 8.8 and 8.9, which run on to the beginning of the third sheet (col. 9) (pl. XLIII.1 and 2), shows clearly that the two sheets were riveted before the engraving of the text, the last under the preceding, as was the case for sheets 1 and 2.

27. Allegro (*Treasure of the Copper Scroll*, pp. 47, 153) understands '"the Entrance" (of the Temple Court), most probably the inner eastern gate'! But there is no explicit proof that this hiding place was even in Jerusalem.

28. Milik, DJDJ III, p. 293: 'Si la lecture et la traduction sont exactes, ce genre d'avertissement au chercheur de trésor serait unique dans le document; comparer pourtant *herem*…'

29. P. Muchowski, *Zwój miedziany (3Q15): Implikacje spornych kwestii lingwistycznych (Copper Scroll 3Q15. Implications of the Controversial Linguistic Problems)*, (International Institute of Ethnolinguistic and Oriental Studies, Monograph Series 4; Posnan, 1993), p. 38: 'Do tamar'.

It is surprising that these observations and comments eluded the editor and all those who have been dealing up until now with the decipherment and study of the scroll. Many errors could have been prevented and the understanding of the text would have gained in precision. But it is also certain that the recent radiography and galvanoplasty have provided very considerable help in the deciphering of the text and in the discernment of the exact layout of the letters in other preserved sections.

Improved Readings

I give below improvements in the readings of the *editio princeps*—there is no question here of their interpretation—improvements that are in general possible thanks to the pieces of information provided by the Laboratoire EDF–Valectra.[30]

Column 1

Line 5 has presented a problem: the reading of the proper name as *bn rbh hšl<y>šy*, 'Ben Rabbah the Šališian', by Milik, followed in part by Wolters ('Ben Rabbah the Third'), is doubtful; admittedly with some difficulty the engraving should be read *bndbk hšl<y>šy* (*daleth* and *kaph* are certain): 'in the third course' (with Allegro).

In line 6, read the sign for 100, not Allegro's *zll*.

In line 7 Milik's readings of *byrk* and *bḥly'* are confirmed, in place of the incorrect *bzrb* and *bḥl'* of Allegro; the second word is probably defectively written for *bḥwly'*, 'in the sand, sediment', rather than to be understood as coming from the root *ḥlh*.

In line 9, certainly read *btl šl kḥlt* with Milik, not the impossible *bḥl šl bḥlh* of Allegro.

In line 9 Milik's *blgyn* and *w'pwdt* have the best graphic support, but certainly not *w'pwryn* of Allegro nor the strange correction *b[[']]l gyn* of Wolters; likewise *mpwgl* should be read in line 11 instead of *mpy gl* (Milik) and for even stronger reasons instead of Allegro's *mpyt lptḥ*.

In line 12, the engraver wrote *mqrt hṭbwl*, and not *nyqrt hṭbylh* of Milik's edition, followed by Wolters and partially by Allegro.

In line 13, the reading *hmsb'* is graphically certain (with Allegro) in place of Milik's *hm'b'*, which is partially followed by Wolters. Probably

30. For the sake of brevity I do not take into consideration here all the numerous variants so far proposed; see the commentary in my edition. In this communication I generally limit my remarks to the *editio princeps* and to the unofficial edition of Allegro.

also *byrk'* with final instead of medial *kaph* should be read, as is the case elsewhere, in preference to *byrd 'l sml* of Milik's edition, which is followed by Wolters with a different word division (*byrd' lsml*).

Column 2

In *hmlḥ (?),* line 1, the engraving is rather that of a *ḥet* if the line is taken into consideration, but in this kind of writing/engraving the *he* and *ḥeth* are often identical. The new documentation cannot provide an argument in favour of *mlḥ* against *mlh.*

In line 3, the engraving favours a reading of *byt hmdh hyšn brwbd* (with Allegro), not *byt hmrh hyšn bdybr* of Milik's edition, nor *hmdḥ* (Wolters), nor *hmdḥh yšw* (Pixner, García Martínez), but then at the start of line 4 *hšlyšy* (Milik) seems certain instead of *hšlšyl* of Allegro.

In line 5 we must certainly read *mtyh 'ṣyn* with Lurie, Pixner and García Martínez, not *bty h'ṣyn* of Milik, correcting the *mem* to *beth*, nor *mtwḥ 'ṣyn* of Allegro, nor *mtn h'ṣyn* of Wolters.

In line 8, read *ḥ[[m]]š 'sr'* with Milik, not *tš' (')sr'* of Allegro nor *tš'sr'* of Wolters.

In line 12, the engraver wrote *b'tw* (incorrect?), not *by'tw* (Milik as in 4.3), and certainly not Allegro's *m'wt.*

In line 13, read *kḥlt* with Milik, not *bḥlh* of Allegro.

In line 14, certainly a dittography of *'mwt* (Milik *'mt* ditto), not *'mh šyṭ* of Allegro.

Column 3

In line 1, only one word is missing, while the first word is a certain reading, *bḥṣ[r* with faint remains of a *ṣade.* The *editio princeps* indicates a place for a small fragment. Milik transcribes what is left of the *nomen rectum* as *..]?y'ṭ* and proposes in the translation 'du *péri*]*bole*' without being more specific about the restoration of this word borrowed from Greek. The absence of any details to indicate the spacings and the traces of the letter preceding the *yod* precludes any decision. One can only postulate the presence of a word of four to five letters, preferably a place name, probably of Greek origin and preceded by *š-* or *šb-/šl-*. However, given the acceptability of the reading of this fragment, there is room to wonder if this word, which designates a precise place, should not simply be read as *dy'ṭ*, 'room, cell, seat of arbitration (or of judgment?)'. This Greek loan-word δίαιτα (without any transcription of the vowel ending) indicates the name of a prison or the seat of the Roman government of

Palestine at Caesarea according to *Esther Rabbah* (Introduction, beginning).[31] It could have indicated a room for arbitration, a court, or for government, comparable to a 'Roman praetorium', for which the existence of a square can easily be imagined.

In line 9, one should probably read *kly dm' wlbyšyn*, in preference to *lkwšy* of Milik; it is a word known in Aramaic to render the Greek λὲβης, 'cauldron, funeral urn', with the copula being inserted, perhaps with an explanatory sense; there is no possibility of reading *wlbwhšyn* of Allegro or *lbwšy*, 'my clothes', of Wolters (the author of the Copper Scroll is in no way involved in these lists as Wolters proposes).

In lines 8 and 11, the engraving of the letter after *lamedh* is probably a *ḥet*, but a *he* cannot be ruled out.

Column 4

In line 1, Milik read *bbwr hgdwl šb[..].qh* and Allegro *bbwr hgd[wl... b]ḥlh*, 'in] a hole(?)'. The new documentation, however, makes the reading *lt* certain and before it that of *ḥeth* rather than of *qoph*. The restoration of the place name which is called for in that case is *k]ḥlt*, which is not surprising, given its occurrence in 1.9, 2.13 and 4.11-12. The space now known thanks to the cast excludes a restoration, such as *šb[mzrḥ* or *m'rb*, but favours *šb[ṣpwn* or *drwm*. In fact, since in 1.9-12 (item 4) the canal and the baths are to the north, while in 3.11-13 (item 16) the pool is to the east, it seems advisable to situate the great pillared cistern itself to the north too. One reads, therefore, with near certainty *šb[ṣpwn k]ḥlt b'mwd*.

In line 2, in carrying forward the numbers read by Milik (as for the letters *šb* on line 1) and preserved on a small fragment unknown to Allegro, there remains space either for 20 + 20, or for the full writing *kk[ryn*.

In line 3 the pattern of the traces of the letters read by Milik on the isolated fragments could have confirmed the reading that seems to be necessary for the space and the meaning, *lbr]k'* (see 2.3).

In line 4, in place of Milik's *'rb'[yn w'ḥ]t*, '41', we must surely read *'rb[' ']srh*, '14'; the remnants are not those of a *taw* (of *'ḥ]t*), but of *samek*, *resh* and *he*.

31. See *Midrash Megillat Esther*: *bdyṭy šl qysryn*, 'in the prison of Caesarea', H. Freedman and M. Simon (eds), *Midrash Rabbah Translated into English with Notes, Glossary and Indices* (trans. M. Simon; foreword I. Epstein; London: Soncino Press, 3rd edn, 1961, vol. 9: Esther–Song of Songs), p. 1 and n. 7.

In line 5, the corner of the number '10' remains at the right of the break to give the reading '55' with the editor, instead of the impossible 40(?) [...*b*]*šd'* of Allegro.

In lines 6 and 7, the engravings of final *nun* for *resh* come from a mistake in reading the original in a script in which the two letters sometimes resemble one another. Thus the reading *hbdyn* (line 6) of Allegro is not to be retained; *hbynyn* of Milik is correct.

In line 8, the *samek* in ligature in the original has not been completely engraved.

In line 9, read *bšyt* with Milik, not *bšyḥ* of Allegro and Wolters.

In lines 11-12 retain the editor's readings *bšyt* and *kḥlt*, not *bšyḥ* and *bḥlh* of Allegro.

Column 5

A fragment not reproduced bore some parts of letters along the break to the left of lines 1 and 2 which gives *tḥ[t*. The dimension of the gap does not support the reading *hmym .[..]*, that is *š[bh]*, 'which is at', assumed by Milik, but which is much too short; nor that of Allegro *[hb'h]*, still a little short; *[hb'h l]* of Beyer would be preferable, but a more frequent expression *š[bm'rb h]* is just as acceptable.

In line 2 Milik's restoration *tḥ[t h'bn]* seems to be called for, as opposed to Allegro's *t[ḥt hym']*.

In line 3, the space would favour *šlw]* (Allegro) since there would not be sufficient space for *ḥmš* (Milik) without having to put the *shin* on the following line.

In line 5, Milik's reading *mzrḥ* is confirmed in place of the impossible *bzr[b(?)]* of Allegro.

In line 6 and *passim*, we prefer to read *'šwḥ*, which is the ancient spelling of the word in the Mesha stele (lines 9 and 23) with Allegro, instead of Milik's *'šyḥ*, which is the spelling in Sir. 50.3, but that was in a period when *waw* and *yod* were often undifferentiated, which led to scribal confusion by copyists, but without any proof of a phonetic change (see below, 11.12).

In line 7, the written form fits Milik's reading *wbtkn 'ṣlm*, which is certain in 11.1 and 4, and not that of *wktbn* (Lurie, McCarter, Wolters),[32]

32. McCarter, 'The Copper Scroll Treasure', and also Muchowski, *Zwój miedziany*; Beyer, '3Q15: Die Kupferrolle (kurz vor 70 n. Chr.)'; É. Puech, 'Quelques résultats d'un nouvel examen du Rouleau de Cuivre (3Q15)', *RevQ* 70 (1997), pp. 163-90; G.B.A. Sarfati, '*btkn 'ṣlm*—A Riddle of the Copper Scroll', *Leshonenu* 36 (1971–72),

but the phrase is to be connected to what precedes (with Allegro), not to what follows as if it were a piece of information about a new entry as is understood by Milik.

In line 9 as well as in 6.8, the reading *hrgb* is necessary (with Allegro) instead of Milik's *hrgm*, followed by Wolters, unless one appeals twice to a copyist's error in the case of the only two uses of the word in this text. The meaning of 'Peter' is well known through the biblical uses of the word, but read *hḥryṣ* (line 8) and '23' with Milik, not *hḥrwṣ* and '13' with Allegro.

In line 13, read *bby'h myrḥw* with Milik, not *bby' hmzrḥy* with Allegro.

In line 14, engraving of *ḥpwn* for *ḥpwr*, already encountered.

Column 6

In line 7 there is room to hesitate between the readings *hbn'* / *hkn'* (Milik), but certainly not *hpn'* of Allegro; the context alone leads to a preference for *hkn'*.

In line 13, read '27' with Milik, not '9' with Allegro.

Column 7

With regard to 7.1-8 Milik notes that 'la lacune n'est pas si grande en réalité qu'elle paraît sur le fac-similé' ('the gap is not really as great as it appears on the facsimile') and that for 7.1-3 'sur les deux bords de la cassure se placent des fragments dont les lettres et chiffres ne sont pas reproduits sur la copie' ('on the two edges of the break are found some fragments whose letters and numbers are not reproduced in the copy').[33] As a result, the word *ḥpwr* should be considered preserved in the original.[34] However, the restoration of *'mwt* does not adequately fill the gap, all the more so since the foot of the second shaft of the *taw* is preserved on the left strip; in this case it is necessary to restore another word, such as *bmzrḥ* or *bm'rb*, either of which is preferable for its length to *bṣpwn* or *bdrwm* or *bptḥ(w)*.

Milik has placed a fragment next to the left edge of the break, at line 2, bearing the number '22'. That would give some space for the rest of the gap, which must have consisted of the number '20' several times, probably

pp. 106-11; H. Stegemann, *The Library of Qumran: On the Essenes, Qumran, John the Baptist, and Jesus* (Grand Rapids: Eerdmans, 1998).

33. Milik, DJDJ III, p. 291.

34. Contrary to Allegro, *Treasure of the Copper Scroll*, p. 151. Wolters ('Literary Analysis', p. 250) reads *ḥ[pwr 'mwt]* and Muchowski (*Zwój miedziany*) reads *ḥpwr ['mwt]*.

up to four times, since in these passages *kk* is always in the abbreviated form. I would propose therefore that it consists of *kk* [20 + 20 + 20] + 20 + 2, that is to say '82'.

In line 3, Milik's reading of *b'm' šl qy[* is certain from the part of the line preserved, instead of *šl my[m* of Beyer, since a *mem* is impossible, based on the remaining traces; Allegro reads nothing there. This reading is confirmed from the editor's decipherment of a supplementary fragment for the right side of the break that he had at his disposal. Without the outline of the traces of the letter after the yod, *qy?[* in the edition, I can only conjecture about a reading for what followed to fit the space, the subject and the phraseology of the scroll. I would propose *qyb[wṣ hmym šl]* or some such phrase.[35]

In line 4, between *hṣpw[ny* and *(h)gd]wl*, a definite reading in agreement with Milik, one should very probably supply a word, since the engraver never leaves so large a space between two words. Allegro's *]wlw* is both unlikely and mistakenly placed by him at the end of line 5; Milik's reading is also to be preferred to Beyer's *h'g]wl* since there is no trace of the *gimel*. I would propose as very probable the restoration of the word *h'šwḥ* at the beginning of the line as a way of bringing more precision to the description.[36]

In line 5, the restoration *rwḥ[wtyw* would also be insufficient, but the reading *dwdy[n* of Allegro and Lurie must be completely rejected because of the remaining letter traces and the sense. The missing word must indicate the starting point and the distance to be measured off and could begin with *mn h-* or *mh-*. In view of the space in question and the frequency of stairs in the large pools (see 12.4), I would propose, for example, *rwḥ[wt mhm'l'/-wt]* or *mn hm'l']*, since the suffix is not indispensable for *rwḥwtyw*.

In line 6, definitely read *'sryn[w'r]b'* with *yod* (Milik read it without a *yod*), not Allegro's *'sryn[šyṭ 'r(?)]b'*, whose reproduction is impossible, nor *'srn [š]b'* of Wolters.

In line 8, the copyist definitely engraved *š'ṣl hmqr[h]šl* and not *š'ṣlh bqr[b]w l* of the *editio princeps*, since the *mem* is certain and the *shin* is

35. The proposal of H. Eshel (at the Manchester symposium) to read *qyp[rws*, followed then by a different restoration, would be possible. However, it is hard to understand the logic of the following sequence: Kypros, Doq, Koziba! Moreover, this reading would conflict with an identification of Mount Gerizim (item 58) in this place according to a late Jewish tradition known to Christians (Madaba map).

36. Nobody has taken note of the excessive size of the gap for *hgd]wl*. Read *'šwḥ* with Allegro, not *'šyḥ* of Milik, Wolters and Muchowski.

possible at the break; however, the overlapping and unplaced fragments make it impossible to be sure of the reading, although it is probable. Allegro read *š'ṣl hmqr[t] šl.*

In line 11, the engraver copied *hmšṭḥ* and seems to have inserted a *waw* between *ṭeth* and *ḥeth*; Allegro read *hmšṭḥ*, but *hmšmrh* of the *editio princeps* followed by Wolters seems ruled out (*mem-resh*?).

In lines 14-15, Allegro read *hby//b'*, but followed Milik for *hkwzy//b'*; the top of the *zayin* is clearly marked to the right of a fold.

At the end of line 15, there is no basis for reading a medial *pe* with Allegro; choose either a cursive *resh* with Milik, or a very open final *pe*.

Column 8

At the beginning of line 1, *b']m'* is certain with Milik, not *bby(?)]b'* of Allegro.

In line 2, Milik's *šmzrḥ* is undoubtedly the reading, instead of *šmyd* of Allegro.

At the end of line 9, the new X-ray images make it possible to read '7', but not based on Allegro's copy, instead of '4' of the edition followed by Wolters.

In line 10, definitely read *bšlp* with Milik, not *bšly* of Allegro.

In line 13, read *'śryn w'rb'* with Milik, not *'śryn 'rb'* of Allegro; also '66' with Milik, not '67' of Allegro.

In line 14, read *bṣwyh* with Milik, not *bṣy'h* of Allegro (with a cursive *aleph*).

Column 9

In line 1, the two *waw*'s of *šwly* and *šwlw* are written as *resh*'s and the *resh* as *zayin* (or *waw*) in line 2, *ḥpwz/w* for *ḥpwr*. But the engraving cannot support the impossible *w'štyn ḥywrwt bšy'h šb' bryn 'ystryn* of Allegro in lines 2-3 or *ḥṭn wgm* of Wolters.

In line 4, the engraver certainly wrote *bḥblt hšnyg*, which should probably be corrected with Allegro to *bḥblh hšnyt*, *taw* for *he* and *gimel* for *taw*, in preference to Milik's *btklt hšny gb*. The engraving *ḥpwn* (final *nun*) for *ḥpwr*, line 5, comes from a mistake in reading; see below.

In line 6, the reading *dm<'> ḥṣ'* with a doubtful *daleth* in the *editio princeps* does not seem convincing. Since *waw* and cursive *resh* are sometimes confused, the engraver has mistakenly copied a normal *resh* for *waw* in *wmḥṣ'*, with Allegro.

In line 7, the engraver did not always differentiate *ḥeth* and *he*, nor *waw* and *yod*, and engraved a semi-cursive *resh* next to a cursive *waw*, which was rewritten distinctly afterwards. *bṣryḥy hḥwryn brwḥ hṣwp' dr{w}wm* seems to render best the copied text instead of *b<ṣ>ryḥ* of Allegro and *hḥwrwn b<ṣ>ryḥ hṣwp' ym* of Milik and partially of Wolters.

In line 8 the script of the *mem-waw* of *'mwt* was engraved *kaph-ayin*, and *waw* for (cursive) *resh* in *šš 'srh*.

At the end of line 10, the copyist certainly engraved *ksp mnḥh rb*, if we want to take into account the differences in the writing of the letters, rather than *mnḥs hrb*, 'a great amount is deposited', which Milik preferred (p. 254), but certainly not *mn hḥrm* (*he*/*ḥeth* and *beth*/*mem*) of Allegro or *mnh ḥrm* of Wolters.

The first word is certainly written *bqw/ym'h*. The form *qym'h* is the reading retained by Allegro, but the meaning is not clear: 'In the "funnel"', by resorting to the Arabic *qam*^{ʿun}; likewise Wolters. Milik preferred to correct the text slightly to read *bqwb'h* and to recognize a place name 'Qob'eh' on the route between Eleutheropolis and Jerusalem,[37] while also indicating that the word *qwm/b'h* could refer to an element of the preceding tomb.[38]

With the reading assured, an effort must be made to give a meaning to the term *qwm'h*, which is unique in Hebrew.[39] For that one should recall that the *ayin* need not be the primitive guttural of the word. We know too that the primitive */ḍ/* is rendered by */ṣ/* in Hebrew, but by */q/* and then by */'/* in the Aramaic dialects, and that an Aramaic influence is perceptible in the language of the scroll. Finally, we must remember that the palatal consonants */g/* and */k/* and the emphatic velar sound */q/* can be interchangeable. As a result, the word *qwm'h* can without difficulty be compared with the Hebrew *gwmṣ*, which is at least related to it, if not its equivalent, being derived in parallel ways from the same primitive Semitic root. We should compare Qoh. 10.8 *ḥpr gwmṣ bw ypwl*, 'Whoever digs a hole falls into it', with the second word translated in the Aramaic targum by *šwḥh*, 'pit',[40]

37. Milik, 'Le rouleau'; Muchowski, *Zwój miedziany*, reads *bqwb't*, 'W dzbanie'.

38. Milik, DJDJ III, pp. 269 and 301. In accordance with his hypothesis, Pixner, 'Unravelling the Copper Scroll Code', the village Qubeyeh is found north of Yarmuk.

39. Reading of Wolters, 'Literary Analysis', p. 250, without any interpretation but 'its funnel' according to Muchowski, *Zwój miedziany*, p. 46. Lurie (see below, n. 46) would read *qym''* = *ṣrwr*.

40. According to G. Garbini, 'Note semitiche', *Annali dell' Instituto Orientale de Napoli* 1 (1959), pp. 85-93, *gwmṣ* would be a borrowing from Eastern Aramaic; this study not having been accessible to me (see *ZAW* 75 [1963], p. 228), I cannot say any more about it.

with Prov. 26.27 *krh šḥt bh ypl*, 'whoever digs a pit falls into it', which is rendered in the targum precisely by *gwmṣ'*, 'hole'. Likewise, the Hebrew *šwḥh 'mwqh*, 'deep pit' (parallel with *b'r*, 'well'), of Prov. 22.14 and 23.27 are translated in the targum once by *gwmṣ' 'mqt'* and once by *šwḥ'* and in the Syriac (Peshiṭta) by *gwmṣ' 'myq'*. But the Hebrew *hpḥd hgdwl*, 'the great pit' of 2 Sam. 18.17 is rendered in the Aramaic targum by *qwmṣ' rb'* and by the Syriac *gwmṣ' rb'* in the Peshiṭta, while the Hebrew *hpḥt*, 'the hole', of Isa. 24.17-18 and of the parallel in Jer. 48.43-44 is rendered by *kwmṣ'* in the targum, but by *gwmṣ'* in the Syriac of the Peshiṭta. It is clearly evident therefore that the forms *g/k/qwmṣ'* refer to the same reality: a pit, a hole, a hollow, a chasm or a well, and in the same way again the Syriac *gwm'th* (with the /'/ of the root) is used to translate the Hebrew *šwḥ*, *šḥt* and *pḥd*, in Greek λάκκος. If the Copper Scroll does not use the word *šwḥ(')*, at least it uses the synonyms *šyt* and *bwr*, or again *'šwḥ*, and so on. As a consequence, the fundamental meaning of the word *qwm'h* should be considered as perceptible and identified. Important consequences follow for the passage from this reading and interpretation, since it is no longer a matter of a new place name but of a hiding place in the same area where numerous caves, recesses, holes and crevices are listed.[41]

In line 11, the copyist certainly engraved *bqwl hmyn hqrwbym lkpt byb* instead of *hqrybyn lkp hbyb* of Allegro or *lkpr nbw* of Milik.

In line 12, the engraving is *mrḥb lpnhm*, which can be understood as *mrḥb lpn[[y]]hm*, in preference to *lpyhm* of Allegro, or *m[[z]]rḥ klpn[[y]]hm* and not *klpyhm* of Milik. The first downstroke of the *he* can be taken as a haplography of the *yod* more easily than as the form of a medial *nun*.

In line 15, follow Milik with *bṣḥy't gr*, not *bṣy't gy* of Allegro, who eliminated the engraved *ḥeth* and changed *resh* into *yod*, not attested elsewhere.

In line 17, the engraver copied *šbmṣdn' btḥ/h[*, not *b'mt h[* of Milik with three doubtful letters (cursive *beth*, *beth* for *mem* and *he*) nor *šbmṣdn' ptḥ[* of Allegro (*pe* is excluded) nor *šbmṣrn 'bt[* of Wolters. Based on the space and the sense I would restore *btḥ[wm h] // drwm*.

41. It is no longer necessary to look for a place name in the Yarmuk Valley (Pixner). It goes without saying that the proposal of *(w)bsp* in parallel to *bqwb'h* to designate a recipient (Beyer) is not to be retained, since on the one hand the form of the word in biblical Hebrew is *qwb't* and on the other *ksp* is the certain reading and has no copula.

Column 10

In line 3 the engraving does not make it possible to decide between *bbwr* of Allegro and *bkyrgr* of Milik, but it does make it possible to exclude *gy* of Allegro and to choose *gr* of Milik and so preferably justifies reading *bbwr gr*.

In line 6, instead of *lsmwl rgmwt* of Milik and *lsmwlw 'mwt* of Allegro, it is recommended that *lsmwl 'mwt* should be read, with the drawing of the tip of the original *aleph* decomposing into the first stroke of a *zayin* and the remainder becoming a *gimel*.

In line 7, a cursive *kaph* (*kkryn*), *waw* shaped like a *zayin* and cursive *nun* (*wšnyn*).

In line 8, the cursive tends to assert itself in *'yk* (*aleph*) and *m'rby* (*resh-beth*), but the doubtful reading *zyt* of Allegro is to be excluded as well as *zrd* of Wolters.

In line 9, *he* for *ḥeth*, decomposition of *aleph* into *waw-gimel*, and of *mem* into *kaph-ayin*. *šḥwr' 'mwt* are certain, partially with Allegro (*šḥwryt*) in place of *šhzdwg' b'zt* of Milik.

In line 13, cursive *resh* in form of *zayin*/*waw* (*ḥpwr*) followed by the same doubling of the *aleph* into *resh-gimel* (perhaps with a visual metathesis of *zayin*/*waw-resh* in this sequence) but *'mwt* is certain with Allegro in place of *rgmwt* of the edition.

In line 15, the new images make it possible to resolve the difficulty in the reading. In place of *by<m> byt ḥmym* of Milik or *hmym* of Allegro and of Wolters, we should read *byṣ'wt hmym* corrected to *b<m>wṣ'wt hmym*. The term *mwṣ'*, 'outlet', already designates the source of the waters of the Gihon in 2 Chron. 32.30 (see Ps. 107.35) and in the Siloam inscription (lines 4-5) under Hezekiah. Then, in place of *šlwḥy* of Milik's edition, which is graphically acceptable but difficult syntactically, and the impossible *šl zḥyl tḥt* of Allegro or *rḥyl* of Lurie, Wolters and Beyer, read most likely a haplography of *šl* before *šlwḥ* (*waw*-cursive *resh*), 'Siloam', followed by *wltḥt hšqt* (see below col. 8 according to pl. XLIII of DJDJ III).

Column 11

In line 1, first *waw* reinserted, *waw* = *zayin* (*zhb*), *resh* = *daleth* (*dm'*) and cursive *aleph* (*'ṣlm*). Follow the edition (DJDJ III, p. 297, not the *addendum* p. 302) with *mqṣw'wt zhb*, or Allegro with *mqṣw'wtyh b-* or Wolters *whb* and *ktbn*.

In line 2, *he* = *ḥeth* (*mtḥt*) and *ḥeth* = *he* and *waw* = cursive *resh* (*hdrwmyt*).

In line 4, *resh* = *yod* (*kly*) and *nun* = cursive *bet* as in 10.8 (*btkn*), cursive *aleph* (*'ṣlm*) with the same formulary as in line 1, not *wtkn* (Milik) or omission of *waw* (Allegro) or of *kaph* (Wolters). The reading *swḥ* must be accepted here and in line 10 in place of *spyḥ* presupposed by McCarter.[42]

In line 5, correction of supralinear *resh*, but in place of *bhbsh* of Milik and *b'ksdr' š(l)* of Allegro, the copyist seems to have engraved *bhksḥ r'š*; it is just possible but very difficult to accept *bhksh,* 'In the "Throne"' (Wolters).

In line 7, faulty beginning of the following entry *bq* (head of the *qoph* only). An entry never begins at the end of a line.

In line 8, read *hsbyn* with Milik, not *hspyn* of Allegro; *bet-kaph* cannot be confused with *pe*.

In line 9, neither the correction of *mem* to *beth* by Milik for *h'bṭ hyrḥy*, nor the reading *h'm ṭhwr ḥw- bw* of Allegro (there is enough room for *bw* at the end of the line) nor *ṭhwrty* of Wolters are acceptable. Since the place name *yrḥw* is certain, the text and the engraving should be taken into account by inserting a *shin* outlined by the pronounced inclination of the base of the *mem*, wishing as it were to reproduce a grapheme read in the original. *[[š]]tḥ yrḥw* should therefore be understood; whether the *shin* is a radical or the relative makes no difference to the sense.[43]

In line 10, the new images do not make it possible to settle whether the reading should be *'w*, *'r*, *'z* or the correction to *'[[r]]z*.[44]

In line 12, the engraver has produced several confusions: in the second word, *waw* is written with the shape of *resh*, as in 9.1, for example, which confirms the reading of *waw* and not *yod* elsewhere (e.g. 5.12) and an initial cursive *aleph* rather than an incomplete *he* (phonetic orthography?) gives the definite reading *h'šwḥyn* (dual?) with the article, not *'šwḥyn* of Allegro. The reading of Milik followed by Wolters assumes too many corrections of the copy, *{'}'šdtyn* (ditto of the *aleph*, *resh*/*waw* for *daleth* and *ḥeth* for *taw*) in order to find the place name 'Beth-Ešdataïn' in a non-attested form (DJDJ III, pp. 271-72).

In line 14, one can envisage two possibilities for errors: either the passage of the sequence *m'* to *ml* by haplography in the process of reading-engraving (notice the oblique stroke of the foot of the *lamedh*, which juts out), and one should therefore read *dm[[' m]]l'h*, 'imposi[tion

42. McCarter, 'The Copper Scroll Treasure', p. 135.
43. See my commentary.
44. For more details, see my edition and the commentary.

of gr]ain', or, with the passing of the beginning of the *ayin* to the foot of the *lamedh* over the first downstroke of an *aleph*, then read *dm[[' ']]l'ḥ*, 'spic(e of a)loe', which would appear materially better than Milik's proposal of *dm[[']]l'h*, which presupposes a phonetic haplography of *aleph*, and better than *dm[[']]l'ḥ*, 'liquid tithe' (with an unexpected spelling), of Allegro.[45] The choice is a delicate one, but on the basis of one hypothesis the word *dm'* has two different meanings in the same sentence.

In line 16, the new documentation would seem to support the reading *rwḥ* as preferable to *dy.*, while the reading *dy[rt]* of Milik or *rw[bd* of Wolters would seem much too long for the space; the reading *bmk'rw*[*t*] of Allegro has no graphic support. One might hesitate choosing between *rwḥ,* 'side', and *dy/wr(?)*, 'enclosure'.

At the beginning of line 17, for want of something better, follow Milik: *ṭyp* with the sense of 'base, platform (of a stove or fireplace)',[46] in place of the unexpected *ṭwp* for *nṭwp* of Allegro. The restoration of the gap as *'l m['rh bh klyn t]š'* by Beyer cannot be retained as such, since no trace of a *lamedh* is perceptible in the preserved space between the lines. The visible traces can correspond to *kaph-samek.* I would propose *'l m['r'] ks[p kkryn]tš' m'wt*, which would fit perfectly into the space.[47] In fact, mention of *ksp* seems necessary in parallel with *zhb* in 12.1.

Column 12

Line 1 remains difficult to read: *kk iiiii* of Milik, while possible, is not certain, but *bkwzyn* of Allegro is excluded by the remaining traces of letters. It seems that *bp* might be likely, and then one could read the letters as in a very cursive style, by way of hypothesis, as *bprwryn*, 'in the vessels'. Then, at the end of the line, accidental omission of *ayin* from *m[[']]rb*.

In line 2 the reading *bydn* of Milik seems to be confirmed by the new documentation, with *daleth* preferable to *zayin-yod.* The feminine plural suffix refers back to *h'bn* and *'l m['r'* of 11.17; and read *hšḥwr'* with Milik, not *hšḥwry'* of Allegro.

45. The translation of Wolters, 'Leah's tribute, Sira's tribute', is not very likely and would be a unique formulation with proper names.

46. Lurie reads *ṭyp-mw'rm*. The translation 'a little' (Wolters, 'The Copper Scroll and the Vocabulary of Mishnaic Hebrew', *RevQ* 14 [1990], pp. 483-95 [492]) does not give the meaning of the passage, but subsequently ('Literary Analysis', p. 251) he reads nothing after *'l[...]*.

47. Pixner does not take into account this partially preserved word.

In line 3, instead of the reading *hbwr* of the edition, which presupposes a correction of the *kaph* and *resh*, read *hkwk* with Allegro.

In line 4, the engraver seems to have re-engraved the top of the *resh* in order to insert the forgotten *yod*. On the other hand, he added the *aleph* to *hm'lh*, 'the step', in order to read *hm'l{h}'*, 'the stairs', instead of correcting the *he* to *aleph* as he did in 1.1 *ḥryb{'}h*, but *hm'lt'* of Allegro has no support. Then the copyist materially engraved *hšyḥ\h* with Allegro instead of *hšyt* of Milik, but the agreement of the feminine adjective presupposes the reading *hšyt* of Milik.

In line 6, omission of *yod* and in line 8, cursive *gimel*. A reading *hbzk* in the two instances (Allegro) seems preferable to that of *hbrk* (Milik) or *hkwk* (Wolters), *hkrk* (Beyer). The cutting of the column makes it impossible to be sure whether the reading *klbyt* is the original in preference to *kl[y] byt*.

In line 10, the copyist engraved *šbnh*, not *šbṣḥ* of Milik or *škynh* of Allegro, *šknh*, 'Shekinah' (Wolters), *šbṣhb* or *šbynḥ* as read by others (neither *ṣade* nor *yod* can be inserted). Finally, *kḥlt* of Milik is a sure reading instead of *bḥlh* of Allegro.

This latest reading of the text engraved on the scroll, based essentially on the new documentation resulting from the work of Mécénat EDF, has made it possible to clarify a certain number of points under discussion. On the whole the clear-cut superiority of the readings of the *editio princeps* of Milik compared to the unofficial edition of Allegro is clear, even if the latter contains some preferable readings here and there. This same observation certainly applies equally to the other more recent editions to which I have had access (Wolters, Muchowski),[48] which have not benefited from the expertise of an eye trained in Qumran palaeography and from direct contact with the originals.

These new readings have an effect on several items: on various aspects of palaeography and the art of engraving, on the language of 'pre-Mishnaic' Hebrew (phonetics, morphology, lexicography, syntax), and, finally, especially on the content of the text, including the identification of the treasures and their hiding places, and the topography of these hiding places.

The composition itself, without context, with neither a developed introduction nor a story incorporating a theme from Jewish folklore,

48. For this work, I was not able to have Lurie's edition at my disposal; it is known to me from the quotations of other authors.

cannot readily support the thesis that it is an imaginary and fabulous treasure-trove, not even if much is made of the mention of 'Aïn Kaḥol (Elijah's fountain on Mount Carmel) on the much later plaques from Beirut, as Milik tried to show in the first edition. Should one therefore decide that it is a list of authentic deposits? And, if so, is it a list of the possessions of the Community or of the treasure of the Temple? Or of the treasures of the Zealots or of the Jewish rebels in the time of Bar Kokhba? Or is it a list of the contributions made by survivors to the (treasury of the) Temple after the destruction of 70? All these responses have been given at one time or another.[49] Is there any indication of a solution?

The Amount of the Deposits

As long as we remain ignorant of the precise value of the talent (*kkr*),[50] it is impossible to value with any precision the total amount of these deposits. We can only get some idea of its important size by adding up the amounts indicated, though we should not disguise their approximate character, given the number of deposits that are not specified. The total adds up to 1644 talents of silver,[51] 404 gold talents,[52] and 3212.5 talents + 20 minas not clearly allocated,[53] to which it is probably necessary to add 100 talents in two incomplete passages,[54] which makes 3312.5 unspecified talents in all. To this total of 5260.5 (or even 5360.5) talents and 20 minas

49. For presentations summarizing these different positions, see, for example, Pixner, 'Unravelling the Copper Scroll Code', pp. 331-40; S. Goranson, 'Sectarianism, Geography and the Copper Scroll', *JJS* 43 (1992), pp. 282-87; and Wolters, 'Literary Analysis', pp. 289-92. Add H. Stegemann, *Die Essener, Qumran, Johannes der Taüfer und Jesus. Ein Sachbuch* (Freiburg: Herder, 1993), pp. 104-108, who favours deposits in the Temple bank in 70 CE, two years after the fall of Qumran.

50. Cf. DJDJ III, pp. 253-54.

51. Namely, 17 (1) + 40 (5) + 70 (8) + 40 (13) + 55 (17) + 200 (19) + 70 (20) + 12 (21) + 7 (22) + 23 (24) + 80 (33) + 70 (38) + 900 (57) + 60 (58). The numbers in parentheses in this and the following notes refer to the itemized sections in which the numbers of talents appear; my numbering system differs slightly from those of Milik and other editors of the scroll.

52. Namely 2 (33) + 300 (48) + 60 (57) + 42 (57) (and perhaps 5 additional talents in 12.1).

53. 900 (3) + 42 (6) + 10 (9) + 22 (11) + 609 (12) + 14 (15) + 14(?) (16) + 32 (25) + 42 (26) + 21 (27) + 27 (28) + 22(?) (29) + 400 (30) + 22 (32) + 17 (35) + 7 (36) + 66 (37) + 23.5 (40) + 22 (41) + 9 (43) + 9 (45) + 12 (46) + 62 (48) +80 (49) + 17 (50) + 40 (54) + 600 (59) + 71 and 20 minas (60).

54. + 40 (16) and + 60 (29).

of gold and silver, there should be added 165 ingots of gold[55] and 19 bars of silver (and) 4 staters.[56] However, on the one hand, we do not know the real value of the talent and the mina at that time (1 talent = 60 or 50 minas = 3600 or 3000 shekels?) and, on the other hand, it is also necessary to distinguish the figures that refer to real weights of metal (see *mšql* in 1.4 [item 1] and 12.9 [item 60]) from those to be understood according to their monetary value, a talent/mina of gold and of silver, though there is no way to show which is appropriate in each case. To these numbered quantities must be added the amounts left unspecified: 'a lot of silver offerings', *ksp mnḥh rb* (item 42), 'consecrated (offering)', *ḥrm* (items 44 and 53), or whose exact amount is written down in a document near the deposit (= inventory 'slip') *(w)btkn 'ṣlm/n* (items 23, 51, 52, 55, 56). Also to be considered are the chests (items 23 and 58), the vessels for taxation, for the collection and for the second tithe (items 4, 14, 34, 51; see too 12 and 59), and the vases (mentioned in items 8, 9, 18, 48, 52, 55 and 56). To these are to be added some books: a scroll in an urn (item 23), books (item 34) and the copy (item 61).[57]

Even without counting the unnumbered quantities or the various silver or gold items, these amounts at first sight seem too fantastic to be thought of as possessions of the Essene religious group. Are they unthinkable? Authors in favour of authenticity commonly make comparisons with other cash amounts from that time: Antiochus IV Epiphanes carried off 1800 talents from the temple (2 Macc. 5.21), Crassus plundered the treasury of the Temple, carrying off 8000 talents of gold and 2000 talents of silver that Pompey had left in the treasury (Josephus, *Ant.* 14.78, 105-10). Even Jonathan Maccabee is accused of having stolen the possessions of the Temple treasury in 150 BC as a manuscript from Cave 4 reports.[58] We know that the importance of the treasure of the Jerusalem Temple had gone the rounds in the ancient Near East. Even if the Copper Scroll had

55. 100 (2) + 65 (7).

56. 6 (10) + 6 (31) + 7 of (/and) 4 staters (39). I now differentiate between *kkr* = 'talent' and the abbreviation *kk* (= *ksp krš*, 'silver *karš*'); see my edition (forthcoming). This new reading changes the total number of talents.

57. Compare the chart in DJDJ III, p. 282: 'Le montant total des quantités spécifiées, abstraction faite des lacunes et des lectures incertaines est de 4.630 talents d'argent et d'or.'

58. Cf. É. Puech, 'Jonathan le Prêtre Impie et les débuts de la Communauté de Qumrân. 4QJonathan (4Q523) et 4QPsAp (4Q448)', *RevQ* 17 (1996), pp. 241-70 (*Hommages à Józef Tadeusz Milik*).

merely alluded to some treasure hidden before the fall of the city and Temple, the Romans still found such amounts to draw from the (unhidden) Temple treasures that, according to Josephus, the price of gold in Syria dropped by half. On the other hand, to gauge the resources of ancient Palestine, Milik refers to the will of Herod the Great detailed in Josephus, *Ant.* 17.317-20 and *War* 2.95-98, namely, 760 talents distributed among Antipas, Philip, Archelaus and Salome.[59] On the basis of such information the disproportionate amounts in the Copper Scroll made it possible for Milik to conclude that the treasure was legendary.

The Abbreviation of Proper Names in Greek

The solution to the enigma presented by the Copper Scroll is to be found, no doubt, at least in part, in the precise study of its text: the topography, the identification of the important site of Koḥlit and the Greek letters. Are the Greek letters symbols[60] or, preferably, the coded proper names of those responsible for certain deposits? With the aid of examples taken from the writings of Josephus, Pixner has proposed identifying proper names in them, and it is easy to increase the possibilities in connection with this proposal: ΚΕΝεδαιος or ΚΕΝεζος, ΚΑΓειρας, ΗΝναφης, ΘΕβουτις, ΘΕοδοωρος, ΘΕυδας, and so on, ΔΙοφατος, ΔΙοδωρος, ΔΙοδοτος, or ΔΙογενες, ΤΡυφων, ΣΚοπας.[61] Only the first two names have three letters, as if it was a matter of giving the key to the reading, from then on two letters being enough for the initiated reader.

59. Milik, DJDJ III, p. 285.

60. E. Ullendorf, 'The Greek Letters of the Copper Scroll', *VT* 11 (1961), pp. 227-28, proposed a reading of the letters as numerals, but his explanation is both more than difficult and also the reading ΘΕ is certain instead of ΞΕ.

61. Pixner, 'Unravelling the Copper Scroll Code', pp. 335-36 and 345 for the priest Theboutis. For Stegemann (*Die Essener*, pp. 106-107) the first two on the list would be members of the wealthy royal house of Adiabene (Josephus, *War* 2.520, 5.474), but is a nickname like Καγειρας so unique? We know the custom of that time concerning the giving of nicknames; see 1 Macc. 2.2-5 for the five sons of Mattathias etc., Acts 12.25-13.1 etc., a custom which we meet again, e.g., in the papyri of Wadi Khabra, *The Documents from the Bar Kochba Period in the Cave of Letters: Greek Papyri*, by N. Lewis, *Aramaic and Nabatean Signatures and Subscriptions*, by Y. Yadin and J.C. Greenfield (Judean Desert Studies, 2; Jerusalem: Israel Exploration Society; The Hebrew University; The Shrine of the Book, 1989): Joseph nicknamed Zaboudos, Judah nicknamed Chthousion, Judah nicknamed Kimber, and so on.

Place Names

The decipherment which I have proposed no longer leaves any possibility of locating any site in Transjordan. All the locations, including Koḥlit,[62] must be situated in Palestine proper: the Holy City and its environs, within a narrowly extended radius in the region south of the city, to Sekakah (with the LXX)—Qumran and Jericho and their environs, and ending up with three sites a little more distant, Mount Gerizin, Beth Sham and Bezek between these two.

It is advisable to set aside the first 16 entries for which the author gives some supplementary indications by means of Greek letters probably alluding to the names of persons in charge. There are 7 of these (items 1, 4, 6, 7, 9, 13 and 16).[63] The deposits of this first group are distributed between *Ḥorebbeh* in the Valley of Achor (items 1, 2 and 3?), three hiding places at Koḥlit and its environs: (item 4) 'in the mound', *btl*, (item 11) 'in

62. Milik, DJDJ III, pp. 274-75, would situate Koḥlit on the western side of Mount Carmel, but that identification is questionable. By way of a hypothesis dare one suggest identifying it with Tell es-Sultan, the ancient tell of Jericho to the north of Hasmonaean and Herodian Jericho, which has a wide perimeter because of important irrigation projects and is contemporaneous with the occupation of Qumran? Does not that solution sufficiently take into account the entries where the deposits of Koḥlit (with water) are mentioned: a tell/mound (item 4), a pool to the east (item 11), a large cistern to the north (item 16), an underground passage to the north (items 20 and 61), and the geographical sequence of place names, 'Valley of Achor, etc.'? 'Un cimetière comparable à celui de *Khirbet* Qumrân-Sokokah est connu du côté nord de Tell es-Sultan' (see K.M. Kenyon, *Excavations at Jericho.* III. *The Architecture and Stratigraphy of the Tell* [London: BSAJ, 1981], pp. 173-74, and É. Puech, 'The Necropolises of *Khirbet* Qumran and of 'Ain el-Ghuwein, and the Essene Belief in the Afterlife', *BASOR* 312 (1998), pp. 21-36. Furthermore, Elisha, the disciple of Elijah who purified the waters of the very abundant spring that wells up at the foot of the tell (2 Kgs 2.19-22), could be the source of the mention of his master Elijah in connection with a spring on Mount Carmel in the Jewish legend from the Middle Ages quoted by Milik. But would this proposition be compatible with the mention of a 'Koḥlit in the Desert' in *b. Qid.* 66a? John Hyrcanus did in fact conquer these 'towns' in Samaria and Idumaea (Josephus, *Ant.* 13.254-58). Tell es-Sultan, although in the oasis of Jericho, is still in the desert. An identification with 'Aïn Feshkha would be more difficult, all the more so since Koḥlit is mentioned five times to four for Sekakah. But nothing in the five attestations of 3Q15 proves that Koḥlit should be understood as a district (despite Goranson, 'Sectarianism', p. 287). Moreover, it does not seem to be a unique name. In the end this place name remains difficult to identify.

63. For another group of 'seven' with Greek names, see the 'seven deacons' of the young Church in Acts 6.3-6.

the pool to the east', *bbrk'*, and (item 16) 'in the great cistern to the north', *bbwr hgdwl*, the others being on the whole probably situated around the very wall of the Temple of Jerusalem[64] and with more difficulty (?) in the region of Jericho, but their location cannot be further specified.

The following group, lacking the indications in Greek, seems to resume the preceding geographical sequence, probably beginning from Koḥlit since item 17 follows the mention of *kḥlt* in item 16 and item 18 resumes with the valley of Achor. There follow items 19 in wadi 'Aṣla, 20 to the north of Koḥlit, 21-24 at Sekakah and its environs, 25 between Jericho and Sekakah, 26-28 in the same region, 29 near a ford of the Jordan, 30 to 31 very probably at Jericho, 32 at Doq to the north-east of Jericho, 33 at the outflow of the waters of Koziba to the west of Jericho, 34 at Jericho(?), 35 a valley in the region, 36 in the Kidron Valley, 37-38 in the valley of Shaveh (one of the tributaries of the Kidron), 39 at Naṭoph and 40-46 in the vicinity of Tekoa-Herodium, 47 at Beth ha-Kerem, 48-50 to the south of Jerusalem (valley of *Job*, monument of Absalom and sources of Shiloah), 51-57 around the ramparts of the city, and finally, 58 at Mount Gerizin,[65] 59 at Beth Sham and 60 at Bezek midway between these two sites, to finish again at Koḥlit (item 61). The distributions of the first and second groupings comply with an order that has its own internal coherence and that can only with difficulty, all would agree, be due to pure coincidence, even if the topographical identifications of the entries in cols. 1-2 are not entirely certain.

If one copies out on a map the identifiable topographical information, it is strikingly obvious that these hiding places occupy a very limited region around Sekakah–Jericho and 'Tekoa-Bethlehem'–Jerusalem and their immediate environs, but with a prominent crossing point between these two groups provided by the Kidron Valley. No doubt the north-east of the Judaean desert could have served as a place of refuge for those resisting at the time of the siege of Jerusalem by the Romans but the

64. According to the translations and identifications of Milik. Even if the Essenes did not sacrifice in the temple, they were not banned from its perimeters, as Josephus reports on the subject of the prophecy of Judah the Essene with regard to the death of Antigonus. Judah saw Antigonus cross the temple on the very day on which he had predicted his death at Straton's Tower; Judah was in the enclosure of the temple with numerous disciples (Josephus, *War* 1.78-80; *Ant.* 13.311-13).

65. The location of Gerizin to the west of Herodian Jericho (see n. 35 above) seems improbable in these sequences. We would have expected its mention at the beginning of the second group.

deposits of 'Jerusalem', of Jericho–Sekakah (= Khirbet Qumran) do not lend themselves to this kind of explanation, any more than those of Mount Gerizin, Beth Sham and Bezek. We must therefore give up identifying the hiding places as deposits from the treasury of the Temple administered by non-Essene high priests before the arrival of Roman troops, one of whose legions followed precisely the route of Beth-Sham–Jericho–Jerusalem.[66] The absence of any mention of other place names in Judaea, especially that of the name of the holy city 'Jerusalem', does not favour the hypothesis that we are dealing with treasures from the Temple administered by Pharisees, Sadducees or Zealots.[67]

Having these goods belong to the Essenes, the Qumran community and other Essene groups in Jerusalem and elsewhere, takes into account far better the geographical distribution of these deposits and the mention of the names of priestly families in these lists; the classical sources on the distribution of the Essenes do not contradict this.[68] This conclusion might explain, in part at least, the connections with the Samaritan milieu that can be seen in the biblical and pseudepigraphal texts found among the Qumran manuscripts.[69] The question comes up at the very least because of the

66. Despite McCarter, 'The Copper Scroll Treasure', pp. 140-41. The mentions of Sekakah (= Kh. Qumran = The Essenes) and of Gerizin, a Samaritan possession, certainly conflict with the idea that the treasure came from the temple and belonged to the Pharisees. If the treasure could not reach the temple because of the beginnings of the war with the Romans, it is surprising not to see any mention of other hiding places more to the south or the west, such as Masada or other cave refuges in the wadis to the south of Ein Gedi. Beth Ḥoron no longer comes into consideration.

67. As is claimed, e.g., by Allegro, *Treasure of the Copper Scroll*, pp. 120-29.

68. Pliny the Elder, *Natural History* 5.17.4; Dio Chrysostom according to his biographer Synesius, *Dio* 5: 'the Essenes, a community of complete happiness, situated beside the Dead Sea'; Philo, *Apology for the Jews* 11.1: 'They dwell in many cities of Judaea and in many villages and in great and populous communities.' If, as it seems, this conclusion is admissible, the lists of the Copper Scroll would give a new and most important insight regarding the settlement of Essenes in the country.

69. Cf., e.g., M. Baillet, 'Le texte samaritain de l'Exode dans les manuscrits de Qumrân', in A. Caquot and M. Philonenko (eds.), *Hommages à André Dupont-Sommer* (Paris: Librairie d'Amérique et d'Orient Adrien-Maisonneuve, 1971), pp. 363-81, esp. 4Q158, 4Q174 and 4Q175; J.E. Sanderson, *An Exodus Scroll from Qumran: 4QpaleoExod^m and the Samaritan Tradition* (Harvard Semitic Studies, 30; Atlanta: Scholars Press, 1986); J.T. Milik, 'Écrits préesséniens de Qumrân: d'Hénoch à Amram', in M. Delcor (ed.), *Qumrân: Sa piété, sa théologie et son milieu* (BETL, 46; Paris–Gembloux: Éditions Duculot; Leuven: Leuven University Press, 1978), pp. 91-106: *Testament of Levi* (pp. 96-97), *of Judah* (p. 101), Judith (p. 101), p. 106; and

mention of Mount Gerizin. The fierce opposition of the Pharisaic priesthood with regard to Gerizin is well known.

This distribution, which seems conclusively established, with no place names in Transjordan (except perhaps 6.14–7.1, 'the ford of the high priest'), in Galilee or in the outlying territory of Judaea, invalidates part of the interpretations of Pixner, Goranson, Stegemann and others. If the caches belonged to the treasury of the Temple as tribute or as the deposits of the rich in the only bank at that time and were hidden two years after the fall of Sekakah–Qumran in 68 CE, as has been maintained,[70] how could those non-Essenes have hidden them at Jericho, which had already been occupied by the Romans since the spring of 68, and at and near Qumran, then guarded by a squad of Roman soldiers (Stratum III of the *Khirbeh*), or have been able to add the scroll to Cave 3, behind or beside the deposits of manuscript-jars and goods belonging to the Essenes,[71] their opponents,

F. Dexinger, 'Samaritan Origins and the Qumran Texts', in A.D. Crown and L. Davey (eds.), *Essays in Honour of G.D. Sixdenier: New Samaritan Studies of the Société d'Études Samaritaines, III and IV* (Studies in Judaica, 5; Sydney: University of Sydney, 1995), pp. 169-84.

70. E.g., Stegemann, *Die Essener*, pp. 105-108, who even describes the Essene hypothesis as 'völlig absurd'!; likewise McCarter, 'The Copper Scroll Treasure', pp. 140-41.

71. Cf. R. de Vaux, 'Exploration de la région de Qumrân', *RB* 60 (1953), pp. 555-58; he speaks of 'd'une lampe, d'éléments de 2 cruches, de 26 couvercles et d'environ 40 jarres'. 'Sous les blocs qui obstruaient l'entrée, peu de tessons ont été trouvés, mais ils étaient très nombreux dans la chambre intérieure… (oû) tous les fragments écrits ont été recueillis', while the scrolls had been left 'près de l'entrée de la chambre intérieure, contre la paroi rocheuse qui faisait le fond de la chambre écroulée'. But in DJDJ III, p. 201, he wrote: 'Ils étaient déposés l'un sur l'autre contre la paroi rocheuse à l'angle nord de la chambre arrière de la grotte; la partie antérieure de celle-ci s'est effondrée… Ils étaient un peu à l'écart de la masse des jarres et des couvercles brisés…' and pp. 7-8: 'Devant cette chambre, une grande quantité de jarres et de couvercles brisés mêlés aux débris du plafond… Dans la chambre arrière de la grotte, niveaux stratifiés de cailloux avec quelques fragments de tissus, de cuir noirci et des fragments écrits, très peu de tessons dans cette région… Juste à l'angle nord de la chambre, deux rouleaux de cuivre inscrits étaient déposés l'un au-dessus de l'autre contre la paroi rocheuse…' These reports by the excavator do not wholly agree. If the written fragments were all found in the rear chamber and the Copper Scroll in front of its entrance against the north wall, the pottery seems to have been discovered in the front chamber (DJDJ III) and/or in the inner chamber (*RB* 1953), but with the scroll apart, before the ceiling had collapsed, one block of which isolated it from the rest of the deposits. W.L. Reed, 'The Qumran Caves Expedition', pp. 8-13, who had participated in the expedition, speaks of the remains of 25 jars of the manuscript-jar type and

who were turning to resistance, had just left the region and definitely hoped to recover their deposits as soon as possible? The hypothesis of deposits from Jerusalem seems to me highly improbable and unrealistic on several levels, in as much as the city was under siege and since movements in its vicinity and at some distance to the south must have been rather limited and closely watched. Nobody could have deposited such quantities without being seen, especially since they would have needed a caravan for transport! On the eve of the fall of the besieged city it is easier to imagine treasures being hidden in the city itself, which was still in the hands of defenders, rather than in the area round about among Essene opponents, or, for even stronger reasons, in the centres under the control of the Roman enemy. Contrary to what has been written, there is no allusion to the author of the text in the scroll itself.[72]

It is generally accepted that the Essenes lived not only at Qumran, but also in Jerusalem and in other cities of the country, and that they held in common the goods that they possessed (Josephus, *War* 2.124-27; *Ant.* 18.18-22). Several of them were priests, starting with the Teacher of Righteousness, and they were therefore eligible to receive their share of tithes, gifts and goods, whether consecrated or not. Such portions might have been sent to them by those who supported them from the beginning and/or who did not wish to make a donation to the wicked priests (CD 3.12) serving in the Temple, which had been defiled since the time of the high priesthood of Jonathan; they might have wanted to avoid becoming the accomplices of such priests. We know that specific rules governed the relationship of the Essenes to the Temple and its offerings: for example, the half-shekel had to be paid just once in a lifetime and not annually (cf. 4Q159 1 6-7 = 4Q513 1-2), or again the priests of the defiled Temple were accused of profanation, greed and fornication (prohibited marriages), in brief, the priests were deemed unfit to touch the *terûmah-dema'* or consecrated objects (cf. CD 4.14-5.11, and esp. 6.11-7.16 with the mention

writes: 'The date of the pottery with which they were associated, and the similarity of several small pieces of inscribed parchment in cave 3Q to the Dead Sea scrolls make it certain that the rolls were placed on the floor of the cave prior to 70 AD' (p. 10). At least some of the manuscripts found in Cave 3 are labelled Essene (3Q9 etc.).

72. For example, Wolters, 'Literary Analysis', pp. 292-93, who thinks that he has found three first-person mentions that could allude to the high priest and his valuable possessions. These are just spurious readings by Wolters, despite his direct examination of the originals.

of *bḥrm* and *bhwn hmqdš*; 1QpHab 8.13; 9.4-5; 12.8-9;[73] and parallel to those, Mk 7.11). 4QMMT^c^ (= 4Q396 1-2 iv) 62-64 recalls the duty of paying the tithe to the priests. And according to 1QpHab 12.8-9 the 'poor' despoiled ones (Essenes) are supposed to possess significant goods.

This way of understanding the facts could account for the entries in the list of hiding places and fits perfectly with almost all the place names listed. One notices that, by and large, the hiding places are situated in places where no Jew would in principle have thought of searching for such goods: sacred deposits in tombs, canals and pools where fluids transmitted impurity, as if these taxes and consecrated gifts were deliberately rendered impure and unusable until their redemption. Such activity could only be directed against possible Jewish looters, who were considered wicked, not against the Romans who were not affected by traditions of this kind. Furthermore, the mention of taxation, second tithe, treasury, consecrated offering (*ḥrm*) and *minḥah*, of priests, Theboutis and so on, of the tomb of Zadok,[74] of the priestly family Haqoṣ-treasurers of the Temple (?), etc., all seem to argue in favour of an Essene interpretation of this composition. The palaeographic dating of the Copper Scroll, very probably towards the middle of the first century CE (certainly prior to the fall of Qumran in 68),[75] and not at the end of the first century or the beginning of the second century CE,[76] as also the locations of the deposits, would support this conclusion more than oppose it.

73. Cf., for example, J.M. Baumgarten, 'Halakhic Polemics in New Fragments from Qumran Cave 4', in J. Amitai (ed.), *Biblical Archaeology Today: Proceedings of the International Congress on Biblical Archaeology, Jerusalem, April 1984* (Jerusalem: Israel Exploration Society; Israel Academy of Sciences and Humanities; ASOR, 1985), pp. 390-99; and E. and H. Eshel, '4Q471 Fragment 1 and *Ma'amadot* in the War Scroll', in J. Trebolle Barrera and L. Vegas Montaner (eds.), *The Madrid Qumran Congress: Proceedings of the International Congress on the Dead Sea Scrolls, Madrid 18–21 March, 1991* (2 vols.; Leiden: E.J. Brill; Madrid: Editiorial complutense, 1992), II, pp. 611-20, where the authors show the Essene restrictions concerning participation in the Jerusalem treasury.

74. This tomb of Zadok is not otherwise described but we know the importance of this name and of the designation of the sons of Zadok *bny ṣdwq* in the Essene milieu.

75. Cf. F.M. Cross, 'Excursus on the Palaeographical Dating of the Copper Scroll', DJDJ III, pp. 217-21.

76. For a dating between the two revolts, cf. Milik, DJDJ III, pp. 283-84. But certainly not during the Second Revolt in 132–35, notwithstanding Lurie (according to Pixner, 'Unravelling the Copper Scroll Code', p. 332), who would make the scroll refer to the proceeds of the treasury of the temple, which had been restored at the beginning of the Second Revolt, and E.-M. Laperrousaz, 'Remarques sur l'origine des

I have only briefly mentioned the research trails that must be followed to show the possibility that these deposits were Essene. There is nothing to stand against this possibility. The deposits were hidden around the Temple and the city where a large group of Essenes resided[77] and at their principal centre, at Sekakah, and at Jericho (in these cases before the destruction in 68 CE).[78] This hypothesis is more probable[79] than those already advanced which propose that the treasures belonged to the Zealots, or to Jewish rebels of the second revolt, or to Pharisees of the period between the two revolts, or were treasures of the Temple in the years before 70 CE.

After this new reading of the scroll, it seems more difficult to prove that these treasures and the scroll in Cave 3 did not belong to the Essenes than the opposite. In this case, the text that now appears to give us some sure readings, also now allows us a glimpse of how we might begin to respond to its enigma.

Finally, the process of inscription on these three metal sheets was on the whole an onerous undertaking and the fact that this rather terse list contains no religious or magical motifs are not points in favour of it being a legendary account.

Conclusion

In light of all this, the Copper Scroll, unique because of its subject matter and way of having been written, turns out to be one of the best-preserved Essene scrolls from the Qumran caves. Only a few words and two incom-

rouleaux de cuivre découverts dans la grotte 3 de Qoumrân', *RHR* 159 (1961), pp. 157-72: treasure of the Jewish rebels.

77. Cf. Pixner, 'Unravelling the Copper Scroll Code', p. 333. There may also be good reasons why the Copper Scroll never mentions the name of Jerusalem, a city that was in the hands of their Pharisee opponents.

78. I cannot see how the Essenes, any more than the Pharisees, would have been able to hide the deposits in Jericho and its immediate vicinity occupied by the Roman legion coming from Beth-Shean-Scythopolis at the end of the Spring of 68.

79. Confirming in that way the first intuition of Kuhn ('Les rouleaux'), contrary to that of 1956, 'Der gegenwärtige Stand der Erforschung', *TLZ* 81 (1956), pp. 541-46, in favour of the treasure of the Temple, a thesis repeated by K.H. Rengstorf, *Ḫirbet Qumrân und die Bibliothek vom Toten Meer* (Studia Delitzschiana, 5; Stuttgart: W. Kohlhammer, 1960), pp. 26-28. But adherence to the opinion that it was Essene treasures was defended by A. Dupont-Sommer, 'Les rouleaux de cuivre trouvés à Qumrân', *RHR* 151 (1957), pp. 22-36.

plete numbers are missing from the text of this scroll. Moreover, in most cases one can restore its terminology with a large measure of probability or at least begin to see the probable solution, especially at 4.1, 2, 3; 5.1, 2, 3; 7.1, 2, 3, 4, 5; and 11.17.

This latest reading has made it possible, it seems to me, to make real headway in the deciphering of this difficult text, even if some obscure points still remain to be cleared up. Those points, however, come less within the province of epigraphy, than of philology and general interpretation. From its contents, the composition reveals itself to be a list of Essene treasures hidden on Essene properties or not far from their dwellings before the arrival of the Roman legions. Those Essene properties were at Jericho–Sekakah, in and around Jerusalem, and at their other centres. The cultic terminology that appears here and there in no way contradicts this being Essene property.[80] In fact, Essenes no longer had to make contributions to the treasury of the Temple, since they were temporarily separated from it, nor did they materially support its illegitimate and impious Sadducean–Pharisaic priesthood, which had plundered the treasury for political purposes.[81] Rather, Essenes supported members of the legitimate Essene priesthood while they waited to take possession of the Temple and to purify it.[82] In the meantime, the Essene 'Community' had become their temple. Finally, it is probable that, when they separated themselves off in the desert, the Teacher and his admirers had brought with them some goods from the Temple itself.[83]

80. Contrary to Wolters, 'History and the Copper Scroll', p. 292.

81. Cf. Puech, 'Jonathan le Prêtre'.

82. Cf. also Pixner, 'Unravelling the Copper Scroll Code', pp. 33-34.

83. After its delivery at the Manchester Symposium this paper was published in French as 'Quelques résultats d'un nouvel examen du *Rouleau de Cuivre (3Q15)*', *RevQ* 18 (1997), pp. 163-90.

Part II

ARCHAEOLOGICAL AND LINGUISTIC STUDIES

6

Aqueducts in the Copper Scroll*

Hanan Eshel

Introduction

Several fortresses were built during the Second Temple period in the region of Qumran, within 20 km of the site (see Fig. 6.1).[1] In the Copper Scroll the aqueducts that brought water to Khirbet Qumran as well as to some of those fortresses are mentioned.[2]

One may assume that the author of the Copper Scroll was familiar with these royal fortresses. During the first century CE these fortresses were guarded by Roman soldiers. Aqueducts led water to all these fortresses. In every fortress cisterns were carved in order to store the water. Those aqueducts were quite notable, and as such were used by the author of the Copper Scroll as a reference to the hidden treasures.

This article is divided into two sections. In the first section I would like to describe briefly four aqueducts that were built in the area of Qumran. In the second part I discuss the parts of the Copper Scroll that are related to aqueducts.

* This paper was written with the support of the C.G. Foundation Jerusalem Project.

1. Y. Tzafrir, 'The Desert Fortresses of Judaea in the Second Temple Period', *The Jerusalem Cathedra* 2 (1982), pp. 120-45; G. Garbrecht and J. Peleg, 'Die Wasserversorgung geschichtlicher Wüstenfestungen am Jordantal', *Antike Welt* 20.2 (1989), pp. 2-20; G. Garbrecht and Y. Peleg, 'The Water Supply of the Desert Fortresses in the Jordan Valley', *BA* 57 (1994), pp. 161-70.

2. I would like to thank D. Amit for his comments on some of the issues discussed in this paper.

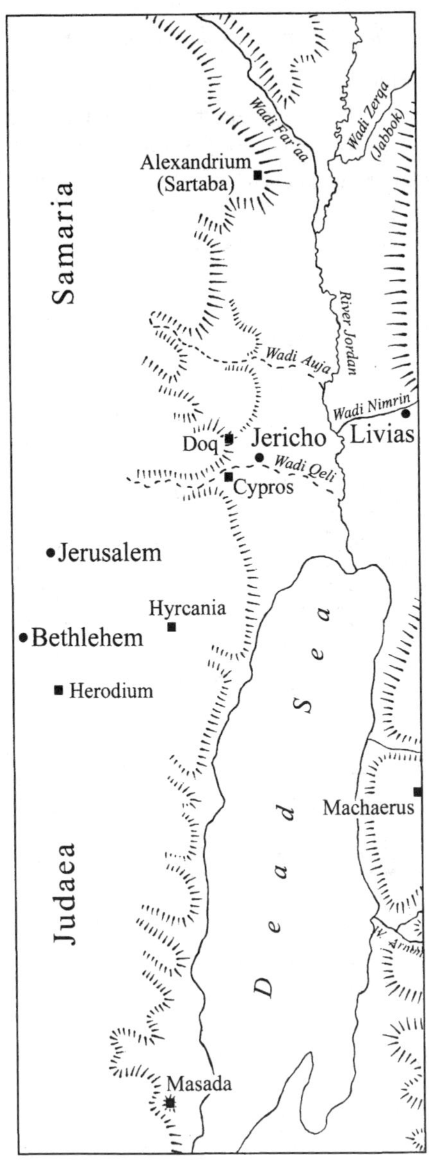

Fig. 6.1. *Map of all the fortresses in the Judaean desert* (Taken from Tzafrir, 'The Desert Fortresses' [see n. 1])

The Aqueducts in the Qumran Area

The Aqueduct to Qumran

A short aqueduct of c. 0.5 km in length, starting under a high waterfall in Wadi Qumran, brought water to Khirbet Qumran (Fig. 6.2).[3] This aqueduct consisted of two parts. The first part was built in Wadi Qumran, keeping its height at a uniform level by means of tunnels and supporting walls. The second part of the aqueduct was built on the plateau.

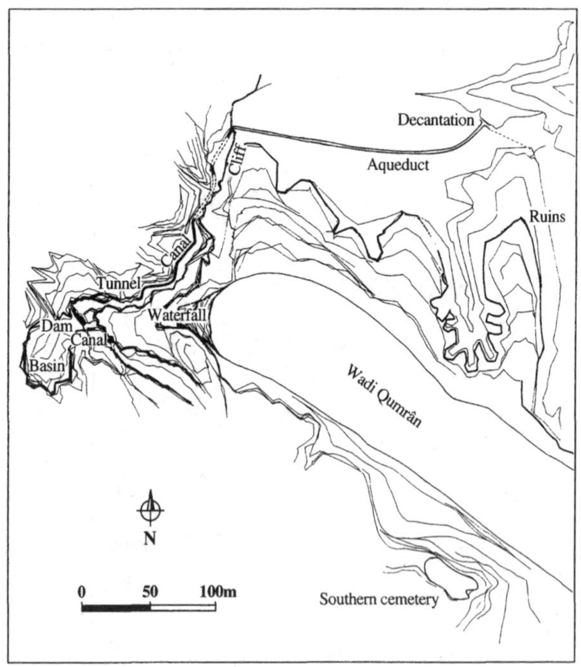

Fig. 6.2. *Map of the aqueduct of Qumran*
(Taken from de Vaux, *Fouilles de Khirbet Qumrân et de Ain Feshkha* [see n. 3])

3. E.W.G. Masterman, 'Notes on Some Ruins and a Rock-cut Aqueduct in Wadi Kumran', *PEQ* 35 (1903), pp. 265-67; R. de Vaux, 'Fouilles de Khirbet Qumran', *RB* 63 (1956), pp. 538-40 [573]; S. Schultz, 'Chirbet Kumran, En Feschcha und die Bukea', *ZDPV* 76 (1960), pp. 53-58; Z. Ilan and D. Amit, 'The Aqueduct of Qumran', in D. Amit, Y. Hirschfeld and J. Patrich (eds.), *The Aqueducts of Ancient Palestine* (Jerusalem: Yad Izhak Ben-Zvi, 1989), pp. 283-88 (Hebrew); R. de Vaux, *Fouilles de Khirbet Qumrân et de Ain Feshkha* (ed. J.B. Humbert and A. Chambon; Göttingen: Vandenhoeck & Ruprecht, 1994), pp. 192, 195-99, 342.

A dam was built under the second waterfall in the wadi, creating a small pool from which the aqueduct started. The dam deflected part of the running water (when there was a flood) from the wadi to the aqueduct. Forty metres beyond the waterfall the aqueduct becomes a subterranean tunnel 13.5 m long. After the tunnel, the aqueduct was built on supporting walls for another 130 m. On the plateau the aqueduct continues for about another 200 m, descending to Khirbet Qumran.

The Aqueducts of Hyrcania

Khirbet el-Mird, Hyrcania, is located 9 km west of Khirbet Qumran.[4] Two water aqueducts brought water to Hyrcania:[5] the northern one, which is 2 km long, started in a wadi north of the site (Fig. 6.3). It started above a waterfall of about 8 m in height. A dam about 4–5 m wide was built in a diagonal direction in order to deflect part of the water to the aqueduct. The width of this aqueduct in its upper part is about 1 m—double the width of the other aqueducts in the Judaean desert. Thus, this aqueduct was designed to receive a vast quantity of flood water in a relatively short time.

The southern aqueduct is 9 km long, starting in Wadi Qidron (Wadi en-Nar). After 1300 m, when the wadi turns south, the aqueduct crosses the wadi and continues on the east side; in the area where in the Byzantine period the St Saba Monastery was built (see Fig. 6.3). The aqueduct leaves Wadi Qidron and changes its direction to the north-east, toward the fortress. The aqueduct then goes through three high bridges and a few small ones. The southern bridge is 7.5 m at its highest point. The highest point of the middle bridge was 17 m, while the northern bridge was 9 m above the wadi.

The two aqueducts meet about 750 m west of Hyrcania. Due to the brittle bedrock in this area, an open canal 500 m long was built. Here two impressive bridges were erected. West of the fortress stood another monumental bridge, through which the two aqueducts passed, bringing water to the cisterns (see Fig. 6.4).

4. J. Patrich, 'Hyrcania', in E. Stern (ed.), *The New Encyclopedia of Archeological Excavations in the Holy Land* (4 vols.; Jerusalem: Israel Exploration Society, 1993), II, pp. 639-41; C.R. Conder and H.H. Kitchener, *The Survey of Western Palestine*, III (London, 1883), p. 212; G.R.H. Wright, 'The Archaeological Remains at el-Mird in the Wilderness of Judaea', *Bib* 42 (1961), pp. 5-6 (5).

5. J. Patrich, 'The Aqueducts of Hyrcania', in Amit, Hirschfeld and Patrich (eds.), *Aqueducts of Ancient Palestine*, pp. 243-60.

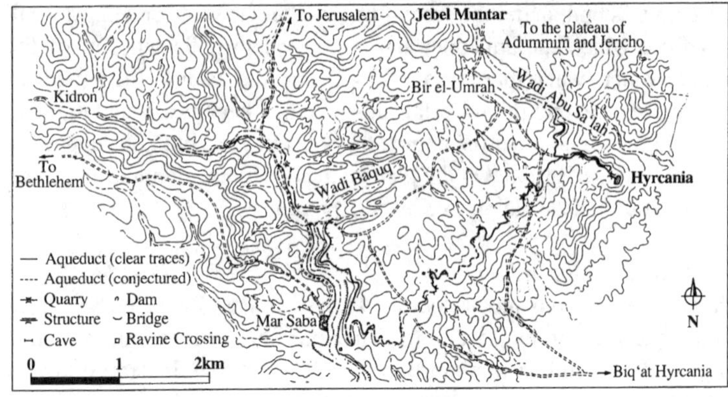

Fig. 6.3. *Map of the aqueducts of Hyrcania*
(Taken from Patrich, 'The Aqueducts of Hyrcania' [see n. 5])

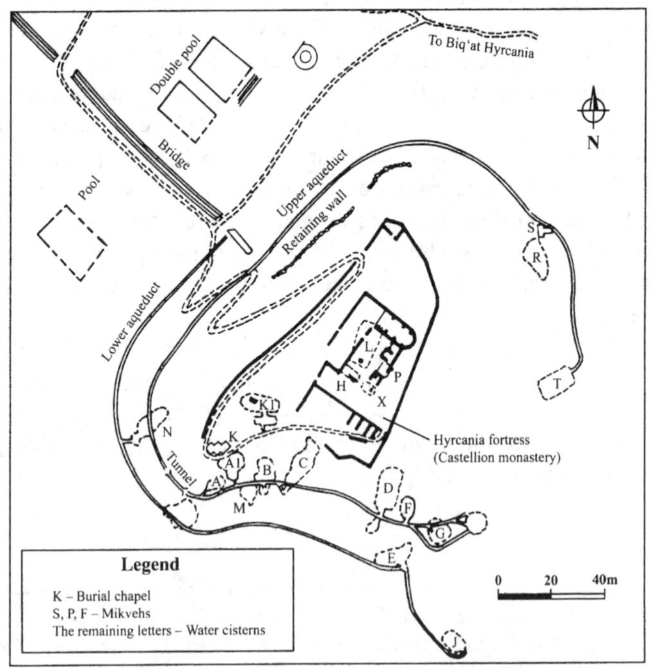

Fig. 6.4. *Map of Hyrcania and its vicinity*
(Taken from Patrich, 'Hyrcania' [see n. 4])

Two water pools were built north of the bridge (see Fig. 6.5). The northern pool measures 19 × 18 × 5 m. The southern pool was not preserved as well as the northern one, but it was slightly smaller, its depth being 2.6 m. A third pool was built south of the bridge.

The aqueducts that carried water to Hyrcania filled 14 cisterns, 12 of which were dug in two lines south of the fortress—8 on the upper line and 4 on the lower level. Two additional cisterns were dug north-east of the fortress. The northern aqueduct was presumably built during the Hasmonaean period, filling the 4 cisterns that are located south of the fortress, on the lower level, while the southern aqueduct, which was built during the Herodian period, filled the other 10 cisterns—8 south of the fortress and 2 in the north-east. Three ritual baths were built near the cisterns (see Fig. 6.4).

Fig. 6.5. *Northern bridge with the pools*
(Taken from Patrich, 'The Aqueducts of Hyrcania' [see n. 5])

The Aqueducts to Tell el-Aqabeh and to Jericho from Wadi el-Qelt
The fortress of Tell el-Aqabeh is located south of Wadi el-Qelt, 12 km north of Qumran.[6] This fortress is usually identified with Cypros.[7] Two

6. E. Netzer, 'Cypros', in Stern (ed.), *New Encyclopedia of Archaeological Excavations in the Holy Land*, I, pp. 315-17.

7. In 1981 we suggested identifying the fortress of Tell el-Aqabeh with Herodium of the hills on the Arabian frontier (Josephus, *War* 1.419); see H. Eshel and Y. Bin-

aqueducts carried water to the fortress of Tell el-Aqabeh (Fig. 6.6). The earlier one, dated to the Hasmonaean period, was built around a hill west of the fortress. This aqueduct was c. 1 km long. It collected rainwater from this hill. During the Herodian period another aqueduct was built, carrying water from Wadi el-Qelt to Tell el-Aqabeh. This aqueduct, 14 km long, passed over a monumental bridge to the fortress (Fig. 6.7). Half a dozen additional bridges and three tunnels were built on the south side of Wadi el-Qelt. This aqueduct brought water to Tell el-Aqabeh, and from the fortress to the fields of the Royal Estate in Jericho.[8]

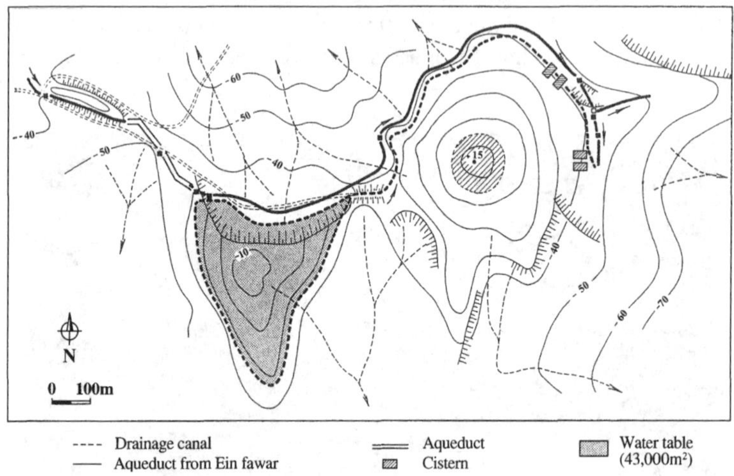

Fig. 6.6. *Map of the aqueduct of Cypros (Tell el-Aqabeh)*
(Taken from Garbrecht and Peleg, 'Die Wasserversorgung' [see n. 1])

Four cisterns were dug in the fortress of Tell el-Aqabeh, two north-east of the site and two east of the fortress. The northern cistern was probably

Nun, 'The Other Herodium and the Tomb of Herod', *Teva va-Aretz* 24 (1981), pp. 65-71 (Hebrew). This suggestion must be reconsidered because two fortresses from the Herodian period were found east of the Jordan. One of them may be identified as the Arabian Herodium; see A. Mallon, 'Deux fortresses au pied des Monts de Moab', *Bib* 14 (1933), pp. 400-407; K. Prag and H. Barnes, 'Three Fortresses on the Wadi Kafrain, Jordan', *Levant* 28 (1996), pp. 41-61.

8. Conder and Kitchener, *Survey of Western Palestine*, pp. 190, 222, 227-28; Z. Meshel and D. Amit, 'Water Supply to Cypros Fortress', in Amit, Hirschfeld and Patrich (eds.), *Aqueducts of Ancient Palestine*, pp. 229-42 (Hebrew).

the smallest one.[9] In the Herodian period the aqueduct carried water to the fortress of Tell el-Aqabeh all year long, and not only during certain days in the winter. Nevertheless, the cisterns were needed because an enemy could block the water in the aqueduct and deflect it at the beginning of a siege. Therefore, the soldiers guarding the fortress in the Herodian period had to ensure that the cisterns were always full.

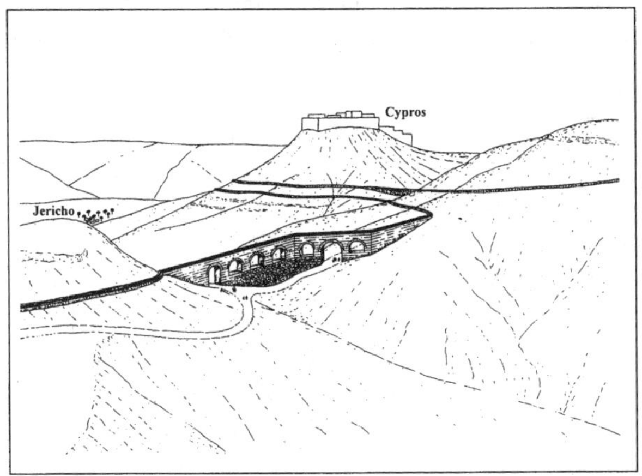

Fig. 6.7. *Drawing of the large bridge carrying the aqueduct leading to Cypros (Tell el-Aqabeh)*
(Taken from Meshel and Amit, 'Water Supply to Cypros Fortress' [see n. 8])

The earliest aqueduct that was built in the Judaean Desert was built north of Wadi el-Qelt. This aqueduct carried water to the Hasmonaean Palace and to the Royal Estate, which were built south of Jericho during the reign of John Hyrcanus I (134–104 BCE).[10] It was 15 km long. King Herod built a 5 km aqueduct along the south side of the eastern part of Wadi el-Qelt, carrying some of the winter water of Wadi el-Qelt to the fields of Jericho. At the end of the Second Temple period, three aqueducts

9. This cistern has collapsed, but in the map of Meshel and Amit, 'Water Supply to Cypros Fortress', p. 234, the northern cistern is smaller than the other collapsed cistern beside it.

10. E. Netzer, 'The Hasmonean and Herodian Winter Palaces at Jericho', *IEJ* 25 (1975), pp. 89-100; *idem*, 'The Winter Palaces of the Judean Kings at Jericho at the End of the Second Temple Period', *BASOR* 228 (1977), pp. 1-14; *idem*, 'Tulul Abu el 'Alayiq', in Stern (ed.), *New Encyclopedia of Archaeological Excavations in the Holy Land*, IV, pp. 682-91; H. Eshel, 'The Historical Background of the Pesher Interpreting Joshua's Curse on the Rebuilder of Jericho', *RevQ* 15 (1992), pp. 409-20.

(one on the north side, one on the south side passing Tell el-Aqabeh and the third being a short aqueduct, on the south side of the eastern part) led the water of Wadi el-Qelt to the Royal vineyards at Jericho. During that period more than 34 km of aqueducts were built along Wadi el-Qelt.[11]

The Aqueduct of Doq at Ras Qarantal

The fortress of Ras Qarantal is located west of Jericho, 16 km north of Qumran (Fig. 6.8). This fortress is identified with Doq or Dagon of the Hasmonaean Period.[12]

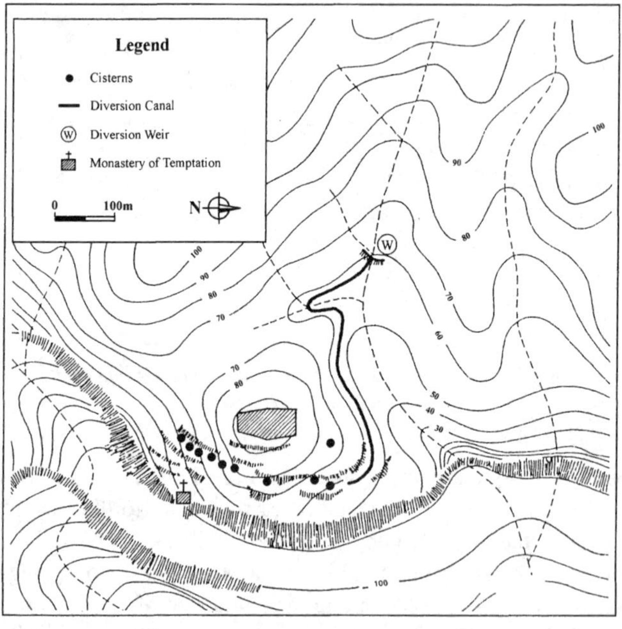

Fig. 6.8. *Map of the aqueduct of Doq*
(Taken from Garbrecht and Peleg, 'Water Supply of the Desert Fortresses' [n. 1])

11. E. Netzer, 'Water Channels and a Royal Estate from the late Hellenistic Period in the Western Plains of Jericho', *Leichtwiess-Institut für Wasserbau der Technischen Universität Braunschweig Mitteilungen Heft* 82 (1984), pp. 1-12; G. Garbrecht and E. Netzer, *Die Wasserversorgung des geschichtlichen Jericho und seiner Könglichen Anlagen* (Braunschweig: Braunschweig Leichtweiss-Institut für Wasserbau der Technischen Universität Braunschweig, Mitteilungen 115, 1991).

12. See Tzafrir, 'Desert Fortresses', p. 122. We have suggested identifying this fortress as Cypros of the Herodian period as well; see Eshel and Bin-Nun, 'The Other Herodium'.

The aqueduct that was built in order to carry water to the fortress of Ras Qarantal measures c. 700 m in length.[13] This aqueduct started at the foot of a small waterfall, running north of the fortress. It carried water to nine cisterns, carved east of the fortress.[14] Most of the cisterns are rectangular and measure between 7.5 m and 14 m long and are 3.5 m to 5.5 m wide. The northern cistern, no. 1, is not bigger than the other cisterns. The content of all these cisterns is 2090 m^3.

Paragraphs in the Copper Scroll that are Related to Water Aqueducts

The Aqueduct of Sekakah

In the beginning of col. 5 of the Copper Scroll we read:

1 ברוש אמת המים [הבאה ל[15]]
2 סככא מן הצפון ת[חת האבן [16]]
3 הגדולא חפור אמות [שלו
4 ש כספ ככ 7

1. At the head of the water aqueduct [which penetrates to]
2. Sekakah[17] from the north, bene[ath the] large
3. [stone,] dig for [three] cubits:
4. seven talents of silver.

As some scholars have already suggested, this aqueduct should be identified with the aqueduct of Wadi Qumran.[18] The dam that was built in this wadi is mentioned before the aqueduct at the end of col. 4:

13. D. Amit, 'The Water System of Dok Fortress', in Amit, Hirschfeld and Patrich (eds.), *Aqueducts of Ancient Palestine*, pp. 223-28 (Hebrew).

14. O. Meinardus, 'Notes on the Laurae and Monasteries of the Wilderness of Judaea (III)', *LA* 19 (1969), pp. 325-26.

15. E. Puech orally suggested the reconstruction ברוש אמת המים [ממערבא ל] סככא, 'At the head of the water aqueduct coming from the west to Sekakah', which is possible.

16. G.B. Sarfati suggested (in a seminar) the reconstruction ת[חת המסמא]. This reconstruction is based on 11.6. The term מסמא is mentioned in the rabbinic literature, meaning 'a stone'; see *m. Kel.* 1.3; *b. Nid.* 69b; and E. Ben-Yehuda, *A Complete Dictionary of Ancient and Modern Hebrew* (Jerusalem: Thomas Yoseloff, 1959), p. 3124 n. 1.

17. The name of Qumran was Sekakah in the First and Second Temple periods; see H. Eshel, 'A Note on Joshua 15.61-62 and the Identification of the City of Salt', *IEJ* 45 (1995), pp. 37-40.

18. See J.T. Milik, 'Le rouleau de cuivre provenant de la grotte 3Q (3Q15)', in M.

13 ביגר של גי הסככא חפור
14 אמת כסף ככ 12

13. In the dam of Sekakah Gorge, dig
14. cubits: twelve talents of silver.

The word יגר means 'a mound', as mentioned in Gen. 31.47, יגר שהדותא.[19] It seems that יגר in the Copper Scroll means 'a dam', where an aqueduct started.[20]

It seems that the first treasure was hidden under a big stone on the plateau, north of the aqueduct, while the second treasure was hidden in the dam of Wadi Qumran.

The Aqueducts of Hyrcania

The dam where the southern aqueduct leading to Hyrcania began is mentioned in 8.8-9 of the Copper Scroll:

8 ביגר של פי צוק הקדרון
9 חפור אמות שלוש ככ 7

8. In the dam of the Kidron cliff
9. dig for three cubits: seven talents of silver.

Therefore it seems that this treasure of seven talents of silver was hidden in the dam of Wadi Qidron (where the southern aqueduct of Hyrcania started).

In 4.3-5, an aqueduct is mentioned. Its destination was not preserved in the Copper Scroll. According to the context I suggest the reconstruction 'to Hyrcania' in line 3. This reconstruction is based on the assumption that there is some geographical order in the Copper Scroll. The next treasure was hidden in עמק עבון, which is probably עמק עבור, mentioned in Josh. 7.24-26, to be identified with el-Buqe'a.[21] The north aqueduct carrying

Baillet, J.T. Milik and R. de Vaux, *Les 'petites grottes' de Qumrân* (DJDJ III; Oxford: Clarendon Press, 1962), p. 263 n. 9; Ilan and Amit, 'Aqueduct of Qumran', p. 287. They also suggested that the יגר is the dam in Wadi Qumran.

19. On the יגר סהדותא see J. Skinner, *Genesis* (ICC; Edinburgh: T. & T. Clark, 1910), p. 401. On יגר in the Copper Scroll as a dam see B.-Z. Lurie, *The Copper Scroll from the Desert of Judah* (Jerusalem: Kiryat Sepher, 1963), p. 83 (Hebrew).

20. The word יגר appears in 8.8, which will be discussed below, and in 6.14: שבמגזת הכוהן ביגר, although I do not understand this description, this יגר can also be a dam of an aqueduct. See Lurie, *Copper Scroll*, p. 94.

21. See J.M. Allegro, *The Treasure of the Copper Scroll* (London: Routledge & Kegan Paul, 1960), pp. 64-68; Eshel, 'A Note on Joshua', pp. 37-38 n. 5. For a

water to Hyrcania passes the hills west of the Buqe'a. If we accept this restoration, we read:

3 באמא הבא[ה להורקניה] בביאתך
4 אמות ארבע[ין ואח]ת כסף
5 ככ 55

3. In the aqueduct which go[es to Hyrcania] when you enter (the site)
4. fort[y-on]e cubits:
5. fifty-five talents of silver.

It seems, therefore, that we can identify this aqueduct as the north aqueduct, carrying water from the area west of the Buqe'a to Hyrcania. The treasure was hidden 41 cubits from the point where the trail met the north aqueduct west of Hyrcania.

The Aqueduct to Cypros or Another Reference to the Aqueduct to Hyrcania

In 7.3 the description of a treasure starts with the words באמא של קי[, in the aqueduct of QY[. There are two possibilities to reconstruct this word. If we reconstruct קי[פרוס—Cy[pros then we should read:

3 באמא של קי[פרוס
4 האשוח הצפו[ני הגדו]ל
5 בארבע רוח[ות לשמ]ולו
6 משח אמות עסרין [ואר]בע
7 ככרין ארבע מאות

3. In the aqueduct of Cy[pros],
4. the nor[th bi]g reservoir [ ]
5. on the four si[des to its le]ft (or: to its north)[22]
6. measure twenty-[fo]ur cubits:
7. four hundred talents.

It seems that the reconstruction [הגד]ול at the end of line 4 is certain. The word משח means 'to measure', namely 'to measure twenty-four cubits, left (or north) of the four sides of the big northern reservoir'. The fortress of Cypros was named after King Herod's mother. If the reconstruction

discussion of Iron Age water irrigation systems in the Buqe'a, see F.M. Cross and J.T. Milik, 'Explorations in the Judaean Buqe'ah', *BASOR* 142 (1956), pp. 5-17; and L.E. Stager, 'Farming in the Judean Desert During the Iron Age', *BASOR* 221 (1976), pp. 145-58.

22. In biblical Hebrew and in Arabic שמאל means north; see BDB, p. 969.

באמא של קי]פרוס is accepted, then the Copper Scroll was composed later than the Herodian Period.

Most scholars identify Cypros with the fortress of Tell el-Aqabeh.[23] There are four cisterns in Tell el-Aqabeh. The north cistern collapsed, but there is no reason to assume that this cistern was bigger than the other three.[24]

I suggested in 1981 that Cypros was the Herodian name of the fortress built at Ras Qarantal, which was named Doq or Dagon during the Hasmonaean period.[25] If this is correct, then a problem arises, since in another description in the Copper Scroll, in col. 7, we read:

11 בדוק תחת פנת המשמרה
12 המנזרחית חפור אמות שבע
13 ככ 22

11. In Doq,[26] under the eastern
12. guardhouse dig for seven cubits:
13. twenty-two talents of silver.

This description raises the question if it is possible that the same fortress be given different names in the Copper Scroll, one representing the Hasmonaean name and the other the Herodian name.[27] Nevertheless the northern cistern at Ras Qarantal is not bigger than the other cisterns.[28] Therefore, we shall consider the possibility of reconstructing in 7.3 באמא של קי]דרון...[and reading, 'In the aqueduct of Qi[dron'.[29]

23. See Tzafrir, 'Desert Fortresses', p. 123.

24. See the map in Meshel and Amit, 'Water Supply to Cypros Fortress', p. 234 and Fig. 6.6 above, in which the north-eastern cistern is smaller than the other collapsed cistern beside it.

25. Eshel and Bin-Nun, 'The Other Herodium'.

26. For the identification of this treasure in the fortress of Ras Qarantal see Milik, DJDJ III, p. 265; Lurie, *Copper Scroll*, p. 97.

27. If we accept the prevailing suggestion to identify Cypros in Tell el-Aqabeh, we will face a similar problem, in light of Allegro's reasonable suggestion of identifying Mount Gerizim of 12.4 with Tell el-Aqabeh. See Allegro, *Treasure of the Copper Scroll*, pp. 75-76. On the polemic use of the toponym Mount Gerizim in the Copper Scroll, see H. Eshel, 'The Samaritans in the Persian and Hellenistic Periods: The Origins of Samaritanism' (PhD dissertation, Hebrew University Jerusalem, 1994), pp. 193-95 (Hebrew).

28. See the plans of these cisterns in Amit, 'Water System of Dok Fortress', p. 226 and Fig. 6.8 above.

29. I would like to thank Dr I. Knohl for this suggestion.

3 באמא של קי[דרון...][30]
4 האשוח הצפו[ני הגדו]ל
5 בארבע רוח[ות לשמ]ולו
6 משח אמות עסרין [וואר]בע
7 ככרין ארבע מאות

3. In the aqueduct of Qi[dron…,
4. the nor[th bi]g reservoir [ ]
5. on the four si[des to its le]ft
6. measure twenty-[fo]ur cubits:
7. four hundred talents.

If we accept this reading, then this passage deals with the south aqueduct of Hyrcania and not with the aqueduct of Cyprus. One problem with this reconstruction is that קדרון is written in col. 8 without a *yod*.[31] Nevertheless this possibility fits the archaeological remains of Hyrcania, and if we accept it, we can identify the אשיח, 'the reservoir', with the big pool north of the bridge west of Hyrcania.[32] Therefore, we may assume that this treasure was hidden 24 cubits north of the northern pool west of Hyrcania.

An Aqueduct at Wadi el-Qelt?

A hint of one of the aqueducts that was built in Wadi el-Qelt may be found in 7.14-16:

14 על פי יציאת המים של הכוז
15 בא חפור אמות שלוש עד הסור
16 ככ 60 זהב ככרין שתים

14. By the mouth of the water outlet of the Koziba
15. dig three cubits to the rock
16. sixty talents of silver, two talents of gold.

30. We may consider reconstructing line 3:

3 באמא של קי[דרון בבואה אל
4 האשוח הצפו[ני הגדו]ל

3. In the aqueduct of Qi[dron when it enters
4. the nor[th bi]g reservoir

31. In some cases we can show that there is no consistency in the Copper Scroll. For example, sometimes the scribe wrote אמת המים, 'water aqueduct' (5.1), and sometimes he wrote only אמא, 'aqueduct' (4.3).

32. The word אשוח can be better understood to be a water pool than a cistern. See the bibliography in J. Hoftijzer and K. Jongeling, *Dictionary of the North-West Semitic Inscriptions* (Leiden: E.J. Brill, 1995), pp. 122-23. See Figs. 6.4 and 6.5 above.

Koziba is probably the name of the eastern part of Wadi el-Qelt since the name of the monastery built there in the Byzantine period was Choziba.[33] If this description describes an aqueduct, it should probably be identified as the beginning of one of the aqueducts built in Wadi el-Qelt.

Appendix: Two Unknown Aqueducts in the Copper Scroll

Two other water aqueducts are mentioned in the Copper Scroll, but I cannot suggest any identification for them. In 1.9-12 we read:

9 בתל של כחלת כלי בלגין ואפרון
10 הכל של דמע והאצר השבעי מעסר
11 שני בפי גל פתחו בשולי האמא מן הצפון
12 אמות שש עד נקרת הטבילה XAΓ

9. In the ruins of Koḥlit, tithe vessels in a flask container and gray
10. (silver coins?)[34] All tithe and stored Seventh-Year produce (and) Second
11. Tithe, in the mouth of the mound its opening is at the edge of the aqueduct on the north
12. six cubits to the crevice (used) for ritual baths XAΓ

Since little is known about Koḥlit other than it was located in the desert, I cannot identify this aqueduct.[35] In the beginning of col. 8 we read:

1 בא]מא שבדרך המזרח בית
2 האוצר שבמזרח אחיה (?)
3 כלי דמע וספרין אל תדקם (?)

1. In the aqueduct which is on the road to the east of the store
2. house, to the east of Ahiya (?):
3. tithe-vessels and books do not appropriate them (?)

33. On Koziba, see Milik, DJDJ III, p. 265; B. Pixner, 'Unravelling the Copper Scroll Code: A Study on the Topography of 3Q15', *RevQ* 11(1983), pp. 323-65 (349 n. 27).

34. Coins that are called 'black silver' are mentioned in the Greek documents of Babatha. Therefore we may assume that אפורן, 'Grays', are some kind of silver coins. See Y. Meshorer, 'The "Black Silver" Coins of the Babatha Papyri: A Re-evaluation', *Israel Museum Journal* 10 (1992), pp. 67-74; N. Lewis, 'Again, the Money Called Black', in R. Katzoff (ed.), *Classical Studies in Honor of David Sohlberg* (Ramat Gan: Bar-Ilan University Press, 1996), pp. 399-401.

35. On Koḥlit in the desert, see *b. Qid.* 66a. I see no reason to accept B. Pixner's suggestion that Koḥlit is the monastic centre of an Essene settlement (Pixner, 'Unravelling the Copper Scroll Code', p. 337). See now B. Zissu, 'The Identification of the Copper Scroll's *Kaḥelet* at 'Ein Samiya in the Samarian Desert', *PEQ* 133 (2001), pp. 145-58; and there is an aqueduct at 'Ein Samiya.

No fortress or site by the name Beth-Achzor is known in the Judaean Desert, and although the aqueduct to Tell el-Aqabeh passes near the Roman road, I cannot identify this aqueduct.

Summary

Several water aqueducts are mentioned in the Copper Scroll. The water aqueduct that led water to Sekakah is to be identified with the aqueduct of Wadi Qumran. Of the other aqueducts in the area of Qumran two projects were long and notable; one carrying water to Hyrcania, and the other built along Wadi el-Qelt. It seems that those two projects are mentioned in the Copper Scroll.

There is evidence that the author of the Copper Scroll was familiar with the Judaean Desert and used the aqueducts of the Second Temple period as reference points for the hidden treasure.[36] It is important to note that although the fortresses were occupied by soldiers at all times, the aqueducts leading to those fortresses were in open areas, and everybody had access to them.

36. Without discussing the disagreements about the authenticity of the Copper Scroll, I would like to note that the only treasure found in Israel that might be connected to the temple, was found in 1960 at Isfiya (or Ussfiya) on Mount Carmel. This hoard is of about 4500 silver coins (3400 Tyrian shekels, about 1000 half-shekels and 160 Roman denarii of Augustus). It was suggested that this hoard is undelivered temple contributions due to the military conflict between the Romans and the Jews in Galilee in 67 CE. See L. Kadman, 'Temple Dues and Currency in Ancient Palestine in the Light of Recent Discovered Coins-Hoards', *Israel Numismatic Bulletin* 1 (1962), pp. 9-11; L. Kadman, 'Temple Dues and Currency in Ancient Palestine in the Light of Recent Discovered Coins-Hoards', in *Congresso Internazionale di Numismatica, 11-16 September 1961, Rome*, II (Roma: Istituto italiano di Numismatica, 1965), pp. 69-76; D. Sperber, 'Numismatics and Halacha', *Israel Numismatic Journal* 2 (1964), pp. 16-18.

7

3Q15: Its Linguistic Affiliation, With Lexicographical Comments

John F. Elwolde

Introduction

The variety, not to say confusion, of readings and interpretations that abounds in respect of the Copper Scroll is probably inevitable. Apart from the quite minuscule amount of linguistic data on which to base interpretation, there are the added and related problems of the concise, and possibly cryptic, style in which the scroll is written,[1] as well as our lack of firm knowledge about the purpose of the scroll as a whole, the social, historical, religious and literary context from which it derives, and the precise reference of each of the propositions stated, or items listed, in the scroll.

My purpose in the present paper is to attempt, first, on the basis of the limited, and usually contested, evidence available, to provide some empirically derived indicators as to the linguistic affiliation of the Hebrew of the Copper Scroll, and, second, to comment on the feasibility of some proposed readings and interpretations. In this dual task, I have restricted

1. Linguistic interpretation of the scroll is made especially difficult by the dearth of 'function' or 'grammatical' words. For example, of the personal and emphatic pronouns, only זה is clearly attested, and that just once, at 12.11; the form אל, either as a preposition, אֶל 'to', or as an adverb of negation, אַל 'not', was always uncertain at 1.13 and 8.3, and has disappeared completely in Wolters's readings (the lack of the preposition אֶל is perhaps explicable in view of the predominance of עַל, under Aramaic influence, in the Hebrew of the period). On the other hand, the scroll does provide us, at 10.9 and 12.2, with our earliest example of אֶבֶן 'stone' modified by an adjective of colour, אֶבֶן שְׁחֹרָא 'black stone', as well as the only example of the colour term אדם 'red' in the entire extra-biblical (pre-tannaitic) corpus, although the syntax of 4.9 seems to me to support Allegro's interpretation of the form as אדמה 'earth'.

myself to lexemes beginning with the letters *alef* to *ṭet*, that is, to the range of the alphabet covered by the first three volumes of the Sheffield *Dictionary of Classical Hebrew*.[2]

The Hebrew of the Copper Scroll

The *Dictionary of Classical Hebrew* is unique in giving systematic treatment to every occurrence of every word in every Hebrew text that antedates the compilation of the Mishnah and therefore provides a valuable tool for tracing links both backwards in time, as it were, between the Hebrew of the Copper Scroll and the language found in the other Dead Sea Scrolls, Ben Sira and the Bible, as well as forwards, to the Bar-Kochba material at Murabba'at and Naḥal Ḥever. It is often merely said that the Hebrew of the Copper Scroll is an early version of 'Mishnaic Hebrew'. My goal in the first part of this presentation is to take a few short steps in refining that statement.

Although the evidence is not sufficient to allow us to draw any conclusions, I have been struck, when examining linguistic connections between the Copper Scroll and the Dead Sea Scrolls in general, with the correspondences of the Copper Scroll and the Temple Scroll in particular.[3] Although they clearly differ in their predilection for or rejection of Greek and Latin loanwords, I have found a few similarities as well. For example, according to the concordance of the Academy of the Hebrew Language (AHL),[4] אמה I 'cubit' occurs 31 times in 12 columns of the Copper Scroll, or 2.6 occurrences per column, and 91 times in the first 46 columns of the Temple Scroll (two occurrences per column).[5] Furthermore, if AHL are

2. Vols. I–III (*Alef–Ṭet*) (ed. D.J.A. Clines; executive ed. J.F. Elwolde; Sheffield: Sheffield Academic Press, 1992, 1995, 1996).

3. An area examined at some length by Professor L.H. Schiffman in his contribution here. Note that S. Morag in his 'Qumran Hebrew: Some Typological Investigations' (*VT* 38 [1988], pp. 148-64) includes the language of the Temple Scroll under the label of 'General Qumran Hebrew'.

4. The Academy of the Hebrew Language (The Historical Dictionary of the Hebrew Language), *Materials for the Dictionary, Series I: 200 BCE–300 CE* (Jerusalem: Academy of the Hebrew Language, 1988).

5. There are also 14 occurrences in cols. 4–9 of the War Scroll. According to the readings of David Wilmot (M.O. Wise, 'David J. Wilmot and the Copper Scroll', in this volume), the noun should also be read at 3Q15 10.6, 13. The facts of אמה are, of course, a striking example of the way in which the Copper Scroll is over-populated by many words occurring just once, and a few that occur disproportionately often.

correct in reading אמה III 'conduit' at 11QT[a] 32.9, then this form will join אמצע 'middle' as a term previously known only from rabbinic literature, but now attested in both Copper and Temple Scrolls.[6]

Working further back, there also appear to be connections to specifically late biblical literature, regarded by some as written in a distinctive form of 'post-classical' or 'Late Biblical' Hebrew (LBH). Included in this literature is the 'early LBH' book of Ezekiel. For example, at 4.6, if one vocalizes, like F. García Martínez, בִּינְיָן 'building',[7] then a link is forged between the Copper Scroll and Ezekiel, the only other pre-tannaitic text in which this word occurs. (The alternative reading, בִּינִין, would represent the first clear attestation of בִּין 'tamarisk' in pre-amoraic Hebrew literature, although the same word has been conjectured at Isa. 44.4.)[8] A possible further connection with Ezekiel, not continued in literature

Another example would be בור 'cistern', which, according to AHL, accounts for seven out of the thirteen pre-mishnaic examples (Wilmot reads another two occurrences at 3Q15 12.8; see p. 310 in this volume). Curiously, the common noun גיא 'valley', according to AHL occurs only fifteen times in the entire postbiblical pre-amoraic corpus, of which three occurrences are in the Copper Scroll and just one in the other scrolls. Incidentally, the Copper Scroll is the only pre-mishnaic document that uses אמה with the written form of numerals 16, 17, 19 and 24. The shared proclivity of the Copper and Temple Scrolls for the use of אמה extends to a specific preference for the expression 'three cubits', found most often in the Bible in Ezekiel.

6. However, E. Qimron believes that AHL simply made a mistake in classifying the Temple Scroll form under אמה III (personal communication via Dr David Talshir [Ben Gurion University of the Negev], to whom I am grateful for help in this matter and others).

7. *The Dead Sea Scrolls Translated: The Qumran Texts in English* (trans. W.G.E. Watson; Leiden: E.J. Brill, 1994), p. 461 ('the two buildings'—'los dos edificios' in the Spanish original: *Textos de Qumrán* [Madrid: Trotta, 2nd edn, 1993], p. 478—which requires the noun to be understood collectively). J. Lefkovits (*The Copper Scroll—3Q15: A Reevaluation* [STDJ, 25; Leiden: E.J. Brill, 2000], p. 162) reads הבתין, which, of course, yields a similar sense.

8. If בבין חציר 'in among grass' is emended to כבין חצור 'like a green tamarisk'. I am grateful to Dr Hanan Eshel for drawing my attention to E. and H. Eshel, 'Fragments of Two Aramaic Documents which were Brought to Abi'or [*sic*] Cave During the Bar-Kochba Revolt', *Eretz-Israel* 23 (1992), pp. 276-85 (in Hebrew). In the second document presented there, we find the first attested usage of the (Aramaic from Greek) noun בָּיִין, either 'palm-branch', that is, the branch of a date-palm tree, or in reference to some other part of a date-palm (see pp. 281-82). Despite the closeness in time of the Copper Scroll and the Bar-Kochba material, the context makes it fairly clear that at 3Q15 4.6 it is still בִּין 'tamarisk' that should be understood, not ביין 'palm-branch'.

subsequent to the Copper Scroll, is the use of אתון 'entrance', as Allegro read at 8.2, the only parallel to which is the *Qere* of Ezek. 40.15. Further possible links to Ezekiel will be raised in subsequent remarks on דרום 'south', שן 'ivory' and ביאה 'entrance'.

Connections with LBH literature other than Ezekiel are found in respect of the common tannaitic term גִּנָּה/גַּנָּה '(vegetable) garden', which is particularly well represented in the late biblical books of Song of Songs, Qoheleth and Esther, and, although not found at all in the 'standard' Dead Sea Scrolls, is attested in the Copper Scroll (11.6) and at Naḥal Ḥever. At 1.11, if J.T. Milik's reading is correct,[9] the Copper Scroll provides us with our only postbiblical (pre-tannaitic) example of the noun גַּל, albeit not in the biblical sense of 'heap', but in the mishnaic meaning of 'door'. For both גִּנָּה/גַּנָּה and גַּל, then, the Copper Scroll would seem to link the late biblical literature directly to the Mishnah, without, as it were, passing through 'Qumran Hebrew'. In fact, the context of 1.11 might support an interpretation of גל as גַּל III 'bowl > spring',[10] posited at Cant. 4.12 (which would thus provide another connection between the Copper Scroll and LBH, but not Rabbinic Hebrew [RH]). At 10.15, בֵּית חַמַּיִם 'sauna' or בֵּית הַמַּיִם 'privy' resumes the late biblical usage of בית in reference to a particular part or quarter of a house, for example, בית הנשים 'harem' in Esther 2 and בית משתה היין 'banquet-hall' at Est. 7.8. We shall comment on the significance of בית המשכב at 11.16 and of בית האוצר in Allegro's reading of 8.1 a little later on.[11]

The word אצל 'beside' is a good example of a form that links the four groups of texts so far mentioned: it occurs up to seven times in the Copper Scroll, twice in the Bar-Kochba material, ten times in the Temple Scroll, and six times in Nehemiah (where אצל occurs with relatively greater frequency, 0.7, than in any other book of the Bible). Similarly, the common tannaitic word דרום 'south', which occurs, working backwards from the Mishnah, five times at Murabba'at, twice in the Copper Scroll,[12] four times in the Temple Scroll, and fifteen times in Ezekiel (13) and Qoheleth (2) combined.[13]

9. It is supported by Lefkovits, *The Copper Scroll*, p. 173.

10. See S. and S. Rin, 'Ugaritic-Old Testament Affinities', *BZ* 11 (1967), pp. 174-92 (187).

11. Lefkovits, *The Copper Scroll*, p. 245, reads, similarly, בית אווצר here.

12. Alongside the new adjectival formation דרומי 'southern'.

13. The form occurs just twice elsewhere in the Bible (Deut. 33.23; Job 37.17).

To conclude this section of the paper, then, we find, on the basis of the very limited evidence available, that the vocabulary of the Copper Scroll, as expected, holds an intermediate place between what is sometimes called 'Late Biblical Hebrew' (including the language of Ezekiel), and 'Mishnaic Hebrew'. However, the relationship with Late Biblical Hebrew does not appear to be mediated through 'General Qumran Hebrew', with the exception of the language of the Temple Scroll. I have noticed no obvious lexical relationship to 4QMMT, although there are clear connections to the Bar-Kochba material, and, of course, to the Mishnah. This limited evidence suggests that, apart from the time difference, features of dialect, register and perhaps subject matter should also be taken into account in any explanation of the apparent discrepancy between the Copper Scroll and the rest of the Dead Sea Scrolls.

Specific Proposals for Readings in the Copper Scroll

I move on now to a number of observations on specific proposals for readings and interpretations. As I shall be concentrating on what I perceive to be mistakes, infelicities or problems in some recent work on the Copper Scroll, I must apologize in advance if the tone sometimes seems negative, and, in particular, if Professor A. Wolters seems rather hard done by.[14] It is simply in the nature of things that someone who has done so much work on the interpretation of the Copper Scroll in recent years will give a critic that much more scope for attack.

I start with what I assume was simply an oversight on the part of Professor Wolters but concerning which a number of comments may still be made. In his paper, 'The Copper Scroll and the Vocabulary of Mishnaic Hebrew',[15] from which I have drawn most of the items for discussion, Wolters notes approvingly[16] that at 1.10 אֵצֶר 'treasure' has been recognized by J.T. Milik[17] as a lexical item 'present in MH but absent from

14. I am grateful to Professor Wolters for sending me detailed responses to some of the points raised in the lecture. With his permission, I have drawn upon these in notes 26, 30, 33, 35, 39, 41, 42 and 46.

15. A. Wolters, 'The Copper Scroll and the Vocabulary of Mishnaic Hebrew', *RevQ* 14 (1990), pp. 483-95.

16. Wolters, 'The Copper Scroll', p. 486.

17. 'Le rouleau de cuivre provenant de la grotte 3Q (3Q15)', in M. Baillet, J.T. Milik and R. de Vaux, *Les 'petites grottes' de Qumrân* (DJDJ III; Oxford: Clarendon Press, 1962), pp. 199-202, 211-302 (pp. 203-10: H. Wright Baker, 'Notes on the Opening of the Copper Scrolls [*sic*] from Qumrân').

BH'. Concerning this surprising statement, the following comments may be made. First, Milik did not read אצר, which is, of course, a common biblical term, but הָאֲצָרָה; second, Milik only regarded the morphology of אצרה as reflecting late biblical and mishnaic practice[18]—the lexeme itself could not be a mishnaism, as it is unattested outside of the Copper Scroll; third, even if a different word division is accepted in order to read אצר השׁבע, which, according to M.R. Lehmann, means 'seventh year treasury',[19] this collocation would be unparalleled in the tannaitic literature; fourth, Lehmann's conjecture seems to ignore the article that, on his reading, precedes אצר השׁבע; forms like האצר השׁבע are of course attested in tannaitic and modern Hebrew, but they are usually only employed in frequent collocations, into which category אצר השׁבע manifestly does not fall.[20]

As a closing aside to this discussion, it is worth remarking that at 8.1, if Allegro was correct in reading בית האוצר, literally 'house of treasury', this would be a further example of the widespread use of בית with reduced semantic function in 'Late Biblical' and 'Rabbinic' Hebrew, a phenomenon documented by A. Hurvitz in various papers.[21] Moreover, this particular construction would furnish another instance of the Copper Scroll linking up late biblical literature, where בית האוצר first emerges (Mal. 3.10; Neh. 10.39; Dan. 1.2), on the one hand, and the tannaitic literature (*m. 'Erub.* 8.4; *m. Soṭ.* 8.2; *t. Pes.* 1.3; *SDeut.* 36, 194, 229), on the other. בית האוצר might also be paralleled in the Copper Scroll itself, at 11.16, by בית המשכב in the sense of 'grave', if that is indeed the correct inter-

18. See Milik, DJDJ III, p. 233.

19. M.R. Lehmann, 'Identification of the Copper Scroll Based on its Technical Terms', *RevQ* 5 (1964), pp. 97-105 (101-102).

20. The phenomenon is occasionally encountered even in the Bible (Gen. 24.67; Josh. 13.7; Judg. 16.14; 1 Kgs 14.24; Isa. 36.16; Ezek. 45.16; my thanks to Martin F.J. Baasten of the University of Leiden for supplying these details). At first glance, the reading of Lefkovits, *The Copper Scroll*, p. 73, הָאוֹצָר הַשָּׁבוּעַ, seems to suffer from the same difficulty. Both his and Lehmann's readings can, of course, be interpreted as appositional constructions, 'the treasure (consisting of) the (produce of) seven years', but it strikes me as implausible that a neologism would be couched in such an opaque form. In his new edition of the Scroll, A. Wolters, *The Copper Scroll* (Sheffield: Sheffield Academic Press, 1996), reads (pp. 32-33) הָאֹצָר הַשְּׁבִעִי 'the seventh treasure', which appears to respect both the palaeographic evidence and the norms of grammar.

21. E.g. 'בית־קברות and בית־עולם: Two Funerary Terms in Biblical Literature and their Linguistic Background', *Maarav* 8 (1992), pp. 59-68. An additional RH example would be בֵּית־הַסְּקִילָה 'place of stoning' at *m. Sanh.* 6.2-4, etc.

pretation. Here, we can also mention בתי העצין at 2.5, as read by Milik,[22] which would seem to be the earliest example of the mishnaic usage of בית meaning 'storehouse'. Indeed, the very collocation found in the Copper Scroll is also attested in the Mishnah.[23] A similar kind of semantic development is found at 2.3, where, if Milik is right in emending to דביר (where most read רובד 'terrace, platform'), the context suggests that the word applies here, without parallel in Bible or Mishnah, to the 'chamber' or 'recess' of a cave.[24]

I turn now to Wolters's interpretation of ביאתא at 3.9, which, he argues, should be taken as the subject of a new sentence,[25] as against Milik, who appears to understand ביאתא as a prepositional adjunct to the preceding sentence, '(hidden) at its entrance'. Wolters disputes Milik's understanding, saying that one would have expected בביאתא in this case, as at 4.3, 5.13 and 11.13. However, he fails to mention 12.1, where the same phenomenon, namely omission of a preposition before ביאה, seems to occur again, at least in the interpretations of Milik and Vermes.[26] Milik's understanding is, of course, supported by the biblical parallels of בית and, more especially, פתח.[27] Incidentally, the latter correspondence suggests that in

22. Lefkovits, *The Copper Scroll*, p. 118, reads מתי העצין; Wolters (*Copper Scroll*, pp. 34-35) reads מתן העצין 'donated firewood'.

23. *m. Soṭ.* 8.2. We might also bear in mind here L.H. Schiffman's observations on the use of בית in 11QT and 3Q15 to mean not 'house' but referring instead to smaller structures; note also Wilmot's reading (see Michael O. Wise, 'David J. Wilmot and the Copper Scroll', in the present volume, p. 310; cf. D.J. Wilmot, 'The Copper Scroll: An Economic Document of First Century Palestine', unpublished), בית הבור 'place of the cistern', at 3Q15 12.8.

24. However, a semantic parallel is provided by L.H. Schiffman in his remarks on עמוד as a *natural* column of stone in the Copper Scroll.

25. 'Notes on the Copper Scroll (3Q15)', *RevQ* 12 (1985–87), pp. 587-96 (594).

26. Geza Vermes, *The Dead Sea Scrolls in English* (Harmondsworth: Penguin Books, 4th edn, 1995), p. 377 ('Sixty talents at its entrance from the west'). Of course, even though my arguments are intended to lend some support to Milik's interpretation on lexical and syntactic grounds, the overall literary shape of the Scroll may well work in favour of Wolters's understanding at 3.9 and 12.1: see his 'Literary Analysis and the Copper Scroll', in Z.J. Kapera (ed.), *Intertestamental Essays in Honour of Jozef Tadeusz Milik*, I (Cracow: Enigma, 1992), pp. 239-52 (246).

27. See P. Joüon and T. Muraoka, *A Grammar of Biblical Hebrew* (Subsidia Biblica, 14.1-2; Rome: Pontifical Institute Press, 2nd edn, 1993), §126h. Note that the construction with בית actually occurs (on the majority of readings) at 10.5: באשיח/ח שיבית הכרם 'in the reservoir that is (at) Bet-hakkerem/the house of the vineyard'; Wilmot (see Michael O. Wise, 'David J. Wilmot and the Copper Scroll', in the

the Copper Scroll ביאה has a purely nominal sense, 'entrance', rather than that of a *nomen actionis*, 'entering'. If so, in this case, the Copper Scroll is closer to the 'Late Biblical Hebrew' usage attested at Ezek. 8.5 than to that of 'Qumran Hebrew', as evidenced by 4QmishmarotA-D (4Q322–24a), where ביאה refers to 'arrival (of priestly courses)', or to that of 'Rabbinic Hebrew', with its well-known employment of ביאה in the sense of '(sexual) intercourse'.

At 9.2, Wolters's reading of חטן to yield חֲטָן, חִטַּן or חַטָּן[28] is questionable not only on the grounds of orthography—reading *ḥet-ṭet-nun-blank* for *ḥet-peh-waw-resh* of both Milik and Allegro seems difficult—but also in connection with various arguments related to meaning and context. Wolters's argument is that חַטָּן (or חִטַּן) means the 'tusks' of an elephant or hippopotamus, citing archaeological evidence from Naḥal Mishmar. This rendering is carried over into Vermes's translation[29] but not that of García Martínez.

First, whereas Wolters might be right in claiming that Milik's interpretation of חפור as an imperative (חֲפֹר 'dig') 'would break the stereotypical pattern', this objection is perhaps less compelling in respect of Allegro's understanding of the same sequence as a passive participle (חָפוּר 'dug', i.e. buried)[30] or Carmignac's interpretation of the form as an infinitive

present volume, p. 310) is alone in reading של בית הכרם '(the reservoir) of Bet-hakkerem'.

28. Following Marcus Jastrow, *A Dictionary of the Targumim, the Talmud Babli and Yerushalmi, and the Midrashic Literature* (2 vols. in one; New York: Judaica Press, 1992 [1903]), Gustav Dalman, *Aramäisch–Neuhebräisches Handwörterbuch zu Targum, Talmud und Midrasch* (Hildesheim: Georg Olms, 3rd edn, 1987 [1938]), and Jacob Levy, *Wörterbuch über die Talmudim und Midraschim* (Darmstadt: Wissenschaftliche Buchgesellschaft, 2nd edn, 1963 [1924]), A. Wolters ('The Copper Scroll', p. 491) vocalizes as חֲטָן or חִטַּן, which Levy and Jastrow derive from חִטָּה and חוט respectively; however AHL, E. Ben-Yehuda, *Thesaurus totius hebraitatis* (8 vols.; New York: Thomas Yoseloff, 1959) and A. Even-Shoshan, *Hammillon heḥadash* (7 vols.; Jerusalem: Kiryath Sepher, 1980) regard the singular as חַט (from the root חטט), with the plural therefore חַטִּין.

29. Vermes, *Dead Sea Scrolls in English*, p. 376 ('two tusks'; in earlier editions, Vermes discussed the Copper Scroll, without offering a translation).

30. Allegro gives the correct form of his reading not in the text itself (*The Treasure of the Copper Scroll* [London: Routledge & Kegan Paul, 1960], p. 49) but in n. 190 (p. 157); because of a different word-division, Allegro actually reads the feminine plural form of the passive participle. Although חפור 'buried' is unattested in earlier Hebrew literature, the Aramaic passive participle חפיר, in the sense of 'one for whom a grave is dug' (Jastrow, *Dictionary of the Targumim*, p. 491), i.e., one who is about

absolute (חָפוֹר).[31] Second, although the collocation שתין חטן in the meaning of 'two tusks' could make good sense in context, the word order is not supported by ככרין שתים 'two talents' at 7.16 or by עזות שְׁתַּיִן or עֲזוֹת שְׁתַּיִן 'two supports' (Milik) at 10.9.[32] The order noun followed by number is respected for other numerals as well, as explained at some length by Thorion.[33]

be buried, might lend some support to Allegro's interpretation. Wolters (see n. 14 above) points out that, apart from its implausibility on palaeographical grounds at 9.2, the form חפור elsewhere occurs only in column C of the scroll.

31. Jean Carmignac, 'L'infinitif absolu chez Ben Sira et à Qumrân', *RevQ* 12 (1985–87), pp. 251-61 (256-57). Carmignac's claim that Milik's interpretation is doubtful because of the general lack of second person address in the scroll fails to consider the structure at 8.3 (on Milik's reading; Allegro understands אל here as the preposition 'to', not the adverb 'not'). S. Segert, in his review of DJDJ III (*RevQ* 4 [1963–64], pp. 279-96) regarded the use of the second person as 'stylized' (p. 294). Note that Bargil Pixner reads an additional imperative form, '*ᵃḇōr*' 'pass' (for which Carmignac would have presumably preferred the infinitive '*āḇōr*), for Milik's '*āḵōr*' 'Achor' at 1.1: B. Pixner, 'Unravelling the Copper Scroll Code: A Study on the Topography of 3Q15', *RevQ* 11 (1983), pp. 323-65 (342).

32. The form *shtayim* (rather than *shnayim*) is, of course, correct in all three cases, as the noun on each occasion is, despite appearances, feminine. Allegro reads *kaddin* 'pitchers' at 7.16 and restores *ammot* 'cubits' at 10.9, but this does not affect the syntactic observations I have made. In a note to 7.16 (*Treasure of the Copper Scroll*, p. 153 n. 160), Allegro comments on the oddity of the structure of a noun followed by number two in the absolute (although he fails to notice its recurrence at 10.9), citing M.H. Segal's *A Grammar of Mishnaic Hebrew* (Oxford: Clarendon Press, 1927), pp. 194-95, where it is claimed that *shtayim/shnayim* are only employed in the construct in 'Mishnaic Hebrew'. This 'regular' construction, with *shne-*, is also attested in 3Q15, at 4.6, 8 and 6.1.

33. Y. Thorion, 'Beiträge zur Erforschung der Sprache der Kupfer-Rolle', *RevQ* 12 (1985–87), pp. 163-76 (173-74). R. Polzin (*Late Biblical Hebrew: Toward an Historical Typology of Biblical Hebrew Prose* [HSM, 12; Missoula: Scholars Press, 1976], pp. 58-60, 81-82) claims that in the Copper Scroll '[t]he substantive is placed before the number sixty times, whereas the number precedes the substantive only once [7.5]' (60), which means that the scroll is firmly in line with the dominant trend in 'LBH' practice but stands contrary to that of 'EBH' and 'RH', which, if they use an absolute form of a numeral, will generally place it before the noun. It must be admitted, though, that in the specific case of *shtayim/shnayim* this latter usage is quite common even in the 'transitional LBH' book of Ezekiel, particularly chs. 40 and 41. Nonetheless, despite the complexity of the issue (as demonstrated by Polzin and drawn to my attention by Professor Wolters [see n. 14 above]), for me the syntax of the numbers in general in 3Q15 and in particular of *shtayim/shnayim* at 7.16 and 10.9 speak strongly against Wolters's interpretation.

Finally, although the word חַט is indeed attested in the tannaitic literature in the sense 'incisor', as against 'molar', of a domesticated beast,[34] neither this nor the limited later usage provides support for the meaning 'tusk' as an item of value, for which one might surely have expected a term such as קרן 'horn' or שן 'tooth' to have been used.[35] The 'Early Biblical Hebrew' terms שן and שנהבים 'ivory' are both maintained in the 'LBH' parallel to 1 Kgs 10.18-20,[36] with שן also appearing in Ezekiel and Song of Songs; an Aramaic form, שנהבותא, has been claimed in a third-century BCE inscription.[37]

At 1.7, Wolters disagrees with Milik's rendering of חַלְיָא.[38] Milik interpreted this as 'perforated stone' ('pierre percée'), in reference to a stone that would have covered a cistern (בור), with a hole in it to let down a bucket. He cites Ben-Yehuda, who argues at considerable length for this meaning in various texts from the Mishnah and Tosefta, an interpretation also accepted, albeit with some reservations, by Even-Shoshan. However, Wolters claims that the meaning of חליא at 1.7 is not the 'perforated stone' at the top of a well but, rather, the 'sediment' or 'sand' that collects underneath it. Although Wolters cites Levy in support of this interpretation,[39] it is an understanding that is explicitly rejected as antiquated by

34. *m. Bek.* 6.4, 12; *Sifra 'Emor* (Lev. 21–24).

35. However, as Wolters (n. 14) points out, 'tusk' is indeed the first meaning given for חט in Dov Ben Abba's *Signet Hebrew–English/English-Hebrew Dictionary* (New York: New American Library, 1978). But note חַיַּת־שֵׁן 'wild beast' (with שו clearly meaning 'tooth' at Sir. 12.13). Although Jastrow (*Dictionary of the Targumim*, p. 1603) cites Bemidbar Rabbah 3.12 in support of שֵׁן as 'ivory' (contracted from שֵׁן שֶׁל פִּיל), I fail to see why שן cannot simply mean 'tooth' there.

36. 2 Chron. 9.21.

37. See H. Donner and W. Röllig, *Kanaanäische und aramäische Inschriften* (3 vols. in one; Wiesbaden: Otto Harrassowitz, 1962), no. 273 (pp. 52, 326-27), and J. Hoftijzer and K. Jongeling, *Dictionary of the North-West Semitic Inscriptions* (Handbuch der Orientalistik. Erste Abteilung. Der Nahe und Mittlere Osten, 21.1–2; Leiden: E.J. Brill, 1995), p. 714, for text and discussion. Note, however (and perhaps in defence of Wolters's position), that neither שנהב nor שן in the required sense appears in any tannaitic source.

38. Wolters, 'The Copper Scroll', pp. 491-92.

39. Wolters's 'sediment' appears to be based on Levy's 'die Sandschichte (eines Brunnens)', which seems to blend, unconsciously, the dominant meaning of חליא, accepted by other lexica as well, namely '(ausgeschnittener) Theil, Ausschnitt' (my parentheses), with that of חול 'sand'; see Ben-Yehuda's comment quoted below. As Wolters (n. 14) points out, though, it is Levy's interpretation, not Ben-Yehuda's (or Milik's) that is represented by twentieth-century translations of the relevant rabbinic

Ben-Yehuda: פירשו המפרשים הקדמונים מלה זו במשמעות חול ועפר. Ben-Yehuda's unspoken criticism is that his predecessors have naïvely associated חליא with חול 'sand'. This 'mistake', if such it is, is not repeated in any other lexicon. Both Dalman and Even-Shoshan support a meaning 'clod' of earth for חליא, but this is hardly the same thing. Jastrow takes a distinctive approach to unifying the different usages of חליא, but one which does not support 'sediment' as a sub-meaning of חליא. Moreover, Wolters's arguments unintentionally misrepresent Milik, for Milik does not appeal to an Arabic cognate instead of a mishnaic parallel, but rather to a well-argued interpretation of the mishnaic evidence by Ben-Yehuda, in the course of which Ben-Yehuda examines some striking cognate expressions from Arabic. Although Wolters's interpretation might, in the end, be the best available in the context of the Copper Scroll passage, and perhaps elsewhere, it could also be argued that Vermes and García Martínez have been rather over-hasty in preferring his understanding to that of Milik.

The context of 11.17 is so fragmentary that in principle there can be no objection to favouring Wolters's vocalization טֵיף, meaning 'a little', over Milik's טִיף 'stand' for a stove, which occurs elsewhere in just one passage in the Tosefta. However, Professor Wolters appears to have missed another possible interpretation of טיף, provided by Allegro at 7.15.[40] Basing

passages, such as those by H. Danby, J.N. Epstein and J. Neusner.

40. Where Milik reads a final *resh* (טוּ/יר 'wall'), Wolters (*Copper Scroll*, pp. 44-45) reads עַד חָטוּף 'plundered loot'. From the perspective of linguistic plausibility, the main weakness in Wolters's reading relates to עַד, which, in the sense of 'booty' is only fairly certain at Gen. 49.27 (and even there עַד might instead signify 'eternity', used adverbially, 'still [devouring]', or have a further different meaning, other than 'booty', such as 'foe', as in the Jewish Publication Society's *Tanakh* [Philadelphia, 1985]); at Isa. 33.23, the text is difficult and perhaps the preposition should be understood; at Zeph. 3.8 עֵד 'witness' may well be intended, or לְעַד could mean 'eternally'. However, the Targum does render שָׁלָל at Isa. 10.2 by עֲדֵי and uses the same form at Isa. 33.23. עַד is not attested (unless in biblical quotations) in the tannaitic literature or the scrolls. In respect of the verb חָטַף, there is rather more evidence in support of Wolters, although some factors do still militate against his understanding. Looking at earlier attested usage, we find, first, that the verb is not attested in the (other) Dead Sea Scrolls or Ben Sira, and is quite rare in the tannaitic literature; more significantly, when, in the Bible, the active form occurs (Judg. 21.21; Ps. 10.9, 9), a person is always specified as object, indicating that the sense is 'prey upon, seize', rather than 'plunder'. The use of the verb in the passive form is not clearly attested until the amoraic period (see below, on the second meaning of חטף), unless we take into account the personal name חטיפא at Ezra 2.54//Neh. 7.56. Because

himself, like Wolters, on an Aramaic cognate, טפיא, Allegro claims that at 7.15 the word means ‘overflow tank’, and it is the same form, somewhat differently interpreted, that lies behind Vermes’s rendering, ‘channel’, at 11.17.[41]

At 1.9, some, very limited, orthographic support for Wolters’s reading ב[ע]ל גין ‘master of nations’[42] comes from the fifth Bar-Kochba letter found at Naḥal Ḥever, which, uniquely among all the Dead Sea material, clearly evidences the plural of גוי in *nun*: שהיו של הגאין. However, to add to Wolters’s problems in reading the text this way, I find that the biblical parallel he cites, בעלי גוים at Isa. 16.8, is not attested in any Qumran rule or *pesher*, and indeed is missing in 1QIsa[a].[43] If the striking expression that Wolters posits really exists, we might have expected it to have turned up more often in our corpus. On the other hand, the word לג as the name of

this is a ‘Late Biblical Hebrew’ passage, if we then accept Wolters’s understanding of 7.15, the Copper Scroll would again provide a link, or fill a gap in the attested data, between ‘Late Biblical Hebrew’ and ‘Rabbinic Hebrew’, both, generally, for the lexeme as such and also, specifically, for its passive usage. Other, tannaitic and amoraic, data lends additional credence to Wolters’s interpretation, although matters are complicated by the fact that the verb in rabbinic literature has three apparently related, but significantly different, senses: (1) ‘seize, snatch’ (e.g. *t. Ket.* 4.9); (2) ‘do in haste’ (e.g. *b. Suk.* 28a); and (3) ‘hastily distribute’ (e.g. *t. Pisḥa* 10.9). Nonetheless, *S. Num.* 157.7 on Num. 31.13, לפי שיצאו נערי ישראל לחטוף מן הביזה ‘it was because the young men of Israel went out to seize some of the booty’ is particularly supportive of Wolters’s understanding as is *t. Šeb.* 7.12 on Gen. 49.2, בנימן זאב יטרף, זו ארצו שחוטפת, בבקר יאכל עד ‘Benjamin is a wolf that tears: this is his land that seizes (other land); in the morning he devours booty’, where, as in Wolters’s reading of the Copper Scroll, עַד is found in collocation with חטף.

41. See Allegro, *Treasure of the Copper Scroll*, pp. 45, 153; Vermes, *Dead Sea Scrolls in English*, p. 377. Wolters (n. 14) points out that his choice of טיף ‘a little’ here is based on the structural parallel with מרחב ‘a wide space’ at 9.12: ‘In both cases we have a rough measure of distance preceding a preposition as part of Column B.’

42. Wolters, ‘Notes on the Copper Scroll’, pp. 590-92; the interpretation is accepted by García Martínez (*Dead Sea Scrolls Translated*, p. 461, and in the Spanish original [p. 477]: ‘the lord of the peoples’/‘el señor de los pueblos’), although it has been abandoned by Wolters himself (‘History and the Copper Scroll’, in M. Wise *et al.* (eds.), *Methods of Investigation of the Dead Sea Scrolls and the Khirbet Qumran Site* [New York: New York Academy of Sciences, 1994], pp. 285-95 [294]).

43. The relevant text does appear, though, in 1QIsa[b]. The form גאים, with *mem* for *nun*, is quite common in DSS. Wolters’s claim that גין, without medial *waw* or *alef*, is also a plural of גוי is to some extent supported by the forms גי at 4QD[a] [4Q266] 10 i 8 (= CD 14.15: גוי) and גיים at 4QBark[a] [4Q434] 1 ii 8, according to the reading of Wacholder and Abegg’s edition (3.310).

a measure or container is extremely common throughout the tannaitic literature and is well represented there in the form found in our passage, that is, לְגִין or לְגִין, without *ḥolem waw* and with plural in *nun*.[44]

At 12.13, Wolters's claim that the text reads not כל־אחד ואחד 'each and every (detail)' but פרוטכל אחד ואחד 'a protocol of the one and the other'[45] has been disputed by Paul Mandel on the grounds that the expression אחד ואחד, without preceding כל־ is not attested elsewhere, whereas כל־אחד ואחד is common in the tannaitic literature.[46] In fact, if כל־אחד ואחד is the correct reading, the Copper Scroll might witness to the development of a structure first attested at 1QS 1.13, where we find the expression כל־אחד מן 'any one of'. In Wolters's defence, however, אחד אחד, without כל־ but also without a conjunction, does occur in 4QShirShabb[f] (4Q405) frag. 20, col. 2, line 14, and Isa. 27.12 may provide a further parallel. Allegro's reading here of כָּל־אֶחָד וְאַחֵר,[47] although attractive, is not, to my knowledge, attested anywhere in the biblical or tannaitic literature.[48] The nearest parallel to Allegro's construction might be זֶה...אַחֵר at Ben Sira 14.18.

At 8.4, Wolters and others, including Allegro, might be correct on orthographic grounds in preferring to read הדר and to vocalize it הַדִּר 'the cattle-shed',[49] over Milik's חרה. However, Milik's interpretation of ח[י]רָה as 'la partie abrupte', depends on a questionable reading of Mekhilta's discussion of the place name Pi-hahiroth. Mekhilta simply says מה היו

44. The spelling without *waw* goes back to Lev. 14.10-24, where the word occurs five times, always in the singular, and to the three inscribed log measures from Susa, to which the same comments apply. The word is not found in any other of the Dead Sea Scrolls or in Ben Sira.

45. A. Wolters, 'The Last Treasure of the Copper Scroll', *JBL* 107 (1988), pp. 419-29 (424-27).

46. P. Mandel, 'On the "Duplicate" of the Copper Scroll (3Q15)', *RevQ* 16 (1993–94), pp. 69-76 (72). In the light of Mandel's paper and due to the fact that one would expect *qof* not *kaf* in 'protocol', Wolters (n. 14) has now dropped this reading.

47. Allegro, *Treasure of the Copper Scroll*, pp. 55, 170; Allegro accepts that the construction with final *dalet* would also make good idiomatic sense.

48. The feminine form, אחרת, occurs at 3.5.

49. Wolters, 'The Copper Scroll', p. 488; Allegro, *Treasure of the Copper Scroll*, pp. 47, 154; García Martínez's 'paridera', that is, a lambing pen (*Textos de Qumrán*, p. 479; 'pen' in the English translation [p. 462]) is too precise (*m. B.Qam.* 6.1: '[sheep] fold'; *m. 'Ed.* 2.2: '[wood] shed', etc.); Lefkovits, *The Copper Scroll*, p. 253, reads כתב חרת 'inscribed writing' instead of בתכ הרה/הדר 'in the midst of the cattle-shed/the rock'.

חירות הללו? 'what were those *ḥirot*?', and then proceeds to describe their shape without at any point saying what objects are actually referred to. It seems fairly clear, though, that the midrash has in mind some kind of cultic pillar, possibly connected with fertility rites, so Yeivin's appropriation of the term in the sense of 'stela' seems more feasible than Milik's 'rocher'.[50] However, Milik's understanding of חירה might be improved upon via a suggestion of G.R. Driver's that underlying the place name Pi-hahiroth is a word חירה, meaning, in its 'original' sense, 'unwalled settlement on the desert edge';[51] Driver also claimed that the same noun can be found at Ps. 84.11, albeit in a rather different meaning of 'courtyard, garden',[52] or 'home'. Although Driver's etymologizing may well be no less fanciful than the rabbinic explanation of Pi-hahiroth, if חירה, in one of Driver's interpretations, does occur at 8.4,[53] it provides an interesting example of a rarely attested Hebrew word that suddenly re-emerges in written records in the postbiblical period. חירה could then be compared with the well-known example of אשוח/אשיח 'reservoir', which has been traced from the ninth-century Mesha inscription to the seventh-century Tel Sirān bottle inscription, the second-century book of Ben Sira, the first-century CE Copper Scroll, and onwards into the Mishnah, evidence that Wolters has judiciously employed for his rendering of שיאח as 'cistern' at 1.13.[54]

It seems fitting to close on that positive note, which may be taken as a token of appreciation to Wolters for his remarkable achievements in encouraging the linguistic study of the Copper Scroll.

50. Or Jastrow's 'cavernous rocks' or Dalman's 'ausgehöhlter Fels'; Yeivin's usage is recorded by Even-Shoshan.

51. 'Once Again Abbreviations', *Textus* 4 (1964), pp. 76-94 (92).

52. 'Courtyard, garden', i.e., the Arabic *ḥair*; the meaning for the Pi-hahiroth passages seems to be more closely connected to that of Arabic *mustaḥir* 'a way leading across a desert, of which the place of egress is not known' (E.W. Lane, *An Arabic–English Lexicon* [London: n.p., 1863], s.v.); see Driver in the work already cited as well as in 'Notes on the Psalms. II. 73–150', *JTS* 44 (1943), pp. 12-23 (16). J. Reider, 'Etymological Studies in Biblical Hebrew', *VT* 4 (1954), pp. 276-95 (279), suggests that the same word, this time with *he* for *ḥet*, is found in הָרוֹת הַגִּלְעָד (usually rendered as 'pregnant women of Gilead') at Amos 1.13.

53. Is it possible that the same word, this time with *yod* included, is to be found at 4QpNah [4Q169] 3.1.6, in association with מענה 'dwelling place'?

54. See A. Wolters, 'The Fifth Cache of the Copper Scroll: "The Plastered Cistern of Manos"', *RevQ* 13 (1988), pp. 167-76. In his data on prosthetic *alef*, Wolters overlooks the possible use in the Copper Scroll of the form אצלם for צלם 'image'.

8

The Meaning of *Dema'* in the Copper Scroll and Ancient Jewish Literature

Armin Lange

The noun *dema'* occurs outside rabbinic literature once in the Hebrew Bible (Exod. 22.28), once in 4Q251 (2 3) and 14 times in the Copper Scroll.[1] During the history of research different opinions concerning its meaning have been expressed even before the Copper Scroll was opened and 4Q251 2 was published.

History of Research

The main point of discussion has concerned from which root *dema'* can be derived. Most scholars have proposed to view it as a derivation of דמע ('to weep'; cf. דמעה, 'tears').[2] *Dema'* is then understood as designating some kind of juice, oil or wine. This is probably supported by the Septuagint, which translates *dema'* in Exod. 22.28 as ληνός, 'winevat'.

1. For 9.6 see below, n. 28.

2. See F. Buhl *et al.*, *Wilhelm Gesenius' hebraisches und aramäisches Handwörterbuch über das Alte Testament* (reprint of the 17th edn; Berlin: Springer, 1962), p. 165; F. Brown *et al.*, *The New Brown–Driver–Briggs–Gesenius Hebrew and English Lexicon with an Appendix Containing the Biblical Aramaic* (Peabody, MA: Hendrickson, 1979), p. 199; *HALAT*, p. 218; and most commentaries on Exodus (e.g. B.S. Childs, *Exodus: A Commentary* [OTL; London: SCM Press, 1974], pp. 479-80; J.I. Durham, *Exodus* [WBC, 3; Waco: Word Books, 1987], pp. 329-30; M. Noth, *Das zweite Buch Mose. Exodus* [ATD, 5; Göttingen: Vandenhoeck & Ruprecht, 6th edn, 1978], p. 152; F.C. Fensham, *Exodus* [De Prediking van het Oude Testament; Nijkerk: G.F. Callenbach, 1984], p. 172; and U. Cassuto, *A Commentary on the Book of Exodus* [Jerusalem: Magnes Press, 1967], p. 294).

For another group of scholars represented by Hoffmann,[3] Perles,[4] and Blau,[5] the Samaritan noun דמע, which means 'best part of, superior', and the Arab noun *dimāgh*, meaning 'brain' demonstrates that in semitic languages a root *dmgh* existed. Because there is no *ghayin* in Hebrew, *dmgh* became the root דמע II, a homonym with דמע I. In rejecting the metaphorical interpretation of *dema'* in Exod. 22.28, Blau asserts,

> not only does the poetic use of 'mourning' in laws appear somewhat improbable, but the parallel *m^{e}lē'a* excludes reference to wine and oil suggested by the etymology... If only *m^{e}lē'a* refers to the vineyard, then *dema'*... must refer to the cereals, i.e. *dema'* describes the cereal tax, *m^{e}lē'a* the tax of the vineyards. But while *dema'* does not designate liquids, it cannot be derived from *dim'ā*, 'tear', either.[6]

This position is probably supported by the Vulgate, which translates *dema'* as *primitiae* meaning 'first fruits'.

After the Copper Scroll had been opened, both positions were applied with some variations to its use of *dema'*. Most influential was Allegro. In his edition of the Copper Scroll he interpreted *dema'* in the context of Mishnaic Hebrew: 'in NH it generally means the priest's share of the produce, a form of Terumah (cf. *bêt had-dema'* "place in the barn set aside for Terumah", Toseph.Ter 1016)'.[7] That vessels (כלין) of *dema'* are often mentioned in the Copper Scroll (1.9; 3.2-3, 9; 5.6-7; 8.3; 11.1, 4, 10, 14; 12.6-7) is explained by Allegro in relation to their sacral value:

> Vessels which had held tithe were no longer usable for secular purposes. Perhaps the reason why these tithe vessels were preserved in hiding and not

3. D. Hoffmann, 'Lexicographische Notizen', *Magazin für die Wissenschaft des Judenthums* 13 (1886), pp. 54-56, esp. p. 55.

4. F. Perles, 'Review of A.A. Cowley, *The Samaritan Liturgy I.II.* Oxford, Clarendon Press, 1909', *OLZ* 15 (1912), p. 218.

5. J. Blau, 'מילון חדש למקרא', *Tarbiz* 25 (1956), pp. 359-61, XI-XII, esp. pp. 360-61; *idem*, 'Über homonyme und angeblich homonyme Wurzeln', *VT* 6 (1956), pp. 242-48, esp. pp. 246-47. Cf. also E. Ben-Yehuda, *A Complete Dictionary of Ancient and Modern Hebrew*, II (16 vols.; New York: Thomas Yoseloff, 1961), pp. 964-65, and N.M. Sarna, *Exodus* שמות: *The Traditional Text with the New JPS Translation* (The JPS Torah Commentary; Philadelphia: The Jewish Publication Society, 1991), pp. 140-41.

6. Blau, 'Wurzeln', pp. 246-47.

7. J.M. Allegro, *The Treasure of the Copper Scroll* (London: Routledge & Kegan Paul, 1960), p. 137 n. 19.

> simply broken to prevent their misuse in the future was to avoid even the smallest sherd being inadvertently used for non-sacred purposes.[8]

He even speculated whether the *dema'* vessels of the Copper Scroll can be compared with the buried cooking pots containing bones found at Khirbet Qumran.[9]

Like Allegro, Lehmann understands *dema'* in the context of Exod. 22.28; *Mek. on Exod.* 22.28 and *b. Ter.* 4a as a synonym for the heave-offering (תרומה).[10] Thus, the *dema'* vessels of the Copper Scroll are in his opinion 'vessels holding תרומה' (p. 97; cf. *t. Ma'as. Š.* 5.1). Because in *m. Ter.* (4.7; 5.5; 7.6; 9.4) *dema'* is

> in a secondary sense...associated with admixtures of תרומה with חולין, id est heave-offerings with food taxed... It follows, that כלי דמע may either be understood as vessels holding portions of the heave-offering, or vessels holding admixtures involving, partially, portions of heave-offerings. As דמע sometimes refers to liquids (e.g. *Mishnah, Ḥagigah* III, 4), the vessels listed in 3 Q 15 may also have been oil of wine barrels.

In their understanding of *dema'* Allegro and Lehmann were supported by Lurie,[11] Sharvit,[12] Greenfield,[13] Safrati,[14] Pixner[15] and Wolters.[16]

8. Allegro, *Treasure of the Copper Scroll*, p. 137 n. 19.

9. Allegro, *Treasure of the Copper Scroll*, p. 148 n. 108.

10. M.R. Lehmann, 'Identification of the Copper Scroll Based on its Technical Terms', *RevQ* 5 (1964), pp. 97-105, esp. pp. 97-99. Quote from p. 98.

11. B.-Z. Lurie, *The Copper Scroll from the Desert of Judah* (Publications of the Israel Bible Research Society, 4; Jerusalem: Kiryath-Sepher, 1963), p. 63.

12. Sh. Sharvit, 'עיונים במילונה של מגילת הנחושת', *Beth Mikra* 31 (1967), pp. 127-35, esp. p. 131.

13. J.C. Greenfield, 'The Small Caves of Qumran', *JAOS* 89 (1969), pp. 128-41, esp. p. 139.

14. G.B.A. Sarfati, 'בתכן אצלם: חידה מן החידות של מגילת הנחושת', *Leš* 36 (1971–72), pp. 106-11, esp. p. 107.

15. B. Pixner, 'Unravelling the Copper Scroll Code: A Study on the Topography of 3Q15', *RevQ* 11(1983), pp. 323-65, esp. p. 343.

16. A. Wolters, 'Notes on the Copper Scroll (3Q15)', *RevQ* 12 (1985–87), pp. 589-96, esp. p. 590; *idem*, 'The Copper Scroll and the Vocabulary of the Mishnaic Hebrew', *RevQ* 14 (1990), pp. 483-95, esp. p. 488; *idem*, 'History and the Copper Scroll', in M.O. Wise, N. Golb, J.J. Collins and D. Pardee (eds.), *Methods of Investigation of the Dead Sea Scrolls and the Khirbet Qumran Site: Present Realities and Future Prospects* (Annals of the New York Academy of Sciences, 722; New York: The New York Academy of Sciences, 1994), pp. 285-98, pp. 293-94; *idem*, *The Copper Scroll: Overview, Text and Translation* (Sheffield: Sheffield Academic Press, 1996), pp. 33-55.

Allegro's position was also accepted in different translations of the Copper Scroll: Beyer, and Maier have translated *dema'* as 'Priesterabgabe',[17] and García Martínez as 'tithe'.[18] McCarter[19] has derived the meaning of *dema'* from its association with תרומה in rabbinic literature, too.[20] But he is of the opinion that *dema'* not only designates the priestly tithe itself, but in a broader sense all forms of contributions for Levites and priests.

At the conference whose proceedings are published in the present volume, S. Pfann tried to support Allegro from archaeological evidence. He proposed that the famous scroll jars found in the ruins and the caves of Qumran were originally used as storage jars for priestly tithes and only secondarily for storing scrolls. Pfann's main evidence is a ט inscribed two times on one of the jars found in Cave 8 before it was fired.[21] In his opinion, the Copper Scroll designates these jars as כלי דמע.[22] Pfann's hypothesis seems to be supported by sherds found at Masada and inscribed either with ת or ט[23] and *m. Ma'as. Š.* 4.10-11; *t. Ma'as. Š.* 5.1, which attest to the use of single letters to designate vessels in which priestly tributes and so on were stored. But in contrast with the sherds found at Masada, the two טs on the jar found in Qumran Cave 8 were not written with ink on its surface but incised into it before it was fired. Because *m. Ma'aś. Š.* 4.11 attests to the prescription that single characters should be used in case

17. J. Maier, *Die Qumran Essener: Die Texte vom Toten Meer* (3 vols.; Munich: Ernst Reinhardt Verlag, 1995), I, pp. 289-95; K. Beyer, *Die aramäischen Texte vom Toten Meer, samt den Inschriften aus Palästina, dem Testament Levis aus der Kairoer Genisa, der Fastenrolle und den alten talmudischen Zitaten. Aramaitische Einleitung, Text, Übersetzung, Deutung, Grammatik/Wörterbuch, Deutsch-aramäische Wortliste, Register, Ergänzungsband* (Göttingen: Vandenhoeck & Ruprecht, 1994), pp. 224-33.

18. F. García Martínez, *The Dead Sea Scrolls Translated: The Qumran Texts in English* (Leiden: E.J. Brill, 1994), pp. 461-63.

19. P. Kyle McCarter, 'The Copper Scroll Treasure as an Accumulation of Religious Offerings', in Wise *et al.* (eds.), *Methods of Investigation of the Dead Sea Scrolls*, pp. 133-48.

20. McCarter, 'Copper Scroll Treasure', p. 134; cf. *idem*, 'The Mystery of the Copper Scroll', in H. Shanks (ed.), *Understanding the Dead Sea Scrolls: A Reader from the Biblical Archaeological Review* (New York: Random House, 1992), p. 239.

21. See M. Baillet, J.T. Milik and R. de Vaux, *Les 'petites grottes' de Qumrân* (DJDJ III; Oxford: Clarendon Press, 1962 [hereafter cited as DJDJ III]), pls. 6-7.

22. For Pfann's position see his article in the present volume.

23. For the sherds found at Masada see Y. Yadin and J. Naveh, 'The Aramaic and Hebrew Ostraca and Jar Inscriptions', *Masada I: The Yigael Yadin Excavations 1963–1965, Final Reports* (Jerusalem: Israel Exploration Society; The Hebrew University of Jerusalem, 1989), pp. 32-33, pl. 26.

of emergency only—clearly not the case since the Qumran jar was inscribed before it was fired—this argues against Pfann. Furthermore, one wonders why only one of the many jars from Qumran intended to contain priestly tributes was marked by an inscription, while the sherds from Masada attest to several marked jars. Thus the ט-inscriptions of the Qumran Cave 8 jar are better understood as an abbreviation designating the jar's owner or something else.

In contrast with Allegro and his supporters, in his *editio princeps* of the Copper Scroll Milik proposed to derive *dema'* from the root דמע I, 'to weep', and to interpret it as a designation for resins or spices:

> The word דמע recurs 15 times... Most often it says 'vessels of *dema'*' followed by the name of a kind of produce. If our identifications of at least some of these kinds of produce are correct, we are dealing with perfumes, incense, resins, and most certainly 'aromatic wood'. Five times 'vessels of aromatic substances' are mentioned and once simply 'the *dema'*'. In i 9 it is unclear whether we should understand '*dema'* of sandalwood' or rather 'sandalwood perfume'... Where the kind of *dema'* is not specified it could be a matter of aromatic substances that are especially pungent, such as incense (*lebona*) and myrrh (*mor*)...
>
> The biblical *hapax legomenon*, דמעך (Exod. 22.28) must, in our opinion, mean the same in the Copper Scroll, namely, 'aromatics, resins', and more generally, 'plants used as perfumes, medicines, seasonings', which make up offerings, no doubt voluntary, made by persons loyal to priests and Temple. It is possible that the *dema'* might have replaced *ad libitum* all kinds of offerings, מלאתך in the same verse.[24]

Milik found only a few supporters. Laperrousaz connects the *dema'* vessels of the Copper Scroll with the balsam trees of En Gedi[25] and the 18th edition of Gesenius's Dictionary translates *dema'* as 'Aroma, Spezerei'.[26] In contrast, the *Dictionary of Classical Hebrew* lists for *dema'* the

24. J.T. Milik, 'Le rouleau de cuivre provenant de la grotte 3Q (3Q15)', DJDJ III, p. 250; cf. also *idem*, 'Le rouleau de cuivre de Qumrân (3Q15)', *RB* 66 (1959), pp. 321-57, esp. pp. 323-28. This interpretation of *dema'* must also be meant when Milik mentions in his famous book, *Ten Years of Discovery in the Wilderness of Judaea*, 'incense and precious substances which are said to be stored in vessels also made of valuable material' (SBT, 26; London: SCM Press, 1959], p. 42).

25. E.-M. Laperrousaz, *Qoumrân: L'etablissement essénien des bords de la Mer Morte. Histoire et archéologie du site* (Paris: Editions A. et J. Picard, 1976), p. 144.

26. W. Gesenius, *Hebräisches und Aramäisches Handwörterbuch über das Alte Testament* (ed. H. Donner and U. Rüterswörden; Berlin: Springer Verlag, 18th edn, 1995), II, p. 255.

meanings ‘tithe’, ‘best part’, ‘juice’ and ‘resin’ and thus integrates both positions by understanding *dema‘* as a polyvalent noun.[27]

The Evidence of the Copper Scroll

Of the 14 occurrences of *dema‘* in the Copper Scroll[28] the context of 5.7 provides no information about the noun. In 3.9; 8.3; 11.1, 4, 10, 14 *dema‘* or the contents of the *dema‘* vessels are specified, but the vocabulary used is in itself difficult to understand. Thus an analysis of the Copper Scroll’s use of *dema‘* should start with 1.9, 10; 3.3; 8.3 and 12.7. Afterwards the occurrences in 3.9; 11.1, 4, 10, 14 will be discussed, while 5.7 can be ignored.

In 1.10-11 the words מעסר שני are crucial for the understanding of *dema‘*. They were interpreted by Allegro,[29] Pixner,[30] Beyer[31] and McCarter[32] as ‘second tithe’. Wolters also understands מעסר שני as a designation of the second tithe but alters the word division in 1.10-11 and reads והאצר השבעי מעסר שני מפוגל, ‘and the seventh treasure, a second tithe rendered unclean’.[33] Because מעסר is linked with a *waw* to the preceding שבע Milik understood it as being part of a number counting the amount of hidden treasure (‘sept [talents] et un dixième’)[34] and thus interpreted מעסר and שני as belonging to two different sentences: ‘It is better to dissociate the two words and take the latter as the imperative of *šnh* ‘repeat’, which precedes the description of the movements of the

27. *The Dictionary of Classical Hebrew* (ed. D.J.A. Clines; Sheffield: Sheffield Academic Press, 1995), II, p. 252.

28. Milik finds a 15th occurrence in 9.6, where he reads דמ<ע> הצא (DJDJ III, p. 293; cf. Pixner, ‘Unravelling the Copper Scroll Code’, p. 352; García Martínez, *Dead Sea Scrolls Translated*, p. 462; and Maier, *Die Qumran Essener*, I, p. 293). But Allegro, *Treasure of the Copper Scroll*, p. 49; Lurie, *Copper Scroll*, p. 108; Beyer, *Die aramäischen Texte*, p. 229; and McCarter, ‘Copper Scroll Treasure’, p. 134, are of the opinion that the first characters in 9.6 should be read as ומחצא, ‘half’, which seems to fit the drawings of both Allegro and Milik better.

29. Allegro, *Treasure of the Copper Scroll*, p. 33.

30. Pixner, ‘Unravelling the Copper Scroll Code’, p. 343.

31. Beyer, *Die aramäischen Texte*, p. 226.

32. McCarter, ‘Copper Scroll Treasure’, p. 137.

33. Wolters, *The Copper Scroll*, pp. 32-33; cf. García Martínez, *Dead Sea Scrolls Translated*, p. 461.

34. Milik, DJDJ III, p. 285.

seeker of the treasure'.[35] Like Milik, Maier did not view מעסר שני as a designation of the second tithe, but read like Wolters השבעי מעסר שני, which he rendered as 'des siebten Zehent, Zweiter'.[36] Two further possibilities for reading and interpreting 1.10-11 exist: to understand שני as *shani* (scarlet)—a colouring matter that was of some importance in the temple cult (cf. Exod. 25.4; 26.1-39, 29; Lev. 14.4, 6, 49, 51-52; Num. 4.8; 19.6)—or to view it as introducing a second treasure hidden also at Tel Koḥlit: 'A second one: from the mouth of a heap is the gate to it at the edge of the aqueduct from the north.'

The structure of the Copper Scroll's descriptions where treasure was hidden argues against understanding the two words ומעסר שני as 'second tithe' because other treasures hidden at a given *locus* are never listed after the weight of the first treasure is given. Thus it seems unlikely that after it has been stated that everything that is hidden at Tel Koḥlit weighs seven (talents) a second tithe is added as also to be found there. Wolters tries to solve this structural problem by reading והאצר השבעי, 'and the seventh treasure'.[37] But this would be a unique expression in the Copper Scroll. Furthermore, before 1.10 only three treasures are listed, not six, which would be necessary so that the one named in 1.10 could be counted as the seventh. ומעסר should thus be understood as a fractional number belonging to the weight given in 1.10, that is, שבע ומעסר, 'seven talents and one tenth'. To interpret the שני of 1.11 as introducing a second treasure must also be doubted because the Copper Scroll never describes and enumerates an additional treasure hidden at the same place (cf. 5.9-11; 11.1-4, 4-7; 12.2-3). The pattern of the Copper Scroll's descriptions of hidden treasure would also be violated if שני is read as שָׁנִי, 'scarlet', because treasures are listed by the Copper Scroll not before but only after a topographical description. Thus, שני should be understood according to Milik as an imperative, but not of שנה II but שנה I. In sum, 1.10-11 must be translated as 'in total *dema'* and treasure seven (talents) and one tenth. Turn aside (change direction)[38] from the mouth of a heap—its entrance is at the edge of the aqueduct from the north'.

35. DJDJ III, p. 235, cf. p. 285.

36. Maier, *Die Qumran Essener*, I, p. 289.

37. Wolters, *The Copper Scroll*, pp. 32-33.

38. For this use of שנה cf. Z. Ben-Ḥayyim, *The Literary and Oral Tradition of Hebrew and Aramaic amongst the Samaritans* (5 vols.; Jerusalem: The Academy of the Hebrew Language, 1977), V, p. 165, § 2.15.5.

The number שבע ומעסר, ‘seven [talents] and one tenth’, also allows us to argue that Milik’s translation of בלגין as ‘bois santal’ in 1.9[39] is wrong because of all the treasures listed in the Copper Scroll only vessels, gold, silver and money are weighed.[40] Thus, in 1.9 no aromatics can be meant by בלגין. It should therefore be understood as a Greek loanword λάγηνος/λάγυνος (‘flask, flagon’; cf. Latin *lagona*).[41] בלגין specifies the type of vessels designated as *dema‘* vessels (‘consisting of[42] flasks’). That in 1.10 a weight is given for the treasure hidden at Tel Koḥlit demonstrates that the flasks in question consisted of gold or silver because only gold, silver and money is weighed in the Copper Scroll. The last word of 1.10 should not be read as ואפרין[43] but as ואפודת[44] because on the Copper Scroll replica produced by Electricité de France[45] a *taw* can clearly be read at the end of 1.10. That Ephodot are weighed here, while otherwise only gold, silver and money are weighed in the Copper Scroll, should not surprise us because ‘the predominant kind of thread woven into it [scil. the Ephod] was gold’ and ‘gold dominated its fabrication’[46] (cf. Exod. 28; 39).

Thus nothing indicates that the *dema‘* vessels mentioned in 1.9-10 contained priestly tribute. On the contrary, what is summarized as ‘in total *dema‘* and treasure seven (talents) and one tenth’ consisted of vessels

39. Milik, DJDJ III, pp. 251, 285.

40. In addition, the Copper Scroll lists several times amounts of talents without any specification. These should probably be understood as amounts of hidden silver.

41. Thus Lurie, *The Copper Scroll*, p. 63; Lehmann, ‘Identification of the Copper Scroll’, p. 99; Sharvit, ‘עיונים במילונה של מגילת הנחושת’, p. 134, and Greenfield, ‘Small Caves of Qumran’, p. 139 (for a detailed critique of Milik’s hypothesis, see pp. 138-39). Wolters proposed understanding בלגין as representing two words, i.e. בל גין, ‘master of nations’. בל would then be a variant spelling for בעל (‘Notes on the Copper Scroll’, pp. 591-92). Later on, he doubted his proposal (‘History and the Copper Scroll’, p. 294) but in his recent edition it can be found again (*The Copper Scroll*, p. 32).

42. The preposition ב should be understood as a *bêth essentiae* (cf. Allegro, *Treasure of the Copper Scroll*, p. 137 n. 20).

43. Thus Allegro, *Treasure of the Copper Scroll*, p. 137 n. 22; Lurie, *The Copper Scroll*, p. 63; and McCarter, ‘Copper Scroll Treasure’, p. 134; cf. also Beyer, *Die aramäischen Texte*, p. 226, and Maier, *Die Qumran Essener*, I, p. 289.

44. Thus Milik, DJDJ III, p. 284; Wolters, ‘Notes on the Copper Scroll’, p. 590; Wolters, *The Copper Scroll*, p. 32, and É. Puech in his lecture at the conference published in this volume.

45. See the CD-ROM of the Laboratoire EDF–Valectra, ‘Photos de la restauration des rouleaux de Qumran’ (Paris: Laboratoire EDF–Valectra, 1996), img0096.pcd.

46. C. Meyers, ‘Ephod’, *ABD*, II, p. 550.

made of precious metal and Ephodot, which were vestments of the High Priest and not priestly tributes. In addition, *dema'* is used in 1.10 in parallel with אצרה, 'treasure', which indicates that its meaning is comparable with אצרה. *dema'* should thus be understood as designating something precious or valuable.

In 3.1-4 כלי כסף וזהב של דמע (lines 2-3) are mentioned. These silver and golden vessels are specified in an aposition as מזרקות כוסות מנקיאות קסאות, 'sprinkling basins, cups, sacrificial bowls, libation vessels'. Because some of these vessels are unsuitable for storing either priestly contributions or resins and spices it seems unlikely that *dema'* in 3.3 designates resins and spices or some kind of priestly contribution. Instead it should be understood as describing the listed vessels as 'valuable' or 'precious'.

For the last two words of 8.3 different transcriptions have been proposed: Milik has proposed אל תֿבֿםּ[47] which he has translated as 'ne te (les) *approprie* pas' (pp. 292-93)—a transcription that he himself characterized as 'tres incertaine' (p. 247). Because this expression would be singular in the preserved text of the Copper Scroll, and because palaeographically the first character of the line's last word could be either ה or ת, while its second could be ב or כ and the remnants of its third character could be attributed to ל, ם or ק, Milik's transcription is doubtful. Wolters has reconstructed וספרי ואלת כס[ף], 'and my scrolls, and a bar of silver',[48] which is possible palaeographically but nevertheless doubtful because the Copper Scroll never speaks of a single bar of silver or gold and because it never uses אָלָה to designate bars, but only the plural forms עשתות (1.5; 2.4) and בדין (2.11; 7.10; 9.3). Recently, based on new photographs É. Puech[49] has read וספרין אל תדקם, 'and scrolls, don't damage them'. However, against him it must be stressed that the photograph published by Milik[50] shows clearly the beginning of a horizontal line at the bottom of the second character of the line's last word. Therefore a ד cannot be read there. In addition to palaeographical problems, Puech's hypothesis must be doubted for linguistic reasons: דקק is never attested in the sense of 'to destroy something'. Its basic meaning is 'to grind/pulverize' (Exod. 30.36; 32.20; Deut. 9.21; 2 Kgs 23.6, 15; Isa. 28.28; 2 Chron. 15.16; 34.4, 7) and the objects ground or pulverized are mostly grain or idols. Even when it

47. DJDJ III, p. 292.
48. *The Copper Scroll*, pp. 46-47; cf. 'History and the Copper Scroll', p. 292.
49. See his lecture published in the present volume.
50. DJDJ III, pl. 63.

is used metaphorically to describe the destruction of people, mountains, or nations, images of grinding are always present in the metaphor (2 Sam. 22.43; Isa. 41.15; Mic. 4.13). In later times the *polpal* of דקק could be used to describe the minute halakhic treatment of a given subject (CD 16.2-3).[51] Thus it seems highly unlikely that the Copper Scroll would have used דקק metaphorically. In addition, a treasure list is not a genre in which metaphoric language is employed and the Copper Scroll is no exception.

Compared with these proposals Allegro's transcription (אל הכלין)[52] seems preferable because it causes no linguistic or stylistic problems and is palaeographically possible. Scroll 3Q15 8.3 should therefore be read כלי דמע[53] וספרי[ן] אל הכלין, 'treasure vessels and scrolls [put] into[54] the vessels'. It specifies the contents of the hidden *dema‘* vessels are specified as scrolls. Again, neither Allegro's nor Milik's interpretation of *dema‘* corresponds with the evidence of the Copper Scroll.

The hypothesis developed above, to understand *dema‘* as meaning something precious, valuable, or treasure is also corroborated by 12.6-7. Here the Copper Scroll mentions כל<י> כסף וכלי זהב של דמע וכסף הכל ככרין שש מאות, 'vessels of silver and gold which are *dema‘* and money—in total six hundred talents'. Because in other contexts only gold, silver and money are weighed in the Copper Scroll[55] and both the vessels and the silver are summarized in 12.7 by הכל, it seems unlikely that the vessels in question contained resins and spices or priestly contributions. Most probably their content was the כסף itself, which should be understood as 'money'. *Dema‘* again seems to designate something valuable or precious.

For 3.9 three different transcriptions have been proposed:

51. דקק is probably also attested in 4Q508 frag. 33 l.1 ([אוׄתׄ דׄקׄנׄוׄ °]). But because of severe damage nothing can be said about its meaning there.

52. Allegro, *Treasure of the Copper Scroll*, p. 47.

53. For the reading וספרי[ן] cf. Allegro, *Treasure of the Copper Scroll*, p. 47 and Milik, DJDJ III, p. 292. McCarter proposes ספרו ('Copper Scroll Treasure', p. 135) while Wolters reads וספרי ('History and the Copper Scroll', p. 292; *The Copper Scroll*, p. 3). But because neither a possessive suffix of the third nor one of the first person can be expected and the final *nun* could well have been sawn away when the Copper Scroll was opened the transcription וספרי[ן] is to be preferred.

54. For a close parallel of this use of אֶל cf. Hag. 1.6.

55. See above, pp. 129-30.

(1) כלי דמע לבֹושין̇[ן] ביאתא,[56]
(2) כלי דמע לכושי ביאתא,[57]
(3) כלי דמע ולבישין̇[ן] ביאתא.[58]

According to the drawings of Allegro and Milik and the photograph published by Milik,[59] palaeographically all three transcriptions are possible. Only the *waw* of ולב/ושין[ן] read by Allegro and Puech should be doubted: what is read as a *waw* is a small vertical stroke found directly under the *lamed* of לבושין. Because there would have been enough space between the preceding דמע and לבושין for a *waw* even inserted later on as a correction, and because the Copper Scroll often ignores the spaces left between two words this stroke should be interpreted as a scribal error probably caused by a slip of the chisel. According to Puech לבישין is to be understood as a Greek loanword derived from λέβης (lat. *lebes*) ('kettle/cauldron'). The Copper Scroll would then list in 3.9 a second type of vessel. Admittedly, the noun λέβης was prominent in ancient Greek literature (the TLG CD-ROM attests 940 occurrences) and was used in the LXX and by Josephus (*Ant.* 8.88; 13.345). But the loanword derived from λέβης and attested in rabbinic literature (לְבֵס var. lec. לפס [*m. Kel.* 14.1; *t. B. mes.* 4], לבוסין [read לְבִיסִין; *Sifre Num.* 158]),[60] is not spelled לביש as proposed by Puech for 3.9 but לבס. It would be surprising to find a noun in every other context always written with ס in the Copper Scroll written with ש. This is all the more true because with two exceptions the

56. Thus Allegro, *Treasure of the Copper Scroll*, p. 37; cf. Pixner, 'Unravelling the Copper Scroll Code', p. 347; García Martínez, *Dead Sea Scrolls Translated*, p. 461; McCarter, 'Copper Scroll Treasure', p. 135; and Maier, *Die Qumran Essener*, I, p. 290. Allegro transcribes the third word as ולבוהשיה[ן] while Wolters reads לבושי ('Notes on the Copper Scroll', pp. 593-54; 'History and the Copper Scroll', p. 292; *The Copper Scroll*, p. 36). The final-*nun* of לבושין, which Allegro marked as damaged and which is rejected by Wolters cannot be found on any photograph of col. 3, but should be seen as destroyed when the scroll was sawn into pieces. Otherwise a first person singular suffix must be read ('my garments'), which is found nowhere else in 3Q15 (according to Wolters it can also be found in 8.3, where his reading is to be doubted for reasons of content [see above, p. 131] and 11.9 where his transcription טהורתי yields a senseless text). Allegro's ה is clearly a printing error.

57. Thus Milik, DJDJ III, p. 287; Beyer, *Die aramäischen Texte*, pp. 225-26.

58. Thus Puech in the present volume.

59. DJDJ III, pl. 53.

60. S. Krauss, *Griechische und lateinische Lehnworter im Talmud, Midrasch und Targum* (2 vols.; repr.; Hildesheim: Georg Olms Verlagsbuchhandlung, 1964 [1898–99]), I, p. 186; II, p. 303.

Copper Scroll always uses ס instead of שׂ.[61] Thus, the transcription לבישין is doubtful. The *hapax legomenon* read by Milik and Beyer might designate ‘Pin d’Alep’, probably used as an incense.[62] Because לבושי is attested only once in Jewish literature and in the immediate context of 3.9 nothing compels us to read it, Milik’s transcription should also be rejected. In contrast, לְבוּשׁ, ‘garment’, is not only widespread in ancient Jewish literature but also yields good sense. Line 3.9 should therefore be read as was first proposed by Allegro: כלי דמע לבושי[ן] ביאתא. The לבושין mentioned specifies the contents of the *dema‘* vessels as precious priestly garments used for cultic purposes.[63] Because garments can neither be understood as priestly contributions nor as resins or spices, Milik’s and Allegro’s interpretations of *dema‘* in 3.9 both seem to be wrong.

For 11.1 (cf. 5.7; 11.4, 9, 11, 15) scholarly discussion focuses on whether בתכן אצלם provides information concerning the distance and direction of the next hiding place (cf. the biblical use of תֹּכֶן in Exod. 5.18; Ezek. 45.11) and belongs thus to the next sentence,[64] whether it gives information of the contents of the *dema‘* vessels mentioned before,[65] or whether בתכן should be read as כתבן אצלם כתבן, ‘their document is beside them’.[66] Against the last proposal it must be stressed that it seems unlikely that in two words, one following directly after the other, the suffix of the third person plural is first written as ן and the next time as ם.

61. Cf. Y. Thorion, ‘Beitrage zur Erforschung der Sprache der Kupferrolle’, *RevQ* 12 (1985–87), pp. 163-76, esp. p. 169.

62. Thus Milik, DJDJ III, pp. 250-51. Cf. Hebrew לֶבֶשׁ (‘*the woolly substance of cedar twigs*, used for wicks’; M. Jastrow, *A Dictionary of the Targumim, the Talmud Babli and Yerushalmi, and the Midrashic Literature* (2 vols. in one; New York: Judaica Press, 1992 [1903]), p. 711) and Akkadian *lukšu* (‘needles of the cedar’; *CAD*, IX, p. 240).

63. McCarter’s translation ‘swaddled vessels of *dema‘*’ (‘Copper Scroll Treasure’, p. 135) results from his interpretation of *dema‘* as a priestly contribution. But vessels containing garments yields more and better sense in a treasure list than swaddled vessels.

64. Milik, DJDJ III, pp. 254, 256, 296-97; Pixner, ‘Unravelling the Copper Scroll Code’, p. 355; García Martínez, *Dead Sea Scrolls Translated*, p. 463; and Maier, *Die Qumran Essener*, I, p. 294.

65. Allegro understands אצלם ‘as a coll. sing. with proth. *'aleph*, of the root *ṣlm* and meaning coins with images stamped on them’ (*Treasure of the Copper Scroll*, p. 148 n. 109), while Beyer translates ‘gemäß dem beiliegenden Inhaltsverzeichnis mit Mengenangabe’ (*Die aramäischen Texte*, p. 231).

66. Wolters, *The Copper Scroll*, pp. 52-53; cf. Sarfati, ‘בתכן אצלם’, pp. 109-11 (‘their description is with them’).

Furthermore, Wolters is forced to emend ותכן אצלם in 11.4—read by him as ותבן אצלם—to וכתבן אצלם. Thus the phrase's first word should be understood as consisting of the noun תֹּכֶן preceded by either ב or כ. Because אֵצֶל is most often attested with the meaning 'beside, with, near' and because תֹּכֶן is known from Exod. 5.18, Ezek. 45.11 and 4Q159 frag. 1, col. 2, line 13 as designating a given measure, the phrase בתכן אצלם should be seen as introducing the description of the next hiding place as to be found 'at a given distance beside them'. In consequence, no information about the *dema'* vessels can be gained from 10.17–11.1. The Copper Scroll simply states that gold and *dema'* vessels are hidden.

In 11.4 the *dema'* vessels' contents are specified as סוח and סנה. Both words are seldom used in Hebrew literature. Thus their meaning is uncertain.[67] Allegro derives סוח from Hebrew סוּחָה, 'offal', and סנה from Hebrew שׂנא, 'hate'. Both nouns would then describe 'some defect *dema'*'.[68] For McCarter the key to the troublesome passage is the fifth word of 11.4, which he reads as ספח (otherwise סנה), meaning סְפִיַחַ, 'aftergrowth', while סוח—read by McCarter as סיח—would designate in parallelism to ספח, '(wild) growth'.[69] But the middle character of ספח/ סנה consists on its left side of one straight vertical stroke only and does not have the upper rounded stroke prominent for פ. סיח is also read by Beyer, who has translated 11.4 as 'Gefäße mit Priesterabgabe von Artemisiastrauch (und) mit Priesterabgabe vom Brombeerstrauch.'[70] Because Milik is able to provide a Jewish–Aramaic parallel for סוח, his interpretation is the most convincing:

> The name is attested in the Aramaic fragments of the Testament of Levi from the Cairo Genizah, in which one of fourteen kinds of wood for the altar, otherwise known as evergreen trees, is called שוחא, equivalent to πίτυν in the parallel Greek text, *piton* in *Jub.* 21[12], πίτυς in Geoponica xi 1 14.[71]

67. Therefore Pixner ('Unravelling the Copper Scroll Code', p. 355) and Maier (*Die Qumran Essener*, I, p. 249) translate neither סוח nor סנה.

68. Allegro, *Treasure of the Copper Scroll*, p. 164 n. 268.

69. McCarter, 'Treasure of the Copper Scroll', p. 135.

70. 'Vessels with priestly offerings of wormwood (and) priestly offerings of blackberry' (Beyer, *Die aramäischen Texte*, pp. 231-32).

71. DJDJ III, p. 251. Cf. also Syriac *sîḥa'* ('tamarisk'; R. Payne Smith, *Thesaurus Syriacus* [Oxford: Clarendon Press, 1879–1901], col. 2610) and Akkadian *sîu*, *sîḫu* ('a tree and its resin'; *CAD* XV, p. 241).

סוח would thus designate the Aleppo Pine,[72] probably to be used as incense. ‘סנה de xi 4 est probablement le séné, “Cassia Senna” (arabe *sanâ*)’,[73] a fragrant herb used for medical purposes and as a colouring matter. Thus, most probably סוח and סנה designate an incense and a herb. But even then *dema‘* must not be interpreted in 11.4 as meaning resins or spices because this would not agree with its use at other places in the Copper Scroll. Instead it should be seen as attesting to the *value* of the incense and the herb.

In line with most scholars, 11.10 (בו כלי דמע א<ר>ז כלי דמע סוח)[74] must be understood on the basis of the interpretation of סוח in 11.4.[75] Therefore Milik is to be supported in his rendering of סוח as ‘sapin’[76] and in his emendation of אז to ארז, ‘cedar’. Because in the context of the Copper Scroll’s use of *dema‘* it seems again unlikely that the noun means ‘resin’ or ‘spices’, it should once more be understood as marking the *dema‘* vessels’ contents as valuable.

In 11.14 the contents of *dema‘* vessels are specified twice: שלו כלי דמ<ע> לאה דמע סירא.[77] Unfortunately לאה is attested in both biblical and rabbinic Hebrew only as a verb and as the name of Leah, the wife of Jacob, while סירה designates a ‘thorn’ or ‘hook’ and *poterium spinosum*.[78] Rabbinic Hebrew attests also to the meanings ‘coat of mail’ (סירא I), ‘thorn’ (סירא II), and ‘surrounded place, court, prison’ (סירה,

72. Cf. García Martínez who translates ‘pine (?) resin’ (*Dead Sea Scrolls Translated*, p. 463).

73. Milik, DJDJ III, p. 251; cf. García Martínez, *Dead Sea Scrolls Translated*, p. 463: ‘cassia [?] resin’.

74. For transcription and emendation see Milik, DJDJ III, pp. 251, 296.

75. Allegro transcribes the אז emended by Milik to א<ר>ז as או and reads סוח again as סיח. This results in the translation ‘vessels of tithe or tithe refuse’ (*Treasure of the Copper Scroll*, p. 53). As in 11.4, Pixner (‘Unravelling the Copper Scroll’, p. 356) and Maier (*Die Qumran Essener*, I, p. 294) do not translate אז and סוח, while García Martínez renders ‘there are vessels of myrtle (?) there, and of the tithe of pine (?) (resin)’ (*Dead Sea Scrolls Translated*, p. 463). Beyer reads סוח as סיח but accepts Milik’s emendation and renders ‘Gefäße mit Priesterabgaben von der [Zeder] (und) mit Priesterabgaben vom Artemisiastrauch’ (*Die aramäischen Texte*, p. 232). Because McCarter reads סוח as סיח, he follows Allegro in reading או and translates ‘vessels of *dema‘* or *dema‘* of (wild) growth’ (‘Copper Scroll Treasure’, p. 135).

76. DJDJ III, p. 297.

77. For the emendation see Milik, DJDJ III, pp. 229, 297.

78. For rabbinic Hebrew cf. Jastrow: ‘thorn, thornbush’; ‘refuse, foul matter’ (*Dictionary of the Targumim*, p. 987).

סירא II).[79] In addition, סירא is known as the name of the grandfather of the author of the book of Sirach (Sir. 50.27; 51.30). Because all this is senseless in a treasure list, neither Pixner[80] nor Maier[81] translate the words in question. Allegro[82] and Lurie[83] read לאה as לאח and interpret it as a *plene* spelling for לַח understood as 'liquid tithe'. For סירא both read סורא, which Allegro renders as 'degenerated tithe'[84] while Lurie views it as teruma doubtful in its purity and thus put aside.[85] Wolters understands both לאה and סירא as names and interprets the line as naming the tribute of two persons, that is, Leah and Sira.[86] McCarter emends לאה to מלאה, which, because of its rabbinic use, would refer to 'the fullness of the stored grain from which the first fruits are taken'.[87] The following דמע סורא[88] would then be a specification, that is, '*dema'* set aside, apart'.[89] All these attempts to understand *dema'* in 11.14 as a priestly contribution contradict its use in 1.9-10, 3.9 and 8.3. Compared with them, Milik's proposal to understand לאה as a Greek loanword derived from ἀλόη[90] has the advantage of avoiding emendations and does not contradict the use of *dema'* at other places in the Copper Scroll. In consequence, סירא should be understood on the basis of the Akkadian term *ḫil* $^{\check{s}am}$*si-ri* as 'l'essence de pin blanc'.[91]

To summarize, the Copper Scroll's key references to the meaning of *dema'* are 1.9-10, 3.9, 8.3. There, priestly garments (1.9-10 [Ephodot]; 3.9) and scrolls (8.3) are described as *dema'* or named as being the content

79. Jastrow, *Dictionary of the Targumim*, p. 987.
80. Pixner, 'Unravelling the Copper Scroll Code', p. 356.
81. Maier, *Die Qumran Essener*, I, p. 295.
82. Allegro, *Treasure of the Copper Scroll,* pp. 53, 164 n. 268.
83. Lurie, *The Copper Scroll*, p. 122.
84. Allegro, *Treasure of the Copper Scroll*, pp. 53, 164 n. 268.
85. Lurie, *The Copper Scroll*, p. 122.
86. Wolters, *The Copper Scroll*, p. 53.
87. McCarter, 'Copper Scroll Treasure', p. 136.
88. McCarter reads סורא instead of סירא ('Copper Scroll Treasure', p. 136).
89. McCarter, 'Copper Scroll Treasure', p. 136.
90. See DJDJ III, p. 251. For the missing *aleph* at the beginning of the word see p. 230 and Krauss (*Griechische und lateinische Lehnwörter*, I, pp. 123, 136-40). In his interpretation of לאה as 'aloe', Milik is supported by García Martínez (*Dead Sea Scrolls Translated*, p. 463) and Beyer (*Die aramäischen Texte*, p. 232).
91. Thus Milik, DJDJ III, p. 251; cf. García Martínez (*Dead Sea Scrolls Translated*, p. 463). Beyer (*Die aramäischen Texte*, p. 232) translates *sîrâ* according to its use in Isa. 34.12; Hos. 2.8; Nah. 1.10; and Eccl. 7.7 as 'Becherblume' (*poterium spinosum*).

of *dema‘* vessels. This contradicts both the widespread interpretation of *dema‘* as ‘tithe’ or more general ‘priestly tribute’ and Milik’s hypothesis to understand it as a designation of resins and spices. Its parallel use with אצרה, ‘treasure’, suggests that *dema‘* describes something valuable or precious. This fits with all the other occurrences of the noun in 3Q15. *Dema‘* should therefore be translated as ‘valuables’ or simply as ‘treasure’. Etymologically *dema‘* can be understood in the context of Samaritan and Arabic as a derivation of the root דמע II, ‘to be superior/best part of’.[92]

Dema‘ *in Exodus 22.28, Rabbinic Literature and 4Q251*

To interpret *dema‘* as designating ‘valuables’ or ‘treasure’ does not contradict its use in Exod. 22.28.[93] The subject of Exod. 22.28b-29 is the offering of the firstborn son and firstborn cattle to the Lord. In contrast with this, the noun *m^{e}le'ah*— in Exod. 22.28a used parallel with *dema‘*— designates in its two other occurrences in the Hebrew Bible (Num. 18.27; Deut. 22.9) the ‘fullness of the winevat’ and the ‘fullness of the yield of a wineyard’, but not an agricultural product to be used as a first fruit offering. Thus it seems difficult to interpret *dema‘* in Exod. 22.28a as such an offering. Better sense is gained if Exod. 22.28a is interpreted as employing metaphorical language: in parallel with the preceding *m^{e}le'ah*, *dema‘* would then designate a treasure to be given to the Lord, that is, the firstborn son. Exodus 22.28 should thus be translated ‘you shall not withhold your fullness and your treasure from me, the firstborn among your sons you shall give me’.

How does this correlate with the use of *dema‘* in 4Q251 frag. 2[94] and in rabbinic literature? For the rabbinic use of *dema‘* as designating ‘the priests’ share of the produce’[95] the *Mekhilta de Rabbi Yishmael* is paradigmatic. In exegesis of Exod. 22.28 it states: ודמעך זו התרומה, ‘“and your *dema‘*” this is the *t^{e}rumah*’.[96] In my opinion this use of *dema‘* can be

92. See above, p. 123.

93. For the different positions on *dema‘* in Exod. 22.28 see the section ‘History of Research’ above.

94. In earlier scholarly literature frag. 2 is counted as frag. 5. For the fragment’s text see Milik, DJDJ III, p. 300, and J.M. Baumgarten, ‘4Q Halakah[a] 5, the Law of *ḥadash*, and the Penteconta Calendar’, *JJS* 27 (1976), pp. 36-46 (36).

95. Jastrow, *Dictionary of the Targumim*, p. 314.

96. For the text cf. J.Z. Lauterbach, *Mekilta de-Rabbi Ishmael: A Critical Edition on the Basis of the Manuscripts and Early Editions with an English Translation,*

explained as being developed from its connotation 'valuables, treasure'. It would not be astonishing if *dema'* was used to describe the valuable part of a product intended to be the priestly share. The first known occurrence of *dema'* with this connotation is 4Q251 frag. 2 line 3: there, the sentence ו]דגן הואה הדמע, 'grain is the *dema'*', can be found in parallel with the prescription that wine is the priest's choice part of the flow. Because both *m^ele'ah* and *dema'* are used in 4Q251 frag. 2 the reference should be understood as a halakhic interpretation of Exod. 22.28.[97]

Introduction, and Notes (3 vols.; Philadelphia: The Jewish Society of America, 1949), III, p. 153.

97. Cf. Baumgarten, '4QHalakah[a] 5', p. 37: 'The identification of *dema'* with grain in l.3 of our text supports the view that it originally meant the "best, fat part" and was applied to cereals. In rabbinic sources it was extended to all *terumah*, the heave-offering given to the priests from oil, wine, and other produce.' For *dema'* as the designation of a priestly contribution in 4Q251 cf. also Milik (DJDJ III, p. 300), R. Eisenman and M.O. Wise (*The Dead Sea Scrolls Uncovered: The First Complete Translation and Interpretation of 50 Key Documents Withheld for over 35 Years* [Shaftesbury: Element, 1992], p. 205), García Martínez (*Dead Sea Scrolls Translated*, p. 87), and Maier (*Die Qumran Essener*, II, p. 192).

9

THE COPPER SCROLL TREASURE: FACT OR FICTION? THE ABBREVIATION כב VERSUS ככרין*

Judah K. Lefkovits

Introduction

The Copper Scroll is a dry document, written in a proto-Mishnaic Hebrew, which is also called Copper Scroll Hebrew.[1] It consists of 60 items, and some of them can be further subdivided. The scroll lists various objects, like dedicated vessels (כלי דמע, made of silver, gold or unspecified metal, perhaps copper), precious metals (silver, gold or unspecified, perhaps copper), garments and documents. These objects were described as being hidden in such places as caves, water-works and burial sites, at various locations in Roman Palestine. The weight of the metals, as well as some

* This subject is discussed in my doctoral dissertation, supervised by Professor L.H. Schiffman, *The Copper Scroll—3Q15: A New Reading, Translation and Commentary* (2 vols.; New York University, 1993 [UMI Order Number 9411113]), II, pp. 1055-1105. It is also elaborated in my book, *The Copper Scroll—3Q15: A Re-evaluation: A New Reading, Translation and Commentary* (STDJ, 25; Leiden: E.J. Brill, 2000), pp. 471-88. I would like to express my appreciation to Mrs Joan R. Allegro, widow of the late John Marco Allegro, for being kind enough to send a copy of material written by her husband immediately after opening the Copper Scroll. The material will be referred to as the 'Provisional Translation and Notes of the Copper Scroll'. Meeting Mrs Allegro was facilitated by the invitation extended by Professor G.J. Brooke (University of Manchester) to participate in the *International Symposium on the Copper Scroll* at the University of Manchester Institute of Science and Technology, 8–11 September 1996. I would also like to acknowledge support given to me by the Memorial Foundation for Jewish Culture during my doctoral and post-doctoral work on the Copper Scroll project. Gratitude is also extended to my brother-in-law, Dr S. Wischnitzer, for his help in editing this paper.

1. S. Morag, 'Qumran Hebrew: Some Topological Observations', *VT* 38 (1988), p. 149.

of the vessels, are stated. Units of weight are mentioned almost 50 times in the scroll, and are mainly found in the last phrase of an item.[2]

The scroll records more than 2600 ככרין (see Table 9.1) and more than 1000 כב (see Table 9.2). As suggested by Allegro[3] and Milik,[4] it is widely (but, I will try to show, wrongly) accepted that כב is an abbreviation for ככרין, 'talents'.[5] Accordingly, the scroll would list more than 3600 talents of silver, gold and unspecified material. The rest of the specified weights are relatively small, except the unknown value of 165 units עשתות זהב, 'unused gold bars'.

2. The various weights are: (1) ככר, 'talent' (sing.), once; ככרין, 'talents' (pl.), 14 times. (2) כב, 30 times, and a single כ once. (3) מנין עסרין, 'twenty minas' (12.9). מנין, the plural of מנה, 'mina', is 1/60 of a ככר. It is known from biblical, mishnaic, and other sources. (4) 100 עשתות זהב, '100 unused gold bars' (1.5-6); עשתות זהב ששין וחמש, 'sixty-five unused gold bars' (2.4). Cf. ביד זה עשתות של זהב, וביד זה פרוטרוט, 'in one person's hand there are gold bars, in the other's hand small change' (*y. Hor.* 3.7). עשתות is the plural of עשת, its weight is unknown. (5) שבע כדין אסתרין ארבע, 'seven pitchers (and) four staters' (9.2-3). אסתרין is the plural of 'stater', a Greek coin or weight about a quarter of a shekel. It is known from the Elephantine documents, and Talmudic-Midrashic literature.

3. Soon after the opening of the first of the two copper rolls (November 1956), Allegro suggested to G.L. Harding (Director of the Jordan Antiquities Department, the originator of the team that discovered the Copper Scroll on 20 March 1955) that כב may be an abbreviation for ככרין (Allegro, 'Provisional Translation'). See also J.M. Allegro, *The Treasure of the Copper Scroll* (London: Routledge & Kegan Paul, 1960), pp. 135-36 n. 8; J.M. Allegro, *The Treasure of the Copper Scroll* (Garden City, NY: Doubleday, 2nd rev. edn, 1964), p. 14. Allegro renders כב as 'talents' throughout.

4. M. Baillet, J.T. Milik and R. de Vaux, *Les 'petites grottes' de Qumrân* (DJDJ III; Oxford: Clarendon Press, 1962 [hereafter cited as DJDJ III]), pp. 221 A-4, 253 C-148, 315, col. 1.

5. E.g., B.-Z. Lurie, *Megillat hanNeḥošet mimMidbar Yehudah* (Jerusalem: Kiryath Sepher, 1963), pp. 79-80, 82-84, 86, 88-89, 91-92, 94-95, 97, 99-102, 108-10, 112-13, 116-17, 124; B. Pixner, 'Unravelling the Copper Scroll Code: A Study on the Topography of 3Q15', *RevQ* 11 (1983), pp. 323-65, plans i-iv (pp. 347-57); F. García Martínez, *The Dead Sea Scroll Translated: The Qumran Texts in English* (Leiden: E.J. Brill, 1994), pp. 461-63; K. Beyer, *Die aramäischen Texte vom Toten Meer: Ergänzungsband* (Göttingen: Vandenhoeck & Ruprecht, 1994), pp. 224-32; G. Vermes, *The Dead Sea Scroll in English* (Sheffield: Sheffield Academic Press, 4th edn, 1995), pp. 375-78; A. Wolters, *The Copper Scroll: Overview, Text and Translation* (Sheffield: Sheffield Academic Press, 1996), pp. 36-55; M.O. Wise, M. Abegg and E. Cook, *The Dead Sea Scrolls: A New Translation* (New York: HarperCollins, 1996), pp. 192-98.

Regarding content, students of the Copper Scroll can be placed into two groups: (1) those who consider it a work of fiction; and (2) those who consider it a genuine document.

Milik claimed that such enormous wealth must be imaginary. Allegro resolved this problem by equating the talent with the mina, thus reducing it to less than 2 per cent of its actual weight, which in turn devalues the treasure by more than 98 per cent. Lurie accomplished the same goal by equating the talent with the Roman pound. These simple solutions are unacceptable, since it is unrealistic to assume that compilers of a secret document would deliberately exaggerate its hidden treasure.[6]

Table 9.1. *The term* ככר(ין), *'talents(s)', in the Copper Scroll*

(1)			[כ]כר	[כ]סף ארבעין	1.14-15
(2)	KEN	שבעשרה	ככרין	שדת כסף וכליה משקל	1.3-4
(3)		71 מנין עסרין	ככרין	הכל משקל	12.9
(4)		שש מאות	ככרין	וכסף הכל	12.7
(5)		ששין ושנין	ככרין	כסף	10.6-7
(6)		שבעין	ככרין	וכסף	2.6
(7)		שלש מאות זהב	ככרין		10.10-11
(8)		22	ככרין		2.15
(9)		42	ככרין		12.3
(10)	HN	42	ככרין		2.2
(11)	ΔI	עסר	ככרין		2.9
(12)		ארבע מאות	ככרינ		7.7
(13)		תשע מאת	ככרין		1.8
(14)		שתימ	ככרינ	ככ 60 זהב	7.16
(15)		ששין	ככרין	זהב ככ 5	12.1

Notes:

a. In line 1.15 parts of the first *kaph* of ככ can be recognized in Allegro's drawing.

b. In line 10.7 the text reads כררין instead of ככרין.

c. In line 12.9 Allegro's drawing has כיכרין, with an extra *yod.*

6. Some scholars accept the face value of the treasure listed in the Copper Scroll; nevertheless, they consider it to be genuine; e.g. Pixner, 'Unravelling the Copper Scroll Code', pp. 339-40. J.E. Harper in his article, '26 Tons of Gold and 65 Tons of Silver', *BARev* 19 (1993), pp. 44-45, 70, by comparing the treasures of the ancient world, concludes that 4630 talents of precious metal could have been part of the Jerusalem Temple treasury.

Table 9.2. *The abbreviation* ככ *in the Copper Scroll*

							M^{dr}	B^{dr}	A^{dr}
(1)		13	ככ			3.13	Y	Y	Y
(2)		32	ככ			5.14	N	N	N
(3)		42	ככ			6.6	?	?	?
(4)		21	ככ			6.10	Y	Y	?
(5)		27	ככ			6.13	N	N	N
(6)		22	ככ			7.13	N	N	N
(7)		4	ככ			8.9	Y	Y	N
(8)		66	ככ			8.13	N	N	N
(9)		23.5	ככ			9.6	Y	Y	Y
(10)		22	ככ			9.9	Y	Y	Y
(11)		9	ככ			9.13	?	?	Y
(12)		9	ככ			10.2	N	N	?
(13)		12	ככ			10.4	N	N	N
(14)		80	ככ			10.14	?	?	Y
(15)		17	ככ			10.16	?	?	Y
(16)		40	ככ			11.08	?	?	?
(17)		מאתים	ככ		כספ	4.10	Y	Y	Y
(18)		שבעינ	ככ		כספ	4.12	Y	Y	Y
(19)		55	ככ		כסף	4.4-5	?	?	?
(20)		12	ככ		כספ	4.14	Y	Y	Y
(21)		7	ככ		כספ	5.4	N	N	N
(22)		23	ככ		כספ	5.11	N	N	N
(23)		70	ככ		כסף	8.16	N	N	?
(24)	TP	40	ככ		כספ	3.7	Y	Y	Y
(25)		60	ככ		וכסף	12.5	N	N	?
(26)		17	ככ	וזהב	כספ	8.6-7	N	N	N
(27)	זהב ככרינ שתימ	60	ככ			7.16	N	N	N
(28)	ככרין ששין	5	ככ	זהב		12.1	N	N	N
(29)			כ[כ...]			7.2			
(30)	ΣK		ככ[...]			4.2			

Notes:

a. This table is organized according to unspecified ככ (1-16), silver ככ (17-25), silver and gold ככ (26), ככ and ככרין in the same line (27-28), and ככ followed by a lacuna (29-30) that can be restored as ככרין.

b. The three columns on the right side indicates whether there was space for emendation according to the three published drawings.

c. Abbreviations: M^{dr} = Milik's drawing; B^{dr} = Baker's drawing; A^{dr} = Allegro's drawing; Y = yes; N = no; ? = questionable.

Those who consider the scroll genuine have various opinions as to whom this massive wealth belonged. Among the suggestions offered are the Qumran sectarians or Essenes, Zealots of Jerusalem, the assumed Temple of Bar Kokhba in Jerusalem, priestly shares collected after the destruction of the Temple, and the Temple itself.

The approach used in this study to resolve the critical problem of the validity of the Copper Scroll is careful comparative analysis of the three published drawings,[7] photographs,[8] as well as examination of the units of weight in light of biblical, talmudic and midrashic literature.

7. The three drawings are Baker's (DJDJ III, pl. xlv), Milik's (which is a corrected version of Baker's; DJDJ III, pls. xlviii, l, lii, liv, lvi, lviii, lx, lxii, lxiv, lxvi, lxviii, lxx), and Allegro's (*Treasure of the Copper Scroll* [1960], pp. 32, 34, 36, 38, 40, 42, 44, 46, 48, 50, 52, 54). The drawing segments in Lurie's work (*Megillat hanNeḥošet*, pp. 53, 59, etc.) are copies of Allegro's drawing. B. Zuckerman (University of South California), who with his brother made magnificent photographs of the Copper Scroll, plans to publish a new drawing (personal communication). Electricité de France reconstructed the Copper Scroll, and handed it over to Queen Nur of Jordan on 11 March 1997 (see *Journal Letter* no. 74 [January 1998]). The new drawings are to be published by É. Puech. In 1978, the late D.J. Wilmot (whose unfinished doctoral dissertation at the University of Chicago, entitled 'The Copper Scroll: An Economic Document of First Century Palestine', will be edited for publication by M.O. Wise) claimed that he was able to trace the published photographs of Milik, and made a new drawing (personal communication; see Lefkovits, Dissertation, I, pp. 84-86 n. 142). It should be noted that where the appearance of the three drawings are identical, it is almost certain that this is an accurate rendition of the scroll, and most probably the new drawings will be confirmatory. Where the drawings differ, the new drawings could be decisive in determining the most accurate rendition. However, where the questionable reading is at the edge of a cut or crack, due to the deterioration of the segments (cf. P.K. McCarter, 'The Mysterious Copper Scroll, Clues to Hidden Temple Treasure?', *BR* 8 (1992), pp. 34-41, 63-64), the new drawings and even the reconstruction of the scroll might not provide enough help. In such a case, one will have to rely exclusively on the original drawings and photographs. It is my opinion that greater accuracy of the drawings and readings could have been achieved had impressions been made (a) of the reverse side of the copper rolls after cleaning but prior to their being cut into segments; and (b) after cutting and cleaning the front side of each segment (cf. Lefkovits, Dissertation, I, pp. 10-11).

8. I obtained photographs of the Copper Scroll from two sources in 1978. (1) The Archaeological Museum of Amman (received through the courtesy of Professor F. Peters of New York University). These resemble the photographs published in *The Allegro Qumran Collection* (ed. G.J. Brooke; Leiden: E.J. Brill, 1996). (2) Photographs made from the original negatives of those published by Milik (DJDJ III, pls. xlix, li, liii, lv, lvii, lix, lxi, lxiii, lxv, lxvii, lxix, lxxi; received through the courtesy of

The vast wealth of the Jerusalem Temple is well known. The following establishes a strong link between the Temple and the Copper Scroll: (1) references to various כלי דמע, 'dedicated vessels', for Temple use, rather than vessels containing priestly shares; (2) references to חרם, 'consecrated', matter for Temple use; (3) references to hiding places, such as waterworks and burial sites, which were controlled by the Jerusalem Court;[9] (4) the use of copper sheets for engraving the text, probably motivated by the concept of ritual purity;[10] and (5) the scroll can be placed in the last decades of the Temple.[11] Probably the scroll lists movable objects of the Temple, hidden before its destruction by the Romans. These were possibly hidden by priests, and in Levitically impure places by Levites.

As noted, it is widely accepted that ככ is an abbreviation for ככרין, the plural of ככר, 'talent'.[12] This logical suggestion automatically increases the wealth mentioned in the scroll. For those who consider the document as fiction, this makes no difference. On the other hand, for those who accept it as genuine, this creates a major problem.

It is difficult to calculate the actual weight of a ככר. In biblical times there were several types of measurements, such as regular, sacred or sanctuary (e.g. Exod. 38.24-26), royal (2 Sam. 14.26) and merchant (Gen. 23.16).[13] While ככר, 'talent', occurs in the Masoretic Text and in the Targumim, it is rarely used in the talmudic–midrashic literature. In fact, it appears only once in the entire Mishnah (*m. Ter.* 8.6).[14]

Professor B.A. Levine, New York University, Mr M. Broshi, Curator of the Shrine of the Book, Jerusalem, and the late Pierre Benoit, École Biblique et Archéologique Française, Jerusalem).

9. *M. Šeq.* 1.1; *t. Šeq.* 1.2, 4-5. Also see Lefkovits, Dissertation, II, pp. 1222-23.

10. Cf. Lefkovits, Dissertation, II, pp. 1215-18.

11. F.M. Cross Jr, in his 'Excursus on the Palaeographical Dating of the Copper Document', DJDJ III, p. 217, dates the Copper Scroll between 25–75 CE.

12. It is also known from Ugaritic, Phoenician, Akkadian and so on. The term ככר has additional meanings, such as ככר לחם, 'loaf of bread' (Jer. 37.21), ככר הירדן, 'Plain of the Jordan' (Gen. 13.10).

13. Cf. 'Rabbi Haninah said, "Whenever silver (shekels) are mentioned, in the Pentateuch they are *sela's*, in the Prophets *litrae*, and in the Hagiographa *centenaria*, except the silver (shekels) of Ephron (Gen. 23.16)…which are *centenaria*"' (*b. Bek.* 50a; cf. *y. Qid.* 1.3 [9b]).

14. In the Palestinian Talmud ככר occurs only four times. See M. Kosovsky, *Concordance to the Talmud Yerushalmi (Palestinian Talmud)* (Jerusalem: The Israel Academy of Sciences and Humanities; The Jewish Theological Seminary of America, 1979–), IV, p. 599. ככר is neither mentioned in the Siphra, nor in the Mekhilta. In the Babylonian Talmud ככר is referred to: (a) in certain calculations connected with

Both Talmudim relate an interesting and relevant incident. In his response to mockery by a Roman notable regarding the calculation of מאת ככר, 'one hundred talents' (Exod. 38.24),[15] rather than the expected two hundred, Rabban Johanan ben Zaqqai replied that the sacred weights were twice the regular ones.[16] This story provides a most essential piece of information. It establishes that during the lifetime of this Tanna, who witnessed the destruction of the Temple, the sacred weights, especially the sacred ככר, were no longer known. This suggests that sanctuary weights ceased to exist by the end of the Temple era. Therefore, it is unlikely that the scroll refers to sanctuary ככר, although it may occur in the Dead Sea Scrolls (e.g. 4Q159).

The basic unit of weight is a shekel. There were שקל הדיוט, 'a common or regular shekel', and שקל קדש, 'a sacred or sanctuary shekel' (*Num. R.* 4.8). The Targumim and Talmudim equate the sacred shekel with סלע, *sela'*, and the Tyrian tetradrachm (Exod. 30.13; *m. Bek.* 8.7).

A regular ככר is equal to 3000 regular shekels or 1500 *sela'*s, or 60 regular minas.[17] Therefore, when attempting to calculate the value of a ככר, one must know the weight of a shekel.

Weiss[18] made detailed calculations of the ancient Jewish measurements and weights. His work is based on biblical and talmudical sources, on the opinions of the *gaonim* and *poseqim*,[19] as well on the Hasmonaean שקל ישראל, 'Israel shekel'. Weiss concludes that the sacred shekel is 14.2

commandments (e.g. *b. Bek.* 5a); (b) in connection with the Menorah (e.g. *b. Men.* 88b); and (c) as a hyperbolical expression (e.g. *b. Suk.* 51b). See H.J. Kasowski and B. Kasowski, *Ozar Leshon hatTalmud* (41 vols.; Jerusalem: The Ministry of Education and Culture, Government of Israel; The Jewish Theological Seminary of America, 1954–82), XVIII, pp. 223b-224a.

15. See the commentaries of Rashi, Rashbam, Ibn-Ezra and *Torah Temimah*.

16. *Y. Sanh.* 1.4 (7a). See the commentaries of *Pene Moshe* and *Mar'eh hapPanim*; *b. Bek.* 5a, and the commentaries of Rabbenu Gershom, Rashi and Tosaphot.

17. The difficult verse in Ezek. 45.12 indicates that the sacred mina (one-sixtieth of a talent) which previously consisted of 50 shekels (cf. the Canaanite system) was increased to 60 shekels (cf. the Mesopotamian system), i.e. an increase by one-sixth (see the Targum; also the commentaries of Rashi, Radak, *Mesudat David*, Malbim; *b. Bek.* 50a, and so on). Accordingly, a sacred talent consisted of 3600 sacred shekels. See also E. Stock, 'Weights and Measures', *EncJud*, XVI, cols. 381-85.

18. Y.G. Weiss, *Midoth uMishkaloth shel Torah (Torah Metrology)* (Brooklyn: Moznaim Publishing, 1984).

19. Rabbis whose rulings were accepted as the definitive Halakhah.

grams plus or minus one-tenth of a gram. Other scholars have arrived at somewhat different conclusions.[20]

Scribal Corrections

There is wide agreement among scholars that כב is an abbreviation for כבין. Yet is this assumption valid? Can it be substantiated? The dilemma concerning whether the Copper Scroll is a genuine document or not essentially depends on the interpretation of the amount of wealth recorded in it. A closer examination of the three published drawings and the photographs point to a number of scribal corrections that may help resolve these problems.

Item 56 (11.16–12.03), which is especially relevant to this discussion, is most difficult. It has both a small and large lacuna, scribal corrections, problems with words, phrase separations, and subdivisions.

(11.16) במבא דינ[רת] בית המשכב המערבי
(11.17) טיף על מן[...........ת]שע מאות
(12.1) זהב כב 5 כברין ששין ביאתו מן המ<ע>רב[21]
(12.2) תחת האבן השחורא כוזין תחת סף
(12.3) הכוך כברין 42

If in line 11.17 the entire lacuna belongs to the first part of that line, then תשע מאות refers to זהב (i.e. 'nine hundred gold [coins]'). If a part of the lacuna belongs to the second part of the line, the last missing word or phrase should define the meaning of תשע מאות (such as כסף, i.e. 'nine hundred silver [coins]'; כלין, i.e. 'nine hundred vessels'; כדין, i.e. 'nine hundred pitchers'; אמות, i.e. 'nine hundred cubits'), while 5 כברין ששין זהב כב is a separate phrase.

As the three drawings show, line 12.1 contains seven letters squeezed in between כב and ביאתו. The letters רי and שש are about half size; the two final *nuns* nearly have a regular shape, while the second *yod* is of

20. E.g. A. Ben-David ('The Hebrew–Phoenician Cubit', *PEQ* 110 [1978], pp. 27-28) weighed 940 Tyrian tetradrachmae and their average was 14.01 g. According to H.P. Benish (*Middot weShi'ure Torah* [Bene Beraq, 1986–87], pp. 423-24, 431, 433-34, 439-40, 444), the sacred weights were in biblical times: shekel 14.16 g, mina 708 g, talent 42.5 kg; and after the increase in the Second Temple era: shekel 17 g, mina 850 g, talent 51 kg. The regular weights were half of these amounts.

21. The last phrase without emendation can be read as ביאתו מן הכרכ (= ביאתו מן הכרך), 'its (masc.) entrance is from the city'.

normal size.[22] Apparently, the scribe originally wrote זהב ככ 5 ככ, left a space of five square letters, then continued with ביאחו. This is not surprising, since elsewhere there are wide spaces between words (cf. 12.9). Later, judging from the shape of the letters, a different scribe corrected the text by squeezing in seven letters plus leaving two spaces for word separation.

Accordingly, the text before correction had [...ח]שע מאות זהב ככ 5 ככ. If ככ is an abbreviation for ככרין, then the scribe could have simply added only ששין in full-sized letters, and the text would read without any noticeable correction as [...ח]שע מאות זהב ככ 5 ככ ששין. Therefore, there must have been a good reason why the scribe inserted the additional three letters, and why he felt compelled to squeeze so many letters into such a narrow space.

The term ככרין occurs 14 times in the scroll (see Table 9.3). Close examination of the drawings and photographs reveals that the original scribes wrote ככ seven times, which were later corrected to ככרין; and once a כ, which was corrected erroneously into כררין instead of ככרין. In three or four cases additional information was also added. In two cases one cannot conclude whether there is a correction or not. There are only four cases in the three drawings where no corrections can be detected.

Close study of the script indicates that more than one scribe engraved the original text.[23] To maintain secrecy, probably scribes with limited Hebrew knowledge were employed. Moreover, the corrections suggest that כ or ככ were intentionally written instead of ככרין, so that the scribes should be unaware of the exact amount. Later, presumably a more trust-worthy person added essential information. All corrections have final *nun*s, either because they need less space than regular ones, or it was revised by a more knowledgeable 'editor'. One may even go a step further and assume that the original text had only כ or ככ. Later, where it was necessary, it was corrected to ככרין.

It can still be claimed that ככ is the same as ככרין and that the text has been corrected only at those places where the 'editor' found room for emendations. However, an examination of the occurrences of ככ indicates that at least in seven cases there is enough room to add or squeeze in the three letters רין (see Table 9.2). Therefore, the text was corrected only where ככ had to be altered into ככרין.

22. This *yod* has an unusual shape in Milik's drawing.

23. This was already realized by Allegro in his 'Provisional Translation and Notes of the Copper Scroll'.

Table 9.3. *According to the drawings of the Copper Scroll: (1) is there a scribal emendation regarding* ככרין*?; (2) can* ככר(ין) *be read as* בכד(ין)*, 'in pitcher(s)'?*

	Was the text corrected?			Corrected reading	Original reading	Can be read as בכדין?		
	M^{dr}	B^{dr}	A^{dr}			M^{dr}	B^{dr}	A^{dr}
1.4	Y	Y	Y	ככרין	ככ	N	N	?
1.8	N	N	?		ככרין ?	Y	Y	Y
2.2	N	N	N		ככרין	Y	Y	Y
2.6	Y	Y	Y	ככרין	ככ	Y	Y	Y
2.9	N	N	N		ככרין	Y	Y	Y
2.15	Y	Y	N		ככרין ?	Y	Y	Y
7.7	N	N	N		ככרינ	Y	Y	Y
7.16	N	N	N		ככרינ	Y	Y	Y
10.7	Y	Y	Y	כררין ששין ושנין	כ	N	N	N
10.10	Y	Y	Y	ככרין	ככ	N	?	N
12.1	Y	Y	Y	ככרין ששין	ככ	?	?	Y
12.3	Y	Y	Y	ככרין	ככ	?	?	?
12.7	Y	Y	Y	ככרין שש מאות	ככ	N	N	N
12.9	Y	Y	Y	ככרין ... מנין עסרין	ככ	N	N	N

Notes:

a. In line 10.7 the corrected text reads כררין instead of ככרין.

b. In line 12.9 Allegro's drawing has כיכרין, with an extra *yod*.

c. The phrase, [כ]סף ארבעין [ב]כר can be read as [כ]סף ארבעין [ב]כד, 'forty silver (pieces) in a pitcher' (1.14-15).

d. Abbreviations: M^{dr} = Milik's drawing; B^{dr}= Baker's drawing; A^{dr} = Allegro's drawing; Y = yes; N = no; ? = questionable.

Those who disagree with this view may argue that it is easier to use numerical symbols than to write out numbers, yet the scribes used both forms seemingly indiscriminately. Likewise, it could be argued that the scribes used ככ and ככרין indiscriminately. However, the fact that some ככs were corrected into ככרין and not others, indicates that these terms are not interchangeable. Therefore, one may conclude that ככ is definitely not an abbreviation for ככרין.

ככר is the largest weight mentioned in the Masoretic Text, and perhaps in the entire rabbinic literature. In addition, the terms ככרין and ככ are used in the scroll in parallel fashion. These two facts demonstrate that ככ is a weight but less than a ככר.

The Aramaic Elephantine documents mention various weights, such as שקל, the Persian כרש (equal to ten shekels), רבע, 'quarter (of a shekel)', and חלר, *hallur* (one-tenth of a רבע). Often these weights are represented by their initials, ש, כ, ר and ח. Likewise, כסף שקל, 'silver shekel', is abbreviated as כש. Moreover, the numerical symbols are practically identical with those used in the Copper Scroll. E.g., כסף כרשן 31 שקלן 8...כ 12 ש 6...כרשן 7 כסף...כרשן 12 'silver 31 karsh 8 shekel …12 k(arsh) 6 sh(ekels)…7 karsh silver…12 karsh';[24] כסף שקל 2, '2 silver shekels' (Cowley, 22, 1.1-3), versus 2 כש, '2 s(ilver) sh(ekels)' (Cowley, 22, 4.59-80); כסף כרשן 10 באבני מלכא כסף ר 2 לכרש, 'silver karsh 10 in royal weight, silver 2 q(uarters) to one karsh';[25] תמסא 1 זי נחש דמי כסף שקל 1 ח 10 ...כס [1 דמי]ן כסף חלרן 20, '1 bronze bowl which valued (in) silver at 1 shekel (and) 10 h(allurs)…[1] cup [valued] (in) silver at 20 hallurs' (Kraeling 7.13-14).[26]

Some of these abbreviations and numerical symbols also occur among the Murabba'at texts. One of them (9, frag. 3) is a list of six lines. Each line starts with a כ for כרש, karsh, rather than כסף,[27] and followed by a numeral, then a ר for רבע.[28]

2	מ	8	ר	ו	כ	(1)
		1	ר	..4	כ	(2)
		1	ר	1	כ	(3)
		..4	ר	4	כ	(4)
	2	…1	ר	5	כ	(5)
		5	[ר]	5	כ	(6)

24. A.E. Cowley, *Aramaic Papyri of the Fifth Century B.C.* (Oxford: Oxford University Press, 1923), 22, 7.120-23 (= Cowley).

25. E. Kraeling, *The Brooklyn Museum Aramaic Papyri* (New York: Arno Press, 1969), 4.20-21 (= Kraeling).

26. An Aramaic customs account from Egypt frequently uses the term כרש(ן). In addition, the genre of this account is very similar to that of the Copper Scroll. See A. Yardeni, 'Maritime Trade and Royal Accountancy in an Erased Customs Account from 475 BCE on the Ahiqar Scroll from Elephantine', *BASOR* 293 (1994), pp. 67-78; B. Porten and A. Yardeni, *Textbook of Aramaic Documents from Ancient Egypt* (4 vols.; Jerusalem: The Hebrew University, 1986–99), III, pp. xx-xxi.

27. Although the כ is explained as 'tetradrachm', it is compared to כרש of the Elephantine documents. See P. Benoit, J.T. Milik and R. de Vaux, *Les grottes de Murabba'at—Texte* (DJD II; Oxford: Clarendon Press, 1961), p. 90.

28. For clarification the lines are represented in columnar form. In the first line the *waw* after the *kaph* may indicate its numerical value 'six'; מ is the abbreviation of מעה, *ma'ah* or מעא, *ma'a'*, a small weight or coin, one-twenty-fourth of a סלע, *sela'* (e.g. *m. 'Erub.* 7.11; *Targ. 1 Sam.* 2.36).

Similarly, a Phoenician inscription from Lapethos, Cyprus (c. 275 BCE) contains the phrase, בכ[ס]ף משקל כר 100 ו 2. Donner and Röllig suggest that כר may be an abbreviation for the Persian weight כרש. Accordingly, it means, ‘in si[lv]er a weight of 100 and 2 kar(sh)’.[29]

A Suggested New Meaning for ככ

In light of the aforementioned discussion, it is reasonable to propose that ככ is an abbreviation for כסף כרש(ין), ‘silver karsh’, like כש for כסף שקל, ‘silver shekel’, in the Elephantine documents. One karsh is 10 shekels, about 71 g. Since a talent consists of 3000 shekels, it is equivalent to 300 karsh. Based on the above, ככ represents a mere fraction of a talent.

The 30 cases of ככ, the most frequently used term in the scroll, can be classified into four groups: 16 cases of unspecified ככ; 9 cases of כסף ככ; 1 case each of 3 phrases that differ; and 2 cases are followed by a lacuna (see Table 9.2).

One may assume that where ככ is unspecified, it refers to כסף כרשין, ‘silver karsh’. In those cases where the word כסף precedes ככ, though one of the *kaph*s seems to be redundant (i.e. כסף כסף כרשין), it means the same, literally, ‘silver silver karsh’. Similarly, in the Elephantine documents occasionally כסף is repeated practically in the same phrase. For example, כל כספא ודמי נכסיא כסף כסף שקלן 7 חלרן 7 פלג, ‘all the silver and the value of the goods are (in) silver: silver 7 shekels, 7 (and) half hallurs’ (Kraeling 2, verso 6-7).

The case ככ 60 זהב ככרין שתים, could mean כסף כרשין 60 זהב ככרין שתים, ‘60 silver karsh, (and) 2 talents of gold’ (7.16).

In Item 56 discussed above, [...ת]שע מאות זהב ככ 5 ככרין ששין would read [...ת]שע מאות זהב כסף כרשין 5 ככרין ששין. If the entire lacuna belongs to the previous phrase, it means, ‘[…, n]ine hundred gold (coins), 5 s(ilver) k(arsh), sixty (unspecified) talents’. If a part of the lacuna refers to [...ת]שע מאות then it can be translated as ‘nine hundred (something), 5 k(arsh) of gold (and) 60 (unspecified) talents’ or ‘nine hundred (something), 5 k(arsh) (and) 60 talents of gold’.

Regarding the phrase כספ וזהב ככ 17, it should be noted that ו– and או are interchangeable, and both could mean ‘and’, as well as ‘or’.[30] Thus this

29. H. Donner and W. Röllig, *Kanaanäische und aramäische Inschriften* (3 vols.; Wiesbaden: Otto Harrassowitz, 1966), No. 43, I, p. 10; II, p. 62.

30. The prefixed ו– often means או in biblical and Mishnaic Hebrew, as well as in the Targumim. Although usually unrecognized, או could mean ו–; cf. או אז...ואז...,

phrase could mean '17 karsh of silver and gold' or '17 karsh of silver or gold' (8.6-7). This may suggest either that the deposit was a mix of silver and gold, or that the compilers did not know whether this cache contained silver or gold.[31] Though it is unlikely, it is also possible to render 17 כספ וזהב ככ as 'one silver (piece) and 17 karsh of gold'.

Perhaps originally ככ was meant to be used for כסף כרש(י)ן, while later it was also used instead of כרש(י)ן by itself. This may be the reason why כסף (in nine cases), as well as זהב (in one or two cases) precede ככ.

The Abbreviation כ

The second half of line 11.7 reads הו חרם followed by a *beth* or *kaph*. After this letter the three drawings differ. Baker's has an almost horizontal line plus a vertical line; Milik's has only an almost horizontal line; and Allegro's has only a straight horizontal line. Milik and Allegro suggest that the letter is a *beth*, and it is a dittography, while Lurie indicates that something is missing.

This letter can be read as a *kaph*, and the horizontal line may be the upper part of an unfinished *kaph*, while Baker's vertical line is the numeral 1. Thus Baker's drawing would read 1 הו חרם ככ (= 1 הוא חרם ככ), '1 karsh of consecrated silver'. Based on the drawings of Milik and Allegro, the numeral after ככ is missing, perhaps a scribal error, and the reading would be הו חרם ככ with a missing numeral. Accordingly, this might be an additional case of ככ in the scroll.

On the other hand, the horizontal line after the *kaph* could be the upper part of an unfinished numeral 10 (cf. the numeral 10 in line 12.9), while Baker's drawing has an additional numeral 1. The single כ could be an abbreviation for כרש. Thus the drawings can be read as follows. Baker: 11 הו חרם כ (i.e. 11 הוא חרם כרש), '11 karsh of consecrated matter'; Milik and Allegro: 10 הו חרם כ (i.e. 10 הוא חרם כרש), '10 karsh of consecrated matter'.[32]

and in Targum Onkelos, ... או בכן ... ובכן, which can be rendered as 'and then…and then…' (Lev. 26.41).

31. This is similar to the phrase בו כלי דמע או דמע סות, 'in it (there are) dedicated vessels and/or dedicated garment(s)' (11.10). See Lefkovits, Dissertation, II, pp. 827, 833-35, 1130-31 (*The Copper Scroll*, pp. 384, 391, 538, 541).

32. There are other Hebrew inscriptions having the abbreviation כ. E.g., an inscription from c. seventh–sixth century BCE, in which every undamaged line except one out of 18 lines, carries a personal name followed by a כ then by a numeral of 3, 4,

These suggestions are similar to the original reading of a single כ, which was later corrected into כרריןששין ושנין (instead of ככרין ששין ושנין, 'sixty-two talents', 10.7). This further supports the concept of scribal corrections. Apparently the 'editor' overlooked emending this item, or perhaps he had no time to correct the entire text. In either case, these could be reasons why so many errors are present in the scroll. Nevertheless, it is likely that the scroll uses a single *kaph* as an abbreviation for karsh.

The above discussion establishes the fact that the scribes of the Elephantine documents (fifth century BCE), the Phoenician inscription, the Copper Scroll and the Murabba'at texts (first–second century CE), which extend across a time interval of five hundred years, all used abbreviations and numerical symbols in a comparable fashion.

On the other hand, one can reasonably ask how the abbreviation of כרש, which is unknown in the entire Hebrew literature, comes to appear in the Copper Scroll.[33] In response, it should be noted that the scroll does contain sets of Greek letters and unusual words.[34] ככ may be another example of a unique element of this document.

The Estimated Weight of the Listed Substances

Table 9.4 shows the estimated weight, in talents, listed in the Copper Scroll according to various scholars. Table 9.5 is based on my revised suggested reading of the text of the Copper Scroll. These calculations assume the following: (1) the weights mentioned are common or regular, rather than sanctuary (which is twice as much); (2) the weight of עשת (*'esehet*) is equated with talent;[35] (3) כ is an abbreviation for כרש (karsh);

5, 7 or 8; such as, 4 בן שחר לאחקם כ, 'son of Shahar for Ahiqam *k* 4'; 3 יועליהו בן עבדיהו כ, 'Yo'aliyahu the son of 'Obadyahu *k* 3' (No. [79]4, recto lines 8-9). See R. Deutsch and M. Heltzer, *New Epigraphic Evidence from the Biblical Period* (Tel-Aviv–Jaffa: Archaeological Center Publication, 1995), pp. 92-102. Although it has been suggested that כ is an abbreviation for כסף, it may well be an abbreviation of כרש.

33. Essentially this question was raised at the *International Symposium on the Copper Scroll* by Dr H. Eshel (Bar-Ilan University).

34. E.g. האסטאנ (11.2), ואפרות, ואפורין or ואפורת (1.9), טיף (11.7), הפרסטלון or הפרסטלין (1.7), בשלף (8.10).

35. Although the actual weight of עשת is unknown, one may assume that it might have been equal to ככר (talent). Based on traditional explanation, Rashi comments on Num. 8.4 that the Menorah of the Tabernacle was beaten out from עשת של ככר זהב, 'one gold mass of talent'.

(4) both ככ and כסף ככ refer to (יו) כסף כרש (silver karsh); (5) a specified amount of silver without a specified weight is considered as regular silver shekel; and (6) the minimal weight of four unspecified *staters* is disregarded.

Table 9.4. *Estimated weight of the listed substances according to various scholars*

Material	Milik	Allegro	Allegro 2nd edn	Lurie	Pixner
Silver[a]	2286	3282	3179	3282	—
Unspecified[b]	2040	—	—	—	—
Gold	307	1280	385	1280	—
Totals[c]	4633	4562	3564	4562	4500

a. Allegro, *Treasure of the Copper Scroll*, pp. 58-59, 135-36 n. 8; Allegro, *Treasure of the Copper Scroll* (1964), p. 42, includes in 'silver' mixed gold and silver plus unspecified material.

b. Milik considers unspecified material as a mixture of silver and gold (see his table in DJDJ III, p. 282.

c. Pixner, 'Unravelling the Copper Scroll Code', pp. 339-40, accepts the total sum of c. 4500 talents of silver and gold.

Table 9.5. *Estimated weight of the listed substances according to Lefkovits*

Material	Talent	'Eshet	Mina	Karsh	Shekel	Kg	Per cent
Gold	302	165	—	—	900	9954	16.7
Silver	789	—	—	1059	—	16881	28.2
Unspecified	1547	—	20	10	—	32959	55.1
Totals	2638	165	20	1069	900	59794	100.0

It is reasonable to assume that unspecified matter is silver, although it may be copper or other metal. Given this possibility, the total listed wealth of the Copper Scroll would be reduced even further. According to the last table, the suggested total weight listed in the scroll is less than 60 tons of precious metal.

In addition, ככר in line 1.15 can be read alternately as בכד (with a *dalet*, rather than a *resh*), 'in a pitcher'. Likewise, several times ככרין, 'talents', can be read as בכדין, 'in pitchers', especially in those cases where there are no scribal corrections (see Table 9.3). Indeed, Allegro in line 7.16, and Beyer in line 10.7, read בכדין, 'in pitchers'. This suggestion further drastically reduces the total weight listed in the Copper Scroll.

Finally, it is possible to read the two letters ככ as כב, בכ and בב. Although these letter combinations are seemingly meaningless, they may refer to an object. Indeed, some Aramaic and even Hebrew words may come close to such options.[36]

Conclusion

In summary, this study strongly challenges the accepted view that ככ is an abbreviation for ככר(ין). It establishes the following.

1. The original text, which was written by more than one scribe, was corrected by other scribes, who often amended the original כ or ככ into ככרין.
2. ככ is clearly not an abbreviation for ככרין, 'talents'.
3. ככ most likely is an abbreviation for כסף כרש(ין), 'silver karsh', or just כרש(ין). Karsh, a Persian weight equal to 10 shekels, is a minute part of a talent of 3000 shekels.

The conclusion of this study that ככ is only a mere fraction of a talent has very important ramifications. Many scholars cannot accept the Copper Scroll as a genuine document on account of the presumably massive wealth recorded in it. The official announcement at the opening and preliminary reading of the scroll refers to 200 tons of gold and silver. This study revises that exaggerated amount to less than 60 tons of precious metal, of which only less than 17 per cent is gold, the rest being silver and unspecified metal that could be copper or other metals. The aforementioned new interpretation strongly supports the view of those who accept the Copper Scroll as a valid historical document. If this is the case, then the status of the Copper Scroll among the Dead Sea Scrolls should significantly increase.

36. For further discussion, see my book, pp. 485-88.

10

The Copper Scroll and Language Issues

John Lübbe

J.T. Milik's principal edition of the Copper Scroll appeared in 1962, some ten years after the discovery of the scroll and six years after its contents had been exposed at the University of Manchester. Milik's work appeared in the third volume of the series Discoveries in the Judaean Desert of Jordan, which was reviewed by Jonas Greenfield in 1969.[1] Milik's work on the Copper Scroll received some harsh criticism. Unimpressed by numerous lexical identifications and semantic solutions, Greenfield was very critical of Milik's general treatment of the language of the text, language which Milik labelled as 'Mishnaic'. In his review Greenfield called for a more sophisticated use of reference sources:

> What actually is the nature of Mishnaic Hebrew? Or better—which Mishnaic Hebrew is Milik talking about? One has the feeling that the reference is to Mishnaic Hebrew as described by M.H. Segal in the English edition of his book (Oxford, 1962) rather than the Hebrew edition (Jerusalem, 1936) which was an advance over it.[2]

In response to Milik's assertion that this is the Mishnaic dialect of the Jordan valley, Greenfield urges caution until more evidence is presented:

> It is the beginning of wisdom to wait until all the so-called 'Mishnaic' texts from Qumran cave 4 and the whole Bar Koseba archive are published before making any sweeping statements about the language of 3Q15 or its place in the history of Mishnaic Hebrew.[3]

1. J.C. Greenfield, 'The Small Caves of Qumran', *JAOS* 89 (1969), pp. 128-41.
2. Greenfield, 'Small Caves of Qumran', p. 137.
3. Greenfield, 'Small Caves of Qumran', pp. 137-38.

Since that time scant attention has been paid to the Copper Scroll. This has apparently been due to the difficulty in interpreting details of its content and explaining the scroll's significance for other issues of a historical sort concerning the history of the site at Qumran, the occupants thereof and the identity of figures mentioned in the scrolls. Recently, general interest in the Copper Scroll has been revived, largely perhaps because it has been used as a vital piece of evidence in Norman Golb's rejection of the traditional view that Qumran was probably occupied by an Essene sect and that the scrolls found in 11 of the surrounding caves were hidden there by the sect shortly before the fall of Jerusalem in 70 CE. Part of Golb's argument concerns the general content of the Copper Scroll, for he would assign the huge treasure listed therein to the Jerusalem Temple rather than to the sect that supposedly occupied Qumran. Golb's arguments are by no means lightweight and the various issues he raises are presented with considerable bibliographical data. Golb's use of the linguistic character of the Copper Scroll is therefore somewhat surprising.

Golb's comments regarding the language of 3Q15 are made in connection with his response to Strugnell and Qimron's suggestion that another composition, 4QMMT, was a letter to the high priest in Jerusalem. Golb not only rejects their suggestion, but also Cross's palaeographic dating of the script of one of the copies of 4QMMT to between 50–25 BCE. Golb recalls that Milik had characterized the language of 4QMMT as 'Mishnaic' and Golb reasons as follows:

> The importance of Milik's observations about the idiom of the *Acts of Torah* [i.e. Golb's name for 4QMMT] resided in the necessary implication that the work was written during the early or middle first century AD, before which no evidence could be found for the existence of such an idiom. Indeed Milik had made use of passages from the *Acts of Torah* to elucidate his discussion of a first-century AD documentary work composed in the same idiom—the *Copper Scroll*. The only other manuscripts written in essentially the same form of Hebrew were the early second century AD Bar Kokhba documentary texts... Milik's description of the nature of the work's idiom in effect clashed with an assertion by his own colleague Cross, who had written, in his study of the palaeography of the Qumran texts, that the handwriting characteristic of one of the *Acts* manuscripts showed that the text had been copied between 50 and 25 BC—unimaginably early for a text verging on early rabbinic idiom.[4]

4. N. Golb, *Who Wrote the Dead Sea Scrolls? The Search for the Secret of Qumran* (New York: Charles Scribner's Sons; London: Michael O'Mara Books, 1995), p. 183.

Although Golb's monograph is replete with bibliographical data, there is little or no evidence in the bibliographical references for the chapters concerning the two scrolls (the one copy of MMT and 3Q15) that indicate that his comment above was adequately informed by the most recent linguistic analyses of the Hebrew language and of the dialects identified in the Dead Sea Scrolls.

In the years separating Greenfield's castigation of Milik's treatment of the Mishnaic nature of the Copper Scroll and the appearance of Golb's monograph, many valuable studies of aspects of the Hebrew language and diachronic descriptions of its development have been published, including diachronic descriptions of Mishnaic Hebrew. Among these publications, the work of E.Y. Kutscher on various linguistic aspects has been seminal, as the recent monograph of A. Saenz-Badillos, *A History of the Hebrew Language*, demonstrates.[5] According to the historical surveys of Hebrew scholarship provided by these two writers,[6] it was due to a lack of evidence that medieval Jewish scholars viewed Mishnaic Hebrew as a corruption of biblical Hebrew. When diachronic descriptions of languages became the accepted linguistic method, A. Geiger described Mishnaic Hebrew as an artificial language created by the rabbis for their religious debates. At the turn of this century M. Segal refuted Geiger's view, which had become widely accepted. Segal argued that Mishnaic Hebrew was a development of biblical Hebrew. The discovery of the Bar Kochba letters brought clarity to the debate by demonstrating that Mishnaic Hebrew had indeed been used as a means of daily communication and was not a mere creation by the rabbis. Evidence has also been presented that is best understood as traces of linguistic developments that stem from earlier phases and dialects, which therefore indicate that forms of Mishnaic Hebrew were probably spoken for generations before they appeared in any written form.[7] Mishnaic Hebrew should not, therefore, be thought of as an extension of biblical Hebrew, but as stemming from a distinct, early dialect.

5. E.Y. Kutscher, 'Hebrew Language', *EncJud*, Supplementary Series 16, cols. 1560-1607; A. Saenz-Badillos, *A History of the Hebrew Language* (trans. John Elwolde; Cambridge: Cambridge University Press, 1993).

6. Kutscher, 'Hebrew Language', cols. 1592-93; Saenz-Badillos, *History of the Hebrew Language*, pp. 161-78.

7. See S. Morag, 'Qumran Hebrew: Some Typlogical Observations', *VT* 38 (1988), pp. 148-64.

Clearly, then, Golb's objection to a BCE dating of the language of the Copper Scroll is an oversimplification of the possible dating of this language. This is not to imply a justification of Cross's dating of a copy of 4QMMT on palaeographic grounds, nor to imply a defence of any particular view of the Copper Scroll (or of MMT). It is rather to assert that the reasoning of Golb on this issue is simplistic, perhaps because it is so tendentious. For Golb seems determined to deny the validity of what he calls 'the traditional Essene theory' and so adduces whatever linguistic evidence suits his case. The most significant aspect of Golb's error is that Golb's argument is purely linear in its basic conception of language development. Unfortunately, such is the main tendency among scholars working with classical languages. The paucity of linguistic evidence for an ancient language as compared to the mass of evidence of a modern, spoken language and the unconscious influence upon philologists of what is a fashionable treatment of an ancient language, combine in this instance to mislead. For it has long been the habit of classical scholarship to search for origins and in the field of languages diachronic descriptions are the order of the day. Thus earlier and later phases of language are mapped in such a way as to represent the developments of that language as though the developments form a segmented, yet continuous straight line, stretching from the earlier to the later phases. Even where this model is modified it is usually by means of straight lines. Thus if the diachronic development of language is portrayed, say, by a vertical line, the synchronic evidence is frequently presented in such a way as to segment that vertical line by means of intersecting horizontal lines. Such portrayals serve a very limited purpose.

Just as earlier generations of scholars were obliged to change their conclusions and, more importantly, their approach to Mishnaic Hebrew per se, it seems that the time has arrived for a more realistic treatment of the language of the Copper Scroll. For since Golb has challenged the view that the Copper Scroll was written by sectarians living at Qumran and has insisted that the language of this scroll cannot antedate the common era, publications have appeared that weigh bits of linguistic evidence and then slide the Copper Scroll along a chronological line, first sliding it closer to one set of texts and then moving it closer to another. Thus a simple comparison was conducted by Al Wolters to determine the proximity of the language of the Copper Scroll to biblical Hebrew on the one hand and Mishnaic Hebrew on the other—a chronological implication being obvious.[8] Having accepted certain lexical items that Milik had, in Wolters's opinion, correctly identified as Mishnaic, Wolters expanded the list from 30 words to 50 by recognizing 10 more lexical items identified by other scholars and another 10 based on his (Wolters's) personal decipherment of the scroll and in some instances his own semantics. Although he acknowledges that the decipherment of 3Q15 is plagued with uncertainty and that the items that he has personally identified and interpreted may prove unconvincing, Wolters claims that his list of 'lexical Mishnaisms' boosts by 26 per cent the list compiled by Qimron of words attested in the Dead Sea Scrolls and Tannaitic and Amoraic literature.[9] This figure is not unimportant, but its significance would be clearer if the vocabulary of the Copper Scroll were also measured with other orientations, for example, as to how many words occur in this scroll and some other source and not in the Mishnah. Wolters sets out in this article to test Milik's description of the language of 3Q15 as 'Mishnaic' and concludes on the basis of simple arithmetic that Milik was correct. When the language of a source is to be identified, it is not identified on the basis of correspondences alone, but also on the basis of distinctions, that is, correspondences and distinctions between the same sources. Furthermore, although Wolters acknowledges that lexical evidence alone cannot decide the precise identity of the language of 3Q15—that is, as to whether it is 'a separate species of Hebrew which is like MH but distinct from it'[10]—he fails to comment on the unusual composition of the text of 3Q15 and that by its very nature an inventory, with its stereotyped phraseology, will be limited for comparative purposes. Thus one would be expecting too much of an inventory that it should yield many of the other signs that the Hebrew of the Dead Sea Scrolls was drifting toward Mishnaic Hebrew. Thus it would be hoping for too much to find that infinitives absolute are being replaced by finite verbs and that there is an increasing use of a form of היה plus a participle. In short, a more complex description of the nature of the document 3Q15 will also tone down the significance of Wolters's statement 'that the Copper Scroll will continue to be the Qumran document with the clear-

8. A. Wolters, 'The Copper Scroll and the Vocabulary of Mishnaic Hebrew', *RevQ* 14 (1990), pp. 483-95.

9. Wolters, 'The Copper Scroll', p. 494.

10. Wolters, 'The Copper Scroll', p. 495.

est affinity of MH'.[11] Viewed against the background of the linguistic drift that is evident in other Dead Sea Scrolls, 3Q15 is not that linguistically unusual given its nature, in contrast to the nature of the other scrolls. For if the view is correct that the biblical and sectarian scrolls from Qumran were written in a Hebrew that was supposed artificially to continue Late Biblical Hebrew, then the use of a form of the vernacular for this secular document may be expected to yield a crop of different lexical items and meanings.

Underlying Wolters's reasoning appears to be the same simplistic model that apparently underlies Golb's fallacious assertion, and such linguistic conclusions are often subsequently used as evidence to bolster a non-linguistic hypothesis regarding the origin and purpose of a document. For the sake of more satisfying linguistic results another model of language should be kept in mind that will not so easily tempt the researcher to draw simplistic conclusions. While the linear conception of a diachronic description is not entirely untrue, it must be remembered that the diachrony of a language is actually composed of a series of synchronic descriptions. Furthermore, languages are now perceived in modern linguistics to be ever-changing systems of communication. The recognition of these changes has given rise to areas of specialization including that of dialectology. The term 'dialect' refers to a variety of language, and within this variety are numerous varieties of that same language that are peculiar to individual speakers, that is, within dialects there are ideolects. Thus a language or phase thereof should not only be thought of in terms of a straight line, but also in terms of a series of concentric circles with overlapping circumferences, so reflecting the extent of usage of that language and the possible influence one variety might have on the others. Such a model is not merely a cross-section of a particular period of the development of a language, but is rather to be understood as representing what is taking place all the time as that language is used by individuals and by communities at different social levels, in different locations. In the light of such complexity, much more evidence will be required before the position of the Copper Scroll and its relationship to other forms and phases of Mishnaic Hebrew can be meaningfully stated. Simplistic comparisons of the sort referred to above are then actually of little use and may rather be misleading because they lack linguistic sophistication.

11. Wolters, 'The Copper Scroll', p. 495.

Muchowski's comparison of the various constructions and vocabulary used in phrases denoting direction is more sophisticated and therefore more satisfactory.[12] Muchowski examined 300 such phrases in the Hebrew and Aramaic sources of Qumran, the Bar Kochba correspondence and the Mishnah. By basing the comparison on such a variety of texts and syntactic constructions, the conclusions drawn will surely paint a more realistic picture of divergences and similarities, allowing a clearer view of the language of the Copper Scroll. But Muchowski also tries to take the evidence too far and thus not only appears to contradict himself, but also betrays an oversimplification of distinctions in language. After tabulating and briefly discussing six categories of differently formulated phrases in 3Q15 that are used to denote direction, Muchowski is able to conclude that 3Q15 differs from the Mishnah in three respects, namely that it uses constructions without a preposition, that it uses the verb צפה rather than פתח of the Mishnah, and that it differs in the manner in which it denotes intermediate direction.[13]

In two places Muchowski also points to differences between the constructions of the Copper Scroll and those of the Bar Kochba correspondence. These two instances concern the same sets of expression in which an expected preposition does not occur. In fact in a parallel set of these expressions in 3Q15 the preposition does occur. Thus 3Q15 has both sorts of constructions with and without the preposition. To conclude that the expressions with the preposition reflect a literary style and those without reflect the spoken language requires elaboration, to say the least. Why should the use of the preposition be a more elevated or formal register of language? What are the characteristics of this register of language for the first century CE if this is the only evidence, or almost the only evidence, for this period? Two other aspects further complicate this issue. If Muchowski is correct that the author tried to standardize the sibilant,[14] alternating between *samekh* and *sin* and that he tried to standardize the final 'e' and 'a' vowels, alternating between

12. P. Muchowski, 'Language of the Copper Scroll in the Light of the Phrases Denoting the Directions of the World', in M.O. Wise, N. Golb, J.J. Collins and D.G. Pardee (eds.), *Methods of Investigation of the Dead Sea Scrolls and the Khirbet Qumran Site: Present Realities and Future Prospects* (Annals of the New York Academy of Sciences, 722; New York: New York Academy of Sciences, 1994), pp. 319-27.

13. Muchowski, 'Language of the Copper Scroll', p. 325.

14. Muchowski, 'Language of the Copper Scroll', p. 320 n. 9.

he and *aleph*, only to drop the process in favour of 'a more phonetic orthography, with which he was probably more familiar', then it seems that the author was not meticulous. Given the attitude of the author and the nature of the document as an inventory, how much should we safely suppose we may discover regarding distinctions between formal literary registers as opposed to informal? In his conclusion Muchowski states that he does 'not suppose that Essenes used only one specific variety of Mishnaic vernacular'[15] and that particular structures in 3Q15 and forms of words 'make the hypothesis plausible that M3Q15 was the spoken language of the Essenes'.[16] Such assertions conflict with the notion of a literary register of language. Too much is being deduced from too little, and given the complexity outlined above of the varieties of language in the form of dialect and ideolect and the paucity of available sources, how can such precision regarding levels of language usage be so facilely assigned? A more sophisticated model of language must inform and restrain scholars in their treatment of language issues pertaining to the Copper Scroll.

15. Muchowski, 'Language of the Copper Scroll', p. 326.
16. Muchowski, 'Language of the Copper Scroll', p. 326.

11

*Kelei Dema*ʻ: Tithe Jars, Scroll Jars and Cookie Jars

Stephen J. Pfann

Introduction

Since the discovery of the Dead Sea Scrolls during the winter of 1947, both caves and jars have been associated with their finding. Due to the fact that a number of the scrolls from Qumran Cave 1 were found in or with jars, it was assumed, and has continued to be so, that the scrolls of the first cave, as well as those of all subsequent caves, were stored in jars. Due to the fact that these specially manufactured jars were hitherto unknown in the history of ancient ceramics, it was further assumed that all such jars had been designed for the long- or short-term storage of scrolls. This paper will examine these two assumptions and will offer new options for understanding the nature of the jars in light of the evidence from the caves of Qumran.

The jars from Cave 1 numbered at least 50 and were found together with nearly as many lids (see Fig. 11.1).[1] In general the jars shared a similarity in form. Most of them were cylindrical in profile with straight to slightly bowed sides, had a footed base, pronounced shoulders, vertical rims, and generally lacked vertical loop handles (see Fig. 11.2). It was soon suggested by R. de Vaux, excavator of the cave, that all the jars of the cave had been intended for storing scrolls.[2] It was inevitable that the term

1. Cf. M. Baillet, J.T. Milik and R. de Vaux, *Les 'petites grottes' de Qumrân* (DJDJ III; Oxford: Clarendon Press, 1962 [hereafter DJDJ III]). Figs. 11.4, 11.5, 11.7 and 11.8 were drawn by the author. The rest of the figures are derived primarily from DJD I, DJDJ III and DJD VI.

2. R. de Vaux, 'La grotte des manuscrits Hébreux', *RB* 56 (1949), pp. 586-609 (593). During the following years, as jars appeared in other archaeological contexts, de Vaux limited his suggestion to the jars similar to the shorter one published by E.L. Sukenik; cf. n. 16.

'scroll jar' would become the favoured term in informal discussions for all such jars found in the Qumran caves, since one of the jars from Qumran Cave 1 was reported to have contained several of the more complete scrolls and since ancient literature mentioned instances of scrolls being stored in jars. Care was given in scholarly publications to avoid the use of the term, but the popular use of 'scroll jar' grew steadily.[3]

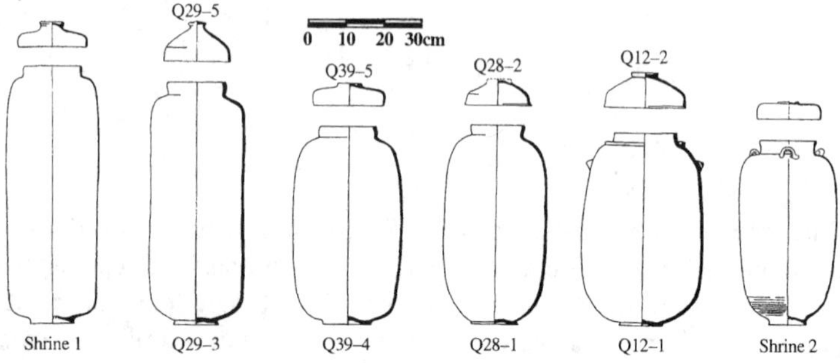

Fig. 11.1. *Jars with lids from the caves*

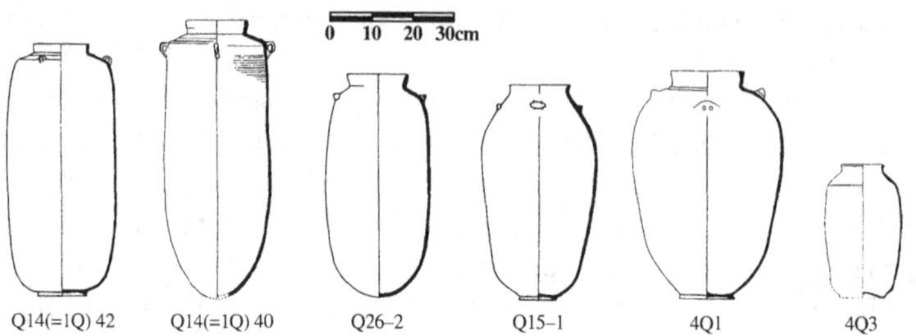

Fig. 11.2. *Miscellaneous jars from the caves*

3. The excavator himself, Roland de Vaux, was, as a rule, careful to avoid the term 'scroll jar' and used the terms 'jarre' or 'jarre cylindrique' instead; cf., e.g., DJDJ III, p. 13, figs. 2-3, and R. de Vaux, J.-B. Humbert and A. Chambon, *Fouilles de Kh. Qumrân et de Äin Feshkha* (NTOA, 1; Freiburg: Universitätsverlag; Göttingen: Vandenhoeck & Ruprecht, 1994), pp. 292-368.

Based upon the fact that somewhat similar jars from the Hellenistic period containing papyrus manuscripts had been found at Deir el-Medineh in Egypt, it was posited that the jars from Qumran were designed specifically for storing scrolls.[4] The term ‘scroll jar’ appeared in print as early as 1950 and its continued popularity among scholars is demonstrated as recently as 1998 in certain technical articles.[5]

Date and Provenance

Before the excavation of the site of Khirbet Qumran, ceramics experts tentatively dated the jars to the late Second Temple period based upon their association with other objects from Cave 1, such as scrolls or lamps, which could be more securely dated on palaeographic or typological grounds. It was during de Vaux’s first season of excavation at Khirbet Qumran that this dating was irrefutably confirmed, when a complete exemplar of this type of vessel was located embedded up to its collar in the floor of locus no. 2, in close association with coins from the early first century CE (cf. Fig. 11.3 below, KhQ 17). At least 19 examples were found at Khirbet Qumran itself.[6] In the subsequent excavations of Qumran and its nearby caves, numerous jars and lids were discovered.[7]

4. J.T. Milik, ‘Le giarre dei manoscritti della grotta del Mar Morto e dell’ Egitto Tolemaic’, *Bib* 31 (1950), pp 304-308, pl. III; reiterated in J.M. Allegro, *The Dead Sea Scrolls: A Reappraisal* (Harmondsworth: Penguin Books, 1964), pp. 86-89.

5. Y. Patrich uses the two terms ‘scroll jars’ and ‘cylindrical jars’ without distinction; cf. ‘Khirbet Qumran in Light of New Archaeological Explorations in the Qumran Caves’, in M.O. Wise, N. Golb, J.J. Collins and D.G. Pardee (eds.), *Methods of Investigation of the Dead Sea Scrolls and the Khirbet Qumran Site: Present Realities and Future Prospects* (Annals of the New York Academy of Sciences, 722; New York: New York Academy of Sciences, 1994), pp. 73-95 (76, 90). However, more recently J. Magness has utilized the term ‘scroll jars’ (but without the quotation marks) in preference to de Vaux’s term ‘cylindrical jars’; see ‘Qumran Archaeology: Past Perspectives and Future Prospects’, in P.W. Flint and J.C. VanderKam (eds.), *The Dead Sea Scrolls after Fifty Years: A Comprehensive Assessment* (2 vols.; Leiden: E.J. Brill, 1998), I, pp. 47-77 (60).

6. In locus 2 (object nos. 24, 40), locus 13 (nos. 758, 764, 768), locus 17 (no. 939), locus 44 (no. 917), locus 45 (nos. 799, 908), locus 61 (no. 1474), locus 81 (nos. 1490, 1492), locus 120 (no. 2661A), locus 124 (no. 2661C), locus 126 (nos. 2198, 2199), and the southern trench (nos. 2493, 2504, 2548). Cf. de Vaux *et al.*, *Fouilles de Kh. Qumrân*, pp. 292, 297, 308, 312, 330-32.

7. Approximately 156 jars and 76 lids were found in the caves; DJDJ III, pp. 13-15.

Jars from Qumran with Lids

Several factors, including (1) the abundance of the jars, (2) their unique form, (3) their general similarity in appearance, (4) their presence only at Khirbet Qumran and in the nearby caves, and (5) the presence of jar fragments in the site's pottery kiln, led to an initial conclusion that the jars had been manufactured at the site of Khirbet Qumran itself.

However, other factors must be considered. Although there are general features that unite the corpus of jars as a unique pottery form, there is also a remarkable diversity of features within the corpus. De Vaux listed 11 jar types and 23 lid types deduced from the numerous jars found during the cave survey of March 1952.[8] The additional jar types found in scroll Caves 1, 4, 7-8 and 11 must be added to de Vaux's initial typology.

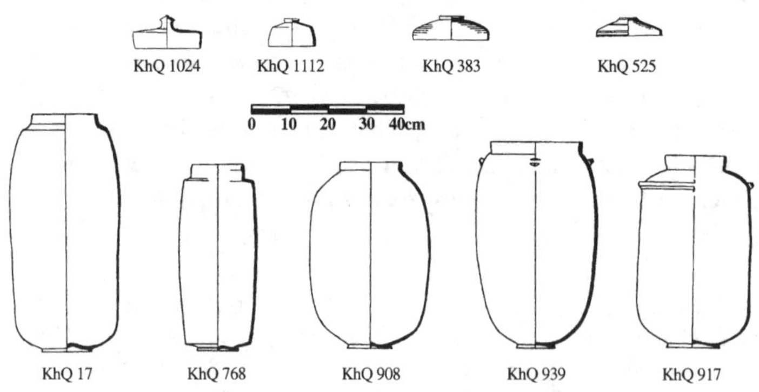

Fig. 11.3. *Jars from Khirbet Qumran*

8. DJDJ III, pp. 13-15. Although de Vaux counts 13 jar types found in the cave survey, only Types 1–11 are significant for this discussion. The distinctions between certain of the forms are not as clear-cut as with others. For example, Types 1–5, 7 and 8 are very similar and might actually form a more loosely described, general type of the cylindrical jar, characteristic of the majority of the jars. This general type, as noted above, has straight to slightly bowed vertical sides, a footed base, pronounced shoulders, vertical rims and the absence of handles. The remaining types (i.e. Types 4 and 9–11), present significant divergences in form. Handles, whether pierced or small loop, are more typical of these more unusual types. (Although there are also examples from the majority type that have such handles [cf. D. Barthélemy and J.T. Milik, *Qumran Cave 1* (DJD I; Oxford: Clarendon Press, 1955), fig. 2.12; E.L. Sukenik, *The Dead Sea Scrolls of the Hebrew University* (Jerusalem: Magnes Press, 1955), fig. 6.2; M.O. Wise *et al.*, *Methods of Investigation*, frontispiece]).

One should also not discount the suggestion that there was a wider distribution of the jars than the limited sphere of Qumran and its surrounding caves alone. Other sites from which examples of such jars have been published are Jericho (Tulul el-’Alayiq),[9] Tel el-Ful,[10] Quailba[11] and likely other sites in, or on the periphery of, the Judaean wilderness.[12] The lids that are generally associated with these jars have been identified among the ceramics from Jerusalem,[13] Ramat Rachel,[14] Bethany[15] and Beth Zur.[16]

The practice of storing documents in jars was not limited to Qumran. There are several references in ancient literature to scrolls that were stored or hidden in jars. A Greek Psalms scroll found in a jar ‘near Jericho’ was used by Origen for one of the columns of the Psalms in his Hexapla.[17]

The world of archaeology beyond the land of Israel has also provided a few examples of scrolls or codices sealed in jars. The Nag Hammadi

9. P. Lapp, *Palestinian Pottery Chronology* (New Haven: American Schools of Oriental Research, 1961), p. 154; R. Bar Nathan, ‘The Ceramics of Jericho’ (unpublished MA thesis, Hebrew University of Jerusalem; Hebrew), pp. 39-40, pl. 17; Magness, ‘Qumran Archaeology’, p. 41; cf. J.L. Kelso and D.C. Baramki, *Excavations at New Testament Jericho and Khirbet en-Nitla* (AASOR, 29-30; New Haven: ASOR, 1955), p. 123.

10. Lapp, *Palestinian Pottery Chronology*, p. 154.

11. Located near Abila in northern Jordan; cf. Lapp, *Palestinian Pottery Chronology*, p. 229 n. 53. Cf. also de Vaux, *Archaeology and the Dead Sea Scrolls* (The Schweich Lectures; London: Oxford University Press, 1973), p. 54, no. 1; F.S. Ma’ayeh, *Annual of the Department of Antiquities of Jordan*, IV–V (Amman: Jordanian Department of Antiquities, 1960), p. 116, and *RB* 68 (1960), p. 229.

12. At least ten sites are listed in the Copper Scroll as containing ‘tithe jars’ (see below).

13. Cf. C.N. Johns, ‘The Citadel, Jerusalem: A Summary of Work since 1934’, *Quarterly of the Department of Antiquities in Palestine* 14 (1950), pp. 144-45, fig. 41.3 (cited in de Vaux, DJD I, p. 10 n. 1), and B. Bagatti and J.T. Milik, *Gli Scavi del ‘Dominus flevit’*. I. *La necropoli del Periodo Romano* (Jerusalem: Franciscan Press, 1958), p. 137, fig. 32, 24-26 (cited in DJDJ III, p. 14 n. 5).

14. Cf. M. Stekelis, ‘Une Grotte funéraire juive à Ramath Rachel’ [Hebrew], *Qovetz* (Jewish Palestine Exploration Society) (1934–35), p. 28, fig. 4, no. 10 (cited in de Vaux, DJD I, p. 10 n. 2).

15. Cf. S. Saller, ‘Excavations in the Ancient Town of Bethany’, *Liber Annuus Studii Biblici Franciscani* 2 (Jerusalem: Franciscan Press, 1951–52), p. 136, fig. 12.5 (cited in de Vaux, DJD I, p. 10 n. 3).

16. Lapp, *Palestinian Pottery Chronology*, p. 181; cf. *BASOR* 150 (1958), p. 19.

17. R. de Vaux, ‘La grotte des manuscrits Hébreux’, *RB* 56 (1949), p. 592 n. 2.

Codices were hidden in jars secreted in the clefts of the rocks.[18] Two jars for which details have been published came from the Ptolemaic Period at Deir el-Medineh in Egypt.[19] At 39 cm in height, both were considerably shorter than the forms from the Qumran caves. One was found covered by a bowl (Suppl. 6121) and the other was covered by a plate; both 'lids' were affixed to the jars' handles with straps (cf. Fig. 11.4). They contained numerous papyrus scrolls written in Demotic and Greek, dating between 171 and 104 BCE.

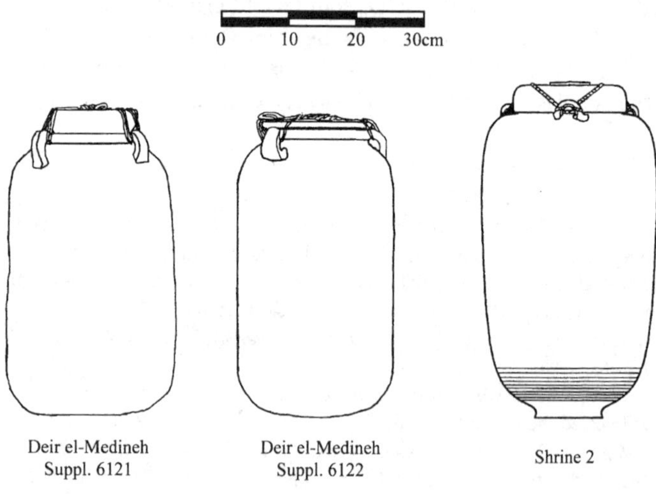

Fig. 11.4. *Deir el-Medineh jars and jar from Cave 1 with fastened lids* (author's drawing)

Although he dismissed the suggestion that most of the cylindrical jars were made for storing scrolls, nonetheless R. de Vaux posited that certain of the shorter jars with loop handles, similar to those from Deir el-Medineh, may have been manufactured for this purpose.[20] On the basis of

18. J.M. Robinson (ed.), *The Facsimile Edition of the Nag Hammadi Codices* (Leiden: E.J. Brill, 1984), p. 5.

19. See n. 4 above.

20. DJD I, p. 9. In particular, he mentions the shorter jar purchased for the Hebrew University by E.L. Sukenik (cf. Sukenik, *Dead Sea Scrolls*, p. 16). Just the same, if this is true, it is curious that the cylindrical jars that were found in the area of the

the foregoing, we would expect that if any of the Qumran jars had been manufactured specifically to contain scrolls, the following characteristics would have been required:

1. An interior height sufficient to cover the tallest scrolls, that is, c. 40 cm (but not much more than that).
2. Diminutive loop or pierced handles, with holes only large enough for affixing the lid (as in the case of the Deir el-Medineh jars).[21]

Statistics on 'Scroll Jars' from Qumran

The only cave in which scrolls can be said with any certainty to have been stored in these jars is Cave 1. At least three of the more-or-less complete scrolls were found in one jar, according to the report of the Bedouin.[22] In addition, it is apparent on the basis of wear patterns, that at least some of them, including 1QS, 1QpHab and 1QM, were protected in jars.[23] How-

scriptorium (loci 1-14, 30) were, for the most part, the tall, slender type, lacking handles (objects 27, 758, 764, 768). No cylindrical jars with small loop handles were catalogued from any area of the site. However, pierced ledge handles were otherwise most prevalent there (present on 12 of 20 jars catalogued).

21. As in the case of Qumran scroll Caves 1 (survey Cave 14), nos. 40, 42 (DJD I, fig. 2.10, 12) and Shrine of the Book No. 2 (Sukenik, *Dead Sea Scrolls*); 4Q1 (R. de Vaux and J.T. Milik, *Qumrân grotte 4.II* [DJD VI; Oxford: Clarendon Press, 1977], fig. 5.2), 7Q5 and 7Q6 (DJDJ III, figs. 6.12 and 5; pl. VIII); 8Q14 (fig. 6.7), and from survey caves: 12-1 (DJDJ III, pl. VI, fig. 3.11), 15-1 (DJDJ III, pl. VI, fig. 3.10); 26-2 (J.A. Sanders, *The Psalms Scroll of Qumran Cave 11 (11QPs^a)* [DJDJ IV; Oxford: Clarendon Press, 1965], pl. V, fig. 3.10). The examples from Qumran Cave 1 have diminutive loop handles while the others have horizontal pierced handles.

22. J.T. Milik, *Ten Years of Discovery in the Wilderness of Judaea* (London: SCM Press, 1959), p. 12.

23. The wavy wear patterns along the bottom or upper edges of these scrolls reveal the pressure points where the rolled document, which stood at a tilt, touched the bottom and side of the jar, leaving damage on one point on the bottom edge and one point on the top edge. The wear patterns of the Cave 11 manuscripts in many ways resemble those of Cave 1, which may indicate that at least some of the Cave 11 manuscripts were stored in the cave standing upright, probably in jars, and leaning diagonally against the jar's side. These include 11QpaleoLev, 11QEzek, 11QPs^a and 11QShirShab. However, only one small jar and two jars lids are published as having derived from this cave, which was first rifled by Bedouin; cf. R. de Vaux, 'Fouilles de Khirbet Qumrân: Rapport preliminaire des 3e, 4e, et 5e campagnes', *RB* 63 (1956), pp. 531-77 (573-74), É. Puech, 'Notes en marge de 11Qpaléolévitique: le Fragment L, des Fragments inédits, et une jarre de la Grotte 11', *RB* 96 (1989), pp. 161-89.

ever, it is likewise apparent that most of the more than 70 manuscripts from Cave 1 had not been protected within jars, as indicated by the bat guano that covered most of them as they lay strewn on the floor of the cave. Thus, it would seem that few of the numerous jars, which are known to derive from Qumran Cave 1, held scrolls at the time of their discovery.[24]

During the excavation of Cave 3, 35 jars (both complete and fragmentary) and 26 lids were recovered. However, none of the 15 manuscripts excavated (including the Copper Scroll) were found in jars.[25] Caves 4a and 4b, which yielded the most abundant manuscript evidence, contained only one complete jar and fragments of only three others (with three typical lids).[26]

In other caves, in which the jars were abundant, no manuscripts were at all evident. This includes Survey Cave 29, which yielded 13 jars and 16 lids, and Survey Cave 39, with 10 jars and 9 lids.[27]

The first exemplar of a 'scroll jar' found *in situ* at Khirbet Qumran was found embedded in the floor up to its collar—hardly a logical place for the safe storage of scrolls.[28] In at least two other cases (loci 13 and 34), there were jars set in the ground with their bottoms broken out.[29] Thus, although the jars were known to contain scrolls in certain cases (namely, certain of those from Cave 1 and possibly Cave 11), it is apparent that these jars were also used for other purposes.

Jar Size

The so-called 'scroll jars' from the Qumran Caves range between 46.5 cm (DJDJ III, fig. 2.4) and 75.5 cm (DJDJ III, fig. 2.1) in interior height. Of the more than 150 jars estimated by de Vaux as having derived from the caves of Qumran, only 47 have been registered. Twenty-three of these are complete.[30]

24. DJD I, pp. 8-10, figs. 2-3; DJDJ III, p. 14.

25. DJDJ III, p. 8, figs. 2-4.

26. DJD VI, p. 17, fig. 5.

27. DJDJ III, pp. 11-12, figs. 2-4.

28. De Vaux, 'Fouille au Khirbet Qumrân', *RB* 60 (1953), pp. 530-61; de Vaux *et al.*, *Fouilles de Kh. Qumrân*, p. 292.

29. De Vaux *et al.*, *Fouilles de Kh. Qumrân*, p. 297.

30. This number increases to 25 with the inclusion of the two jars of Allegro. However, measurements for those jars are unavailable. The statistics presented here are based upon the measurements of the 23 complete jars from the caves that have been published to date (cf. DJD I, DJDJ III and DJD VI, and Sukenik, *Dead Sea Scrolls*, figs. 4 and 6), and those of the six complete jars from Khirbet Qumran (cf. *RB* 60

The jars, as a rule, are far too tall and wide to have been purposely designed to house scrolls, as Table 11.1 illustrates.[31] As can be seen from the table, the Thanksgiving Scroll (1QH^{a}) was the tallest. Yet even this, the tallest of the scrolls from the caves of Qumran (c. 36.5 cm, cut from a cowhide), is dwarfed by the shortest jar of this type from the caves (46.5 cm; a difference of 10 cm, or more than one-fourth the height of the scroll).[32] Shrine 2, the one jar from the Qumran caves that most closely approximates the form and size of the noted manuscript jars from Egypt, would have had the capacity to contain all seven scrolls from Cave 1, with

[1953], fig. 2.4, and ‘Fouilles au Khirbet Qumrân’, *RB* 61 [1954], pp. 206-36, figs. 5.3, 4, 7, 9). Other jars which have been published in photos but without dimensions include the following: (a) A jar, very similar to Shrine 2, from the collection of the Oriental Institute of the University of Chicago. A color photo is given as a frontispiece in Wise *et al.*, *Methods of Investigation*. This is one of the few existing jars that has survived with its lid. (b) A second jar excavated by Y. Patrich from a cave situated between Qumran Caves 11 and 3; cf. Patrich, ‘Khirbet Qumran’, pp. 73-95 and fig. 7 (NB: The designation ‘Cave 24’ should not be confused with the cave of the 1952 survey bearing the same number).

31. The heights are approximated for scrolls whose upper or lower portions have deteriorated. The approximate diameters are calculated by first measuring the length or perimeter of the last turn of the wound scrolls. That measurement (which is equal to the scroll’s outer perimeter) is taken from the widest distance found between recurring wear patterns at the end of the scroll (perimeter/circumference = $\pi\partial$ [diameter]).

The height of scrolls seems to be limited by the size of herd animals. Personal microscopic examination of the hair follicle patterns of numerous sheets from the scrolls of Qumran reveals that skins were normally made from hides of flock animals that had been dehaired and split lengthwise down the back to form two separate sheets. Occasionally, in exceptional cases, the hide was cut crossways from side to side, as is borne out through hair follicle analysis of manuscripts such as 4QEn^{g}. When smaller, pocket-sized scrolls were made, numerous sheets could be cut, lengthwise or widthwise, from a single hide. Cf. S. Pfann, ‘298. 4QcryptA Words of the Maskil to All Sons of Dawn’, in T. Elgvin and others, in consultation with J.A. Fitzmyer, *Qumran Cave 4.XV: Sapiential Texts, Part 1* (DJD XX; Oxford: Clarendon Press, 1997), pp. 2-5, figs. 1-3.

The examination of the direction, size and shape of the hair follicles that cover the upper surface of the fragmentary scrolls has also proven to be a valuable tool for (a) identifying the proper placement of fragments over the area of a given sheet and (b) identifying the type of herd animal from which the sheet has derived.

32. The width of a sheep or goat skin (divided into two rectangular sheets) would not exceed 30 cm in height. In excess of that, it could be assumed that the source animal was bovine, as in the case of 1QH^{a}, confirmed recently by examination of the hair follicles and by DNA analysis.

Table 11.1. *Scroll heights and widths in centimetres*

Scroll	*Height*	*Width*
1QS	24.1	5.1
1QIsa[a]	26.2	7.9
1QapGen	31.0	5.5
1QH[a]	c. 36.5	6.4
1QIsa[b]	c. 33.5	5.4
1QM	c. 26–29	5.3
11QpaleoLev	29.5	—
4QpaleoEx[m]	32.0	—
4QNum[b]	c. 30.0	—

room to spare. Needless to say, other jars that are taller and wider, particularly at the base, would dwarf even the tallest scrolls. The unsuitability of the large cylindrical jars is illustrated in Fig. 11.5 in jar Q8(3Q)-7, where even medium-sized scrolls would have toppled and lain in a pile with other scrolls at the bottom of the jar.[33] For contrast, each of the seven

33. Although a single jar could conceivably have held all seven scrolls, it is still possible that each of the scrolls was stored in its own jar, or even that a number of jars held a number of scrolls.

A corollary of the assumption that the scrolls were stored in specially made jars was the assumption that they were stored in these jars rolled on sticks, in which case there might have been justification for using taller jars for storing scrolls. However, in general in antiquity, libraries stored scrolls on shelves, often within 'cubby-holes'. The use of sticks as spools for scrolls was not a common practice in the Roman period. Rather, evidence to the contrary can be provided. Of the 12 scrolls which survived in a rolled state (some of which were in jars in Cave 1), none were preserved with a stick. These scrolls were 1QIsa[a], 1QIsa[b], 1QpHab, 11QT[a], 11QpaleoLev[a], 11QPs[a], 11QShir-Shab, 11QtgJob, 11QapPs (where the end of the scroll was tightly bound to form a spool), 11QNJ, 11QEzek and 4QXII[g] (cf. PAM 41.964). The damage patterns on the lower edge of several of the scrolls from Cave 1 indicate that they stood erect on the bottom edge of the scroll (again confirming that there was no spool in use). A wavy damage pattern along the bottom edge indicates that the pressure along the edge was uneven. In these cases, the scroll seems to have been leaning diagonally with the top resting against the jar's side (cf. the damage pattern at the top of 1QS which lay against the side). Nor were any such sticks preserved in the caves, despite the fact that many scrolls, textiles and leather straps survived. On the panel from the second-century CE Dura Europos synagogue, 'Ezra reads the Law', the scroll is depicted without a stick. See A.R. Bellinger, F.E. Brown, A. Perkins and C.B. Welles, *The Excavations at Dura-Europos: Final Report VIII, Part I* (New Haven: Yale University Press, 1956), pl. LXXVII. The earliest example of scrolls mounted on sticks or spools dates from the

scrolls has been positioned in Shrine 2 in this illustration to reflect the actual orientation and contact points of each scroll in the jar based on the damage patterns evident on the scroll itself.

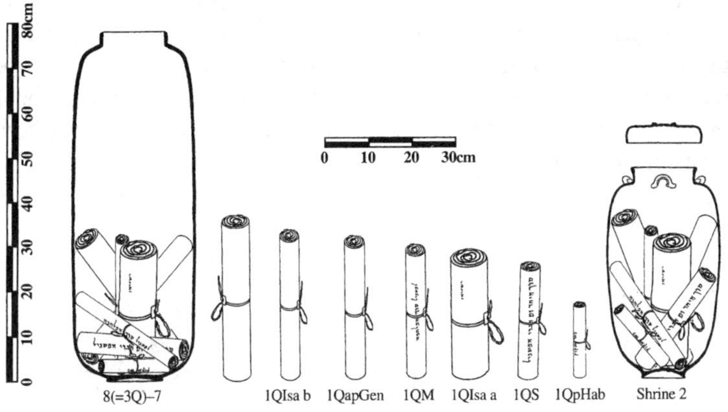

Fig. 11.5. *Comparison of jar capacities and the various sizes of scrolls from Qumran's Cave 1* (author's drawing)

Given the small percentage of scrolls that had actually been stored in jars, the presence of jars set into the ground at Khirbet Qumran for purposes other than scroll storage, and the discrepancy in height and width between the jars and the scrolls, I would suggest that scroll storage was not the intended use of the vast majority of these jars. What then was their intended use at the time of their manufacture?

The Original Purpose of the Jars

A significant clue as to the intended use of these jars lies in one example from Qumran Cave 3 (= Survey Cave 8). Jar no. 10 had the letter *ṭet* incised into the neck and shoulder before it was fired, indicating that it was manufactured to be a tithe vessel (see Fig. 11.6).

Byzantine Period (from the charred scrolls found in the synagogue at Ein Gedi, though again, not found in jars). In *The New Encyclopedia of Archaeological Excavations in the Holy Land* (ed. E. Stern; 4 vols.; Jerusalem: Israel Exploration Society, 1993), II, p. 408, D. Barag dates the end of stratum III A, i.e., the charred remains of the Torah niche, to the mid-fifth century CE.

The practice of inscribing letters onto jars set aside for priestly tithes and offerings is described in the Tannaitic literature. Compare, for instance, *M. Ma'as. Š.* 4.11: 'If a vessel was found on which was written a *qof*, it is *Qorban*; if a *mem*, it is *Ma'aser*; if a *dalet*, it is *Demai*; if a *ṭet*, it is *Ṭevel*; if a *taw*, it is *Terumah.*'[34] The use of the names or letters was to distinguish jars related to the tithe for various uses. The practice of placing a *taw* or *ṭet* on the shoulders of standard storage jars to indicate that its contents were either for the *terumah* (priestly tithe from produce) or *ṭevel* is attested at Masada on standard storage jars that otherwise bear no distinctive features.[35]

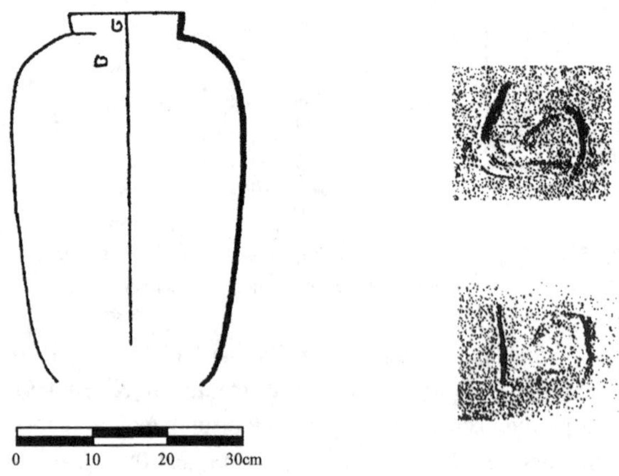

Fig. 11.6. *Jar inscribed with the letter* 'ṭet' (= 'tevel') *from Qumran Cave 3*

34. The text goes on to explain that the reason for using only letters for these terms (i.e. instead of spelling out the entire word) was in order to avoid persecution for practising Jewish law. That is, during times of oppression, the letters could be explained as representing the initials of individuals, as opposed to being connected in some way with religious practice. (Nevertheless, normally the ownership of vessels was signified by complete names and not initials.) *M. Ma'as. Š.* 4.11 continues: 'For in the time of danger people wrote *taw* for *Terumah.* R. Jose says: They may all stand for the names of men.' It is possible that the jars from Cave 7 with the word רומא may actually bear an abbreviated form of the word תרומא rather than the unlikely designation 'Roma'.

35. Cf. Y. Yadin and J. Naveh, *Masada I: The Aramaic and Hebrew Ostraca and Jar Inscriptions* (Jerusalem: Israel Exploration Society; Hebrew University of Jerusalem, 1989), pl. 26.

Fig. 11.7. *Jars inscribed with the letters* ‘ṭet’ (= ‘tevel’) *and* ‘taw’ (= ‘terumah’) *from Masada* (author’s drawing)

Fig. 11.8. *‘Priestly tithe’ inscribed on a jar fragment from Masada* (author’s drawing)

At Qumran, the system was less complex. The inclusive phrase כלי דמע was used to designate the jars used for the general *terumah*. The distinctive and rather uniform shape of the tithe jars from Qumran would have rendered the *taw* mark of *terumah* unnecessary as a distinguishing feature. The only instances where a mark would have been of use were those in which the jar was intended for another, more specific purpose, for example, to contain food products that were *ṭevel*, as in the case of Jar no. 10 from Cave 3.[36]

In order to ensure the purity of a jar and its contents for priestly consumption at a standard acceptable to the Qumran community, special jars

36. *Ṭevel* (טתבל) designates produce from which the priestly and Levitical dues have not been set aside. Cf. *b. Ber*. 35b: ‘The *ṭevel* is not subject to tithes, until it is brought home (for consumption or storage).’

and lids were made that would be designated solely for priestly tithes. Jars were manufactured that were large enough to contain at least one, two, or three *seah*s of produce (approximately 15, 30 or 45 litres, respectively).[37] The jars were generally made without loop handles. They were carried in the arms, hugged close to the chest (cf., e.g., Fig. 11.9, showing John Allegro clutching such a jar). This method of carrying was intended to protect the jar against possible nicking or breakage, which would render it and its contents halakhically unclean and unfit for priestly use or consumption.

Fig. 11.9. *John Allegro with a scroll jar*

The mouths of these jars were sufficiently wide to allow the filling and extraction of dry produce with measuring cups (perhaps of stone), without nicking the rim or spilling the contents. Lids that were wide enough to enclose the rim needed to be affixed to the jar in order to prevent impure items from falling in. In many specimens, the lid was tied down to two or three pierced ledge handles on the jar's shoulders. The lids were also made of kiln-hardened clay so that the jar could be opened and closed numerous times without the risk of disintegration (as would happen with the more commonly used and smaller clay jar stoppers).

37. For the volume of the *ephah* based upon the volume of inscribed jars from Qumran, see Milik, 'Appendice: Deux jarres inscrites provenant d'une grotte de Qumrân', in DJDJ III, pp. 37-41.

Subsequent Use of Tithe Jars

The possibility of a subsequent use of the jars for commodities other than the tithe (such as scrolls) is noted in *M. Ma‘as. Š.* 4.11:

> Even if a jar was found which was full of produce and on it was written ‘*Terumah*’, it may yet be considered common produce, because I may assume that last year it was full of produce of heave-offering and was afterward emptied.

This helps to explain why jars that were originally produced to contain priestly tithes might subsequently be buried in the floor or used to carry scrolls. Halakhic purity, necessary for their original function of containing tithes, rendered them likewise suitable for transporting or hiding sacred scrolls (in particular those containing the Divine Name), as long as the purity of the jars was preserved.

Evidence from the Copper Scroll

The term כלי דמע is mentioned several times in the Copper Scroll. דמע is found alone in 3Q15 1.10 and 4QHalakah frag. 5, line 3. The phrase כלי דמע, designating tithes of herbs and wood, occurs in 3Q15 1.9; 3.9; 8.3; 11.1, 4 (2×), 10 (2×), 14 (2×) and, designating vessels that were wrought of silver and gold, in 3Q15 3.3; 12.7. The collective phrase כלי דמע is found in 3Q15 5.7. In the Copper Scroll כלי דמע evidently refers, then, to a specific form of jar associated with the collecting and storing of goods associated with priestly portions.

Dema‘ in other Jewish sources designates tithes in general. In rabbinic literature the terms *terumah* and *dema‘* are used interchangeably. Cf. *Yal. Exod.* 351: ‘*Terumah* has three names: *reshit* (ראשית), *terumah* (תרומא), and *dema‘* (דמע).’ *Bet dema‘* (בית דמע) designates a place in a barn set aside for the *terumah*.

In the Copper Scroll, no scrolls were listed as being hidden with these jars. The single scroll mentioned in the Copper Scroll as being hidden within a jar is hidden in a קלל (3Q15 6.4-5), not in a כלי דמע. In references where tithe jars are mentioned along with their contents, they are said to contain products subject to the tithe (generally herbs; cf. 3Q15 11.1, 4 [2×], 10 [2×] and 14 [2×]). Even when the contents are not explicitly mentioned, the contents, or the jars themselves, are implied as being part of the tithe (3Q15 1.9-10; 5.6-7).[38] This is also the case where gold or silver tithe vessels (or vessels for the tithe) are mentioned (3Q15 3.3; 12.6-7 כלי כסף וכלי זהב של דמע).[39] This would make the jars themselves have inherent value, for monetary reasons in the case of silver and gold vessels, and because of their function within the priestly sphere in the case of clay vessels.[40]

Conclusion

Are these rather unique jars, then, scroll jars, tithe jars, or both? Based on the foregoing, it would seem that most, if not all, of these jars were indeed originally intended at Qumran to be used by the Levites as tithe jars to gather and transport tithed produce and are described as כלי דמע in the Copper Scroll. Certain of the shorter cylindrical jars with small handles from Qumran may have been manufactured specifically to contain scrolls. However, since there are also tall jars with small loop handles and short jars without handles, the combination mentioned above may be coincidental. Of the varieties found at Qumran, the shorter jars with small loop handles would have been best suited for the purpose of transporting and hiding scrolls, even if their original use had been to contain priestly tithes.

While most cylindrical jars might have been tithe jars, they were certainly not all intended to be scroll jars. A few might have been used as

38. Cf. 3Q15 5.6-7 כאלין של דמע כחבן אצלם, 'Tithe vessels and their accounts with them', seems to indicate that written records would accompany each jar, and denote its contents and their amounts.

39. Cf. *M. Ma'as. Š.* 4.10: 'If a vessel was found on which was written "*Qorban*", R. Judah says if it was of earthenware, it is itself common and what is in it is *Qorban*. But if it was of metal it is itself *Qorban* and what is in it is common. But they said unto him: it is not the custom of people to put what is common into what is *Qorban*.'

40. The priestly derivation of the founders and leadership of the Qumran community is clear in their literature. The ongoing need of the associated lay community to tithe to Levites and priests within their communities did not cease, although the bringing of sacrifices to the Temple was discouraged. Most of the offerings received by the community seem to have been produce and money, as is evident in the jars with amounts of grain marked, and from the coin hoards at Khirbet Qumran. Also, cf. treasures and the references to כלי דמע in the scrolls.

According to Abu Dahoud, one of the Bedouin excavators who was involved with de Vaux's excavation, many of the jars were partially filled with the remains of insects and cocoons; cf. W. Fields, 'Discovery and Purchase', in *Encyclopedia of the Dead Sea Scrolls* (New York: Oxford University Press, 2000), p. 208. If the jars held grains or herbs, it can be presumed that the insects found a veritable feast.

scroll jars though it is unlikely that that was their intended use at their time of manufacture.

To sum up, I would like to use an image from contemporary life to help illustrate the point: One might choose to store buttons in an empty cookie jar, in which case the owner might decide to call the jar a ‘button jar’ because of its contents. However, once the buttons are emptied out, the form of the jar will still be a cookie jar.

12

The Architectural Vocabulary of the Copper Scroll and the Temple Scroll

Lawrence H. Schiffman

From the earliest discussions of the Copper Scroll it was realized that its vocabulary shared aspects of the later Hebrew dialect generally termed Mishnaic Hebrew or Middle Hebrew.[1] In fact, the presence of large numbers of what appeared to be lexical items from this later dialect led many to state incorrectly that the Copper Scroll had actually been composed in the Mishnaic dialect generally in evidence in the rabbinic texts from the tannaitic period. In these discussions, issues of morphology and syntax were generally ignored and the language was classified based on its lexicon alone.

The same problems were raised in relation to two other important texts, the Temple Scroll and 4QMMT. In the case of the former, aspects of the grammar and syntax required that the text be classified generally with other Qumran Hebrew documents.[2] Indeed, the Temple Scroll is somewhere in between the Hebrew of the Masoretic text and that of the Qumran sectarian writing practice,[3] but its vocabulary has decidedly 'Mishnaic'

1. J.T. Milik, 'Le rouleau de cuivre provenant de la grotte 3Q (3Q15)', in M. Baillet, J.T. Milik and R. de Vaux, *Les 'petites grottes' de Qumrân* (DJDJ III; Oxford: Clarendon Press, 1962), pp. 222, 275-76. Milik's full study of the language is on pp. 221-59. The Mishnaic connection seems to have eluded J.M. Allegro, *The Treasure of the Copper Scroll* (London: Routledge & Kegan Paul, 1960), pp. 29-30, where he recognizes the links with other Second Temple period texts.

2. Cf. E. Tov, 'The Orthography and Language of the Hebrew Scrolls Found at Qumran and the Origin of these Scrolls', *Textus* 13 (1986), pp. 31-57.

3. L.H. Schiffman, 'The Temple Scroll in Literary and Philological Perspective', in W.S. Green (ed.), *Approaches to Ancient Judaism* (BJS, 9; Chico, CA: Scholars Press, 1980), pp. 143-58.

elements.[4] In many cases, whereas the sectarian documents as a whole use archaizing biblical terminology,[5] this scroll uses that known from later usage. 4QMMT was also mistakenly identified as being in Mishnaic Hebrew.[6] Actually, this document has the grammar and syntax of Qumran Hebrew, but numerous terms used here are known from later tannaitic texts.[7]

Various historical explanations have been given for these facts. However, my purpose here is not historical, but philological. In this chapter I seek to investigate a variety of lexical items and terms that occur in both the Copper Scroll and the Temple Scroll, in the hope that both texts will thereby be illuminated. The chapter will be limited to the discussion of architectural terminology since both of these texts, in very different ways, relate to architecture.[8]

Architectural Terms in the Copper Scroll and the Temple Scroll

In what follows I investigate one by one, in alphabetical order, the architectural terms that occur in both texts.[9]

4. Y. Yadin, *The Temple Scroll* (3 vols.; Jerusalem: Israel Exploration Society, Hebrew University, Shrine of the Book, 1983), I, pp. 33-39.

5. C. Rabin, *Qumran Studies* (Scripta Judaica, 2; London: Oxford University Press, 1957), pp. 108-11.

6. Milik, DJDJ III, p. 225.

7. A thorough study of the language of this text by E. Qimron appears in E. Qimron and J. Strugnell, *Qumran Cave 4.V: Miqṣat Ma'aśe ha-Torah* (DJD X; Oxford: Clarendon Press, 1994), pp. 65-110. See also the discussion of 'Halakhic Terminology' on pp. 138-42.

8. Architectural terms also appear in the New Jerusalem texts. See M. Broshi, 'Visionary Architecture and Town Planning in the Dead Sea Scrolls', in D. Dimant and L.H. Schiffman (eds.), *Time to Prepare the Way in the Wilderness: Papers on the Qumran Scrolls by Fellows of the Institute for Advanced Studies of the Hebrew University, Jerusalem, 1989–90* (Leiden: E.J. Brill, 1995), pp. 9-22.

9. The Temple Scroll citations follow the numeration of Yadin, *The Temple Scroll*, II, and the text follows the editions of both Yadin and E. Qimron, *The Temple Scroll: A Critical Edition with Extensive Reconstructions* (Beer Sheva-Jerusalem: Ben Gurion University; Israel Exploration Society, 1996). Architecture is emphasized in J. Maier, *The Temple Scroll: An Introduction, Translation and Commentary* (JSOTSup, 34; Sheffield: JSOT Press, 1985), although I generally prefer the analysis of Yadin. For the Copper Scroll, the chapter is based on the readings and numeration of J.K. Lefkovits, *The Copper Scroll—3Q15: A New Reading, Translation and Commentary* (2 vols.; PhD dissertation, New York University, 1993), now published

בור. In Copper Scroll 1.6 this word appears for a 'cistern', and in 2.1 it occurs in the phrase בור המלח, 'salt pit', referring to a pit for storing salt. This pit is located below steps. This term also appears in 2.7 where it refers to a pit or cistern that has been filled with vessels and money. Another בור is mentioned in 2.10 and still another under the wall (חומה) in 2.10. In 4.1 there is mention of הבור הגדול, indicating that there was also a small cistern. Another cistern appears in 10.3. This same usage is found in both biblical and Mishnaic Hebrew. In 11QT^{a} 46.14, its only occurrence in the Temple Scroll, it means a 'pit' within a latrine, 'into which the excrement will descend' (line 15).[10]

בית. This word in the Copper Scroll can mean just a 'building' as in 2.5 where the בתי העצין are storehouses for wood, and these are located in a courtyard. A בית אוצר, 'storehouse', is mentioned in 8.1. The בית המים of 10.15 is either a water storage facility or a toilet facility. In 11.12 בית האשוחין can also be a water facility of some kind. בית המשכב is apparently a burial structure in 11.16, some kind of a tomb. Two buildings (בתין) are mentioned in 4.6. This same meaning is found in the Temple Scroll, where, for example, the stairhouse can be termed a בית (11QT^{a} 31.8[11]), as are many other structures. Interesting in our context is the use of בתים ומקורים, 'roofed buildings',[12] to designate latrines in the Temple Scroll (11QT^{a} 46.14). The usage in 7.9 of בית הקץ, which seems to be a summer house or summer palace, is more literal. The usage of בית for

in a revised form as *The Copper Scroll—3Q15: A Reevaluation: A New Reading, Translation and Commentary* (STDJ, 25; Leiden: E.J. Brill, 2000). The discussion that follows is everywhere indebted to the excellent and detailed commentary by Lefkovits. A discussion of the vocabulary of the Copper Scroll is found in Milik, DJDJ III, pp. 236-75, with architectural terms discussed on pp. 247-49. My classification differs from that of Milik, and my readings are substantially different due to the vastly improved readings of Lefkovits. Another new reading of the Copper Scroll is A. Wolters, *The Copper Scroll: Overview, Text and Translation* (Sheffield: Sheffield Academic Press, 1996).

10. Trans. Yadin, *Temple Scroll*, II, p. 199; cf. Yadin, *Temple Scroll*, I, pp. 294-304. See also A.I. Baumgarten, 'The Temple Scroll, Toilet Practices, and the Essenes', *Jewish History* 10 (1996), pp. 9-20, who in my view has exaggerated the importance of this aspect of sectarian identity.

11. Also restored by Yadin in 11QT^{a} 30.3-4 and read by Qimron in 30.5. The reading of the top of this column varies markedly in the two editions.

12. Note the use of *vav* of explication. See GKC § 154 n. 1 (b).

'house' in the normal sense is also found in the Temple Scroll.[13] This usage is most common in both biblical and Mishnaic Hebrew.[14]

חצר. In 1.6 this appears to refer to a 'courtyard' for residence, since it has a cistern (בור) in it. A courtyard appears also in 2.5 where there is a storehouse for wood. But the court of 1.6 is referred to as the Court of the Peristyle, probably referring to a colonnaded structure. So we cannot be certain if it was a residential area. Another חצר is mentioned in 3.1. In the Temple Scroll this term appears regularly to refer to the courts of the Temple. This word is used in the same ways in both the Bible and Mishnaic literature.

מסבא. In 1.13 this term for a 'spiral staircase' (from the root סבב) appears.[15] Some readings find this word also in 11.6, in which case a cache would have been located below a 'large staircase' (המסבא הגדולא). This term (spelled מסבה) also appears in 11QT[a] 30.5[16] and 10,[17] 31.8, and in the plural in 42.8.[18] The Temple Scroll designates the building in which this staircase is housed as בית. But this seems to be termed שיא by the Copper Scroll in 1.13, although this term may mean 'top'. This usage is not found in the Bible, but does appear in Mishnaic Hebrew.

מעלות. This term occurs in Copper Scroll 1.2 meaning 'stairs', and is used this way in the Temple Scroll: 11QT[a] 46.7, singular use as a collective; 30.4, 10; 31.9; and 42.7 (בית מעלות). It also refers to steps in 2.1 where a salt pit is under the steps. It seems that the singular[19] מעלהא in 12.4 refers to a stairway, but it can also refer to one step. This term is found in biblical and rabbinic usage.

13. For example, see the laws of the impurity of the dead in 11QT[a] 49.5–51.10 and L.H. Schiffman, 'The Impurity of the Dead in the Temple Scroll', in L.H. Schiffman (ed.), *Archaeology and History in the Temple Scroll: The New York University Conference in Memory of Yigael Yadin* (JSPSup, 8; Sheffield: JSOT Press, 1990), pp. 135-56.

14. I omit use of בית in place names from consideration here.

15. Spellings with *'alef* in place of *he'* to mark the final long vowel on feminine nouns are common in the Copper Scroll.

16. Following Qimron, *Temple Scroll*, p. 45. Yadin also reads it in line 4.

17. Again with Qimron, but not Yadin.

18. Qimron reads it partially also in 10.13.

19. Note that the long vowel of the feminine noun is indicated twice, with the original *he'* and with an added *'alef*.

מקצע. In the Copper Scroll this term appears in 2.13 as a 'corner'. In the *plene* spelling, מקצוע appears in many passages in the Temple Scroll where it denotes the interior corners.[20] So dimensions from 'corner' to 'corner' where this term appears indicate the inside dimensions.[21] In Copper Scroll 11.1, therefore, the four corners (מקצועותיה) of some structure probably refer to the inner corners.

מקרה. This term appears in the Copper Scroll 7.8 for a roofed chamber that is part of a summer house or palace (בית הקץ). A roof, designated by this same term, is mentioned in 11QT[a] 36.6 and 10, where it seems to refer to an arched structure. Such a ceiling is supported by pillars (עמודים) in 11QT[a] 34.15. That this word can refer to the ceiling, that is, the inside of the roof exposed to what is below, is apparent from the fragmentary 39.2. The word also occurs in 5.6.[22] The plural מקרות is found in 33.9. The word מקרה appears in the Bible once (Eccl. 10.8), but does not seem to occur at all in rabbinic usage where it has been replaced by תקרה, 'ceiling'.

סף. This term for 'threshold' appears in the Copper Scroll in 2.12. Here there is mention of הסף הגדול under which is the entrance to the cistern itself under a wall. In 11.8 הסבין may be equivalent to הספין, 'thresholds'. If so, this would be referring to a grave below the thresholds. In 12.2 there is reference to the סף of a burial niche (כוך). The term סף also appears in the Temple Scroll. In 11QT[a] 36.9 it is below the משקוף, which is the upper part of the doorway. The synonymous form אסף appears in the plural also in 49.13 meaning the same. There, משקוף also appears as the upper part of the doorway. This term is regular in biblical Hebrew but has effectively been replaced in Mishnaic usage by אסקופה.

עמוד. This term for pillar appears in 4.1 with no further information. In 6.1 it refers to a pillar that seems to be between the two openings of a cave. Such a pillar would be a natural one, rather than the usual columns designated by this word that are created to fit the architecture. In 11.3 the pillar is mentioned as part of an *exedra* associated with a gravesite. This word is used for columns or pillars numerous times in the Temple Scroll and is regular in both biblical and Mishnaic usage.

20. See, e.g., Yadin, *Temple Scroll*, II, p. 154, to 11QT[a] 36.6-7.
21. Yadin, *Temple Scroll*, II, p. 132.
22. The reading in Qimron, *Temple Scroll*, p. 14, is more complete.

פנה. In Copper Scroll 3.5 this term refers twice to the 'corner', apparently of a square courtyard. In 3.10 it is not possible to know what the corner refers to. This is the case also in 11.2 where the reading is very difficult. This term appears in the Temple Scroll numerous times. It seems that this term in this scroll refers always to the outside corners, so that measurements given according to these 'corners' are exterior. In Copper Scroll 7.11 פנת המשמרה, 'the corner of the guardpost', most likely refers to the outer corner. While this word is regular in biblical usage, it appears to be used by the Rabbis only as a reflex of biblical material, not independently.

פתח. In 1.8 this word signifies an 'entrance', most probably of the cistern, but perhaps of the courtyard referred to there. In this general meaning it is regular in both biblical and Mishnaic usage. In 1.11 it refers to the opening of a heap (גל), presumably. It occurs again in 6.2-3 in relation to a cave with two openings, apparently with a pillar between them. In 6.9 it is also the opening to a cave. In 10.10 it refers to the entrance to a water storage facility (ים). In 6.9 a hidden entrance is referred to as צפון פתחא, which opens to a deep pit (שית). The use of פתח to refer to an opening or entrance also occurs in the Temple Scroll. In 11QT[a] 41.14 and 46.6 it refers to the openings of the gates (פתחי השערים). According to one reading, 31.7 refers to the 'entrance (פתח) [of the roof(?) of the *heikhal*'.[23] In any case, the Temple Scroll usage and that in the Copper Scroll seem to be the same.

קבר. In 3.11 and 5.12 of the Copper Scroll this term appears for a 'grave'. The קבר צדוק in 11.3 is a particular, known gravesite as is the case with קבר בני העבט located in Jericho in 11.9. One of the features of the grave of Zadok in 11.3 is an *exedra*. The same usage of קבר appears in the Temple Scroll (11QT[a] 50.6, 11). Another קבר is located apparently below the threshold in 11.8. The plural[24] קברין appears in 12.11 where the graves are located at the mouth of the deep pit (שית). The usage in 11QT[a] 50.6 results only from the biblical parallel, but the use in 50.11 indicates actual usage by the author of the scroll or his source. Indeed, this word was regular in both biblical and rabbinic usage. It is interesting that in prescribing cemeteries throughout the land (11QT[a] 4.11-14), the scroll

23. So Yadin, *Temple Scroll*, II, p. 135, whose translation I follow. Qimron's reading does not find this word as he reads לפרור [ה]היכל.

24. Plural in ין- is regular in Mishnaic usage as well as in the remnants of Northern Israelite Hebrew found in MT.

uses the verb קבר and refers to the cemeteries by the general term מקומות, 'places'.

קרקע. This term for 'ground' appears in both texts. In 1.7 it refers to the bottom of a pit (בור) but in 1.14 it is simply the ground. In 10.4 it refers to the bottom of a cistern normally filled with water. It appears in 11QT[a] 49.12 where it refers to the floor of a house. In the Bible it only appears for a 'floor', but in Mishnaic usage it refers to the 'ground' or even to the earth itself, in the sense of 'real estate'.

רובד. This term appears in the Copper Scroll where it seems to refer to a row of stones (2.3). It also appears in the Temple Scroll but in a somewhat different meaning. In 11QT[a] 4.1-6 it refers to the successively higher pavements on which the levels or chambers surounding the Temple building are built. In this sense it is a 'pavement'.[25] The same meaning is found in 46.5, which speaks of a pavement surrounding the outer court of the Temple (the third court in this scroll's plan) that is 14 cubits wide. It is apparent from these parallels as well as those in rabbinic literature that this term in the Copper Scroll must designate rows of stone that protrude so that there is created a stepped structure of some kind, and the third level protrudes out from what is below. The noun רובד does not occur in biblical usage. In rabbinic Hebrew it is a 'pavement', often arranged in a stepped structure, so that some translations use the imprecise term 'terrace' to describe it.

שער. The Copper Scroll uses this term for 'gate' in 2.7 where it must refer to a formal gate as opposed to the more informal פתח (see above). The Temple Scroll speaks of the architectural details of the gates that led into the three concentric courtyards of the Temple as well as into some of the buildings in the Temple as designed according to the scroll. This usage is regular in both biblical and Mishnaic Hebrew.

תל. In Copper Scroll 1.9 this word refers to a 'mound'. Its use in 11QT[a] 55.10 for a destroyed city is simply a reflex of the biblical usage in Deut. 13.17. Indeed, this usage is found in the Bible and is also common in Mishnaic Hebrew.

25. Yadin, *Temple Scroll*, II, p. 12, translates 'terrace', but his interpretation is the same.

Architectural Terms in the Copper Scroll that are not Used in the Temple Scroll

The following architectural terms appear in the Copper Scroll, but not in the Temple Scroll. In some cases their usage is such that we might have expected them in the Temple plan of the Temple Scroll. For some words, it will be noted that alternative expressions are used while these terms are not. Unlikely readings are omitted.

אוצר. This word for a 'storehouse' (here in the phrase בית אווצר) occurs in 8.2 with the strange orthography אווצר.[26] This word does not occur in the Temple Scroll, but it is common in both biblical and rabbinic usage.

אכסדרן. This is the Greek ἐχέδρα which appears in Latin as *exedra*. Basically, this word has two meanings.[27] It can refer to a hall with seats, or to a colonnaded entry into a house or building. In our case, it is clearly the second, designating a pillared entryway into a tomb. Rashi's translation into Old French, 'portico', seems to capture the meaning best. This word is used in Copper Scroll 11.3 where it appears with a medial *nun* in final position as is not so infrequent in the Qumran scrolls. It does not occur in the Temple Scroll, although the term פרור denotes a similar structure in several passages. A פרור עמודים, 'pillared stoa', is mentioned in 11QT[a] 35.11, although it is a cultic structure. It should be noted that the Hebrew and Aramaic scrolls from Qumran are virtually free of Greek loanwords, in contrast to Mishnaic Hebrew, which is suffused with them.

אמא. This term for 'canal' or 'aqueduct' is common in Mishnaic Hebrew but does not appear in the Bible. It occurs in the Copper Scroll several times, as in 1.11, where there is reference to the bottom of the aqueduct, or in 4.3 where no details are provided.[28] In 5.1 reference is to אמת המים and a similar phrase is found in 7.3. In 8.1 the canal is associated with a road. This word does not appear in the Temple Scroll where העלה (11QT[a] 32.12) may be a substitute known from the Bible.

26. Perhaps this spelling indicates a pronunciation with consonantal *vav*.

27. See S. Krauss, *Griechische und Lateinische Lehnwörter im Talmud, Midrasch und Targum* (2 vols.; Hildesheim: Georg Olms, 1964), II, pp. 44-45.

28. Both these passages use final *'alef* instead of *he'* to indicate the final long vowel.

אשווח. This is a term for a pool that occurs in the Copper Scroll in 5.6. In 7.4 and 10.5 it is spelled אשוח. In 11.12 the plural occurs in בית האשוחין, House of the Pools.[29] This word is not found in the Bible but occurs in the Mesha Inscription (lines 9 and 23). The similar term אשיח is known from Ben Sira 3.3. It is not known in rabbinic sources. This term would have no place in the Temple Scroll.

ביאה. This is a term for 'entrance' in 3.9 of the Copper Scroll. It does not occur in the Bible but is found in rabbinic texts. Not only is this unusual usage absent from the Temple Scroll, but the more common מבוא, known from both biblical and Mishnaic Hebrew, does not occur there either.

ביב. This term for a 'gutter' or 'pipe' occurs in Copper Scroll 9.11, but not in the Temple Scroll. In Copper Scroll 12.8 it appears in the feminine as ביבא, unless this is Aramaic influence. This word is not found in the Bible but is common in Mishnaic usage.

ברכה. This biblical and Mishnaic term for 'pool' of water occurs in the Copper Scroll in 2.13 and is often restored in 10.17, but it is not found in the Temple Scroll. In general, water systems are not discussed much in the Temple Scroll.

חוליא. This term for a 'trench' or the dirt piled up around a trench or hole is well known from Mishnaic usage and appears in Copper Scroll 1.7. It does not occur in the Bible. It does not appear as such in the Temple Scroll, but the term חיל which is found there (11QT^{a} 46.9) is understood by Yadin as a 'fosse', that is, 'a kind of very wide ditch'.[30]

חומא. This term for a 'wall', as in the wall of a city, appears in Copper Scroll 2.10 and might have been expected to appear in the Temple Scroll. Only קיר, however, is found throughout. חומה is common in both biblical and rabbinic usage.

חריץ. This term for 'ditch', found in 5.8 of the Copper Scroll, is a Mishnaic usage that is not paralleled in the Bible where this word designates only 'that which is cut' or a 'sharp instrument'. This word is not found in the Temple Scroll. The term חיל is used in that scroll to refer to a barrier constituted of a large ditch.

29. See the discussion in Lefkovits, *A Reevaluation*, pp. 392-97.
30. Yadin, *Temple Scroll*, I, p. 275.

טור. This biblical word for a 'row' occurs in 7.15 of the Copper Scroll but not in the Temple Scroll. This usage is not found in Mishnaic Hebrew.

יד. This word means a monument in the expression יד אבשלום in 10.12, and this usage is not found in the Temple Scroll. This usage is found in the Bible but seems not to have been in use in Mishnaic Hebrew.

ים. The Copper Scroll 10.8, 15 and 11.13 uses this word to designate a water storage facility. This term does not occur in the Temple Scroll. It is found, however, in the Bible and continues to be used for a tank or reservoir in Mishnaic usage.

ירך. This biblical term for 'side' appears in Copper Scroll 1.7 and 9.8 but nowhere in the Temple Scroll. It is not used in this meaning in Mishnaic Hebrew.

כרך. This term for a 'walled city' is known in Mishnaic Hebrew and used in Copper Scroll 12.1, but it does not occur in the Temple Scroll. It is not found in the Bible and may indeed be a loanword from Aramaic.

מבוא. This is a term for an 'entrance' or 'alley' in Mishnaic Hebrew and it appears in Copper Scroll 11.16. It does not appear in the Temple Scroll. While biblical texts use this word in the sense of 'entrance', it is not used for an alley leading to houses as in rabbinic usage.

מגזה. This term occurring in Copper Scroll 6.14 is some form of a 'bridge' or 'passageway' for the high priest. This term is otherwise known from Aramaic, but does not appear in the Temple Scroll, nor in biblical or rabbinic Hebrew.

מדף. The Copper Scroll uses this term in 3.12-13 for a 'board', but the Temple Scroll uses instead לוחות. This is a simple case of the use of a Mishnaic term in the Copper Scroll and a biblical term in the Temple Scroll.

מזקא. This term for irrigation canal is known only from Aramaic and occurs in Copper Scroll 2.9 but not in the Temple Scroll. It is not used in biblical or Mishnaic Hebrew. It might theoretically have found a place in the Temple Scroll but תעלה and מחלה are used. The plural מזקות occurs in 10.3.

מערה. This word, the normal word for 'cave', appears in the Copper Scroll in 2.3, 6.7 and 7.8 but would have no place in the Temple Scroll. In 6.1 it appears in the construct in [מ]ערת העמוד, 'the cave of the pillar'. מערה is common in both biblical and Mishnaic Hebrew.

מצד. This word means a fortress in Copper Scroll 9.17 but does not occur at all in the Temple Scroll where no such military structures are discussed, even in the laws pertaining to the king and his army. This word appears in both biblical and rabbinic usage.

משכן. In Copper Scroll 6.11 this term designates either an 'abode' or perhaps a grave. While the verb שכן occurs numerous times in the Temple Scroll to indicate the indwelling of the divine presence,[31] the noun משכן occurs in no usage at all. This is despite the fact that the Temple plan here is an attempt to replicate the Tabernacle and desert camp of Israel.[32] While משכן appears all over the Bible, it is virtually limited in rabbinic usage to designation of the biblical tabernacle.

משמרה. This word for 'guardpost' occurs in 7.11 of the Copper Scroll but has no real place in the Temple Scroll. This word is not found in the Bible, but in Mishnaic Hebrew it refers to the times of the watch, not to the place of watching. Biblical משמר does refer to the 'guardpost'.

נדבך. This term for a 'row of stones' appears in Copper Scroll 1.5. It is found in late biblical usage and continues into Mishnaic Hebrew. It might easily have been used in the Temple Scroll but is not.

נטף. Copper Scroll 9.1 uses this term for a 'water pool', and it does not occur in the Temple Scroll, where it would have no place since drainage systems for rain water are not discussed there. While this root is attested in biblical and Mishnaic Hebrew, this noun is not found there at all. There is, however, in the Bible a segholate נטף meaning 'drip' which is no doubt related.

31. Cf. L.H. Schiffman, 'The Theology of the Temple Scroll', *JQR* 85 (Qumran Studies; 1994), pp. 118-23.

32. L.H. Schiffman, 'Architecture and Law: The Temple and its Courtyards in the Temple Scroll', in J. Neusner, E.S. Frerichs and N.M. Sarna (eds.), *From Ancient Israel to Modern Judaism, Intellect in Quest of Understanding: Essays in Honor of Marvin Fox* (BJS, 159; Atlanta: Scholars Press, 1989), pp. 267-84.

ניקרת הטבילה. This expression for a natural immersion pool appears in Copper Scroll 1.12 instead of the usual term מקוה used in Mishnaic Hebrew for a ritual bath.[33] The noun נקרה means 'cleft (in the rock)', so we can translate the phrase as 'a cleft for immersion', that is, a rock pool. This word is used in both biblical and Mishnaic Hebrew, but not for an immersion pool. The Temple Scroll, like the Bible, acts as if there is no such thing as an artificial ritual bath and assumes that immersion only takes place in natural water sources, hence there is no word used for this purpose.

נפש. This term for a 'grave' or 'tomb', known from Mishnaic Hebrew, appears in 1.5 of the Copper Scroll, whereas the biblical term קבר is regular in the Temple Scroll. The usage for 'grave' does not occur in the Bible.

פרסטלון. This is the Greek word περίστυλον, 'peristyle' or 'colonnaded structure' that appears in 1.7 of the Copper Scroll. No Greek words at all appear in the Temple Scroll, but the difficult word פרור is used for the same kind of colonnade or stoa,[34] and this synonymous term is common in the Temple Scroll.

צריח. This unusual term for 'catacomb' is used in the Copper Scroll as in 2.5; 8.11, 14; 9.4 and 7 but is not found in the Temple Scroll. This usage may possibly be found in biblical Hebrew,[35] but it seems not to have carried over to Mishnaic Hebrew.

שובך. Normally this term refers to a 'dovecote', but here it seems to be an alternate spelling for שופך, a 'drain canal', as it occurs in Copper Scroll 9.1 and 17. It does not appear in the Temple Scroll although other terms are used. The verbal root שפך appears regularly in both biblical and Mishnaic usage meaning 'pour', but the noun is used for 'waste water' only in Mishnaic Hebrew.

33. Cf. the expression גבא בסלע (CD 10.12) for a cleft in the rock in which rain water has accumulated and which is used for immersion. Line 11 there specifies the minimum of water for immersion as a מרעיל (=מרחל), which was equivalent to the 40 seahs required for the volume of a ritual bath by tannaitic law. See S. Lieberman, *Greek in Jewish Palestine* (New York: Philip Feldheim, 1965), p. 135 n. 151. These passages are preserved only with lacunae in the Qumran MS 4QD[a].

34. Yadin, *Temple Scroll*, II, p. 21.

35. Lefkovits, *A Reevaluation*, p. 274.

שולים. Usually in the construct שולי, this term occurs in the Copper Scroll in 1.11, 4.9 and 9.1. In 7.5, 9.1 and 11.7 it appears with *defective* spelling to be read *shulaw*. In all these passages it appears with the Mishnaic meaning, 'bottom', as opposed to the usage in the Bible for 'rim, hem'.[36] It does not appear in the Temple Scroll.

שיא. This word appears in Copper Scroll 1.13 for 'tower', or 'top' of the stairhouse. It is not used in the Temple Scroll. This is a biblical word not used in Mishnaic Hebrew.

שית. Whatever the reading of this difficult word for a 'pit' in 3.8, 4.11, 9.14 and 12.10 of the Copper Scroll, it does not occur in the Temple Scroll. This term can designate a pit of clay in 4.9 or an upper pit in 12.4. The usage of שית for 'pit' is rabbinic and is not found in the Bible.

Architectural Terms that Appear in the Temple Scroll that are not Used in the Copper Scroll

In this section I list alphabetically, with their definitions, those architectural terms that are found in the Temple Scroll, but that do not appear in the Copper Scroll.

אבני גזית, singular אבן גזית. Dressed stones (3.7). This is a biblical expression (1 Kgs 5.31; Ezek. 40.42; 1 Chron. 22.2).

אדשכים, singular אדשך*. Wooden beams (41.16; 42.03). This word is otherwise unattested.[37]

אולם. Portico of the Temple (4.8). This term is biblical and is used also by Mishnaic sources.

גג. Roof (31.6-8; 39.2; 42.9-10; 44.7; 46.2; 65.6). This term is common in biblical and Mishnaic usage.

דלת. Door (6.8; 13.4; 36.11; 39.3; 41.16; 49.12). This word is found in both biblical and Mishnaic Hebrew.

36. Lefkovits, *A Reevaluation*, pp. 616-19.

37. See Yadin, *Temple Scroll*, II, p. 175. This word is listed for the first time in a dictionary, I believe, in D.J.A. Clines (ed.), *The Dictionary of Classical Hebrew* (Sheffield: Sheffield Academic Press, 1993–), I, p. 137. It is defined as 'rafter or perhaps doorway'.

דף. Board (10.10[38]). This word is postbiblical. One of its meanings is 'board' in Mishnaic Hebrew.

היכל. Temple building (30.5, 7-8; 31.6-7; 35.8, 10). This is a biblical term that continues in Mishnaic use to refer to the Jerusalem Temple building.

חדר. Room (42.01-02;[39] 42.3, 5-9; 44.3-12). This term is used in both biblical and Mishnaic Hebrew.

חלונים, חלונות, singular חלון. Windows, lockers (5.7; 6.5, 8;[40] 33.11). This term is regular in biblical and Mishnaic usage.

כיור (*kiyyur*). Entablature (5.7, 10; 6.5, 8; 36.10).[41] This usage is not found in the Bible but appears in Mishnaic Hebrew.

לוח. Board (7.1-3, 5; 34.1). This is a biblical usage, for the most part replaced by דף in Mishnaic Hebrew where לוח usually refers either to the tablets of the Ten Commandments (in the plural) or to an everyday writing surface.

לולאות. Loops[42] (8.3[43]). This biblical usage for the loops of the curtains of the Tabernacle continues to be used for this purpose in rabbinic sources.

מזוזה. Doorpost (49.13).[44] This is a biblical usage that continues into rabbinic Hebrew except that there its most common meaning is the parchment affixed to the doorpost.

38. In the reading of Qimron, *Temple Scroll*. For alternatives, see Yadin, *Temple Scroll*, II, p. 42.

39. Yadin's numeration in *Temple Scroll*, II, p. 177; cf. the fragment designated by him as Rockefeller 43.366 (p. 172), which preserves this text and serves as the basis for the restoration. This MS is numbered 4Q365 and the relevant passage is published under this number in Qimron, *Temple Scroll*, p. 59.

40. The first three passages are restored.

41. Passages using the homograph כיור (*kiyyor*), 'sink', 'basin', are omitted as this is not an architectural usage.

42. This word is variously understood as derived from a singular *לולי (BDB, p. 533a), לול (KB, II, p. 504b) or לולאה (Even-Shoshan), which is a form not attested in classical Hebrew that is used in modern Hebrew.

43. Reading with Qimron, *Temple Scroll*, p. 17.

44. Related is the use of מנעול, 'lock', which I do consider an architectural term.

מחלה. Pipe or drain (32.13). This biblical term is also common in Mishnaic Hebrew.

מקדש. Temple (*passim*).[45] This is a biblical term that continues in Mishnaic usage to refer to the Temple in Jerusalem.

נשכות, singular נשכה. Chambers (41.17; 42.05, 3, 5, 9; 44.3,[46] 6, 8, 10, 12; 45.6). This biblical term is replaced in Mishnaic Hebrew by the alternative biblical form לשכה.

עיר. City, building complex (*passim*).[47] This word is common in both biblical and Mishnaic usage.

עליה. Upper chamber (6.6; 31.6). This usage is regular in biblical and Mishnaic Hebrew.

פרור. Stoa, colonnaded structure (5.13; 30.8;[48] 35.9-10; 37.6, 9; 42.1, 2,[49] 4, 8-9). This is a biblical term for a structure, apparently colonnaded, that is mentioned in connection with Solomon's Temple (2 Kgs 23.11; 1 Chron. 26.18 [פרבר]). In Mishnaic usage the same word refers to the outskirts of a city. In its biblical meaning, it has been traced to a Persian derivation.[50]

קיר. Wall (*passim*).[51] This word is common in biblical and Mishnaic Hebrew.

תא. Chamber, cell (36.6;[52] 38.15; 40.10). This term is used especially for cells in the Temple structure in biblical and Mishnaic terminology.

תעלת. Drainage channel (32.12). This biblical term has been replaced by אמה in Mishnaic Hebrew.

45. The many references are listed in Yadin, *Temple Scroll*, II, p. 449.
46. Restored.
47. For references, see Yadin, *Temple Scroll*, II, p. 453.
48. Restored by Qimron, *Temple Scroll*, p. 45.
49. Restored in 42.2 by Qimron, *Temple Scroll*, p. 60.
50. BDB, p. 826b.
51. A full list appears in Yadin, *Temple Scroll*, II, p. 457.
52. Restored.

Conclusion

The lists analyzed above indicate that numerous architectural terms that were common in late Second Temple times found their way into both the Temple Scroll and the Copper Scroll. These terms, of course, were common among Hebrew-speaking and Hebrew-writing Jews throughout the Land of Israel in this period. These usages were drawn, as is to be expected, from the typical vocabulary of the times. It is for this reason that many of them appear in Mishnaic Hebrew as well as in these two scrolls.

At the same time, we need to account for the numerous cases in which this terminology might have appeared in the Temple Scroll and does not. In general, the impression we get is that Second Temple architectural terminology is less pervasive in the Temple Scroll than in the Copper Scroll. This is to some extent because of the biblicizing tendencies of the scroll, which seeks to appear as God's revelation to Israel. Of course the Mishnah and other tannaitic sources show an even fuller presentation of this vocabulary, to the virtual exclusion of the older biblical alternatives that in some cases appear in the Temple Scroll instead of the later terms.

All of this leads to an inescapable conclusion. The Temple Scroll is an older document and reflects an earlier stage in the development of the postbiblical Hebrew vocabulary. The Copper Scroll was composed at a later date, by which time this vocabulary had already replaced numerous terms. This process is only at its beginning in the Temple Scroll and also in 4QMMT, but is much more advanced in the Copper Scroll.

Are any of these documents in Mishnaic Hebrew? Vocabulary does not make a language, unless it is joined by morphology and syntax. None of these documents can yet be called Mishnaic, but the Copper Scroll certainly comes as close as possible. The architectural vocabulary certainly shows that the progress toward Mishnaic Hebrew was already well advanced in the Maccabean and Herodian periods.

Part III

Interpreting the Copper Scroll

13

The Process of Writing the Copper Scroll

Meir Bar-Ilan

The Copper Scroll is one of the most unusual compositions found at Qumran, and it is plausible that for this reason it has received less attention than any other scroll.[1] In a recent dissertation devoted to this scroll, a work of over 1300 pages, the scroll was defined in the summary as 'mysterious',[2] a description that for me is sufficient to call into question the method of the research used. The goal of this paper is to analyse the unique literary nature of this scroll—the listing—in order to propose a new way of understanding how the scroll was written.

The Question of the Authenticity of the Copper Scroll

One of the questions that has disturbed researchers who have dealt with the Copper Scroll and that has held up research into it is the question of the scroll's authenticity. It is clear that very different treatment and discussion is required whether the composition is considered to be a literary fabrication or a day-to-day inventory. But the inability to arrive at a consensus on this topic has prevented progress in research. The issue of the nature of the scroll has depended on a single question: does the quantity of the treasures mentioned in the scroll reflect realia or are these amounts simply imaginary? Or, put in slightly more detail, should the

1. In spite of following everything connected with Qumran in general and the Copper Scroll in particular, I have found only a few publications devoted to this scroll (most of them found in my bibliography at http://faculty.biu.ac.il/~barilm/bibcoppe/html). See E. Tov, 'On the Status of Research: The Qumran Scrolls in Light of New Research', *Sciences of Judaism* 34 (1994), pp. 37-67 (Hebrew).

2. See Judah K. Lefkovits, *The Copper Scroll—3Q15: A New Reading, Translation and Commentary* (2 vols.; PhD dissertation, New York University, 1993).

scroll be studied as imaginative literature alongside traditional haggadic material that deals with the hidden vessels of the Temple or with the description of Jerusalem in the future, or should it be studied in relation to the geographical and historical realia of the first century CE?[3]

Two major contributions have led to the definition of the Copper Scroll as being concerned with authentic geographical and historical realia. First, the research of several scholars, among them B.-Z. Lurie, has set the Copper Scroll alongside rabbinic legends dealing with the hidden treasures of the First Temple, prior to its destruction. These legends derive, apparently, from the actual hiding of these treasures during the final days of the Second Temple (not as Lurie posits from the time of the revolt of Bar Kosiba, a point of view that can be refuted outright).[4] Second, J.E. Harper

3. Tractate *Kelim*, in A. Jellinek, *Bet ha-Midrash*, B (Jerusalem: Bamberger and Wahrmann, 1938), pp. 88-91 (Hebrew). It is worth noting that several pseudepigraphic writings from the days of the Second Temple moved the time of their appearance to the end of the First Temple, like the Letter of Baruch and the Vision of Ezra, so that the shifting of the storing of treasures to the days of the First Temple changes the writing to 'folklore' but reflects pseudepigraphic tendencies (some examples penetrated the literature of the Sages). For more on the storage of the vessels of the Temple in general and on this book in particular, see L. Ginzberg, *On Jewish Law and Lore* (Tel Aviv: Dvir, 1960), p. 270 n. 16; P. Churgin, *Researches in the Period of the Second Temple* (New York: Shulsinger Bros, 1950), pp. 157-60; S. Lieberman, *Tosefta Kifshuta* (10 vols.; New York: Bet ha-midrash le-rabanim sheba Amerika, 1973), VIII, p. 733; Y. Yadin, *The Temple Scroll* (3 vols.; Jerusalem: Israel Exploration Society, Institute of Archaeology of the Hebrew University of Jerusalem, Shrine of the Book, 1977), II, p. 21 (citing private correspondence with S. Lieberman). Also see Marilyn F. Collins, 'The Hidden Vessels in Samaritan Traditions', *JSJ* 3 (1972), pp. 97-116.

4. B.-Z. Lurie, *The Copper Scroll from the Judaean Desert* (Jerusalem: Kiryat Sepher, 1963) (Hebrew). The current basis for dating the scroll relies on its palaeography (of the first century CE), but Lurie was prepared to recognize research that disputes this possibility because of the erection of the temple in the time of Bar Kosiba. See Y. Cohen, 'The Construction of the Temple by Bar Kochba', *Jerusalem* 6 (1904), pp. 306-17 (Hebrew); Y. Goldman, 'The Destruction of the Third Temple', *Jerusalem* 7 (1907), pp. 70-76 (Hebrew); M. Auerbach, 'Sacrifices after the Destruction of the Temple', *Jeschurun* 10.3-4 (1923), pp. 23-29 (Hebrew); M. Beer, 'One Bit of Evidence Regarding the Question of Non-renewal of Sacrificial Worship in the Days of Bar Kochba?', in S. Cohen, Z. Kaplan, Y.Y. Hacohen-Avidor and S. Markovitz (eds.), *Isolated from his Brothers: Words of Torah, Meditation, Research and Appreciation, a Memorial to God's Hermit Rabbi David the Cohen of Blessed Memory* (3 vols.; Jerusalem: Nezer David, 1978), III, pp. 196-206 (Hebrew). Also see Y. Tabori, *The Festivals of Israel in the Period of the Mishna and the Talmud* (Jerusalem: Magnes Press, 1995), p. 99 n. 65 (Hebrew).

has done research on the plausibility and the reasonableness of the quantity of the treasures that were stored.[5] These two points of view, together with attempts at identifying some of the places mentioned in the scroll, nullify, almost by themselves, wild fancies that were attached to the scroll from the very start. The intent of this chapter is to strengthen the authenticity of the scroll by regarding it as a list.

The Uniqueness of the Scroll as a List: Explanation of the Process of the Writing and its Sitz im Leben

We know that the Copper Scroll differs from all the other Qumran scrolls in several respects: (a) the material of the scroll, copper, is unlike the other scrolls that are written on parchment or paper; (b) the scroll's palaeography: the script differs from the usual script of Qumran (at that time); (c) its language is closer to Mishnaic Hebrew than almost all the other Qumran texts; (d) its content: treasures hidden underground; (e) its genre: a list. Actually, each one of these distinctive aspects of the scroll requires explanation, and surely the combination of these aspects in one scroll emphasizes its uniqueness. Nevertheless, it is the intent of the following to focus on only one aspect of the scroll: the nature of the scroll as a list. Even though this phenomenon has been mentioned previously, it has not received enough attention. Furthermore, I will attempt to explore the significance of this phenomenon as an instrument for the understanding of the process by which this scroll was composed. The nature of this scroll as a catalogue was diagnosed many years ago, in fact, from the very first moment it was discovered.[6] So too, M.R. Lehmann, for instance, noted that the style of the scroll is that of a list.[7] But, until now this definition has not played a significant role in serious research.

Apparently, the first scholar to deal with the list-like character of the Copper Scroll in appropriate detail was the late David Wilmot.[8] Indeed,

5. J.E. Harper, '26 Tons of Gold and 65 Tons of Silver', *BARev* 19.6 (1993), pp. 44-45, 70.

6. K.G. Kuhn, 'Les rouleaux de cuivre de Qumrân', *RB* 61 (1954), pp. 193-205.

7. M.R. Lehmann, *Essays and Travels* (Jerusalem: Mosad Harav Kook, 1972), pp. 152-60 (Hebrew); *idem*, 'Identification of the Copper Scroll Based on its Technical Terms', *RevQ* 4 (1964), pp. 97-105.

8. See A. Wolters, 'Literary Analysis and the Copper Scroll', in Z.J. Kapera (ed.), *Intertestamental Essays in Honor of Józef Tadeusz Milik* (Kraków: Enigma Press, 1992), pp. 239-52, esp. 242-43; see further M.O. Wise in this volume.

within the last few years A. Wolters has devoted several research articles to the Copper Scroll, in which he supports the approach taken by Wilmot.[9] But he does not fully explain the advantage of this approach. That is to say, Wolters has shown that the structure of the Copper Scroll is of a list of 64 (or 60, according to Lurie or Lefkovits) locations where various treasured articles and gold were hidden; and he has indicated that each of the entries is a combination of a fixed number of 'fields' on the list—according to modern terminology—and they are: (a) designation of the location; (b) additional information for designation of the site; (c) directions for digging; (d) the distance (usually indicated in *amot*); (e) description of the treasure; (f) additional remarks regarding the place of hiding; (g) two or three Greek letters. Thus the scroll is not a 'free' literary prose creation; instead, it is a work designed acccording to a fixed and defined (preset) structure. Even if none of the 60 items is complete in containing entries for all seven subjects or 'fields' that exist in the scroll, the form of the description was preset, and the author was not permitted to express himself freely. Indeed, Wolters has shown that the Copper Scroll could have been written in seven columns, a fact that emphasizes that we cannot regard this as a text with a free form but a text with a rigid structure.

Along these lines, it should be mentioned that previous scholars who have studied this scroll did not dwell sufficiently on the nature of the scroll as a list. Further on I will attempt to examine the list genre in general, and the import of this genre as it applies to the Copper Scroll, in particular. I do so in order to examine and combine the above findings as they apply to the uniqueness of the Copper Scroll. All this can enable us to reach some new conclusions regarding this scroll.

9. A. Wolters's other articles are as follows: A. Wolters, 'Notes on the Copper Scroll', *RevQ* 12 (1985–87), pp. 595-96; *idem*, 'The Fifth Cache of the Copper Scroll: "The Plastered Cistern of Manos"', *RevQ* 13 (1988), pp. 167-76; *idem*, 'The Last Treasures of the Copper Scroll', *JBL* 107 (1988), pp. 419-29; *idem*, 'Apocalyptic and the Copper Scroll', *JNES* 49 (1990), pp. 145-54; *idem*, 'The Copper Scroll and the Vocabulary of Mishnaic Hebrew', *RevQ* 14 (1990), pp. 483-95; *idem*, *The Copper Scroll: Overview, Text and Translation* (Sheffield: Sheffield Academic Press, 1996); *idem*, 'The Shekinah in the Copper Scroll: A New Reading of 3Q15 12.10', in S.E. Porter and C.A. Evans (eds.), *The Scrolls and the Scriptures: Qumran Fifty Years after* (JSPSup, 26; Sheffield: Sheffield Academic Press, 1997), pp. 382-91.

The Scroll as a List

A 'list' is a literary genre, a form of writing texts, apparently the most ancient of all forms of writing.[10] In writing the list, the author records a series of entries without conjunctions or verbs (except when dealing with a list of verbs), in order to present the reader with a specific 'inventory'. For instance, a scribe might write a supply list of items in the royal treasury, or a list of words as part of an exercise for a student, or a list of 'early ancestors', or genealogical lists, and so on. A large amount of the most ancient texts are arranged as lists. Also in Jewish literature this genre has left its mark: the opening of Chronicles, the *Scroll of Ta'anit*, the list of basic, major forms of labour in the Tractate Shabbat, and so on.[11]

When a specific text is composed as a list, the following implications derive from its essential nature as a list:

1. Generally, a list has a cumulative nature: it is not written all at once. Instead, it is written in the sequence of a number of entries that may be separated over a span of time (or place). Thus, for instance, a list of groceries, much like a list of ancestors or a list of nations, is nothing more than a summary of several lists that were prepared and summarized, not written all at once. If we speak of a genealogical order, it is understood that such a list is a cumulative collection that by its very nature and chronological order cannot possibly be written all at once.
2. A list has an inherent order and internal organization of some kind (something that is absent from a conventional prose text). For instance, an alphabetical list is prepared according to the conventions of the alphabet of that language; a list of words in a dictionary is prepared according to the alphabet. However, a list of dates or kings is prepared on another basis. The order could be, generally, as we see in history books, a chronological order,

10. See J. Goody, *The Domestication of the Savage Mind* (Cambridge: Cambridge University Press, 1977), pp. 74-111.

11. On the list as a literary genre in ancient cultures and in Jewish sources, see M. Bar-Ilan, 'The Character and Origin of the Scroll of Taanith', *Sinai* 98 (1986), pp. 114-37 (Hebrew); Peter W. Coxon, 'The List Genre and Narrative Style in the Court Tale of Daniel', *JSOT* 35 (1986), pp. 95-121; M.S. Jaffee, 'Writing and Rabbinic Oral Tradition: On Mishnaic Narrative, Lists and Mnemonics', *Journal of Jewish Thought and Philosophy* 4 (1994), pp. 123-46.

or as we see in the *Scroll of Ta'anit*, a calendrical ordering, within the yearly cycle. An ordering of facts according to a hierarchy is yet another way of listing, in which items are listed according to their importance, their age, and even there we can discern secondary patterns: ascending or descending in importance (bottom up or top down).

3. The ordering of the entries in a list can characterize the type of list and the purpose of its composition. An inventory is unlike a list of students in a class, and it is worth remembering that books can be listed in various forms: by author, by title, by subject, by date of acquisition, and so on.
4. A list is not necessarily read in a linear manner, as is a prose text. It also has meaning when read in other ways (for instance, according to 'fields' such as the accumulation of treasures, and so on).

This summary of the characteristics of lists is presented in order to provide a key to understanding the Copper Scroll.

Thus, for instance, Wolters has pointed out that each of the sections that describe a place of hiding was composed of 'data fields', with a maximum of seven items. That is to say, the list was combined from a large compilation of smaller lists (64 in number, according to his theory), a frequent occurrence in lists (just as a larger narrative is assembled from smaller episodes). Each section consists of a shorter uniform listing even though there are sections containing incomplete, partial data fields that are not uniformly formatted. For example, only some of the sub-lists have Greek symbols (at 1.4, 12; 2.2, 4, 9; 3.7; 4.2). Another example is that the sixth data field[12] exists in the first 15 sections and in the last 13 but is missing in all the others except section 24. In other words, the text of the Copper Scroll is assembled from a large list consisting of several shorter lists having a more or less set structure. In some cases it is possible to recognize the secondary division of the longer list (more below). Indeed, this examination is insufficient to clarify all that can be learned from the listing character of the scroll. For this we need to examine a specific phenomenon in the scroll: the duplication of some of the place names in it.

12. Column F in the reading of Wolters, 'Literary Analysis and the Copper Scroll': the field that includes the details of the hiding place.

The Duplication of Place Names

In order to understand the significance of the scroll as a list, the following discussion will focus on a single 'data field': the hiding places of the treasures, though deliberately without consideration of the geographical identification of these places. As mentioned, this 'data field' appears at the beginning of every entry and the study of its content can serve as a key to the understanding of the nature of the scroll and the way it was composed.

First, it must be admitted that the description of the places is very vague; only a native familiar with the paths of the land could have listed the names in this way. Furthermore, most of the names are not actual names but rather mnemo-technical indicators, that is, they are references to the places for personal use only. For example, 'in the pit beneath the wall' is not an exact location but a reminder, since every wall has a certain length, and the wall of Jerusalem is many kilometres long. It is clear that the writer noted this indication of location only as a personal reminder. Similarly, 'in the external valley' and 'at the top of the rock' are not clearly defined places. Indeed it is reasonable to assume that the person who stored the treasure away was not interested in providing details about where his treasures were hidden, and if in the future most of the 'locations' mentioned in the scroll could not be identified, this should not be a cause for wonder or a consideration in establishing the degree of the scroll's authenticity.

Examination of the list of the names of the caches reveals that a number of names from the 60 (or 64) were written more than once. Two categories can be distinguished among them. The first is exemplified in the name 'Sekakah', which appears in items 20, 21, 22, 24 (4.13; 5.2, 5, 13). In other words, we are dealing here with the hiding of treasures adjacent to a place called Sekakah. The second category is the non-consecutive duplication of names for places. Thus, for instance, 'the valley Achor' (Ekun) and 'Kaḥlit' (which could be pronounced 'Koḥlit', 'Keḥelet', or some other way) appear more than once. 'The valley Achor' is mentioned in item 1 (1.1) and in item 17 (4.6).[13] 'Kaḥlit' is mentioned in items 4 (1.9), 11 (2.13), 19 (4.11) and 60 (12.10). Thus the names Sekakah, the valley Achor and Kaḥlit are mentioned a number of times in the list of hiding places.

13. In Pixner's opinion the correct reading for 1.1 is 'which is in the valley, pass over'. Pixner divides the scroll according to considerations of geographical location and finds five cycles (in the 64 places): B. Pixner, 'Unravelling the Copper Scroll Code: A Study on the Topography of 3Q15', *RevQ* 11 (1983), pp. 323-65.

What is the significance of the duplication of the names? Pixner suggested that the name 'Kaḥlit' might be understood as a nickname for a settlement of Essenes.[14] Whatever the precise case, for Pixner it is reasonable to locate every 'Kaḥlit' at a different geographical location. Clearly, according to this approach one is not dealing with duplication because 'four Kaḥlit existed' and each occurrence deals with a different 'camp'. However, I see this interpretation as taking the text beyond its literal meaning and basically contradicting the principles involved in the writing of the places in the scroll, in which the names do not seem to have a double meaning. More seriously, this form of writing would not enable the person hiding the caches to identify the places when war subsided. In fact, S. Goranson has also disputed Pixner's position and claimed that the name indicates a district, a region.[15] However, the definition of any name as a district does not help the person hiding the cache since every place has to be unambiguous with a distinctive meaning so that the treasure can be recovered from storage. Therefore it is preferable to assume that 'Kaḥlit', without any known geographical identification, is the name of a specific place (not necessarily the place mentioned in *b. Qid.* 66a) reached by the person who hid the caches and his group in the course of storing the treasures. On this basis they went to the valley Achor twice and Kaḥlit four times.

It is worth noting here that even if it is assumed that the scroll is the creation of a single author alone, it reflects the activities of a team, since the amount of treasure was well beyond the ability of any single person to watch over, at least from the point of view of anyone responsible for the beasts of burden (donkeys, camels or mules). In order to carry the treasures from their source (in the Temple) to the secret places in the ground, it was necessary to transport them on a number of animals. To provide for guarding the treasure during the course of the trip and because of the physical effort involved in digging a pit, burying and covering up the treasures, many people obviously had to share the secret of the burial expedition. In other words, even if there was only one recorder (apparently not the case), the real situation for the hiding of the treasures required a team.

On the basis of all this, what significance lies in the repeated appearance of some named burial places? It appears that the answer is self-evident: those who hid the treasures did not carry out just a single expedition but

14. Pixner, 'Unravelling the Copper Scroll Code', p. 337.

15. S. Goranson, 'Sectarianism, Geography and the Copper Scroll', *JJS* 43 (1992), pp. 282-87 (287).

reached their storage sites in a number of cycles (at least four). Thus, the burial expedition departed from the source of the treasures (the Temple) with the articles meant for storage, buried them, and then returned to the starting point (the Temple), loaded other treasures on the animals, and set out again on the next cycle of their burial expedition. In this frame of 'cycles' it sometimes happened that the burial expedition returned to one of the places where it had been in the past and buried additional treasure there. In other words, the non-consecutive repetition of the names of places is instructive, on the one hand with regard to how those hiding the treasures executed their mission and, on the other, with regard to the form of the writing of the scroll.[16]

Indeed it is obvious that anyone hiding a large treasure will not hide it all at once to avoid drawing too much attention to it (on the principle of not putting all one's eggs in one basket). Those hiding the treasures did their work covertly, since a long caravan carrying a large bulky load draws attention to itself, in complete contrast to the actual objectives of those doing the hiding. Clearly those hiding the treasures realized that they could not afford to draw too much attention to themselves and that they had to attempt to make the operation as inconspicuous as possible. Just as those hiding the treasures took care to bury them in dozens of places, exercising understandable caution, so it is reasonable to suppose that they did not remove all their treasures at once, for fear of disclosure, robbery or some other concern. No less important a reason for the division of the storage operation into many separate events was the great bulk of the hidden treasures, estimated at tens of tons. Obviously, it would be difficult if not impossible to hide this large quantity in a single operation. In other words, the logic behind the storage shipment required the operation to be divided into a number of stages, and the treasures to be hidden not only in dozens of places, as can be inferred from the body of the text, but also in a number of storage cycles in order to spread the risk of discovery.

Stated otherwise, the internal structure of the scroll (the duplication of names) as well as internal considerations deriving from the unique content of the scroll (the hiding of a great quantity of treasures) tells us that the scroll reflects activity taking place in several stages. Indeed it can be

16. This repetition is bound to assist in renewed research into the identification of the places in the scroll. And even if unambiguous identification of the places does not become possible, at least the analysis of the route of the storage expedition and the manner in which the scroll was written should eliminate as impossible various suggestions that have been made up to now.

assumed that the scroll was written in this way at different times. The delivery expedition reached the storage location, ascertained that no one saw them (perhaps at night), buried the vessels, while the man in charge of the expedition listed for himself a summary of the operation: treasure Y was buried at location X, and so on. The expedition then proceeded to another location and repeated the writing process. Thus the list reflects non-consecutive writing processes in the pattern of lists, corresponding to the progress of the actual execution of the project.[17]

It is possible that the writer himself was replaced, as inferred from a change in the internal structure of repetitions of listings recognized as having a uniform and consistent structure (with or without signs in Greek). Another possibility is that the writer was not replaced but that, since he wrote the description of the places over different periods of time in the course of the various 'storage expeditions', he subconsciously changed (through addition or deletion of details) his writing pattern (while remaining meticulous in writing the entire scroll in a uniform and substantive style). In any case, even if it is assumed that at the end the tentative list was edited and reworked into the list now in our hands (that is, we are dealing with a reworked text) this plausible assumption makes no difference in the understanding of the scroll, since we are still dealing with a uniform pattern of writing: burial and recording, burial and recording, the writing of the list agreeing with its implementation at each location.

Duplication as Indicating the Joining of 'Repeated Lists'

The analysis of the text elaborated above does not hinge in any way on particular geographical identifications, but it appears that a more penetrating understanding of the text could be achieved if its analysis incorporates the assumption that the treasures mentioned in the text are the treasures of the Temple, obtained from the Temple in Jerusalem. But it must be emphasized that the manner of the writing of the scroll does not depend on this assumption. Those who want to tie the source of the treasures to Qumran or to locate the places as in Transjordan or the Carmel are free to do so, but on condition that they identify a sequence of places near each other.

According to the assumption that the Temple was the source of the treasures, it follows that the man responsible for the Temple treasures left

17. Cf. a close example in King Shishak's expedition to Israel: B. Mazar, *Canaan and Israel* (Jerusalem: Mosad Bialik, 1974), pp. 234-44 (Hebrew).

the Temple with the storage expedition as its head. This expedition had to bury a large quantity of objects and therefore performed its task in many cycles. They left Jerusalem, buried the treasures under their care and, on completion of their task, they returned to the Temple for another similar mission.

As stated above, a number of places are mentioned more than once. The proposed explanation ties the duplication into the way the scroll was put together, a list entered in the course of implementation in the area (like a list of grocery items and their prices at the supermarket) and additional contact with the same place in the course of more than one storage trip.

As for the reason for the writing of the scroll, a brief note is in order. Some claim that it is hard to imagine why already at the beginning of the war, any of the defenders would consider scattering the Temple treasures in various places, at a time they thought the city would remain in their hands forever.[18] Regarding this, it can be said that the proponent of this opinion does not recognize the thinking of quartermasters and those responsible for equipment; they do all they can to preserve their treasures. Furthermore, even if there were people who thought Jerusalem would remain in their hands, this does not eliminate the possibility that there were others who considered it dangerous to keep all the treasures in the Temple and that it was preferable to bury the treasures in different places in order to ensure their survival. In this connection attention has to be paid to the subordinate nature of the treasures. We are not talking about the Temple candelabrum or other unique ritual objects that have no replacement, but 'ordinary' objects, part of the Temple inventory, whose removal from the Temple would neither be noticed nor impede the daily service at the Temple. In other words, the hiding of treasures of secondary importance in diverse locations before war reflects a precautionary measure as the exercise of responsibility by some of the Temple priests who were responsible for its treasures.

Concluding Summary

The association of the Copper Scroll with actual events does not depend on the geographical identification of the places mentioned therein but rather on its literary analysis. The Copper Scroll is a collection of lists of hidden inventory, lists written by the man (or men) responsible for a

18. See Goranson, 'Sectarianism, Geography and the Copper Scroll', p. 285.

'salvage campaign'—the hiding of the treasures of the Temple for their preservation in case the Jerusalem Temple should fall to the enemy. The 'duplicated' places are those places that the storage expedition visited more than once. It is only natural that in circular journeys (especially in the conditions of the Judaean Desert) there should be places that are traversed more than once either in the same or slightly different journeys.

Analysis of the literary character of the scroll as a list with the resulting implications explains the historical character of its writing. Identification of the scroll as a list shows that it is not a polished literary document but a list generated in the course of its implementation, matching the progress of the storage expedition chronologically and geographically, reflecting the actual sequence of the procession of those hiding the treasures.

The distinctiveness of the scroll in all of its components refutes almost in itself the conclusion of anyone who sees the scroll as an integral part of the texts from Qumran, and this (conclusion) on the basis of its proximity (to other texts).[19]

A final note. After more than 40 years of research, it appears that the time has come to cease talking about the 'puzzling' or 'mysterious' nature of the Copper Scroll. If we set aside for the moment the controversy over the reading of not too small a number of words, a controversy resembling the status of the reading of the texts from Qumran, we find that the bounds of the 'unknown' in the scroll are now basically limited to the exact identification of the places where the treasures were hidden. However, those exact identifications the writer kept to himself. In any case there is no difference in this respect between the places in the Copper Scroll and various places mentioned in the Bible that also remain unidentified.

19. Such is the opinion of Goranson. It is worth noting too that many archaeological finds reach researchers only through antiquities thieves so that one cannot know the context in which they were found. Nevertheless, a great deal can be learned about the find without depending on its relationship to nearby finds. Similarly it is worth mentioning that non-sectarian texts have also been found at Qumran, so that any conclusion based on proximity alone is risky and does not stand up to criticism. The attempt to identify characteristics of one cave or another has not succeeded (see Tov, 'On the Status of Research'). Goranson also seeks the support of Tov, but on this point he disregards the fact that Tov's analysis is based on the methods of writing and the language of the texts. In this area it is certain that the Copper Scroll differs entirely from the other texts.

14

Inclusio and Symbolic Geography in the Copper Scroll

Ruth Fidler

The notions here entitled *Inclusio* and Symbolic Geography have received only little attention in studies of the Copper Scroll. Nevertheless, I think that both may be worth some further exploration. In this chapter these notions will be considered, first in general terms and regarding their possible relevance to the Copper Scroll, then with reference to the expression that they apparently find in the text of the scroll, and finally from the aspect of their bearing on reading 3Q15 as a literary text.

Preliminary Considerations

Symbolic Geography?

Geographical terms in the Copper Scroll are usually not entitled 'symbolic'. This is understandable, given the current tendency to treat them primarily as plain (and/or partly encoded) geography,[1] and, moreover, as

1. J.M. Allegro, *The Treasure of the Copper Scroll* (London: Routledge & Kegan Paul, 1960), chs. 4-6 and below, n. 4; J.T. Milik, 'Le rouleau de cuivre provenant de la grotte 3Q (3Q15)', in M. Baillet, J.T. Milik and R. de Vaux, *Les 'petites grottes' de Qumrân* (DJDJ III; Oxford: Clarendon Press, 1962), pp. 199-302, esp. D: 'Sites et monuments' (pp. 259-75); B.-Z. Lurie, *The Copper Scroll from the Desert of Judah* (Jerusalem: Kiryath Sepher, 1963) (Hebrew); B. Pixner, 'Unravelling the Copper Scroll Code: A Study on the Topography of 3Q15', *RevQ* 11 (1983), pp. 323-65; P. Kyle McCarter Jr, 'The Mysterious Copper Scroll: Clues to Hidden Temple Treasure?', *BR* 8 (1992), pp. 34-41, 63-64, esp. p. 40. Also consulted on several issues: J.K. Lefkovits, *The Copper Scroll—3Q15: A New Reading, Translation and Commentary* (2 vols.; PhD dissertation, New York University, 1993; printed by UMI Dissertation Services, Ann Arbor MI, 1996); now published in a revised form (STDJ, 25; Leiden: Brill, 2000). The book by R. Feather (*The Copper Scroll Decoded: One Man's Search for the Fabulous Treasures of Ancient Egypt* [London: Thorsons, 1999]) came to my attention too late to be considered here.

a key to discovering the habitat and affiliation of the author and of the treasures described.[2] The latter task—severely hampered by textual and other difficulties[3]—is still far from accomplished. However, one point of (relative) consensus seems to emerge: the Copper Scroll toponyms, whatever and wherever they may be, reveal something about the author who styled them the way he did. They may reflect his origin, background or residence, possibly also his thinking or purpose.

The present use of the term 'symbolic' should be understood within this general framework. More specifically, it is intended to suggest that some location statements may possess—owing to their wording or position in the scroll—a meaning *beyond* the plain geographic reference necessitated by genre and context (i.e. a list of caches). The idea of such extended meaning presents itself especially in those toponyms that are loaded with traditional connotations accumulated from earlier—patently biblical —literature. Indeed, the occurrence of such toponyms in 3Q15 has been duly noted both generally[4] and in comments on pertinent items, for example, עמק עכור (1.1), סככא (4.13; 5.2, 5, 13), קדרון (8.8), בית הכרם (10.5), הר גריזין (12.4).[5] However, the traditional material was usually examined for its possible contribution to matters of geographic identification rather than to the overall significance of the item in question within its Copper Scroll context. Now, this chapter experiments with reversing this order of priorities. I am interested in such questions as, 'What made an author in

2. Milik concluded from the geographical terms and other details in 3Q15 that the author lived in Jericho, was not an Essene (DJDJ III, pp. 276-77) and that the treasures described were purely legendary (pp. 274-75, 278-84). Pixner ('Unravelling the Copper Scroll Code', pp. 325-27) reached the opposite conclusions. Findings similar to those of Pixner, connecting the scroll to the Essene community at Qumran and other sites east of the Jordan River, are presented by S. Goranson, 'Sectarianism, Geography and the Copper Scroll', *JJS* 43 (1992), pp. 282-87; 'Further Reflections on the Copper Scroll', in this volume.

3. Apart from difficulties related to reading the text and to historical geography—on which see Allegro, *The Treasure of the Copper Scroll*, p. 63; Milik, DJDJ III, pp. 259-60—there is the problem of identifying toponyms as distinct from common nouns: the various interpretations offered by the authorities mentioned in this and the previous notes to such graphemes as בחריבה (1.1), כחלת (1.9; 2.12; 4.11-12) or בית המרה (2.3) may illustrate the point.

4. E.g. Allegro, *The Treasure of the Copper Scroll,* p. 63: 'our scroll sometimes locates its treasures by biblical names'. Allegro associated this with the author's 'habit of using alternatives or synonyms for the more common place names, perhaps with a view to disguising them from the unauthorised reader'.

5. See the above mentioned commentaries on these toponyms.

the first century CE begin his list of sacred treasures with a cache in עמק עכור, a toponym traditionally associated with the violation of sacred property (= חרם; Josh. 7.24-26)?' I have less interest (or expertise) in establishing the geographical reference of עמק עכור, for example, as *el-Buquei'ah* south-west of Jericho[6] or as *Wadi Nuwei'imeh,* north-east of it.[7]

To summarize, it should be borne in mind that 'symbolic' (or 'eschatological'[8] or 'mythic') geography as outlined above is not meant to supersede the plain (or partly encoded) geography essential for the Copper Scroll, but to complement it, perhaps as a *pesher* (or פרוש[ה]? cf. 12.12)[9] of a sort.

Inclusio?

The possible presence of such a symbolic–eschatological *pesher* will be examined here with reference to the two ends of the scroll. Comparison between the opening and the closing sections reveals several parallels in vocabulary, style and subject matter, suggesting an *inclusio*.

Inclusio is one type of symmetrical design, wherein the symmetry is observable 'at both ends of a literary work'.[10] Thus defined, it has been pointed out in the laws of Deuteronomy (Deut. 11.31–26.16),[11] in the major collections which make up the book of Jeremiah,[12] as well as in smaller units of prophecy[13] and narrative, down to a single verse.[14]

6. M. Noth, 'Das Deutsche Evangelische Institut für Altertumswissenschaft des Heiligen Landes: Lehrkurs 1954', *ZDPV* 71 (1955), pp. 1-59 (52); Allegro, *The Treasure of the Copper Scroll*, pp. 64-68, 172, fig. 3.

7. Milik, DJDJ III, p. 262 (D 3); Lurie, *The Copper Scroll from the Desert of Judah*, p. 55.

8. Allegro, *The Treasure of the Copper Scroll*, p. 64.

9. פרוש(ה)—'explanation' or 'interpretation' may be a suitable term for this extended meaning, although this is not to say that the additional copy (משנא הכתב הזא) mentioned in 12.11 would have necessarily included such an interpretation. See further below, n. 36.

10. A. Rofé, 'The Arrangement of the Book of Jeremiah', *ZAW* 101 (1989), pp. 390-98, quoting from p. 391.

11. A. Rofé, 'The Arrangement of the Laws in Deuteronomy', *ETL* 64 (1988), pp. 265-87. It is shown that themes and terminology that open the collection recur at the end (e.g. 'rest from enemies': Deut. 12.10; 25.19).

12. Rofé, 'The Arrangement of the Book of Jeremiah', pp. 390-94. Rofé claims that *inclusio* (in terms of genre, date, style and/or the addressees of the prophetic words) is the typical arrangement in all four collections, i.e., chs. 1–24; 25–36 [30–33]; 37–45; 46–51.

13. E.g. Amos 2.14-16; 3.1-14, 4-8; 5.18-20; 6.1-7. For these and other examples

A more elaborate form of this symmetrical arrangement ('ring composition')[15] may embrace the whole (or extensive parts) of a literary work, exhibiting a scheme of concentric rings. In the book of Ruth this architecture has been symbolized as: ABCC′B′A′.[16] The same scheme may be observed in a single legal-poetic saying: שפך דם האדם/ באדם דמו ישפך (Gen. 9.6),[17] where it highlights the 'symmetry' between crime and punishment. Similar patterns may obtain in literary units of other types and sizes, such as a single narrative and a narrative cycle.[18]

Biblical literature apart, symmetrical design is known also in the Epic of Gilgamesh,[19] in Homeric epic and in later Greek and Latin literature,[20] evidently cutting across categories of genre, period and culture.

in the book of Amos see S.M. Paul, *Amos: Introduction and Commentary* (Mikra Leyisra'el, Tel Aviv: Am Oved; Jerusalem: Magnes Press, 1994), pp. 8, 54, 56, 61, 63, 96, 101, 105 (Hebrew). Paul refers to this device as מעטפה ספרותית, i.e., 'a literary envelope'.

14. E.g. Ruth 4.6, 7, as shown by Y. Zakovitch, *Ruth: Introduction and Commentary* (Mikra Leyisra'el, Tel Aviv: Am Oved; Jerusalem: Magnes Press, 1990), pp. 107-108 (Hebrew). Zakovitch refers to this device as מבנה המסגרת, i.e., 'the frame structure'.

15. This term is used by Rofé, 'The Arrangement of the Book of Jeremiah', p. 391, as synonymous with *inclusio.* The intention above is somewhat wider, bearing in mind the possibility of recurring, concentric 'rings', mentioned forthwith.

16. Each letter representing a section of the book. See S. Bertman, 'Symmetrical Design in the Book of Ruth', *JBL* 84 (1965), pp. 165-68, esp. p. 167.

17. R. Weiss, 'Chiasm in the Bible', *Studies in the Text and Language of the Bible* (Jerusalem: Magnes Press, 1981 [1962]), p. 260 (Hebrew); Rofé, 'The Arrangement of the Book of Jeremiah', p. 391.

18. Both can be demonstrated from the Jacob narratives: see, e.g., the analysis of Gen. 28.11-19a by R. Rendtorff, 'Jakob in Bethel', *ZAW* 94 (1982), pp. 512-13 and the comments on the 'inclusive structure' of the whole Jacob story made by T.L. Thompson, *The Origin Tradition of Ancient Israel.* I. *The Literary Formation of Genesis and Exodus 1–23* (JSOTSup, 55; Sheffield: Sheffield Academic Press, 1987), pp. 161-62: 'individual conflict tales are linked together, not successively but concentrically'. On the Jacob cycle as well as further examples and bibliography see also M. Fishbane, 'Composition and Structure in the Jacob Cycle (Gen. 25.19–35.22)', *JJS* 26 (1975), pp. 15-38, esp. pp. 19-20.

19. J.H. Tigay, *The Evolution of the Gilgamesh Epic* (Philadelphia: University of Pennsylvania Press, 1982), pp. 5-10. Tigay discusses 'the frame' of Tablets 1–11, which is formed by the repetition of certain lines, themes and motifs.

20. Bertman, 'Symmetrical Design in the Book of Ruth', p. 168; Fishbane, 'Composition and Structure in the Jacob Cycle', p. 19; both with relevant bibliography.

We cannot determine here whether it was 'a psychological disposition [to perceive a] balanced relation', 'an aesthetic preference which finds... repetition...pleasing'[21] or 'the observation of nature, above all of living beings', that developed 'the human sense of symmetric harmony'[22] and so inspired this literary architecture. Whatever its inspiration, the parallelism or harmony in question is not tantamount to sheer repetition of identical elements, as in some styles of embroidery or tapestry. Rather, the idea seems to be the existence of *some relationship* between the parallel or symmetrically juxtaposed elements. This relationship may well involve contrast, as (in Gen. 9.6, cited above) between crime and punishment or (in the book of Ruth) between 'past' (Ruth 1.1-5) and 'future' (4.18-22), or a reversal of fortune from affliction (1.19-21) to blessing (4.14-17).[23]

Some of these observations may be valid also for the *inclusio* in the Copper Scroll context, to which I now turn. Following this, the discussion of symbolic geography will be resumed (yet another instance of the human bias towards symmetrical arrangement).

Textual Data

Inclusio?

In Table 14.1 are gathered several parallels between the opening sections of the Copper Scroll (in the left column) and its closing sections (in the right column). The text of the quotations and the enumeration of the sections follow Milik's unless otherwise stated.[24] The words or phrases which occur in both the beginning and the end are underlined (e.g. בחלת, כלי דמע, תחת המעלות). Those whose distribution in the scroll is also restricted to these parts have a double underline (e.g. משקל, שדא, תשע מאות). The comments on the parallels below follow the order of the opening sections.

Comments

(1) Section 1 is closely paralleled by section 61 in style, content and

21. Bertman, 'Symmetrical Design in the Book of Ruth', offers both these explanations.

22. Rofé, 'The Arrangement of the Book of Jeremiah', p. 392.

23. Bertman, 'Symmetrical Design in the Book of Ruth', pp. 166-67.

24. Milik, DJDJ III. Some variant readings are indicated in the following notes. Parts of the text where the reading is difficult and controversial have been omitted, when not essential for comparisons. The original line division has been ignored.

structure. Both are devoted to a שדה (chest?),[25] silver and vessels that are hidden under some steps. Although שדה (= שדא, שדת) seems to be the only lexeme which is exclusive to these two sections,[26] the accumulation of similar phraseology is remarkable. It almost begs the question concerning a possibly meaningful relation between the toponyms עמק עכור and הר גריזין (to be taken up later).

(2) Section 1 also resembles section 63—in the style of its 'summarizing statement with respect to the treasure'.[27] As shown by Wolters, these are the first and the last such statements in the Copper Scroll and the only two instances of the word מִשְׁקָל.[28] It is interesting that they are followed by similar (converse?) numbers: 17 and 71. These numbers are represented in different manners though, so the point need not be pressed. Another linguistic feature of the 'summarizing statement with respect to the treasure' will be mentioned in comment (4).

(3) Sections 3 and 58 exhibit numerical identity: 900. This is significant because it happens to be also the highest number of talents (?)[29]—in fact, the highest number of anything—that occurs in the scroll. Like nearly

25. Or sedan-cart (?). On the exegetical possibilities with respect to שדה see, e.g., the discussion of Lefkovits, *The Copper Scroll—3Q15*, pp. 116-20.

26. שדא was read also in 4.5 (but marked doubtful) by Allegro, *The Treasure of the Copper Scroll*, pp. 38-39, followed by Lurie, *The Copper Scroll from the Desert of Judah*, p. 80. Most authorities, however, have taken the sequence of signs in question as part of the numeral (= 55, rather than Allegro's 40).

27. For this terminology see the analysis of the recurring pattern of the Copper Scroll carried out by Al Wolters, 'Literary Analysis and the Copper Scroll', in Z.J. Kapera (ed.), *Intertestamental Essays in Honour of Jósef Tadeusz Milik* (Qumranica Mogilanensia, 6; Kraków: Enigma Press, 1992), pp. 239-52. The pattern explicated by Wolters has seven components or 'types of material', several (never all!) of which recur in a fixed order in each of the sections. Here I refer to one of the three forms of the sixth component ('column F' = 'additional comment on the hiding place or treasure') as defined there, p. 246.

28. Wolters, 'Literary Analysis and the Copper Scroll', p. 246. More generally, Wolters notes here another feature that is relevant to the idea of *inclusio*, namely that the type of material grouped as 'column F' tends to concentrate in the beginning and the end of the Copper Scroll: 'found only in the first 15 and in the last 13 sections'. Here, however, *two* exceptions should be mentioned: section 24—וכתבן אצלם—as indicated by Wolters, but also section 45—כל שבה חרם (pp. 249, 251 in the text following his article).

29. In section 3 the number seems to denote talents (of unidentified matter). Section 58 was similarly restored by Milik (talents of silver), while others refer it to the gold of 12.1 in the form of talents (Allegro) or coins (Lurie, Lefkovits).

Table 14.1. Inclusio *features in the Copper Scroll*

Opening sections			Closing sections		
Section	Lines	Text	Section	Lines	Text
1	1.1-3	בחריבה שבעמק עבור[a] תחת המעלות[b] הבואת למזרח... שדת כסף וכליה[c]	61	12.4-5	בהר גריזין תחת המעלהא של השית העליונא שדא אחת וכלכליה וכסף ככ 60
(1)	1.4	משקל ככרין שבעשרה [=17]	63	12.9	...הכל משקל ככרין 71 מנין עסרין
3	1.6-8	...ככרין תשע מאת	58	11.17	...ככ] תשע מאות
4	1.10-11	בתל של כחלת כלי דמע בלגין ואפודת הכל של הדמע... פתחו[d] בשולי האמא מן הצפון...	64	12.10-13	בשית (...?) בצפון כחלת פתחא צפון... משנא הכתב הזא ופרושה...
			62	12.6-7	בפי המבוע של בית שם כל(י) כסף וכלי זהב של דמע וכסף הכל ככרין שש מאות...

Notes:

a. The reading ...שבעמק, עבור (for Milik's שבעמק עבור), proposed by Pixner, 'Unravelling the Copper Scroll Code', p. 342 n. 2, while palaeographically possible, remains unconvincing in every other respect.

b. The same phrase occurs also in section 6 (2.1). The next word, הבואת, represents an unusual spelling of הבאות, 'which go (eastwards)', i.e., the steps (מעלות). So Milik, DJDJ III, pp. 228 (B 7a), 285. The reading חבואה, 'hidden', i.e., the silver chest (שדת כסף), proposed by Lurie, *The Copper Scroll from the Desert of Judah*, p. 53, seems unwarranted. Lurie's modern Hebrew translation (p. 58) ignored the following word, למזרח, 'eastwards'.

c. Milik read here וכלוה (indicating the second *waw* as uncertain): 'dont le total'. The reading כליה, followed above, has also been rendered as 'its contents' (Allegro, *The Treasure of the Copper Scroll*, pp. 33, 134 n. 6, deriving from √כול and noting the parallel in 12.5). However, Lefkovits points out (*The Copper Scroll*, p. 116), rightly, I think, that parsing as כלי-plural, is quite acceptable. Hence the word may be rendered 'its components' (Lefkovits), or 'its vessels' (Al Wolters, *The Copper Scroll: Overview, Text and Translation* [Sheffield: Sheffield Academic Press, 1996], p. 33), depending on the meaning assigned to שדה, on which see above, n. 25.

d. פתח occurs also in 1.8; 6.2, 3, 9; 10.10 (= sections 3, 27, 28, 49). However, only in sections 4 and 64 is it accompanied by a third person suffix (hence the double underline above). This morphological affinity was amply noted by Lefkovits, *The Copper Scroll*, pp. 189, 205, 925-26, 935. The fact that 'its opening' is related to the north—(ה)צפון, is another special feature of these sections. See further below, n. 34.

all the high numbers (i.e. 100 and up), it is a round number of a less 'realistic' appearance.[30] Whether these and other numerical data[31] could support a theory of 'mixed authenticity' regarding the Copper Scroll treasures is a question that cannot be fully discussed here. Is it possible, however, that placing the most impressive number of talents both in the beginning and towards the end of the scroll was meant to strike a 'grand-overture-and-finale' kind of note?

(4) Section 4 has in common with sections 62 and 63 a special stylistic feature of what Wolters termed the 'summarizing statement with respect to the treasure': all three introduce this statement with the word הכל.[32]

(5) Section 4 bears a more general resemblance to section 64. Associated with the enigmatic toponym כחלת, each of these hiding places has 'its opening'[33] further defined by some relation to the north.[34] Moreover, both sections may contain some reference to the content of the *whole*

30. There is apparently only one exception to the 'rule' that high numbers are round, namely the number 609 in section 13 (3.4). There are also several (approximately 10) low *and* round numbers (40, 70, etc.); but most numbers (approximately 30) are low and not round (17, 42, etc.). Pixner, 'Unravelling the Copper Scroll Code', p. 339, raised the possibility that the very high numbers might be 'tactics to divert attention'. Be this as it may, it is important to take into account that the Copper Scroll contains *different kinds of numbers*. Therefore, it would be somewhat inaccurate to describe the Copper Scroll numbers *in toto* as having 'specificity and concrete feel' (M.O. Wise, 'David J. Wilmot and the Copper Scroll', p. 299 below], arguing against Milik).

31. It is remarkable, for example, that the seven sets of Greek letters, which are sometimes thought to indicate 'real rather than legendary' treasures (Pixner, 'Unravelling the Copper Scroll Code', p. 335), usually occur with the more natural-looking numbers, and never with the high and round ones.

32. I am indebted to Al Wolters for this observation (made in response to my presentation at the Manchester Symposium, 9 September 1996). In his article, 'Literary Analysis and the Copper Scroll', p. 246, Wolters did note this introduction of the summarizing statement 'with the word (h)kl' in: 'sections 4 (a), 13, 45, 62 and 63'. However, it is precisely in sections 4 (1.10), 62 (12.7) and 63 (12.9) that we find הכל (hence the double underline above), whereas in sections 13 (3.4) and 45 (9.16) the word is כל.

33. This morphological parallel has already been noted above (Table 14.1 n. d).

34. A simpler relation to the north occurs in section 27 (6.3), which refers to 'the northern opening' (=[ב]פתח הצפוני). According to some readings of section 4, לפתח (*sic*) is detached from the sequel (...ובשולי), so that there is no connection between 'the opening' and the 'north'. See Allegro, *The Treasure of the Copper Scroll*, p. 33, and Lurie, *The Copper Scroll from the Desert of Judah*, pp. 62-65.

Copper Scroll. In section 4 such a generalization was read by Lehmann. The term אפודת, he argued,

> holds the key to the riddle of the Copper Scroll... Akin to Biblical פדות and Talmudic פדיון [אפודת means] 'redemption'... Coming at the beginning of the scroll, it may be taken as a description referring to practically *all* the items, listed throughout the inventory, or at least to those categories of taxes, gifts, tithes and consecrations which under Jewish law are subject to redemption...such items had been redeemed for money or precious metal and had been centrally gathered and accumulated for the purpose of delivery to Jerusalem and/or the Temple, but for political or Halakhic reasons could not be taken to their legal destination...[and] had to be, temporarily or permanently, committed to Genizah...[35]

In section 64 we have a different kind of generalization, revealing the need for further information and explanation for the *whole* document, establishing the existence of another copy that contains such matter, and stating its location. It seems, then, that in one way or another this section must also be credited with some 'key to deciphering the Copper Scroll'.[36]

The parallels and similarities between the two ends of 3Q15 pointed out so far may be of some significance when one tries to work out the quality and import of this enigmatic document. As already indicated, this frame may have the effect of making the reader aware of some relation that obtains between the parallel or similar parts. Now it only(!) remains to see what this relation might be. My own impression here is affected also by the special significance of the toponyms עמק עבור and הר גריזין, which seems to be highlighted by this frame (as suggested above, in comment 1).

Symbolic Geography?

Opening with עמק עבור seems too perfectly suited to the whole Copper

35. M.R. Lehmann, 'Identification of the Copper Scroll Based on its Technical Terms', *RevQ* 5 (1964), pp. 97-105 (99). More recently, Lehmann's conclusions regarding the technical terms in the Copper Scroll were embraced by McCarter Jr, 'The Mysterious Copper Scroll', pp. 63-64, and reiterated by Lehmann himself in a less technical publication: 'Where the Temple Tax Was Buried: The Key to Understanding the Copper Scroll', *BARev* (November/December 1993), pp. 38-43. A highly critical response to Lehmann's conclusions—especially the recent ones—was made by L. Morawiecki, 'The Copper Scroll Treasure: A Fantasy or Stock Inventory?', *The Qumran Chronicle* 4.3-4 (1994), pp. 169-74.

36. Thus Al Wolters, 'The Last Treasure of the Copper Scroll', *JBL* 107 (1988), pp. 419-29 (419). The theory developed there on the nature of the interpretative key to which section 64 refers is quite unique and too elaborate to be discussed here.

Scroll context to be dismissed as coincidence or explained away by the proximity to Qumran.[37] עמק עכור, literally the 'Vale of Trouble (or Curse)', is the place where sacred treasures were, once before, withdrawn from public view, buried in the ground and eventually also described by the person responsible (namely, Achan, when interrogated by Joshua):

> אדרת שנער אחת טובה ומאתים שקלים כסף ולשון זהב אחד חמשים
> שקלים משקלו...
> והנם טמונים בארץ בתוך האהלי[38] והכסף תחתיה (Josh. 7.21)

The *inclusio* sections of the Copper Scroll resemble this list also in their use of משקל (sections 1 and 63) and of the indefinite pronoun אחת (section 61), noted above. Moreover, the items enumerated by Achan are defined in the biblical story as part of the חרם (consecrated property): Josh. 6.17-18; 7.1, 11-15, a term that occurs several times also in 3Q15 and may be of some consequence for establishing the status of the property described.[39] Of course, the 'Genizah'—so to speak—performed by Achan differs somewhat from that which is recorded in the Copper Scroll: it is blatantly unlawful, intended to disguise the illegal possession of חרם objects, and inevitably results in a national calamity that can only be redressed when the perpetrator and all his household have been destroyed.

37. For this explanation of the fact that 3Q15 begins with עמק עכור see Milik, DJDJ III, p. 278: 'Notre écrivain commence avec une cachette de sa région (n° I, i 1-4) et poursuit avec quatre dépôts aux sites disparates' ('Our author begins with a cache in his region and continues with four deposits in various sites'). It may be of some interest that according to Milik (pp. 259-75, 278-79), the scroll has a geographical *inclusio*: the beginning and the end (= sections 1-5; 61-64) stand outside the pattern of four zones in which, Milik argued, most of the caches were arranged. Both these parts he described as 'divers', since they could not be attributed to any one particular area. Milik's theory was rejected by Pixner, who drew up a different plan of topographical zones: 'Unravelling the Copper Scroll Code', esp. pp. 333-34, 336, 341-60.

38. The present text has a conflated reading. Probably אהלי, 'my tent', *or* האהל, 'the tent', should be read. See *BHS*.

39. Thus Lehmann, 'Identification of the Copper Scroll Based on its Technical Terms', pp. 102-105. The occurrences of חרם in the Copper Scroll according to him are 9.10, 16 and 11.7, the first of which being read like Allegro (against Milik). The same three readings are followed by Wolters, 'The Copper Scroll and the Vocabulary of Mishnaic Hebrew', *RevQ* 14 (1990), pp. 483-95 (488-89) (with a reference to an earlier publication); up to his most recent: *The Copper Scroll: Overview, Text and Translation*, pp. 48, 52, and by Lefkovits, who notes the Copper Scroll's use of the term חרם in his comments on עמק עכור of 1.1: Lefkovits, *The Copper Scroll*, pp. 101, 126 n. 18, 674-75.

The narrative ends (vv. 25-26) with an aetiology of the name עמק עבור, deriving it from עכר, 'disturb, trouble',[40] but echoing also the name of the trouble *maker* עכן (Achan). In some later texts the paronomastic relation between עכן and עמק עבור apparently gave way to etymological identity. Thus the person's name was written עכר—rather than עכן—in 1 Chron. 2.7, and similarly (Αχαρ etc.) in the Septuagint and Syriac versions of Joshua 7 and in Josephus' *Ant.* 5.33; or, conversely, the place became עמק עכון, the spelling that appears in its second mention in 3Q15 (4.6 = section 17). If the form עמק עכון is indeed to be explained as contamination from עכן,[41] then perhaps it could be taken as a sign of the author's knowledge of the biblical tradition. To be sure, other explanations of עמק עכון are quite possible,[42] but the inference concerning the author's familiarity with biblical tradition need not depend on this one instance.

To summarize, if one had to choose a place that might be naturally associated with the Copper Scroll on a biblical-symbolic level of meaning, then עמק עבור would be an obvious candidate. It is one of the few sites in which biblical historiography locates the burial of sacred objects, both temporarily (Josh. 7.21) and 'to this day' (v. 26),[43] these objects being carefully reported in a manner that even bears some stylistic resemblance to the *inclusio* frame of the Copper Scroll. It may be objected that the connotations of עמק עבור are too negative to have been intended by our author as a framework for his own list. This is a valid point, unless it can be shown that the negative aspect has its own contribution, that it is, in other words, *part* of the framework.

I turn now to the closest parallel of the עמק עבור section at the other end of the Copper Scroll, namely section 61 (as shown in comment 1, above). The toponym found here, הר גריזין, appears to be contrasted to

40. BDB, p. 747.

41. This explanation was offered by Milik, DJDJ III, p. 257 (C 200).

42. The variants עבור/עכון may be seen simply as an instance of phonetic interchange within 'the למנ״ר group of sounds (voiced sonorous)' (Lefkovits, *The Copper Scroll*, p. 987). The most obvious case for comparison in the Copper Scroll is חפון for חפור (4.7; 5.14; 8.14 etc.). Muchowski argues for 'affective dysorthography' brought about by the circumstances of transmission (dictation at 'some tempo and rhythm', emotional disturbances) as well as by the performance of final [R] in Hebrew of the first century CE. See P. Muchowski, 'Dysorthographic Forms *ḥăpôn* and *'ākôn* in 3Q15', in Kapera (ed.), *Intertestamental Essays*, pp. 131-33.

43. It is possible to understand the MT (Josh. 7.24-26) as indicating that the חרם treasures stolen by Achan were buried *with* him in עמק עבור, under the heap of stones erected on that occasion. See Milik, DJDJ III, p. 263 (D 5).

עמק עבור in both topography (mountain versus valley) and biblical connotations (blessing versus curse).[44] It is remarkable that the main national-blessing context of Mount Gerizim (Josh. 8.33)[45] is adjacent to the national-calamity context of the 'Vale of Trouble' (Josh. 7). The usual identification of Mount Gerizim as the ancient Samaritan centre near Shechem, followed by Milik,[46] is somewhat problematic for those who interpret the Copper Scroll as a perfectly authentic record of the Jerusalem Temple treasures or dues.[47] Hence the idea of locating our scroll's Mount Gerizim (and Mount Ebal) in the vicinity of Jericho, following another ancient tradition.[48] Connotations travel freely, though. The line of interpretation pursued here may 'legitimately' incorporate biblical Shechemite connotations that might have been provoked by הר גריזין, *even if* the geographical reference of this name (or pseudonym) is non-Shechemite.

Thus it is not without interest that the area of Shechem is also associated with a biblical report concerning an act of 'Genizah': the 'foreign gods' and earrings of Jacob's household buried under the terebinth tree near Shechem (Gen. 35.4; a ritual implicit also in Josh. 24.23-27). The report in Gen. 35.4 uses a verb (טמן = 'hide, conceal, esp. in *earth*')[49] of the root found also in Achan's confession, quoted above, concerning the illegally possessed חרם objects (Josh. 7.21: = טמונים, 'are hidden'). In contrast with

44. On the possible use of *inclusio* or ring composition to express contrast or reversal see the end of the previous section.

45. Mount Gerizim is mentioned also in Deut. 11.19 and 27.12, both of which anticipate the ritual performed in Josh. 8 as preparatory instructions. In Judg. 9.7 the strange choice of Mount Gerizim as the 'pulpit' of Jotham's address to the Shechemites may presuppose its mountain-of-blessing status paradoxically or satirically, since the blessing has turned into a curse. For a recent discussion of the episode as political satire see Z. Weisman, *Political Satire in the Bible* (Semeia Studies, 32; Atlanta: SBL, 2000), pp. 26-36.

46. Milik, DJDJ III, p. 274 (D 69). The same identification was followed by Pixner, 'Unravelling the Copper Scroll Code', p. 357 n. 49; and—for totally different reasons —by Lefkovits, *The Copper Scroll*, pp. 892-93 (with further bibliography).

47. The problem was first noted by Allegro, *The Treasure of the Copper Scroll*, p. 75, who felt prompted 'to seek…a pseudonym…or preferably a place nearer Qumran or Jerusalem'.

48. This tradition is echoed in: *b. Soṭ* 33b; *y. Soṭ* 7.3; *Sifre Deut.* 56 (R. Eli'ezer); Eusebius, *Onomasticon* 64.9-20 (cf. also 65.9-21); the Madeba mosaic map; see Allegro, *The Treasure of the Copper Scroll*, pp. 75-76, and Lurie, *The Copper Scroll*, pp. 123-24, for the details.

49. BDB, p. 380.

Achan's action, however, the concealment of the 'foreign gods' is anything but illegal. Rather, it signifies passage to a higher form of religion, stipulated in a covenant (Josh. 24 in particular) and requiring the Genizah of obsolete objects of worship. In any case, there is no theft—nor any other taboo infringement—involved in this Shechem–Mount Gerizim tradition. Finally, it seems that the contrast between the different biblical sites of concealed valuables was basically kept in postbiblical legend: the 'illegal' stigma of עמק עכור, on the one hand, and the 'sacred', 'Genizah' flavour of Mount Gerizim, on the other.[50]

It can be concluded that הר גריזין—treated by our author, either consciously or intuitively, as the positive counterpart of עמק עכור—is combined with the latter to form a suggestive 'frame' within which the whole work moves. Movement from 'The Vale of Trouble' to The Sacred Mount can be understood as 'progress'; hardly *The Pilgrim's Progress*, to be sure, but a hopeful one, nevertheless. That עמק עכור *could* have been found an appropriate point of departure for some message of hope is evident from its occurrences in prophetic eschatology: Isa. 65.10 and Hos. 2.15 [Heb. 17]. It is with the Hosea verse in particular that 3Q15 may be seen as having a *pesher* relationship.[51]

(והלכתיה המדבר...) ונתתי לה את... עמק עכור לפתח תקוה

(...I will go with her into the wilderness)...
Turning the Vale of Trouble into the Gate of Hope...[52]

Further Observations

The features of the Copper Scroll pointed out in the section above belong to the kind that is usually associated with literary creation. This is plain from the other examples provided for these features, down to the last citation. If it is granted that what we have here is more than a random set of textual curiosities, then some questions inevitably arise concerning how this line of interpretation may affect our understanding of the nature of the Copper Scroll and its author. It hardly needs to be stated that no solutions to these problems can be offered on the basis of the present sample

50. See the details supplied by Milik, DJDJ III, pp. 263 (D 5), 274 (D 69).

51. Cf. my comment on symbolic geography above, p. 212.

52. The translation follows the NEB. The margin has the alternative: '...Emek-achor to Petach-tikvah.'

analysis.[53] Nevertheless, I hazard the following, inevitably tentative, observations:

(1) *The 'list' genre*: The Copper Scroll has been characterized as a 'list', 'inventory' and the like, even before its opening in 1956.[54] More recent publications, especially when rejecting Milik's legendary folkloristic theory, have tended to regard the term 'list' as a strict genre definition. According to the findings of the late David J. Wilmot's dissertation, as reported by M.O. Wise,

> 3Q15 is...by genre, no work of literature or folklore. It is a genuine business document. It is a list...a temple inventory list... The Copper Scroll clearly falls into the category of non-literary text, of document... Milik argued that the Copper Scroll is a product of human imagination, a work of literature. Yet if so, why does it lack the format, layout and content of literary productions?[55]

A similar position is presented by Wolters:

> The Copper Scroll is not a 'literary' work in the modern sense of belonging to a category of *belles lettres* or high art. But it does qualify as literary in the more basic form-critical sense of belonging to a specific genre and of displaying recognizable patterns of structure and arrangement... Whatever the scroll may lack in the ordinary ornaments of literary prose is counterbalanced by the less charming but nevertheless literary virtues of economy and symmetrical structure.[56]

53. The analysis sampled in this paper may perhaps be developed further. The cache subsequent to the one in הר גריזין (section 62, in Milik's enumeration), is located in בית שם (12.6). This phrase was understood by Allegro (*The Treasure of the Copper Scroll*, pp. 55, 169 n. 305) as a reference to the Temple, literally 'House of [the] Name'. In the latest edition of the Copper Scroll by Al Wolters, *The Copper Scroll: Overview, Text and Translation*, pp. 54-55, the beginning of section 64 (12.10) is read ...בשית שכנה, and rendered: 'In the cavern of the Presence...' These readings are not followed by other scholars, as far as I have seen. Nevertheless, both of them seem especially interesting in relation to the interpretation offered above.

54. K.G. Kuhn, 'Les rouleaux de cuivre de Qumrân', *RB* 61 (1954), pp. 193-205; See also the research reviews on this point by Wolters, 'Literary Analysis and the Copper Scroll', pp. 240-43, and Wise, 'David J. Wilmot and the Copper Scroll', in the present volume.

55. Wise, 'David J. Wilmot and the Copper Scroll', in the present volume. Wilmot's conclusion was based on a wealth of comparable documents from the Graeco-Roman period.

56. Wolters, 'Literary Analysis and the Copper Scroll', pp. 239, 247.

The present paper suggests, nevertheless, that the Copper Scroll is not totally devoid of the 'ornaments of literary prose'. This hardly puts it in the 'category of *belles lettres* or high art', yet there may be a little more to it than factual documentation, structure and arrangement. It is just possible that on certain occasions the recommended division of 'written materials …from antiquity…into…literary and non-literary texts'[57] does not yield neatly distinct categories. Making an inventory of temple treasures put away in a time of national distress may well be such an occasion. Is it feasible that this inventory would have been prepared without some religious sentiment creeping in?

(2) *The authenticity of the Copper Scroll treasures* is not necessarily undermined by reading it in a more 'literary' style, since 'literary' is not equivalent to 'fictitious'. The features pointed out above have much to do with the order of the sections. They may indicate, for example, that authentic records were subjected to some 'literary' editorial activity. However, it cannot be ruled out that such records were also 'reinforced' or 'solemnized' by the addition of 'folkloristic' fictitious entries.[58]

57. Wise, 'David J. Wilmot and the Copper Scroll', in the present volume.

58. As already suggested (above, nn. 30-31), the possibility of 'mixed authenticity' recommends itself also on other grounds.

15

Further Reflections on the Copper Scroll

Stephen Goranson

Introduction

In my article, 'Sectarianism, Geography, and the Copper Scroll', after conceding that much about this text remained enigmatic to me, I asserted that the Copper Scroll belonged to the Essenes, that it did not list items *from* the Jerusalem temple, and that some of its items were probably located east of the Jordan River.[1] Now I can offer a few further supporting observations, as well as a new guess concerning the function of the Copper Scroll's Greek letters.

To my knowledge it is still the case that no evidence has been presented that contradicts the most plausible scenario, namely that the Copper Scroll and the Cave 3 texts on leather (which include sectarian texts) were deposited by members of the same group. The fact that the Copper Scroll and various scroll jars were within clear sight of one another makes most implausible the hypothesis that the Copper Scroll might have been deposited after the leather scrolls and by someone unrelated to the deposit of the leather scrolls; as has often been observed, such a hypothesis ignores the fact that this cave would not have appeared to such a depositor as a safe hiding place.[2]

1. S. Goranson, 'Sectarianism, Geography, and the Copper Scroll', *JJS* (1992), pp. 282-87.

2. In this respect I agree, among others, with F.M. Cross, *The Ancient Library of Qumran and Modern Biblical Studies* (Grand Rapids, MI: Baker Book House, 1980), n. 29 on pp. 22-25; B. Pixner, 'Unravelling the Copper Scroll Code: A Study on the Topography of 3Q15', *RevQ* 11 (1983), pp. 323-65; and A. Wolters, 'History and the Copper Scroll', in M.O. Wise, N. Golb, J.J. Collins and D. Pardee (eds.), *Methods of Investigation of the Dead Sea Scrolls and the Khirbet Qumran Site* (Annals of the New York Academy of Sciences, 722; New York: New York Academy of Sciences, 1994),

This is not the occasion for an extended defense of the view that the Qumran text collection is an Essene accumulation, but allow me to state that I find the identification persuasive, that I have defended it in previous and in forthcoming publications, and that I assume here that Qumran was one of the places where Essenes lived. This is also not the occasion for an extended defense of the proposal that Alexander Jannaeus was regarded by the Essenes as a wicked priest, and that Judah, who, according to *b. Qid.* 66a, asked Alexander to give up the priesthood, was regarded by Essenes as a teacher of righteousness.[3]

Koḥlit *and Sites East of the Jordan*

This is, however, an occasion to continue consideration of the term *koḥlit* (כחלת) which appears both in the Copper Scroll and in *b. Qid.* 66a. According to the latter, Alexander Jannaeus returned from conquering 60 towns in *koḥlit*, which in this case is most plausibly identified as an area east of the Jordan River.

In my view, Pixner's article on the Copper Scroll made a relevant and useful contribution in calling special attention to this important term *koḥlit*, even though I find his interpretation of it not persuasive. In addition to my previous reservations about his interpretation of the term as applying to three separate monastic centers (rather than to one district),

pp. 285-98. In note 11 of my previous article (cited above) I mistakenly wrote that the report by J. Patrich on his Cave 3 excavation was forthcoming, when, in fact, it was already in print in *Excavations and Surveys in Israel* 6 (1988), pp. 66-70. However, his new information—concerning, for instance, the date of one collapse from the cave's roof—substantially matches what I had heard from him orally and does not change my view that the Copper Scroll depositor must have been comfortable leaving that text along with other texts only because all the texts belonged to his own group.

3. Provisionally, see, e.g., Strabo, *Geography* 16.2.34-40; I. Friedlaender, 'The Rupture between Alexander Jannai and the Pharisees', *JQR* NS 4 (1913–14), pp. 443-48; M.J. Geller, 'Alexander Jannaeus and the Pharisee Rift', *JJS* 30 (1979), pp. 202-11; and E. Main, 'Les Sadducéens vus par Flavius Josèphe', *RB* 97 (1990), pp. 161-206; E. Main, 'For King Jonathan or Against Him? The Use of the Bible in 4Q448', in M.E. Stone and E.G. Chazon (eds.), *Biblical Perspectives: Early Use and Interpretation of the Bible in Light of the Dead Sea Scrolls: Proceedings of the First International Symposium of the Orion Center for the Study of the Dead Sea Scrolls and Associated Literature, 12–14 May, 1996* (STDJ, 28; Leiden: E.J. Brill, 1998), pp. 113-35. See now S. Goranson, 'Others and Intra-Jewish Polemic as Reflected in the Qumran Texts', in P.W. Flint and J.C. VanderKam (eds.), *The Dead Sea Scrolls after Fifty Years: A Comprehensive Assessment*, II (Leiden: E.J. Brill, 1999), pp. 534-51.

Pixner's interpretation is made unlikely by his translation of 3Q15 1.9 ('On the hill of *Koḥlit*...') because this appears to imply that a hill or tell appears within such a *koḥlit*. Such is not plausible, as it would require either an unusually small tell or an unusually large monastery. K. Beyer translates כחלת as 'schwarzes Objekt', which seems unlikely.[4] V. Jones has also proposed a meaning based on the potential color association, as a reference to a 'blue aura'.[5] Rather, a district remains the most probable meaning.

J. Lefkovits has helpfully indicated a possible, restored fifth instance of the term כחלת in 4.1.[6] Lefkovits provides a useful discussion of the term, but does not determine a definite meaning or location, but he writes that it may be identical with the wilderness of כחלת mentioned in *b. Qid.* 66a; Lefkovits, following Rashi, interprets this as being within the wilderness of Judah.[7] But if this *baraita* has a historical basis, the military campaign of Alexander Jannaeus was more probably east of the Jordan River.

Pixner proposed that the mention of *naḥal hagadol* in 3Q15 10.3-4 could well refer to the Yarmuk River. Lefkovits provides massive and quite helpful commentary, but when it came to *naḥal hagadol*, he wrote (p. 728), 'It is a mystery to which river or wadi the Great River refers', not noting till later the suggestion that it may be the Yarmuk River.[8]

Several of Pixner's other proposed locations east of the Jordan are not persuasive, but the idea is worth pursuing. There is no reason *a priori* to neglect other apparently weighty trans-Jordanian possible readings. For example, not only J.T. Milik, but also F.M. Cross read Kefar Nebo at 9.11

4. K. Beyer, *Die aramäische Texte vom Toten Meer. Ergänzungsband* (Göttingen: Vandenhoeck & Ruprecht, 1994), pp. 224-33.

5. See D.C. Browning Jr, 'The Strange Search for the Aṣhes of the Red Heifer', *BA* 59 (1996), pp. 74-86, and Vendyl Jones, 'The Copper Scroll and the Excavations at Qumran', reprinted from his newsletter *The Researcher* (February 1996) on the web site, The Vendyl Jones Research Institutes (http://www.vendyljones.org.il).

6. J.K. Lefkovits, *The Copper Scroll—3Q15: A New Reading, Translation and Commentary* (PhD dissertation, New York University, 1993), available from University Microfilms in two volumes. This seems a plausible reading, with the first letter and part of the second restored; the fourth letter could be a *taw* though it is understandable that *he* and *ḥet* are also possible.

7. His main discussion is on pp. 183-87.

8. As an aside, it could be expected that, if a Syria–Israel peace treaty were negotiated, one of the many consequences would be to make excavations near the Yarmuk, including in northern Jordan, more practicable.

and considered the site, with a waterfall, appropriate.[9] This suggestion of sites east of the Jordan is not intended to dismiss but to supplement the arguments, for example, that several sites (e.g. Sekakah) apparently are in and around Qumran.[10]

A conjecture that perhaps Essenes were named after a village east of the Jordan is attested, with variations, at least as early as 1604 by Nicolas Serarius.[11] The claim that Essenes were named after Ossis east of the Jordan was made by C. Salmasius in 1629.[12] If there is any connection between such place names—Essa or Ossis, spelled עסיא and אסיא—and the Essene group name, the place was more likely named after the group than vice versa. A. Neubauer reasonably concluded that the village of Essa, mentioned in rabbinic literature along with other sites having hot baths, was located east of the Lake of Tiberias.[13] It would make sense for R. Meir to go there, as claimed in *Gen. R.* 36, a site with hot baths, east of the Tiberias Lake, to recite the book of Esther. Of course the lack of any extant copies of Esther at Qumran is well known. Callirhoë, east of the Jordan and near the Dead Sea, has also been suggested as an alternate to the reading that takes this as a reference to Asia Minor.[14] And Essenes and/or Ossenes were said by Epiphanius to have survived post-70 CE in Perea, trans-Jordan.[15]

9. F.M. Cross, 'Reuben, First-Born of Jacob', *ZAW* 100, supplement (1988), pp. 46-65 (51-52).

10. As shown, e.g., by H. Eshel, 'A Note on Joshua 15.61-61 and the Identification of the City of Salt', *IEJ* 45 (1995), pp. 37-40.

11. N. Serarius, *Trihaeresium*, Book 3, ch. 1, is cited here from the anthology edited by J. Triglandius, *Trium scriptorum illustrium de tribus Judaeorum sectis syntagma* (Delft, 1703), p. 106.

12. Cited here from his *Plinianae exercitationes in Caii Iulii Solini Polyhistoria* (Paris, 1629; repr., 1689), pp. 430-34; and see my 'Sectarianism, Geography, and the Copper Scroll', p. 287.

13. A. Neubauer, *La géographie du Talmud* (Paris: Michel Lévy Frères), pp. 38, 273, 308-309.

14. G. Vermes, 'The Etymology of "Essenes"', *RevQ* 2 (1959–60), pp. 427-43 (443), suggested a third option: that R. Meir was neither in Asia nor in a town named Essa (or Ossa), but 'among the Essenes'. For the suggestion of Callirhoë, see N.I. Weinstein, *Beiträge zur Geschichte der Essäer* (Vienna: Ch. D. Lippe, 1892), pp. 9-11. See also S. Wagner, *Die Essener in der wissenschaftlichen Diskussion* (BZAW, 79; Berlin: Alfred Töpelmann, 1960), pp. 119-20 and M. Jastrow, *Dictionary of the Targumim...* (repr.; New York: Judaica Press, 1985), pp. 93, 1098.

15. *Panarion* 19.2.1 on Ossenes in Peraea; cf., e.g., 20.3.1 on Ossenes in the land beyond the Dead Sea; and heresy 53 on the Ossene-related Sampsaens in Peraea and

A burial complex on the outskirts of Abila included three ceramic inkwells, one of which was similar to those at Qumran, but more importantly, it also contained a cylindrical, 'scroll-type' jar.[16] De Vaux noted this jar as the only parallel to the Qumran type known to him.[17] This discovery is of interest additionally because it is located in the proposed 'land of Damascus' area. Unfortunately, apparently, records of that salvage dig were lost. Jodi Magness notes only one other parallel, from Jericho, and she rejects some other suggested comparanda.[18] A photo by J. Trever of a display case in the Amman museum seems to include the tallest of the Abila inkwells.[19] The case includes two jars; is one merely of Qumran provenance (i.e. is one the Abila jar?). Pottery, of course, as well as any distinctive burials or water installations that may be found in the area would be of interest. In any case it would appear to be worth publishing, if the object (or photos, drawings, descriptions, or measurements of it) does turn up.[20]

Qumran Hoards

Jodi Magness's redating of the end of Qumran Period Ib to '9/8 BCE or some time thereafter' is persuasive.[21] The hoard of Tyrian silver tetra-

Moabitis. I assume here that these 'Ossenes' are related to 'Essenes' (derived from עושי התורה).

16. F.S. Ma'ayeh, *ADAJ* 4–5 (1960), p. 116 and pl. V.1. The plate shows three inkwells or inkpots but unfortunately does not show the jar.

17. R. de Vaux, *Archaeology and the Dead Sea Scrolls* (London: British Academy; Oxford University Press, 1973), pp. 54-55 n. 1. See also 'Chronique archéologique', *RB* 67 (1960), p. 229.

18. J. Magness, 'The Community at Qumran in Light of its Pottery', in Wise *et al.*, *Methods of Investigation of the Dead Sea Scrolls*, pp. 39-50 (41).

19. In S.A. Reed, 'Survey of the Dead Sea Scrolls Fragments and Photographs at the Rockefeller Museum', *BA* 54 (1991), pp. 44-51 (48).

20. For further information on the excavations at Qweilbah (= Quailba), near Abila, see now J.D. Wineland, *Ancient Abilah: An Archaeological History* (BAR International Series, 989; Oxford: Archaeopress, 2001), pp. 15-16.

21. 'The Chronology of the Settlement at Qumran in the Herodian Period', *DSD* 2 (1995), pp. 58-65, quote from p. 64. See also A. Kushnir-Stein, 'Another Look at Josephus' Evidence for the Date of Herod's Death', *Scripta Classica Israelica* 14 (1995), p. 73-86, for a possible refinement during that period; this argues that Herod died not before Passover 4 BCE but during winter 4–3 BCE, which would be relevant to the periods of Qumran if the events surrounding the death of Herod played a role in the destruction of Qumran at the end of Period Ib or in the resettlement afterward.

drachmas found at Qumran in locus 120 was evidently buried soon before the end of period Ib. When the same (Essene) group resettled the site shortly afterward, it is likely that the depositor, the Essene treasurer, had died. At any rate the coins (which are the type used for Temple dues) were not dug up throughout the next seven or so decades of Essene occupation of the site, suggesting that this hoard location was no longer known. Experiences such as this one could have encouraged the practice of record keeping, to prevent such further losses in the future. Saving funds apparently had a long history within the Essene movement.

The items listed in the Copper Scroll apparently include funds and objects *for* the (or a) Jerusalem temple; there is no evidence that any of these items were *from* the Jerusalem Temple. An assumption that, since Jewish temple items are mentioned, it necessarily relates to either the standing pre-70 Temple or to a Bar Kochba-intended one, seems unwarranted. Apparently the Essenes collected for a hoped-for, future, alternately organized Temple.[22]

The Greek Letters

I wonder if the seven sets of Greek letters found at the ends of seven items relate to removals or withdrawals of deposits. All seven appear in the first four of the twelve columns; all in the first of three sheets of copper; and all ranging from the first to the fifteenth of the sixty items (using the numbering of Lefkovits). If the text was not written at one sitting, the earlier items could represent the earliest deposits. Since only some of those earliest deposits are marked with Greek, this could represent removals of some of those deposits. The Greek might indicate abbreviated names of persons, as previously suggested, or times of removal; my suggestion concerns not so much the deciphering of the Greek letters individually as in seeking a plausible function for them overall, as applied to only seven items.

If this is the case, the Essenes decided to move some deposits to safer areas (either to a central treasury or to re-interments, whether in the same or in regrouped lots). For example, the silver chest or sedan chair mentioned in 1.3 (in one of the items marked with Greek) could be the

22. For an example of differing Essene legal positions regarding the temple, see J.M. Baumgarten, 'The First and Second Tithes in the Temple Scroll', in A. Kort and S. Morschauser (eds.), *Biblical and Related Studies Presented to Samuel Iwry* (Winona Lake, IN: Eisenbrauns, 1985), pp. 5-15.

same silver chest listed in 12.5, though with a differing amount deposited with it.

Another possibility is that some or all of these seven specially marked items may have been uncovered by others—either Romans or other non-Essenes. The Greek could be used as easily distinguished endnotes. It would be hard, after all, to erase an entry on copper, in order to cancel a listed deposit. Finally, I admit that these suggestions concerning the Greek letters are all highly speculative.

New Light on the Copper Scroll and 4QMMT

Israel Knohl

The Copper Scroll is an enigma that has yet to be deciphered. In this study, I would like to suggest a new solution to this riddle, based on a careful inspection of the different items mentioned in the scroll. The investigation will be undertaken with the aid of information available in biblical and rabbinic sources. I will further suggest a new understanding of a perplexing, fragmented passage in 4QMMT. It is my opinion that the reconstruction and interpretation of this passage will provide us with the key to many problems concerning 4QMMT and the Copper Scroll.

The Treasures of the Copper Scroll

The Copper Scroll lists mainly treasures of gold and silver, but some other objects are also mentioned. Among these are: *dema'* vessels (כלי דמע, 1.9-10; 3.2, 9; 5.6; 8.3; 11.1, 4, 10, 14; 12.6-7); *ḥerem*, consecrated offering (חרם, 9.16); and second tithe (מעסר שני, 1.10-11). *Dema'* and *ḥerem* are priestly gifts[1] that could be given to the Temple or directly to the priests.[2] Thus, we can infer from the reference to the *dema'* vessels and *ḥerem* that the origin of the treasures is either in the Temple, or a priest's

1. For *dema'* as a priestly gift see M.R. Lehmann, 'Identification of the Copper Scroll Based on its Technical Terms', *RevQ* 5 (1964), pp. 97-105 (97-98); J.C. Greenfield, 'The Small Caves of Qumran', *JAOS* 89 (1989), pp. 128-41 (139); J.M. Baumgarten, *Studies in Qumran Law* (Leiden: E.J. Brill, 1977), pp. 131-33; E. Qimron, 'The Biblical Lexicon in Light of the DSS', *DSD* 2 (1995), pp. 310-14. For *ḥerem* see Num. 18.14.

2. See G. Alon, *Jews, Judaism, and the Classical World* (Jerusalem: Magnes Press, 1997), pp. 89-102; A. Oppenheimer, *The Am Ha-aretz* (Leiden: E.J. Brill, 1977), pp. 29-42; E.E. Urbach, *The Halakha: Its Sources and Development* (Jerusalem: Magnes Press, 1986), pp. 44-49.

private house. On the other hand, the second tithe (מעסר שני) is not a priestly gift. According to the law in Deut. 14.22-23 it should be eaten by its owners.[3] However, since there was a tradition determining that the second tithe should be consumed in the Temple, it is possible that it would also be kept in the Temple.[4] On the other hand, priests, like all other Israelites, may hold the second tithe in their houses.[5] Thus, the treasures mentioned in the scroll come either from a priestly house or from the Temple.

The inventory in the scroll may shed light on the sectarian identity of the people who concealed the treasures. At one point, *dema'* vessels are mentioned as placed beside a Torah scroll (ספר, 8.3). Pharisee Halakha forbids the keeping of *dema'* -(*terumah*) near Torah scrolls,[6] whereas the Sadducees did not accept this rule.[7] We may therefore infer that the priests

3. The term 'second tithe' is applied to the tithe mentioned in Deut. 14, already in *Jub.* 32.9-11 and Tob. 1.7. This is the usual term for this tithe in rabbinic literature. The Septuagint and Pseudo-Jonathan to Deut. 26.12-13, however, apply the term 'second tithe' to the tithe that is given to the poor. Since there is no reasonable motive to hide this type of tithe, it seems better to assume that the scroll refers to the tithe of Deut. 14. For possible reasons for the concealment of this tithe see n. 5.

4. *Jub.* 32.11 rules that the 'second tithes' should be eaten in the Temple. The same view can be inferred from the Temple Scroll (43.2-17), which discusses the eating of the second tithes in its description of the Temple court.

5. Two different reasons can be suggested for the storing and hiding of מעסר־שני, 'second tithe': (1) the Temple Scroll (43.2-17) rules that the 'second tithe' should be eaten only on the days of festivals; hence, it should be stored until a suitable time; (2) the word that follows the term מעשר שני should probably be read מפוגל (see A. Wolters, 'The Copper Scroll and the Vocabulary of Mishnaic Hebrew', *RevQ* 14 [1990], pp. 483-95 [493 n. 69]). Lefkovits rejects this reading since the rabbinic terms מפוגל ,פיגול refer only to sacrifices and not to tithes; see J.K. Lefkovits, *The Copper Scroll—3Q15: A New Reading, Translation and Commentary* (PhD dissertation, New York University, 1993), p. 204. However, the rabbinic use of the term פיגול, which is based on Lev. 7.18; 19.7, is not the only possible application of this word. In Isa. 65.4 and Ezek. 4.14, it has the meaning of 'unclean, impure'. Thus we can accept Wolters's suggestion to read מעסר שני מפוגל as 'a second tithe rendered unclean'. Rabbinic law forbids the eating of an unclean second tithe (see *Sifre Deut.* 103; *b. Yeb.* 73b). Rabbinic Halakha rules that a second tithe, brought to Jerusalem and there become unclean, should be redeemed and eaten (*m. Ma'as. Š.* 3.9; *b. Pes.* 36b). Yet we may assume that the sectarian priests held the view that it is impossible to redeem an unclean second tithe, and it should be kept and stored by its owners.

6. Since they ruled that ספר, 'the holy book', would defile the *dema'-terumah* (see *m. Zab.* 5.12).

7. The Sadducees objected to the view that the holy books defile the hands (see *m. Yad.* 4.6).

who hid the treasures listed in the Copper Scroll were of a non-Pharisee origin.

In 3Q15 3.3-4 there is a list of four types of vessels: libation bowls, cups, jugs and jars (מזרקות כוסות מנקיאות קסאות). All these vessels are Temple vessels,[8] and they are the only vessels of the Temple service that are mentioned in the scroll. On the one hand, this may support an argument that the treasures are not the Temple treasures, since, if the treasures originated in the Temple, why would these vessels be the only Temple vessels mentioned in the scroll?[9] On the other hand, if these are the treasures of a private priestly house, how can we understand the existence of Temple vessels in private hands? For at least two of the vessels listed, we seem to have a solution to this problem. The jugs and the jars (מנקיאות קסאות), which are mentioned in the Pentateuch as libation vessels (Exod. 25.29; 37.15; Num. 4.7), are specifically connected in the rabbinic literature to the water libation during the festival of Tabernacles.[10] As is well known, the sectarian priests objected to the Pharisee water libation custom.[11] Two distinguished scholars[12] have argued that the reference in *m. Sanh.* 9.6 to the person who 'steals the jar' (הגונב את הקסוה) should be explained in light of the dispute between the sects. The jars were taken by the sectarian priests in order to prevent the performance of the Pharisee custom of water libation during the Feast of Tabernacles. In my view this assumption can be supported by the tradition in the Tosefta (*Zeb.* 1.12), which rules that the water libation can be performed not only by means of jugs and jars, but also by using other vessels: ניסוך המים...בין בהין בין

8. קשות and מנקיות are mentioned in the Bible only as Temple vessels. The same is true for מזרקות with one exception (Amos 6.6). The כוסות do not appear in the Bible as Temple vessels; however, we see them in cultic use, in rabbinic texts (see *m. Zeb.* 8.8, 12; 13.8; *t. Zeb.* 3.6; 8.20, 25). Since the other three vessels in this group are clearly Temple vessels, we have to assume that the כוסות mentioned here had the same origin.

9. If the scroll in fact contains a list of Temple treasures, should we not also expect to find other vessels that were in use in the Temple, such as כפות, מחתות?

10. See *t. Zeb.* 1.12; *b. Suk.* 48b.

11. See *m. Suk.* 4.9; *t. Suk.* 3.16; *b. Suk.* 48b.

12. See A. Geiger, 'Biblische und Talmudische Miscellen', *Jüdische Zeitschrift* 5 (1867), pp. 98-117 (108-109); D. Hoffmann, *Die Sechs Ordnungen der Mishna*. IV. *Seder Nesikin* (Berlin: H. Itzkowski, 1924), p. 187 n. 59. See further A. Kohut, *Aruch Completum*, VII (Vienna: Menora, 1926), p. 143; Ch. Albeck, *The Mishna, Seder Nezikin* (Jerusalem: The Bialik Institute, 1953), p. 454; Alon, *Jews*, p. 118 n. 59; Urbach, *The Halakha*, p. 34.

בקערה בין בקיסוא בין במניקיות. This rule seems to reflect the response of the Pharisees to the stealing of the jugs and the jars by the sectarian priest. In order to enable the performance of the water libation the Pharisees allowed the use of vessels other than the jugs and jars (מנקיות קסוות) that are specifically mentioned in the Torah as libation vessels. In light of these rabbinic traditions, we may identify the jugs and jars of the Copper Scroll as the Temple libation vessels taken by the sectarian priests in order to prevent the performance of the Pharisee custom of water libation. However, we do not have sufficient explanation for holding the other two types of Temple vessels mentioned in the scroll (מזרקות כוסות), which were used mainly for receiving the sacrificial blood.[13] Hence, we have to leave open the possibility that the treasures are Temple treasures, and that for some unknown reason only these four types of vessels were taken from the Temple for concealment. In any case, it is clear that the people who stored the treasures were priests who served in the Temple, and had an immediate connection to its vessels.

I shall conclude this part of the study by suggesting that the objects mentioned in the Copper Scroll seem to fit very well with the Talmudic traditions on the non-Pharisee priesthood in Jerusalem. Moreover, these objects with all their details, it seems to me, are the best evidence for the authenticity of the treasures mentioned in the scroll. It is hard to believe that a person writing a list of legendary treasures would take the trouble to deal with four different types of *dema'*[14] and other minute details of sacred gifts.

Thus, the most likely conclusion is that the treasures listed in the scroll are real treasures, either of an extremely wealthy priestly house in Jerusalem, or of the Temple. This conclusion opens up another question: why were some of the treasures buried in the Qumran area, and why was the scroll with the list of the treasures and the sacred gifts concealed in a Qumran cave? To try to solve this mystery I turn now to 4QMMT.

4QMMT B8-9

At the beginning of the second section of 4QMMT (B8-9) is a short passage that deals with זבח הגויים, that is, offerings made by non-Jews.

13. For כוסות see above, n. 8; for מזרקות see Temple Scroll 23.12; 26.6; *m. Yom.* 4.3; 5.4.

14. See דמע סוח דמע סנה 11.4; דמע לאה דמע סירא 11.14; the exact meaning of these terms is not clear.

The text is not well preserved, but the editors reconstruct it as follows:

> ועל זבח הגויים [אנחנו חושבים שהם] זובח[ים] אל הי [...] שא היא
> [כ]מי שזנת אליו...

> And concerning the sacrifice of the Gentiles [we are of the opinion that they] sacrifice to the […] that it is like (a woman) who whored with him…

The editors note that they cannot explain the text of this passage fully, but that the context suggests that the author of the scroll is denouncing the custom of accepting Gentile offerings.[15] This general statement is undoubtedly correct. All the halakhic rulings in the scroll pertain to matters in which the halakha of the sect was at odds with the rabbinic–pharisaic halakha. Since we know that the Pharisees accepted Gentile offerings,[16] we may conclude that the subject is mentioned in MMT in order to dispute the rabbinic ruling, that is, to prohibit this custom. It is possible that the

15. See E. Qimron and J. Strugnell, *Qumran Cave 4.V. Miqṣat Ma'aśe ha-Torah* (DJD X; Oxford: Clarendon Press, 1994), pp. 46-47, 149-50. Qimron and Strugnell are undoubtedly correct in their understanding of זבח הגוים in 4QMMT as sacrifices offered by Gentiles to the God of Israel and not as Gentiles' sacrifices to the idols. Their interpretation is supported by the context of this issue in the composition. The halakhic section in 4QMMT starts with a prohibition against bringing Gentiles' grain to the Temple (B3-5). Then there is a discussion of the following three issues: cooking of certain sacrifices in the Temple (B5-8), Gentiles' sacrifices (B8-9), and the time for eating the cereal-offering (B9-13). It is clear that we are dealing here with issues related to the worship of the God of Israel in his Temple, and not with an idol cult. Thus, there is no direct connection between the issue of זבח הגוים in 4QMMT and the discussion of Gentiles' sacrifices in CD (see J.M. Baumgarten, *Qumran Cave 4.XIII. The Damascus Document (4Q266-273)* [DJD XVIII; Oxford: Clarendon Press, 1996], pp. 130, 151, 173). This discussion is partially preserved in three fragments of CD (4Q269 frag. 8 ii; 4Q270 frag. 3 iii; 4Q271 frag. 2). The combination of the three fragments enable us to reconstruct the following: אל יבא איש את...בדם זבחם... [ו]כסותו בטהרתו. It seems that we have here a prohibition against using a garment defiled by the blood of a Gentile offering (to idols)—בדם זבחם (see Baumgarten's note, DJD XVIII, p. 151 line 20). This interpretation is supported by the analogy with the next two issues discussed in CD: the prohibition against using metals, which the Gentiles had made into graven images, and the prohibition against using a garment defiled by the corpse of a human being.

16. See the sources and studies listed by I. Knohl, 'The Acceptance of Sacrifices from Gentiles', *Tarbiz* 49 (1980), pp. 341-47 (Hebrew); Y. Sussmann, 'The History of Halakha and the Dead Sea Scrolls, *Tarbiz* 59 (1990), pp. 11-76 (33 n. 97) (Hebrew).

Qumranic prohibition on Gentiles' offerings was based on a Qumranic version of Lev. 22.25.[17]

I shall begin by examining the phrase כמי שזנת אליו, 'like (a woman) who whored with him', which appears at the end of the passage. The phrase זנה אל is very rare, appearing only three times in the Hebrew Bible (instead of the more regular זנה עם and זנה אחרי), all in the same chapter of the book of Ezekiel: 'you played the whore with your neighbours, the lustful Egyptians', 'you also played the whore with the Assyrians', and 'you multiplied your harlotries with Chaldea' (Ezek. 16.26, 28, 29). Ezekiel uses the phrase זנה אל to disparage the alliances Israel has forged with its neighbours, thus desecrating—in his eyes—its matrimonial bond with God.[18]

We can assume, then, that the phrase כמי שזנת אליו, 'like (a woman) who whored with him', refers to an alliance forged with another nation. But what has this to do with the general topic of the sacrifice of the Gentiles? In my opinion, the answer is linked to the fact that in the Roman period we hear about sacrifices offered daily in the Temple in Jerusalem for the well-being of the foreign emperor and the Roman people (Josephus, *War* 2.194-97). According to Philo (*Leg. All.* 157, 317), the animals used for these offerings were donated by the emperor from his private stock.[19] It appears, then, that the author of the scroll holds that

17. On the basis of some late midrashic passages and a Karaite commentary, I assumed, years ago, that the sectarian law prohibited the acceptance of sacrifices from Gentiles (see Knohl, 'The Acceptance of Sacrifices', pp. 346-47). I noted there that some of these sources based their view on Lev. 22.25. There is a possibility that the Qumranites relied in this issue on their own version of that verse. The MT reads משחתם בהם; the Samaritan Pentateuch has משחתים; but in 11QPaleoLev we read [משח]תים הם.The Qumranic version can be explained as the result of a wish to solve the linguistic difficulties found in the other two versions. However, as was correctly noted by D.N. Freedman and K.A. Mathews (*The Paleo-Hebrew Leviticus Scroll* [Winona Lake, IN: Eisenbrauns, 1985], p. 41), in the Qumranic version the word [משח]תים can be interpreted also as a nominal form 'they are corruptions/corrupt ones'. It is possible then that the Qumranites interpreted the phrase as a reference to the Gentiles. Thus, even unblemished sacrifices donated by Gentiles should not be accepted since the donors are corrupt, משחתים הם.

18. See M. Greenberg, *Ezekiel 1–20* (AB; NewYork: Doubleday, 1983), pp. 282-83, 298-99.

19. According to Josephus (*Apion* 2.77) the sacrifice was paid for by the Jews. Schürer, following E. Meyer, attempted to reconcile the contradictory testimonies of Philo and Josephus by suggesting that the sacrifice was financed by the taxes the Jews paid the emperor (see E. Schürer, *Geschichte des Jüdischen Volkes* [Hildesheim: Georg Olms, 1970], II, p. 362). In any case, Josephus says in his account of the events of the

these offerings provided by Gentiles and sacrificed for the well-being of Gentiles are prohibited. Thus, he denounces his opponents for accepting the emperor's animals and sacrificing them.[20] This action is viewed by the author of the scroll as prostitution and a violation of the conjugal bond between God and Israel.[21] In light of this, I suggest we try to incorporate this view—that the passage is a polemic against offerings for the well-being of the emperor—in our reconstruction of the text.

Let me begin by saying that I accept the reading and reconstruction offered by the editors.[22] I would merely like to change a single letter, and even this in accordance with the guidelines established by Qimron and Strugnell. In their opinion, the remnant of the second letter of the second word on line 9 is in all likelihood either a *waw* or a *yod*, though it may also be a *mem* or a *kaf* (DJD X, p. 9, note to line 9). Of these I prefer the third possibility. I believe this word should be reconstructed as [ה]מושל, 'the ruler',[23] which is the common appellation for the Roman rulers both in the

year 66 (*War* 2.2-3) that by the decision not to accept sacrifices from Gentiles the sacrifice for the emperor welfare was also stopped. This may serve as an indication that the sacrifice for the emperor's welfare was included in the general definition of זבח הגוים, 'Gentiles' sacrifices'. Talmudic traditions also speak in this connection about sacrifice(s) sent by the emperor (see *b. Giṭ.* 56a; *Lam. R.* 4.3).

20. The author speaks about these sacrifices as current practice [שהם] זובח[י]ם '[that they] sacrifice'. For this reason, we have to rule out the possibility that we have here a reference to the practice of the Persian or Seleucid periods.

21. A similar protest is preserved in the Midrash (see S. Schechter, ' 'Agadat Shir Hashirim', *JQR* 7 [1895], pp. 145-63 [163]). The author of this midrash holds that the sacrifices offered for the well-being of the Romans are the cause of the dissolution of the marriage of God and Israel (see S. Lieberman, *Greek in Jewish Palestine* [New York: Jewish Theological Seminary of America, 1942], pp. 179-84; Alon, *Jews*, p. 43; Y. Baer, 'Jerusalem in the Times of the Great Revolt', *Zion* 36 (1971), pp. 127-90 (131-32) (Hebrew).

22. The editors comment (DJD X, pp. 9, 47, 150) that the reading of the two words כמי שזונת, זבח, is materially uncertain. However, we can support the reading זבח by the word זובח(י)ם, which was partially preserved in 4Q395, l.4 (p. 15). As for the reading כמי שזונת, in my view the letter *zayin* is clearly there, making this the most plausible reading.

23. Materially, it is possible also to reconstruct המלך, 'the king', or הכתי,הכתיאי (the Kittean). But these options are problematic. It is difficult to assume that the writer would refer to the Roman emperor simply as 'the king', and not as 'king of the Kitteans' (cf. 1QM 15.2). The problem with הכתיאי is that the singular form of כתיאים, כתיים is unknown in the Dead Sea Scrolls (הכתי is found in the Arad inscriptions, see Y. Aharoni, *Arad Inscriptions* [Jerusalem: The Bialik Institute, 1981], p. 37).

Pesharim (see 1QpHab 4.5, 10, מושלי הכתיאים, 'the Rulers of the Kitteans'; 4QpNah l.3 מושלי כתיים), and in the sectarian polemic preserved in the Mishnah at the end of tractate *Yadayim*.[24]

Furthermore, there is a fragmentary pesher that seems to use this word as an appellation for the Roman emperors and rulers within a specific reference to the offerings they donated to the Temple in Jerusalem. 1QpPs frag. 9 is reconstructed by M. Horgan[25] as follows:

[מהיכלך על ירושלים לך יובילו מלכי]ם שי פשרו על כול מש[לי]
[הכתיאים אשר]לפניו בירושלים גערת [חיית קנה]
[עדת אבירים בעגלי עמים מתרפס ברצי] כסף פשרו חיית ק[נה היא]
[כ]תיאים ל... [ ]

1. [FROM YOUR TEMPLE AT JERUSALEM, KING]S [BRING] GIFTS [TO YOU] the interpretation of it concerns all the ru[lers of]
2. [the Kittim, who]before him in Jerusalem. YOU REBUKED [THE BEAST OF THE REED THICKET]
3. [A HERD OF BULLS AMONG CALVES OF PEOPLES TRAMPLING] SILVER the interpretation of it: the beast of the r[eed thicket is]
4. [the K]ittim

24. 'קובל אני עליכם פרושים שאתם כותבין את המושל עם משה בגט', 'I cry against you, O Ye Pharisees, for ye write in a bill of divorce the name of the ruler together with the name of Moses'. The complaint is against the custom of dating documents according to the years of the Roman rulers. The term 'the ruler' (המושל) in this mishnah refers primarily to the Roman emperor, since the usual practice was to count the years with reference to the emperor (see S. Lieberman, *Tosefta Ki-fshutah* [10 vols.; New York: Bet ha-Midrash lerabanim Sheba-Amerika, 1973], VIII, p. 890 n. 13; ''Agadat Shir Hashirim 1.7', *JQR* 6 [1894], pp. 672-97 [685] and the reference to the years of Nero in P. Benoit, J.T. Milik and R. de Vaux, *Les grottes de Murabba'at* [DJDJ II; Oxford: Clarendon Press, 1961], p. 101). Ch. Rabin (*The Zadokite Documents* [Oxford: Clarendon Press, 1954], Addenda to 6.10) pointed to the expression מושלי הרשעה in *b. B. Qam.* 38a (this expression is to be found in MS versions of the Talmud; in the printed editions it was replaced by מלכות רומי, note also the version of the Escorial MS in the parallel story in *y. B. Qam.* 4.3 4a: מלכות הרשעה). This talmudic tradition clearly dates after 70 CE (see S. Rosenthal, 'שני דברים', *I.L. Seeligman Memorial Volume* [Jerusalem: Magnes Press, 1983], pp. 475-76), thus למושלים מושלי הרשעה, of *b. B. Qam.* are the Roman rulers of the imperial period. See also the use of המושל הגדול in J.Z. Lauterbach (ed.), *Mekhilta de Rabbi Ishmael* (3 vols.; Philadelphia: Jewish Publications Society, 1933), I, p. 150, where the reference is probably to the emperor (see Z. Frankel, 'Mechilta', *MGWJ* 3 [1854], pp. 191-96 [193]).

25. M.P. Horgan, *Pesharim: Qumran Interpretations of Biblical Books*, (Washington, DC: Catholic Biblical Association of America, 1979), part 1, p. 14.

Psalm 68.30 refers to offerings brought by alien kings to Jerusalem.

The pesher interprets the biblical מלכים, 'kings', as [מש]ל[י], 'the rulers'.[26] Since the Kittim are mentioned in line 4 of the fragment, Milik and Horgan restored 'Kittim' also at the beginning of line 2. It seems that the pesher thus refers to gift-offerings[27] that were sent by the Roman rulers to be sacrificed before God in Jerusalem.[28] It is possible that the offerings referred to here are the daily sacrifices for the welfare of the emperor and the Romans,[29] which were supplied, as noted above, by the emperor. Another possibility is that we have here a reference to occasional sacrifices by Roman rulers in Jerusalem.[30] One may argue also that the pesher does not refer to any historical events but to Roman offerings in the apocalyptic messianic future.[31] At all events, we have here the use of the word [מש]ל[י]

26. In his *editio princeps* of 1QpPs, J.T. Milik restored מל[כי]... (D. Barthélemy and J.T. Milik, *Qumran Cave 1* [DJDJ I; Oxford: Clarendon Press, 1955], pp. 81-82). However, Horgan correctly comments that the *lamed* is unlikely, and she suggests the restoration [מש]לי. The traces of the letter on the left side of line 1 seem indeed very much like the right upper corner of *šin*. Thus Horgan's restoration is the most plausible. It is true that the regular form of this word in the pesharim is *plene*, מושלי; however, the spelling משלי is attested in 1QIsa[a] (Isa. 28.14). The use of [מש]לי as a synonym for מלכים in 1QpPs is significant. It is possible that מושלי כתיאים, כתיים in 1QpHab and 4QpNah are really references to the Roman rulers in the republican time (see E. Schürer, *The History of the Jewish People*, III.1 [rev. and ed. by G. Vermes, F. Millar and M. Goodman; Edinburgh: T. & T. Clark, 1986], p. 403). However, the use of [מש]ל[י] in 1QpPs as a synonym of מלכים and the talmudic use of מושלי, המושל הרשעה as an appellation for the Roman emperor (above n. 24), indicate that the term מושל continued to function in the imperial period, now as an appellation for the emperor.

27. For שי as sacrifice in Ps. 68.30, see Ps. 76.12, and *Targ. Ket.* for Ps. 68.30.

28. J. Carmignac, 'Notes sur les Pesharim', *RevQ* 3 (1961–62), p. 526, argues that we have to restore פניו instead of לפניו at the right end of line 2. If we accept this argument it is possible that the word פניו was part of a phrase such as לראות פניו בירושלים, which is a common biblical term for pilgrimage. If we follow Milik's reading לפניו we should think about a phrase such as לזבוח לפניו בירושלים.

29. According to Philo (*Leg. Gai.* 317) the daily sacrifice consisted of two lambs and one steer. Thus, the phrase 'calves of peoples' could be interpreted as a reference to the steers supplied by the emperor and offered for his and the Romans' welfare.

30. For instance the sacrifice of Marcus Vespasianus Agrippa (Josephus, *Ant.* 16.14). Josephus tells us that Agrippa sacrificed 100 oxen; thus his sacrifice can also be described as 'calves of peoples'.

31. The Rabbis understood Ps. 68.30-31 as a description of gifts or sacrifices that will be offered to the Messiah by the Romans (see *b. Pes.* 118b; *Exod. R.* 35b; *Ag. Ber.* 59; *Cant. R.* 1.3). This interpretation is based on the understanding of the biblical

as a substitute for the biblical מלכים within a reference to offerings sent by the Roman rulers to Jerusalem. This may support our reconstruction of the verse in 4QMMT.

Thus, the reconstruction yields the following:

ועל זבח הגוים [אנחנו חושבים שהם] זובח[ים] אל המ[ושל] שא היא [כ]מי שזנת אליו

> And concerning the sacrificing of the Gentiles, [we are of the opinion that they] sacrifice to the [ruler], that is like (a woman) who whored with him.

The passage contains an interdiction against receiving the offerings of non-Jews, with a special denunciation of the sacrifice performed in the Temple for the well-being of the Roman emperor. Indeed, according to this sect, the sacrifice is not offered for the well-being of the emperor, but is actually made *to* the emperor himself [אל המ[ושל. The offering, then, is nothing less than an act of harlotry מלכים and a breach of the covenant between God and Israel.

4Q513

Our interpretation of the 4QMMT passage may shed light on another obscure passage in the Dead Sea Scrolls. 4Q513 contains several halakhic polemics of the sect against its opponents. J.M. Baumgarten has found in the fragments of 4Q513 references and connections to several issues that are known to us from other sources as points of halakhic disagreement between the Qumranites and their opponents.[32] 4Q513 frag. 2ii also

phrase חית קנה, 'the beast of the reed' as an appellation for Rome. God rebuked the beast and rejected its offerings. The interpretation of חית קנה as an appellation for Rome is related in the Babylonian Talmud to R. Yosi, who lived in the second century AD. It seems that this interpretation of חית קנה goes back to the Second Temple period and is probably at the base of our pesher, היא...כיתיאים] חיית ק[נה. We may assume that, like the rabbinic tradition, the author of the pesher held that God rebukes the beast and rejects its offerings. The fact that the pesher version is גערת, 'You rebuked', instead of גער, 'rebuke' (MT), suggests that the pesher refers to past or present events, rather than to the messianic future. In this sense the pesher thus probably differs from the rabbinic traditions. It is worth noting that in later generations this interpretation of חית קנה probably led to the forming of the talmudic legend about the founding of Rome, on a reed in the sea (*b. Šab.* 56b; *y. 'Abod. Zar.* 1.2, 39c).

32. J.M. Baumgarten, 'Halakhic Polemics in New Fragments from Qumran Cave 4', in J. Amitai (ed.), *Biblical Archeology Today: Proceedings of the International Congress of Biblical Archeology* (Jerusalem: Israel Exploration Society, 1984), pp. 390-99.

contains a polemic. The first three lines of the fragment were read and reconstructed by M. Baillet as follows:[33]

להגיעם בטהרת [הקו]דש כיא טמאים [המה]
בעלות לבני הנכר ולכול הזנות אשר [אשר]
רא[ה] לו להאכילם מכול תרומת הש[ ]

The expression בעלות לבני הנכר was interpreted by Baillet as a reference to sexual relationships with non-Jews. Baumgarten[34] followed this line, and suggested that we have here a reference to daughters of priests who were married to non-Jews. According to this view, which was adopted also by L.H. Schiffman,[35] the writer criticizes priests who marry their daughters to Gentiles. These priests are unworthy to touch the sacred purities ([ואי]ן להגיעם בטהרת [הקו]דש) and they should be deprived of priestly gifts (תרומת הש[למים]). Baumgarten argues that the basis for this rule is in the verse in Lev. 21.9: ובת כהן כי תחל לזנות את אביה היא מחללת. This verse was interpreted literally: the harlotry of a priest's daughter will profane her father and will cause the suspension of her family's priestly privileges. This interpretation of Lev. 21.9 is plausible, but I doubt that it is behind the expression בעלות לבני הנכר in 4Q513. There are clear indications that 4Q513 is a Qumranic sectarian document;[36] we should try therefore to understand it on the basis of Qumranic Hebrew. The verb בעל is not used elsewhere in Qumranic literature as a term for sexual relationship, unless in biblical or reworked biblical texts.[37] Furthermore, the form

33. M. Baillet, *Qumrân grotte 4.III (4Q482–4Q520)* (DJD VII; Oxford: Clarendon Press, 1982), pp. 288-89.

34. Baillet, DJD VII, p. 393.

35. L.H. Schiffman, 'Ordinances and Rules', in J.H. Charlesworth (ed.), *The Dead Sea Scrolls*. I. *Rule of the Community and Related Documents* (Tübingen: J.C.B. Mohr; Louisville, KY: Westminster/John Knox Press, 1991), pp. 145-76 (159 n. 14).

36. This can be shown both by the content of 4Q513 (see Baumgarten, 'Halakhic Polemics', pp. 396-97), and by its scribal markings (see E. Tov, 'Scribal Markings in the Texts from the Judean Desert', in D.W. Parry and S.D. Ricks [eds.], *Current Research and Technological Development on the Dead Sea Scrolls* [Leiden: E.J. Brill, 1996], pp. 46, 49, 53).

37. In 11QT[a] 65.7 we have כי יקח איש אשה ובעלה, while the MT of Deut. is כי יקח איש אשה ובא אליה. The scroll version is probably a replica of Deut. 24.1. When there is no biblical text at the basis of the rule of 11QT[a], we find the word שכב for denoting sexual relationship (45.11). This word, שכב, is the term used regularly also in other Qumranic writings for sexual relationship (e.g. 4Q266 frag. 12, line 6; 4Q270 frag. 2, col. i, line 17; 4Q270 frag. 4, line 20; 4Q270 frag. 5, line 19; 4Q271 frag. 3, line 3, line 12; 4Q271 frag. 5, col. i, line 17).

בעול(ים) is used twice in Qumranic writings[38] with the meaning of 'to be learned, to be used to', that is, in a non-sexual context. Therefore, it is difficult to accept the view that the word בעלות in 4Q513 means a sexual relationship. Baumgarten claims that the expression בעלות לבני נכר is an echo of the phraseology of Mal. 2.11, בעל בת אל נכר, '(Judah) has consorted with the daughter of a foreign god'. However, this observation doesn't solve the problem: the verse in Mal. 2.11 refers to sexual connection between a Jewish man and an alien woman, but here, according to Baumgarten's interpretation, we are dealing with the opposite case. The direct basis for our fragment, according to Baumgarten's interpretation, is Lev. 21.9 and not Mal. 2.11. Thus, we should expect the writer to use the phraseology of Leviticus rather than that of Malachi. Lev. 21.9 uses the verb זנה for the illicit relationship of the priest's daughter. Thus, if the rule in 4Q513 was really based on this verse we should expect to find זונות עם בני הנכר rather than בעלות לבני הנכר.[39] The difficulty is aggravated when we recognize that expressions similar to those of Lev. 21.9 (הזנות, בחללם) indeed appear in the fragment but they refer to (male) priests and not to priests' daughters!

For these reasons, I would like to offer a different interpretation of this fragment, based on a different understanding of the expression בעלות לבני הנכר. In my view the word בעלות should be derived from the word עלה, 'burnt offering',[40] rather than בעל, 'sexual intercourse'. Thus, the expression should be translated 'by burnt offering to the Gentiles'. The author of 4Q513 claims that the priests became impure [כי טמאים [המה by sacrificing burnt offerings to the Gentiles בעלות לבני הנכר and לכול הזנות for 'all the fornication'. This combination of 'burnt offering to the Gentiles' and 'all the fornication' in 4Q513 is similar to the combination

38. See CD 14.9, 1QM 6.12 (see Y. Yadin, *The Scroll of the War of the Sons of Light and the Sons of Darkness* [London: Oxford University Press, 1962], p. 289).

39. The difficulty was noted by Schiffman ('Ordinances and Rules', p. 159 n. 14), who writes, 'It should be observed that the vocabulary and formulation of the verses which serve as the basis of this ordinance from Leviticus do not seem to have shaped the text.'

40. The short spelling עלה is attested in Qumran, in both biblical and non-biblical texts (see 11QpaleoLev 4.25; 14.9; 4QLev^b 1.14,17; 22.28; 23.12 [E. Ulrich and F.M. Cross, *Qumran Cave 4.VII: Genesis to Numbers* (DJD XII; Oxford: Clarendon Press, 1994), pp. 179, 182, 184]; 4Q220 frag. 1, lines 3-4 [H.W. Attridge *et al.*, in consultation with J.C. VanderKam, *Qumran Cave 4.VIII: Parabiblical Texts, Part 1* (DJD XIII; Oxford: Clarendon Press, 1994], p. 57).

of 'the Gentiles' sacrifice' זבח הגוים and 'like a woman who whored with him' כמי שזנת אליו in 4QMMT.

The construction ...עולה ל, 'burnt offering to X', is usual in biblical Hebrew. X always denotes the party to whom the burnt offering is sacrificed.[41] Thus in the case of עלות לבני הנכר we are not dealing with sacrifices of Gentiles (עלות בני הנכר), but with sacrifices directed to the Gentiles. Who are the Gentiles who are worshipped by burnt offerings?

The similarity noted above, between 4QMMT and 4Q513, may help us in solving this problem. I think that in these two documents we are dealing basically with two aspects of the same issue. As is well known, Augustus ordered that the imperial cult, established in his time in the eastern provinces of the Roman Empire, should consist of two elements: worship of the emperor and worship of the Goddess Roma (Suetonius, *August*. 52). Thus, Herod established a temple in Caesaria with statues of Augustus and the goddess Roma (Josephus, *War* 1.414; *Ant.* 15.339). In Jerusalem this pagan form was replaced by sacrifices for the welfare of the emperor and of the Roman people.[42] We know from Philo and from the Midrash that these sacrifices were burnt offerings.[43] Hence, I would like to identify the 'burnt offering to the Gentiles' in 4Q513 with the daily sacrifices of burnt offerings for the welfare of the Romans practised in Jerusalem. The author of the Midrash condemns this sacrifice as a burnt offering for (the name

41. The usual form is עלה לה, 'a burnt offering to God' (Lev. 23.18 etc.). The same pattern is used also regarding idolatry עלה...לאלהים אחרים (2 Kgs 5.18) עלות לבעל (Jer. 19.5). The phrase וזה מזבח לעלה לישראל (1 Chron. 22.1) does not refute this notion: it is the altar for the burnt offering that is described as לישראל (for Israel) not the burnt offering itself!

42. The dual meaning of the sacrifices is clear in Josephus's account (*War* 2.195-98). He also states that these sacrifices are offered twice daily. It is reasonable to assume that they were offered at about the same time as the daily Temple offerings of the Temple, i.e., in the morning and in the afternoon. This can be inferred from the Midrash (above n. 21), which speaks of a burnt offering of two lambs, one for Rome and one for Jerusalem, which were sacrificed on different corners of the altar: שני טלאים, אחד לצפון המזבח לשם ארהומי ואחד לדרום המזבח לשם ירושלים. As Baer ('Jerusalem', p. 132) correctly noted, 'the burnt offering for Jerusalem' is probably the תמיד, i.e., the daily offering.

43. Philo (*Leg.* 317) states that two lambs and one steer were sacrificed daily as burnt offerings. In light of the Midrash which speaks about 'one lamb for Rome' we may assume that two lambs were offered twice a day for the welfare of the Romans and a steer was offered (probably in the morning) for the welfare of the emperor.

of) Rome[44] לשם ארהומי. In the same way 4Q513 condemns this sacrifice as a burnt offering to the Gentiles הנכר עלות לבני. As I have noted above, the same observation is expressed in 4QMMT regarding the sacrifice of a burnt offering for the welfare of the emperor ([שהם] זובח[ים] אל [המ]ושל, 'they sacrifice to the emperor'). 4QMMT and 4Q513, like the author of the Midrash, see no difference between the pagan form of worship to the Roman emperor and the goddess Roma and the ritual of sacrificing in Jerusalem to the welfare of the emperor and the Romans.

4Q513 argues that the priests involved with this sacrifice became impure and they should not approach the purity of holiness. What is the biblical basis for this claim? As mentioned above, Baumgarten remarks that the expression בעלות לבני הנכר echoes the phraseology of Mal. 2.11 (בעל בת אל נכר). I believe that the verses in Malachi indeed supply the main scriptural basis for this claim in 4Q513. In the eyes of the author of 4Q513, the sacrifices for the welfare of the Romans are actually a burnt offering to the Romans (עלות לבני הנכר), and there is no real difference between the sacrifice in Jerusalem and the sacrifice to the goddess Roma in Sebaste or Caesaria. Hence, whoever made this sacrificial offering can be perceived as one who had committed fornication with the foreign goddess Roma (בעל בת אל נכר).[45] Accordingly, using pesher methodology, we may apply the words of Mal. 2.11-12 to the alliance between Judaea and Rome with its accompanying sacrifices. This act may be described as a betrayal, an abomination and a desecration of the holiness of God: בגדה יהודה ותועבה נעשתה בישראל ובירושלים כי חלל יהודה קדש ה' אשר אהב, 'Judah has been faithless, and an abomination has been committed in Israel and in Jerusalem; for Judah has profaned the sanctuary of the Lord'. Thus a priest who took part in it should be deprived of the right to bring sacrifices to God: יכרת ה' לאיש אשר יעשנה...מגיש מנחה לה' צבאות, 'May the Lord cut off anyone who does this...to bring an offering to the Lord of hosts'.

Further connection between Mal. 2.11-12 and 4Q513 can be seen in line 5: מאכליהם נשא עוון כי החל. Even though the meaning of the phrase is

44. See above nn. 21, 42. According to *m. Zeb.* 4.6, a sacrifice should be offered for (the name of) God, otherwise it is not a legal sacrifice.

45. The Qumranic version of Deut. 32.8 is יצב גבלת עמים למספר בני אלהים (see P.W. Skehan, 'Qumran and the Present State of Old Testament Studies', *JBL* 78 [1959], pp. 21-25 [21]). The divine rulers of the nations, are described as בני אלהים, 'the sons of God'. Thus the goddess Roma can be described as בת אל נכר, 'a daughter of a foreign God' or 'a foreign Goddess'.

not clear, it is undoubtedly[46] a reflection of Lev. 19.8 ואכליו עוונו ישא כי את קדש ה׳ חלל ונכרתה הנפש ההיא מעמיה, 'All who eat it shall be subject to punishment, because they have profaned what is holy to the Lord; and any such person shall be cut off from the people'. Lev. 19.8 in turn is the Pentateuchal base for some of the phrases in Mal. 2.11-12.

Two other tiny fragments of 4Q513 (frags. 8-9) seem to be connected with the same matter. As has been noted by Baillet, these two fragments should be attached to each other.[47] Their combination gives the following text:

]]הגיש[ ]
]]גוים אשר
]]עלה
]]שאת

The word הגיש and similar derivations of the root נגש are used nine times in the book of Malachi as a term for the act of sacrificing. In light of this, we may read the word עלה in this fragment as 'burnt sacrifice'.[48] Since the previous line has the word גוים, 'Gentiles', we may assume that these fragments also deal with burnt offerings to Gentiles or of Gentiles, using some of Malachi's terminology.

4Q513 condemns the sacrifices for the welfare of the Romans as an act of fornication. Since this sacrifice was usually (in pagan Temples) offered to the goddess Roma, 4Q513 can follow the phraseology of Mal. 2.11-12, by describing the Jewish priests as the male partners in these illicit relationships (טמאים [המה]...לכול הזנות). 4QMMT, on the other hand, condemns the other element of the imperial cult, sacrifice for the welfare of the emperor. Thus, following the spirit of Ezekiel 16, it describes the Jews as the female partner in the relationship (כמי שזנת אליו). This difference results from the fact that the polemics of the two documents are directed to slightly different persons. 4Q513 attacks the priests who sacrifice the burnt offerings. To argue for their deprivation of priestly rights, the author must use the model of Malachi that contains this element (יעשנה...מגיש מנחה יכרת ה׳ לאשר). The criticism of 4QMMT seems to be directed, as is usual in this document,[49] against the Pharisees, who were,

46. See Baillet, DJD VII, p. 289.

47. See Baillet, DJD VII, p. 291.

48. For the short spelling עלה see above n. 40.

49. See Sussmann, 'The History of Halakha', pp. 27-28; Qimron and Strugnell, DJD X, pp. 175-77.

as attested by Josephus,[50] supporters of the sacrifices for the welfare of the emperor. In this case the regular metaphor of the prophets, describing Israel as the unfaithful woman, fitted the polemic very well.

The Date and Addressees of MMT

If my reconstruction of the passage dealing with זבח הגוים, 'the Gentiles' sacrifice', is correct, it provides us with an upper limit for the time of the composition of 4QMMT. The author refers to the sacrifice for 'the ruler' as current practice (שהם] זובח[ים] אל המ[ושל). Thus we can rule out the possibility that the reference in the scroll is to sacrifices in the past, for rulers in the Persian or Hellenistic periods. Hence, we have to think on the imperial cult of the Roman period. Roman emperor worship began in the eastern provinces during the reign of Augustus, in the year 29 BCE. Herod was one of the greatest supporters of this worship;[51] hence, it is reasonable to assume that he was the initiator of the substitute of the emperor cult in Jerusalem.[52] It seems that he started to take part in the worship of Augustus no later than the year 27 BCE, when he established games honouring Augustus's name in Jerusalem, and founded Sebaste, with a temple bearing Augustus's name.[53] We do not have a clear indication in the sources when the sacrifice for the welfare of the emperor and the Romans was

50. Josephus, *War* 2.411. The negative view in the Midrash mentioned above may attest for some objection in the Pharisaic camp (see Alon, *Jews*, pp. 43-44); however, that does not represent the Pharisee mainstream (cf. *m. 'Ab.* 3.2). The claim (see C. Roth, 'The Debate on the Loyal Sacrifice', *HTR* 53 [1960], pp. 93-97) that the leaders of the Pharisees supported the cessation of the offering for the welfare of the emperor has no real basis in the sources. For the positive view of the rabbinic Halakha regarding Gentile offerings in general, see above n. 16.

51. See W. Otto, *Herodes* (Stuttgart: Metzler, 1913), p. 67; L.R. Taylor, *The Divinity of the Roman Emperor* (Middeltown, CN: American Philological Association, 1931), p. 171; M. Stern, 'Herod and the Herodian Dynasty', in S. Safrai and M. Stern (eds.), *The Jewish People in the First Century* (Assen: van Gorcum, 1974), p. 241.

52. See Baer, 'Jerusalem', p. 131; E.M. Smallwood, *The Jews under Roman Rule* (Leiden: E.J. Brill, 1981), pp. 83, 148.

53. For 27 BCE as the date of the games, see Smallwood, *The Jews*, p. 84 n. 78. Cf. A. Schalit, *König Herodes* (Berlin: de Gruyter, 1969), p. 421 n. 959, who also notes the year 27 BCE as the time when Herod had begun his involvement in the imperial cult. The establishment of the games and of the city Sebaste in 27 BCE are probably connected to the new title of the emperor 'Augustus'. The giving of the new title in January 27 BCE was an important factor in the development of the imperial cult (see Taylor, *The Divinity*, pp. 156-58).

established in the Jerusalem Temple. All we know is that it was during Augustus's reign. In light of the clear connection between the games and the imperial cult in the eastern provinces, we may assume that the sacrifice in Jerusalem was established at the same time as the games, that is, c. 27 BCE.[54] Thus the year 27 BCE can be suggested as the upper limit for the composition of 4QMMT.[55]

The lower limit of composition is provided by the earliest manuscript of the scroll, 4Q398, recently dated by Strugnell and Yardeni between the years 50–1 BCE.[56] 4QMMT, then, was composed between the years 27 and 1 BCE. The conclusion regarding the composition of 4QMMT in the early Herodian period is supported, in my view, by the evidence of the manuscripts. We have fragments of six different manuscripts, all dated by the editors to the Herodian period.[57] If 4QMMT was composed, as many scholars think, in the early Hasmonaean period, we could have expected to find at least one Hasmonaean manuscript.

From its content, it appears that 4QMMT was sent to a leader who possessed influence over the Temple service, most likely a high priest who also held some political power.[58] As I have suggested above, the time framework for the composition of 4QMMT is 27–1 BCE. For most of this

54. For the connection between the games and the imperial cult see Schürer, *The History*, p. 45 n. 89; D. Fishwick, *The Imperial Cult in the Latin West* (2 vols.; Leiden: E.J. Brill, 1991), II, pp. 574-84. The dating of the sacrifice in Jerusalem to the time of the beginning of the relationship between Augustus and Herod can be supported by the description of the Midrash (above n. 21), which sees the sacrifice as a symbol of making a covenant with Rome (see Y. Rosenthal, *Sinai* 57 [1965], p. 92; Baer, 'Jerusalem', p. 132).

55. If 4Q513 contains a condemnation of the sacrifice for the welfare of the Romans, it would make the year c. 27 the upper limit for the composition of 4Q513. On the basis of paleographic criteria, Baillet dated this document to shortly before 50 BCE. However, Dr Ada Yardeni, who kindly inspected the script of 4Q513 at my request, dated it to the early Herodian period (i.e. 50–1 BCE). This dating fits my interpretation.

56. See J. Strugnell, 'MMT: Second Thoughts on a Forthcoming edition', in E. Ulrich and J. VanderKam (eds.), *The Community of the Renewed Covenant* (Notre Dame: University of Notre Dame Press, 1994), p. 70. This dating is close to the one given by F.M. Cross (50–25 BCE) in his important study 'The Development of the Jewish Scripts', in G.W. Wright (ed.), *The Bible and the Ancient Near East* (Garden City, NY: Doubleday, 1961) p. 149, no. 4.

57. See Qimron and Strugnell, DJD X, pp. 3, 14, 18, 21, 25, 34, 38.

58. See Sussmann, 'The History of Halakha', p. 38 n. 120.

period (23–6 BCE)[59] the high priest was שמעון בן ביתוס, Simon the son of Boethus, Herod's father-in-law, and the founder of the Boethus dynasty of priests.[60] Simon and his house, the Boethus house of priests (בית ביתוס), were, I believe, the recipients of 4QMMT.

In their discussion of the identity of the 'You' group in 4QMMT, Qimron and Strugnell write:

> If we assume that the work is to be explained as reflecting the history…of the Qumran community, we must look for a time when the 'we' group i.e. the writers, were in 'eirenic' discussion with the 'you' group—a group not so different from themselves as to be incapable of being won over to the writers' positions and practices… The 'we' group recommended their own purity practices to the 'you' group in contrast to the contrary practices of the 'they' group… (DJD X, p. 114).

I believe that Simon and his house fit this characterization very well: Simon the son of Boethus hailed from Alexandria, and his appointment to the office of high priest suited Herod's policy of marginalizing the Hasmonaeans and their supporters by introducing new elements from the Diaspora communities.[61] Simon could not expect to get the support of the priestly circle in Jerusalem. The Jerusalem priestly families—the Sadducees—were traditional supporters of the Hasmonaeans, against whom the appointment of Simon seems to have been directed. Simon could form a coalition with one of the other two main Jewish sects: the Pharisees or the Essenes in Qumran. From their point of view, the Qumranites could look on the Boethus priests as newcomers who were not involved in past struggles in Judea, and thus as possible partners for 'eirenic' discussion.

The Qumran community, then, would have perceived the changes in the Jerusalem priesthood[62] in Herod's time as an opportunity to return to a

59. For the dating of Simon's appointment to the year 23 BCE see Smallwood, *The Jews*, p. 91 n. 109.

60. The genealogy of the priestly house of Boethus is discussed by E.M. Smallwood, 'High Priests and Politics', *JTS* 13 (1962), pp. 14-34 (34); D.R. Schwartz, *Agrippa I, The Last King of Judea* (Tübingen: J.C.B. Mohr, 1990), pp. 185-89.

61. See Smallwood, *The Jews*, pp. 64-65, 90-91; M. Stern in S. Safrai and M. Stern (eds.), *The Jewish People in the First Century* (2 vols.; Assen: van Gorcum, 1974), I, pp. 270-75; II, pp. 600-11.

62. I presented part of this study in April 1996 at Harvard Divinity School. Professor F.M. Cross, who attended my lecture, raised the possibility that Simon was a descendant of the priestly house who served in the Onias Temple (בית חוניו) near Leontopolis. If the Boethus family came from this priestly house, they could have gained the support of the Qumranites by being true heirs of the old high priesthood. I

position of power and influence over Temple activities.[63] They sent an epistle to the new high priest, Simon the son of Boethus, to try to persuade him to reject the customs supported by the Pharisees (the 'they' group) that had been introduced into the Temple service[64] and to adopt the old priestly traditions that they upheld.

Simon and his house were probably trained in priestly traditions similar to the Qumranic ones, traditions that go back to the biblical period.[65] The Qumranites are presumably referring to this knowledge of the priestly traditions when they write to Simon, 'For we have seen (that) you have wisdom and knowledge of the Torah' (שר[א]ינו עמך ערמה ומדע תורה, 4QMMT C27-28). Thus, it seems that Simon and the house of Boethus,

would like to refer in this connection to Stern's remark (*The Jewish People*, I, p. 274 n. 1) about Simon's predecessor in the Jerusalem Temple, Jesus the son of Phiabi. Stern notes that the name Phiabi (which is Egyptian) is to be found in a Jewish inscription from Tell el-Yehudia near Leontopolis (for a recent discussion of this inscription, see W. Horbury and D. Noy, *Jewish Inscriptions of Graeco-Roman Egypt* [Cambridge: Cambridge University Press, 1992], pp. 69-74). It is possible to suppose that Herod nominated high priests from the Egyptian line of Onias in order to gain an advantage over the Hasmonaeans, who came from an inferior priestly family (on the connections between Herod's father and the Oniades, see Josephus, *Ant.* 14.131; *War* 1.190).

63. I accept the identification of the Qumranites with the Essenes. Thus, in my view, Herod's respect for the Essenes (Josephus, *Ant.* 15.371-79) could also contribute to the change of atmosphere.

64. According to talmudic tradition (*b. Šab.* 15b) Hillel began his leadership 100 years before the destruction of the Temple. Hence, we should see him as the head of the Pharisees in the year 27 BCE. However, as was noted by Alon (*Jews*, p. 330), the number of '100 years' seems to be schematic, and Hillel was probably appointed later. It is thus possible that the Pharisaic representatives at that time were Hillel's predecessors 'the Sons of Bathira' (בני בתירא), who probably held an official position in the Temple (see E.E. Urbach, *The World of the Sages* [Jerusalem: Magnes Press, 1988], p. 313 n. 26 [Hebrew]). Several scholars (Alon, *Jews*, pp. 328-34; Urbach, *World*, pp. 313-14; Stern, *The Jewish People*, I, pp. 614-15), are of the opinion that we should connect the 'sons of Batira' of the Talmud with the Babylonian family settled later by Herod in Batanea, who founded there a village named Bathyra (Josephus, *Ant.* 17.23-28). If we accept this view, we would have another example of Herod's policy of introducing Diaspora Jews to the administration of the Temple. As was noted by Alon (*Jews*, p. 331) it seems that 'the Sons of Bathira' were supporters of the Herodian dynasty and of the Romans. Hence, they probably supported the offerings for the welfare of the emperor and the Romans.

65. See below n. 70.

who were devoted to the priestly rules and traditions,[66] accepted, in principle, the major views[67] of the Qumran community regarding the Temple and the sacrifices[68] and thus established an alliance between the Boethus priests and the Qumran community. This coalition is in my view the party known variously in the rabbinic literature as בית סיין, בית סין, ביתסין, ביתוסין.[69]

66. For the archaeological evidence of the devotion of the priestly families in Jerusalem to the purity laws, see N. Avigad, *Discovering Jerusalem* (Jerusalem: Shiqmona, 1981), pp. 124-28, 174-83; Sussmann, 'History of Halakha', n. 203.

67. Though the Boethus priests adopted the halakhic views of the Qumranites, political considerations doubtless prevented them from accepting their position regarding offerings by non-Jews and the sacrifice for the well-being of the emperor. Thus, the sacrifice for the emperor's well-being continued until the year 66 CE. Another issue in 4QMMT was also impractical for the Boethus priesthood—the solar calendar. As leaders of the Temple of all Israel they could not accept this sectarian calendar. Yet it seems that at some point they tried to find a compromise between the two systems. This, in my view, is the explanation for one halakhic opinion associated with the Beithseen (ביתסין) in rabbinic literature. According to this tradition, the Beithseen argued that the word 'Sabbath' in the biblical phrase 'from the day after the Sabbath' (Lev. 23.15) should be interpreted as a reference to the 'Sabbath of Passover' (שבת הפסח; see the sources and the discussion by Sussmann, 'History of the Halakha', p. 30 n. 81). The term 'Sabbath of the Passover' is vague, but its most obvious reference is to the Sabbath, which falls during the days of the Passover festival and not the one after (otherwise we should have שבת שאחר הפסח). We thus have evidence that the Beithseen used to perform the Omer harvest and to start the counting of the days from the Sunday during the festival of Passover. This custom seems to be a compromise between the Pharisaic practice to start counting after the first day of Passover, and the Qumran rule, to start on the first Sunday after the end of the festival. In my view, the reference in this case is to the Boethus priests who tried to find a way between their allegiance to the Qumranic priestly traditions and the pragmatic need to follow the view of the majority of the people.

68. As was noted by Sussmann, 'History of the Halakha', p. 26 n. 66, all the issues dealt with in 4QMMT are connected to the Temple and the priesthood. Other issues that are discussed at length elsewhere in the Qumran literature, e.g., Sabbath observance, legal and moral rules, are not mentioned in MMT.

69. For an exhaustive discussion of the talmudic traditions about the ביתסין see M.D. Herr, 'Who Were the Boethuseans?', in *Proceedings of the Seventh World Congress of Jewish Studies, Studies in Talmud, Halakha and Midrash*, pp. 11-20 (Hebrew); Sussmann, 'History of the Halakha', pp. 42-55. The name of the priestly house Boethus (ביתוס) is spelt in two good manuscripts of tannaitic literature as בייתס, ביתס: see Sh. Naeh, *The Tannaitic Hebrew in the Sifra according to Codex Vatican 66* (dissertation submitted to the Hebrew University, Jerusalem, 1989). The plural form of the latter spelling is ביתסין; however, this form ביתסין can also serve as a shortened

form of בית (א)סין, 'The house of Essenes'. The possible dual meaning of the name ביתסין enables us to see this term as the designation of a coalition of the two groups: the house of Boethos and the house of the Essenes. This assumption may explain some inner contradictions in the rabbinic traditions. From the philological point of view, we have on the one hand evidence for the spelling ביתסיין בית סיין, which supports A. de Rossi's proposal (*Meor Einayim* [Vilna: Phin and Rosenkrantz, 1863], p. 29) to explain this term as a reference to בית אסיין, 'the house of the Essenes' (see J.M. Grintz, 'Anshei Ha-Yahad-Isiyim-Beit (A)sin', *Sinai* 32 [1953], pp. 11-43 [11-12]; Lieberman, *Tosefta Ki-fshutah*, IV, p. 870; Sussmann, 'History of the Halakha', pp. 54-55). However, as was pointed out by M.Z. Fox (*Sinai* 114 [1994], pp. 162-64), the derivatives of this term in the talmudic literature (מפני הביתסין מעשה בביתסי אחד but not מעשה באחד מבית סיין, מפני בית סיין), support the explanation of the name ביתסין as a term derived from the name ביתוס thus referring to the Boethus priesthood (the derivation of ביתסין from ביתוס is to be found first in *ARN* [ed. S. Shechter (New York, 1967), p. 26]; the first modern advocator of this view was A. Geiger, *Sadducaer und Pharisaer* [Breslau: H. Skulch, 1863], p. 29). Similar ambiguity exists in the traditions regarding the dispute over the counting of the Omer days: on the one hand, we have the tradition that the ביתסין argued that the counting should start on שבת הפסח (see above n. 67). As noted above, this term seems to suggest a custom of performing the Omer harvest on the Sunday within the Passover days, a custom that differs from the Qumranic one. Thus it fits the view that the ביתסין are a group other than the Qumran Essenes. But, on the other hand, the general remark in the Mishna (*m. Men.* 10.3), מפני הביתסין שהיו אומרין אין קצירת העומר במוצאי יום טוב, 'because of the Beithseen who used to say the Omer may not be reaped at the close of a Festival day', seems to be directed against the Qumranic view, according to which the Omer harvest will never fall on the day after the day of Passover (see Baumgarten, 'Halakhic Polemics', p. 396 n. 30; Sussmann, 'History of the Halakha', n. 81). The explanation for the ambiguity of the sources seems to be the complexity of the group called ביתסין, taking this term to refer to a group formed, as we have suggested, by a coalition of two groups. In some cases the reference is mainly to one component, and in other cases to the other. In this way we may also solve the serious objections put forward by Herr against the identification of the ביתסין with the Essenes. The tradition in *ARN*, mentioned above, seems to refer mainly to the Jerusalemite component of the coalition, i.e., the priestly house of Boethus. Thus the reference that Beitus used vessels of silver and gold (שהיה משתמש בכלי כסף ובכלי זהב) fits well our knowledge of the wealth of this family (see below nn. 74, 77). The argument in *ARN* regarding the disbelief of the ביתסין in life and divine retribution after death may be true for the priestly house of Boethus. It is true, as Herr argues, that the Qumranites believed in the immortality of souls. However, since ideological issues are not mentioned in 4QMMT we may assume that the coalition between the Qumranites and the house of Boethus was based on agreement in the legal realm only. We should see the house of Boethus also behind the references in the talmudic literature to the ביתסין, ביתסי, who are involved in the Temple worship (see *t. Suk.* 3.1, 16) . On the other hand, the reference in *ARN* to the

The Qumranites and the house of Boethus shared, on the one hand, a common political interest as Herod's clients and supporters. In this respect they had a common political struggle against the veteran Jerusalem priesthood, that is, the Sadducees, who were the supporters of the Hasmonaeans.[70] On the other hand, all priestly groups (the Sadducees, the Qumranites and the Boethus priests) had a common halakhic debate with the non-priestly party, the Pharisees.

I conclude this section of my study with a summary of my view regarding the composition of 4QMMT. The 'halakhic letter' known as 4QMMT was written around the year 23 BCE[71] by the leadership of the Qumran community. The letter was sent to the new high priest in Jerusalem, Simon the son of Boethus, and to his family 'the house of Boethus'. 4QMMT achieved its goal: common political interests and shared priestly traditions enabled the formation of an alliance[72] between the rich priests from Jerusalem, and the ascetic community (עדת האביונים) of Qumran.

Beithseen (ביתוסין) as a sect formed at the same time with the Sadducees, fits the Essenes of Qumran (see Josephus, *Ant.* 13.171-73) rather than the Herodian house of Boethus. Thus, we have an example to explain the ambiguity in *ARN* itself.

70. The rivalry between the Sadducees and the Beithseen was mainly political. The Beithseen supported Herod while the Sadducees supported the Hasmonaeans. In the halakhic realm it seems that there was a basic agreement on issues related to the Temple and its worship practices. This agreement, which is grounded probably on old priestly traditions (see I. Knohl, 'Post-Biblical Sectarianism and the Priestly Schools of the Pentateuch', in J.T. Barrera and L.V. Montaner [eds.], *The Madrid Qumran Congress* [2 vols.; Leiden: E.J. Brill, 1992], II, pp. 601-609), is the explanation for the similarity between some of the halakhot mentioned in 4QMMT and several Sadducean rules mentioned in the talmudic literature (on these parallels see J.M. Baumgarten, 'The Pharisaic–Sadducean Controversies about Purity, and the Qumran Texts', *JJS* 31 [1980], pp. 157-70; Sussman, 'History of the Halakha', pp. 28-31). The solar calendar of the Qumranites was probably rejected by the Sadducees (see Sussmann, 'History of the Halakha',p. 49 n. 166; A.I. Baumgarten, 'Who Were the Sadducees? The Sadducees of Jerusalem and Qumran', in I.M. Gafni, A. Oppenheimer and D.R. Schwarz (eds.), *The Jews in the Hellenistic–Roman World: Studies in Memory of Menahem Stern* [Jerusalem: The Zalman Shazar Center for Jewish History, 1996], pp. 396-405 [Hebrew]), and the same is probably true regarding the severe Qumranic Sabbath laws (see I. Knohl, *The Sanctuary of Silence* [Philadelphia: Fortress Press, 1995], p. 224 n. 93).

71. I assume that 4QMMT was sent to Simon upon his nomination as high priest. 4Q398 is thus an early copy, written within about 20 years from the composition of the original letter.

72. The combination of religious and political interests at the base of the alliance probably caused the Qumranites to moderate their criticism of the sacrifices for the

The Copper Scroll and the House of Boethus

J.M. Allegro begins his discussion of the identity of the group who buried the treasures enumerated in the Copper Scroll and placed the scroll in the cave, as follows:

> It is possible that the Qumran Essenes had past acquaintances among the Jerusalem priesthood to whom, in this hour of danger, they were willing to lend their local knowledge of the Judaean desert for the concealment of sacred treasures and the scroll. Yet, such contact between Qumran and the city, in view of what we know about the Essenes and the strictness of their self-imposed exile, is difficult to envisage. Furthermore, the display of such trust by the Jerusalem priesthood in this fanatical fringe sect, to the point of entrusting them with Temple secrets, seems hardly credible. [73]

In light of what I have suggested regarding the alliance between the Boethus priests of Jerusalem and the Essenes of Qumran, we may accept the hypothesis that Allegro rejects. We may identify the Boethus family (whose wealth is legendary in the talmudic tradition)[74] as the non-Pharisee house of priests, who were either the owners of the treasures described in the Copper Scroll, or those priests who took and concealed Temple treasures and vessels. It would appear that with the outbreak of rebellion and civil war in Jerusalem (66 CE),[75] the Boethus priests turned to their old

welfare of the emperor and the Romans. It is hard to believe that they maintained their demand to dismiss the priests involved in this sacrifice while their allies in Jerusalem were performing these offerings. Thus, we may assume that 4Q513, which expresses that demand, had been written prior to 23 BCE. The supposed date of the composition of 4Q513 would be 27–23 BCE. As I have noted above (n. 55) this date fits the palaeographic evidence. The fact that 4Q513 and 4QMMT were probably written about the same time helps to explain the similarity in the terminology of these two documents (see Qimron, DJD X, pp. 96-97).

73. J.M. Allegro, *The Treasures of the Copper Scroll* (London: Routledge & Kegan Paul, 1960), p. 120. For a similar argument see A. Dupont-Sommer, *The Essene Writings from Qumran* (Oxford: Basil Blackwell, 1961), p. 386.

74. See *t. Yom* 1.14 (ed. S. Lieberman, p. 226); *y. Ket.* 5.11, 30a; *b. Yom.* 18a; *b. Suk.* 52b; *b. Yeb.* 61a; *b. Ket.* 104a; *b. Giṭ* 56a; *Lam. R.* 1.47 (ed. S. Buber, p. 86).

75. This date concurs with the conclusions of F.M. Cross's palaeographic study of the text, i.e., that the scroll was composed between the years 50 and 70 CE (see M. Baillet, J.T. Milik and R. de Vaux, *Les 'petites grottes' de Qumrân* [DJDJ III; Oxford: Clarendon Press, 1962], p. 219). Dupont-Sommer argues (*Essene Writings*, p. 388), that 'the Qumran buildings were attacked and destroyed by the Romans in June A.D. 68…if it is the Temple treasure, we have to accept that it was evacuated and

allies at Qumran, and enlisted their aid in hiding the treasures and guarding the scroll with the list of the treasures—the Temple vessels and the sacred gifts. The anxiety of the Boethus priests to preserve the priestly gifts, even at a time of such extreme crisis, may serve as further indication[76] of their devotion to the laws of the Torah.

Twice in the scroll mention is made of 'silver and gold *dema'* vessels' (3.2-3; 12.6-7). If these vessels indeed served the priests of the Boethus dynasty, this constitutes a surprising confirmation of the rabbinic tradition,[77] according to which Boethus 'used vessels of silver and gold' (שהיה משתמש בכלי כסף ובכלי זהב).

The Copper Scroll offers evidence for the existence of a friendly relationship between the Qumranites and a non-Pharisee priestly house in Jerusalem in the last decades before 70 CE. This may serve as further support for my reconstruction and interpretation of 4QMMT as a document leading to the formation of an alliance between the Essenes of Qumran and the priestly house of Boethus in Jerusalem.

handed over to the Essenes at least some time before the abandonment of Qumran… Now at that moment Jerusalem was not yet invested… Would it have even occurred to the Temple authorities to disperse the Temple wealth outside the precincts of Jerusalem, which was the most strongly protected city in Palestine and which they were determined to defend to the end?' In light of this argument, it seems preferable to assume that the hiding of the treasures outside of Jerusalem may have been motivated by the wish to save them from the civil war inside the city and not from the Romans.

76. See above n. 66.

77. *ARN*, A. 5 (ed. S. Schechter, p. 26; the quote follows the Oxford MS no. 408). See also the discussion by M. Kister, '*Avot de Rabbi Natan*, Studies in Text, Redaction and Interpretation' (PhD dissertation, Hebrew University, Jerusalem, 1993), p. 154.

17

THE ORIGIN OF 3Q15: FORTY YEARS OF DISCUSSION

Piotr Muchowski

Introduction

Although 40 years have elapsed since the discovery of the Copper Scroll, the question of its origin remains unresolved. None of the several hypotheses that have been offered in this regard has met with universal acceptance. This state of affairs results on the one hand from the fact that the text contains no direct information related to the historical context in which it was written, and on the other from lack of general agreement about the relevant data and their importance.

This lack of agreement is evident, first, in relation to the topographic interpretation of the place names mentioned in the text, many of which do not occur in other sources. Four proposals concerning them have been offered so far; however, they contradict one another on a number of points and do not agree even upon the locality of such a place as Mount Gerizim. Second, the results of palaeographic studies, which date the text at 25–75 CE (Cross) or 30–130 CE (Milik),[1] are ignored by some scholars, who relate the scroll to the Bar Kokhba Revolt. Third, archaeological information, according to which the Copper Scroll and the other Cave 3 deposits were found in different spots, is either interpreted as indicative of its separate origin or considered to be irrelevant; there is also disagreement as to the possibility that the Copper Scroll was placed in the cave after 68 CE, later than the remaining deposits. Fourth, the actual or real existence of the hoards mentioned in the text, and of their potential owner, is called

1. F.M. Cross, 'Excursus on the Palaeographical Dating of the Copper Document', in M. Baillet, J.T. Milik and R. de Vaux, *Les 'petites grottes' de Qumrân* (DJDJ III; Oxford: Clarendon Press, 1962), pp. 217-22 (217); J.T. Milik, 'Le rouleau de cuivre provenant de la grotte 3Q (3Q15)', DJDJ III, pp. 198-302 (217).

into question. Fifth, there are problems surrounding the language of the text—in particular, whether it can represent the vernacular of the authors of the Qumran scrolls. Finally, the reading of the text and especially of its key fragments, such as Note 4, gives rise to controversies that are of the utmost importance for the discussion. Positions assumed by individual scholars with regard to the above-mentioned questions, for the most part motivated by differences of interpretation and the inevitably subjective preference for one out of two or several possibilities, provide grounds for those hypotheses about the origin of the Copper Scroll that are currently being discussed.

In my endeavour to present the most important of those hypotheses, I have decided to relate some aspects of the general dispute, introducing the main theses and arguments put forward by different authors. In view of the lack of consent mentioned above as to the facts, it seems to me advisable to refrain from polemical statements as regards individual hypotheses. I shall limit myself to some general critical remarks in the conclusion. The hypotheses are classified according to their attitude towards the authenticity of the treasures mentioned in the Copper Scroll, and according to their assumptions concerning the origin of the document. Thus divided, they fall into a few major categories.

The Copper Scroll Treasure as Legend

The first hypothesis is that which treats 3Q15 as a legendary account. It was formulated by J.T. Milik, the author of the official edition of the Copper Scroll (published in 1962).[2] One of the fundamental claims of this hypothesis is that 3Q15 is not an Essene document at all. According to Milik, evidence for this lies in the fact that the scroll was found in a spot apart from the other manuscripts in the cave, and so constitutes a separate find; there are also some specific features that set it apart from the Qumran manuscript corpus, such as the clumsy and hesitant style of writing, confusion of script types and letter shapes, careless text layout, phonetic spellings, and a peculiar way of transcribing final vowels.

Another aspect of Milik's approach was to consider that 3Q15 is a piece of folklore written after the destruction of the Second Temple of Jerusalem (70 CE), in the dominant atmosphere of the time, when the impending arrival of the Messiah and the reconstruction of the Temple were awaited.

2. Milik, DJDJ III, pp. 198-302.

According to this argument, the caches listed in the text should be considered fictionally as containing the Temple treasure, hidden away at the time of its destruction. The total quantity of the riches mentioned, even excluding gaps in the text and uncertain readings, amounts to 4630 talents of gold and silver. Such a figure, as Milik put it, 'certainly surpasses all the individual and communal resources of Palestinians at any time'.[3] Milik referred to those passages in Josephus and in 2 Maccabees that give us some idea of the size of the wealth owned by the Temple and by high officials in the Roman period (*Ant.* 12.175; 14.78, 105-10; 17.317-20; 2 Macc. 3.10-11; 5.21). These sources inform us, among other things, that in the mid-first century BCE the Temple possessed about 2000 talents in cash and about 8000 talents in gold, and that Antipas of Perea and Galilee had an average annual income of about 200 talents. In the light of these data Milik concluded that the treasures described in the Copper Scroll were too vast to be genuine.

Milik dated the origin of the document in the interval between the First and Second Revolts against Rome, about 100 CE. The dating was based both on the palaeographic analysis of the handwriting of the catalogue, which, according to Milik, suggests a date within 30–130 CE, and topographic evidence, which seems to indicate that 'certain places are in ruin as a result of the war' of 66–73 CE. Also, for Milik, the freedom of movement in the Jerusalem Temple 'implied by the descriptions is easier to understand after that date'.[4] It should be noted at this point that the localization of some toponyms within the Temple is controversial.

Milik's hypothesis about the legendary character of the catalogue has found numerous adherents, some of whom have presented different views on matters of detail while accepting its general tenets. For example, S. Mowinckel and F.M. Cross assumed that 3Q15 was an inventory of the treasure of the first Temple,[5] L. Moraldi, M. Delcor and also F.M. Cross argued that the document was of Essene origin,[6] whereas T.H. Gaster suggested that the Copper Scroll might represent some kind of humorous

3. Milik, DJDJ III, pp. 282-83.

4. Cf. Milik, DJDJ III, p. 283.

5. Cf. S. Mowinckel, 'The Copper Scroll: An Apocryphon?', *JBL* 76 (1957), pp. 261-65 (262-63); F.M. Cross, *The Ancient Library of Qumran and Modern Biblical Studies* (Garden City, NY: Doubleday, 1958), pp. 16-18.

6. Cf. L. Moraldi, *Manoscritti di Qumran* (Torino: Unione Tipografico–Editrice Torinese, 1971), p. 714; M. Delcor, 'Littérature Essénienne', *DBSup* 9 (1979), pp. 828-960 (955); Cross, *Ancient Library*, pp. 16-18.

literature.[7] Earlier, in 1957, H. del Medico, another supporter of the folkloric character of 3Q15, proposed that the scroll could have been an accessory used by the Sadducees in initiation ceremonies.[8]

The Copper Scroll Treasure as Authentic

Among the hypotheses assuming the authenticity of the hoards mentioned in the catalogue, three principal conceptions can be distinguished. The first of them maintains that 3Q15 is an inventory of the treasury of the Essene movement. This theory was first presented by K.G. Kuhn.[9] In 1953, having examined the reverse side of the scrolls, still uncut, at the Palestine Archaeological Museum, he hypothesized that the document was a list of the places where the Essene treasure had been concealed. Kuhn assumed that the treasure had been made up chiefly of the personal property of newly accepted members, given up to the communal fund, and also of donations contributed by sympathizers. Further, Kuhn ventured the supposition that in the face of the approaching outbreak of the First Revolt against Rome the community administrator had buried all the valuables and then made a catalogue that, should he and those in the know die, would help the surviving members to retrieve the treasure.

A. Dupont-Sommer gave his support to this theory;[10] he too claimed that the Copper Scroll was an inventory of the genuine riches of the Essenes. He rejected as groundless editorial reservations about the depth of the hiding places and the size of the hoards. He invoked the passages in Josephus quoted by Milik (*Ant.* 14.78, 105) as evidence for his opinion that the sums the Jerusalem Temple had at its disposal were larger than those mentioned in the catalogue. He pointed out to the allusions to communal property in 1QS 7.6-8 and 1QpHab 12.9-10. The Essenes were

7. Cf. T.H. Gaster, *The Dead Sea Scriptures* (Garden City, NY: Doubleday, 1976), pp. 533-36. He claims that such a literary piece, addressed to 'the hearts and minds of men who were looking to an imminent restoration of the past glories of Israel' (i.e. the Essenes), could have been based on the received legend of the First Temple treasure; he also points to *Masekhet Kelim* and the relationship of the scroll to the writings of Josephus.

8. Cf. H.E. del Medico, *L'énigme des manuscrits de la Mer Morte* (Paris: Plon, 1957), p. 259.

9. Cf. K.G. Kuhn, 'Les rouleaux de cuivre de Qumrân', *RB* 61 (1954), pp. 193-205.

10. Cf. A. Dupont-Sommer, 'Les rouleaux de cuivre trouvés à Qumrân', *RHR* 151 (1957), pp. 22-36.

dispersed almost all over Palestine and according to Dupont-Sommer the places listed in 3Q15 form a map of their settlements. He speculated that as a risk-reducing precaution the bursar had divided the treasure up among separate groups, then compiled two lists that contained a catalogue of the caches, and concealed them.

A second theory assumes that the treasure of 3Q15 was the property of the Jerusalem Temple. After the report on the contents of the Copper Scroll had been announced (1 June 1956), K.G. Kuhn modified his original hypothesis.[11] Assuming that the deposits belonged to the Temple, 'one of the most famous and wealthiest in all the contemporary world',[12] he suggested that the priests had entrusted them for safe-keeping to the Essenes, who had communities all over the country, so that the treasure would not be despoiled by the Romans.

J.M. Allegro developed this view in his book *The Treasure of the Copper Scroll*,[13] where he assumed that the scroll was an inventory of sacral treasure belonging mostly to the Jerusalem Temple and hidden by the Zealots probably in the spring of 68 CE. Allegro speculated that the catalogue might also include the spoils of the Zealots obtained from their raids on Judaean desert settlements. He quoted a passage from the Mishnah (*m. Sanh.* 10.6) that says that when a town was to be destroyed all consecrated objects had to be redeemed, the tithe abandoned to destruction, and the second tithe and the holy scriptures concealed.[14] Allegro proposed that the catalogue had been engraved on copper sheets by some Zealots camping at Qumran. They based their compilation on reports received from Jerusalem and other garrisons, and then concealed the finished document. These events took place, allegedly, during their three-month occupation of Qumran before the arrival of the Romans. The choice of copper for the purpose could have been motivated, according to Allegro, either by the physical durability of the metal or by its resistance to ritual uncleanness (*m. Kel.* 11.3). His identification of the Zealots as the owners of the treasure is based on the assumption that nobody else had free access to the Temple treasury and at the same time, as warfare escalated slowly, remained in control of the places mentioned in the catalogue.

11. Cf. K.G. Kuhn, 'Bericht über neue Qumranfunde und über die Öffnung der Kupferrolle', *TLZ* 81 (1956), pp. 541-46.

12. Cf. Kuhn, 'Bericht über neue Qumranfunde', p. 545.

13. J.M. Allegro, *The Treasure of the Copper Scroll* (London: Routledge & Kegan Paul, 1960).

14. Allegro, *Treasure of the Copper Scroll*, pp. 61-62.

Similar views were expressed by C. Roth, who said:

> Eleazar ben Simon managed to get into his hands in the course of the operations in the early autumn of AD 66, 'the Roman spoils, the money taken from Cestius, and a great part of the public treasure'. In due course he and his Zealot followers entrenched themselves in the Temple, where for some time they were in control. Thus presumably they would have had in their custody a great part of the sacred treasure as well. As danger approached (whether from their internal opponents, John of Gischala and his followers, or from the Romans), it would have been natural for them to conceal their treasure in some safe place and make a record of what they had done.[15]

The theory that the treasure of 3Q15 belonged to the Jerusalem Temple was also supported by G.R. Driver,[16] who assumed that the riches had been accumulated during the period of relative political stability between 63 BCE and 66 CE. Their evacuation from the Temple and subsequent concealment took place between the autumn of 66 CE and the summer of 68. Driver thinks that

> This would not necessarily be the time when sectarian and other scrolls were put away in the caves at Qumran; but a date c. AD 100, which has been suggested, would certainly be too late, if only because no satisfactory reason can be found for the operation at that time.[17]

He accepted the possibility that at a later date somebody had buried the remaining documents in the same cave where 3Q15 had been deposited.

The author of a third idea was E.-M. Laperrousaz.[18] Assuming that 3Q15 contains a list of real treasures, he agreed with Milik that it had been compiled after 70 CE and hidden away in Cave 3 later than the other documents unearthed there. He rejected the theory that the treasure was of Essene provenance. He took the catalogue to be a description of the places where Simon Bar Kokhba had concealed the treasure in his possession, presumably in the autumn of 134 CE, after his departure from Herodium. The insurgents, mindful of the plundering of Jerusalem in 70 CE, had decided to scatter the treasure all over Palestine, first of all in the Judaean

15. Cf. C. Roth, *The Historical Background of the Dead Sea Scrolls* (Oxford: Basil Blackwell, 1965), pp. 44-45, 67.

16. Cf. G.R. Driver, *The Judaean Scrolls: The Problem and a Solution* (Oxford: Basil Blackwell, 1965), pp. 30-36, 373-93.

17. Cf. Driver, *Judaean Scrolls*, p. 375.

18. Cf. E.-M. Laperrousaz, 'Remarques sur l'origine des rouleaux de cuivre découverts dans la grotte 3 de Qumrân', *RHR* 159 (1961), pp. 157-72.

Desert, where they had withdrawn under Roman pressure. It was probably at that time that a list of those places was concealed in Cave 3 by one of their groups stationed at Qumran.[19]

Laperrousaz's view was to a large extent shared by B.-Z. Lurie.[20] By referring to various passages in rabbinic literature he attempted to prove that during the Bar Kokhba Revolt there had been a provisional temple in Jerusalem that possessed valuable cultic objects and considerable funds. Its resources would have consisted mainly of donations from Jews of the Diaspora who supported the revolt and intended to reconstruct the Sanctuary. He speculated that during the final phase of the insurrection, as the Romans approached Jerusalem, the decision to conceal the valuable and sacred objects had been taken:

> As time was running short, the job was carried out hastily and frantically. For that reason no organising principle is visible in the course of the rescue operation. We can suppose that the custodians assembled the treasures, packed them into chests, trunks and assorted vessels, and wrapped them up in whatever was at hand. Thus they delivered to groups of priests all the sacred things which could be rescued...[21]

Lurie suggested that a secret expedition set out in the direction of the still free Jericho region. On its arrival there it turned for help to the numerous priestly families living in the area. The treasures were hurriedly buried away on the property of dependable people, in caves, in various cisterns, canals, and so on, which typically occur in areas with advanced water systems like that of Jericho. At the same time, probably in difficult conditions, an inventory of the deposits was made. It is worth noting here that Lurie localized all the toponyms appearing in the text in the area south-east of Jerusalem.

19. Matters testifying to the cultic character of at least some of the deposits are explained by him in the following way: 'One may in particular suppose that the reference is to worship-related objects which derive from the temple provisionally rebuilt by Ben Kosba. But are we not entitled to ask if the latter, following the example of Moses after his fight against the Midianites (Lev. 31.48-54), Joshua during the capture of Jericho (Josh. 5.18-19, 24; 7.11, 13), David in the course of his campaigns against hostile nations (2 Sam. 8.11-12; 1 Chron. 18.7) did not sacrifice to Yahweh part of the spoils taken from his enemy during his victorious operations like the one that resulted in the destruction of Deiotarian's 22nd Legion, brought from Egypt' (Laperrousaz, 'Remarques', p. 151).

20. Cf. B.-Z. Lurie, *Megillat ha-nehošet mi-midbar Yehudah* (Jerusalem: Kiriat Sefer, 1963).

21. Cf. Lurie, *Megillat ha-nehošet*, p. 15.

Apart from the theories presented above it is necessary to mention one proposed by M.R. Lehmann.[22] It set out to prove that 3Q15 was a list of funds accumulated from the redemption of religious taxes and tributes, which were to have been sent to Jerusalem but were instead deposited in genizas because of the city's inaccessibility. The objects would have been buried between the First and the Second Revolt against Rome, either permanently or temporarily, pending the rebuilding of the Temple. In the course of the Bar Kokhba Revolt, in the face of imminent disaster, it was probably found necessary to compile a durable record of the size of the collection and its hiding places. Lehmann reached such a conclusion by analysing the following terms: (a) דמע (= *terumah*, the part of grain set aside for the priests);[23] (b) אצרה שבע (the public treasury, containing the produce of the sabbatical year or its equivalent);[24] (c) מעשר שני (the second tithe);[25] (d) חרם (consecrated objects dedicated to the material

22. Cf. M.R. Lehmann, 'Identification of the Copper Scroll Based on its Technical Terms', *RevQ* 5 (1964), pp. 97-105.

23. This type of offering was not, in principle, subject to redemption. The owner had to keep it at the priest's disposal but was not obliged to deliver it to Jerusalem (*b. Ḥul.* 134b; Maimonides, *Hilkhoth Terumoth* 12.17). In the postexilic period there was, however, a custom of transporting the *terumah* to the Temple (Neh. 10.38-40; Mal. 3.10); hence perhaps immediately after 70 CE people continued to feel a spontaneous need to contribute the *terumah* or at least its equivalent for the purpose of reconstructing the Temple. Apart from that, the following factors may have led to the replacement of the *terumah* with money: (a) if the *terumah* was combined with other forms of taxation and inseparable from them, the priest had to pay for them (*m. Ter.* 5.1; *m. 'Or.* 2.6; Maimonides, *Hilkhoth Terumoth* 13.2); perhaps such a *dema'* had to be delivered to Jerusalem; (b) a non-priest who intentionally or unintentionally had eaten *terumah* had to pay back its value in compensation (if the act was not deliberate, he had to add 20 per cent of its value) (Lev. 5.16; 22.14; *m. Ter.* 6.1).

24. The term is attested in *t. Šeb.* 8.1, where it is said that the court appointed custodians for the collection and distribution of the sabbatical year's produce. Their duty was to leave a portion of the foodstuffs necessary for the population and deliver the rest to the *'oṣar* (public treasury). There was probably a central treasury to accumulate the produce of the sabbatical year or the money from its redemption (*t. Šeb.* 7.3, 5). Since Jerusalem was inaccessible, the gathered products had to be con-cealed because their use for lay purposes was forbidden (*t. Šeb.* 7.5; 6.29).

25. According to Deut. 14.22-26 it had to be consumed in Jerusalem either in its original state or redeemed with money. The regulations effective after 70 CE are given in the Mishnah: 'If somebody had fruit at that time and the hour of its removal had arrived, the Shammai school said, "He must redeem it into money" and the Hillel school said, "He must either redeem it into money or leave it unredeemed". Though the two schools differed slightly on the matter of redemption, they both agreed that

sustenance of the Temple);[26] (e) אפודרת (redemption money or metal for votive gifts).[27]

All the opinions recounted so far were expressed in the 1950s and 1960s. No fresh or significant proposals were made in the relatively few publications on 3Q15 that appeared in the following decade. A limited revival of research on the Copper Scroll began in the 1980s with the publication of articles by N. Golb[28] and B. Pixner.[29]

N. Golb used the Copper Scroll as an argument in favour of his theory, which challenged the Qumran–Essene hypothesis. He supported the authenticity of the hoards. He emphasized those features of 3Q15 that betrayed its documentary character: the non-literary language, succinct style, occurrence of authentic Judaean desert toponyms, references to books and to a duplicate of the scroll (according to him, an autograph), the choice of copper as the writing material and the inexpert execution. He excluded the possibility that such enormous resources might have belonged to the Essenes, and regarded Jerusalem as their place of origin. He assumed that both before and after the siege of the capital, steps had been taken to

either the produce or its equivalent had to be buried' (*m. Ma'as. Š.* 5.7).

26. In *m. 'Arak.* 8.1 Rabbi Jehuda ben Batyra states that if the ultimate destination of the *ḥerem* had not been made clear, it belonged to the Sanctuary (a different opinion, however, is expressed by the Sages and Maimonides, who attribute it to the priests: *Hilkhoth Erkhin we-Haramin* 6.1). *Ḥerem* devoted to the Temple (as opposed to that set aside for the priests) was subject to redemption (Maimonides, *Hilkhoth Erkhin we-Haramin* 6.4). This would mean that 3Q15 contains a list of amounts of money of precious metal obtained from redeeming various objects, movables and immovables, devoted to the maintenance of the Temple. In *b. 'Abod. Zar.* 13a, *Bek.* 53a, *Yom.* 66a and *Šeq.* 22a, it is said that after the destruction of the Temple *ḥerem* offerings were forbidden. If made, the pledged object had to die or perish; if it was redeemed, the money or precious metal had to be disposed of in the waters of the Dead Sea. If defaced, the money could be invalidated by means of any other body of water. Considering that many of the hiding places listed in 3Q15 are connected with various canals, reservoirs and so on, it might be assumed that they contain defaced coins from the redemption of *ḥerem* (*b. Pes.* 28a).

27. The root of this word, according to Lehmann, is פדה, related to פדות and פדיון, 'redemption', attested in the Bible and the Talmud. Since it occurs in the first column, it may refer to all the items listed in the catalogue or at least to the category of objects that according to Judaic law were subject to redemption.

28. Cf. N. Golb, 'The Problem of Origin and Identification of the Dead Sea Scrolls', *Proceedings of the American Philosophical Society* (1980), pp. 1-24.

29. Cf. B. Pixner, 'Unravelling the Copper Scroll Code: A Study on the Topography of 3Q15', *RevQ* 11 (1983), pp. 323-65.

remove, at least in part, the enormous treasure accumulated mainly in the Temple. Basing his opinions on the passages in 3Q15 that mention caches located near Jericho (5.12-14; 6.1-6; 8.1-3), in juxtaposition with information about manuscripts discovered in the area, obtained from Origen (third century CE) and the Nestorian patriarch Timothy (ninth century CE), Golb expressed the opinion that 'at some time in the first century Hebrew manuscipts were hidden away in various places in the Judaean wilderness and the plain of Jericho, not only in the Qumran caves, and that burial of objects of material value, palpably emanating from Jerusalem took place in the same area at the same time'.[30] This suggests that all the deposits were of the same origin. The location of many of the caches in the vicinity of aqueducts, sewers, and so on, which were probably part of the Jerusalem water system, with drains leading to the Dead Sea, also points to a connection between the hoards and the capital.

The basis for Pixner's views was his inspection of Cave 3, which allowed him to determine that '[t]he leather manuscripts and CS were both deposited by the same people of Qumran and at the same date, i.e. in the year 68 AD'.[31] He claims that 3Q15 is an inventory of the treasure of the Essene bank, hidden by the members of the community either before the war of 66–70 CE or at its beginning, and dug out after it:

> The original (or duplicate) of the treasure catalogue, mentioned at the end of the CS contained many more details. Since this duplicate was apparently never destroyed, it was probably used to retrieve all the mentioned treasures soon after the war was over.[32]

In addition to archaeological finds and topographical identifications (according to which most of the hiding places were located in areas inhabited by the Essenes, e.g., in the Essene quarter of Jerusalem), Pixner's arguments in favour of this hypothesis included above all the precise and matter-of-fact style of the document (Cross's opinion), which dates its handwriting within the period 25–75 CE, and the use of Greek letters.[33] The language of the scroll, Pixner seems to imply, is the collo-

30. Cf. Golb, 'Problem of Origin', p. 7.

31. Cf. Pixner, 'Unravelling the Copper Scroll Code', p. 335.

32. Cf. Pixner, 'Unravelling the Copper Scroll Code', p. 359.

33. Cf. Pixner, 'Unravelling the Copper Scroll Code', p. 335: 'Another indication that the CS is something else than a catalogue of fantastic treasures are the Greek letters… I share H. Bardtke's view that these curious letters make much more sense if the hidden treasures were real rather than legendary.'

quial language used in the first century. He quotes Milik to point out that certain documents discovered in Cave 4 were also written in the same dialect.[34] Pixner's explanation for the occurrence in the list of objects related to worship is the fact that among the members of the Essene sect there were priests and Levites entitled to collecting tithes from people associated with the movement. I believe it is worth quoting some of the arguments highlighted by him that make it likely that there were material resources in the Essenes' possession: (a) the treasure would have belonged not to a particular community but to the whole sect with its 4000 members; (b) new members yielded their personal property to the communal fund; (c) priests and Levites were entitled to collecting tithes and other tributary payments from people associated with the movement; (d) the sect may have been collecting funds for purposes connected with the imminent eschatological war; (e) over the 200 years of their history the Essenes, thanks to their hard labour and frugal lifestyle, may have amassed considerable wealth (witness the Qumran archives themselves); (f) the Essenes may have established their own bank, like that of the Temple, where people who were ideologically close to the movement would have invested their capital.[35]

Opinions about the origin of the Copper Scroll presented after 1983, mostly as digressions in polemics against N. Golb, have as a rule supported previously formulated hypotheses and have not, to my mind, contributed to any significant changes in the state of knowledge on the issue.

Concluding Remarks

The arguments for the documentary character of the scroll and for the genuineness of the deposits it describes are, in my opinion, convincing. At the same time I assume that the problem of its origin should not be analysed with recourse to data that are not regarded as relevant by common consent or whose significance is uncertain. Here belong, first of all, the facts that Cave 3 was used as a hiding place for a second time after 68 CE and that the scroll was placed at a certain distance from the other deposits; here we should also place, I believe, the problem of the language of the scroll. To be sure, there is no evidence to my knowledge (or, at any

34. Cf. Milik, DJDJ III, p. 222.
35. Cf. Pixner, 'Unravelling the Copper Scroll Code', pp. 339-40.

rate, no conclusive evidence) that the Mishnaic usages of 3Q15 has parallels in the remaining Qumran texts, but, taking into consideration the non-literary language of 3Q15 and the Mishnaisms occurring in other Qumran documents, one cannot rule out the possibility that the scroll represents the colloquial language of the authors of the Qumran archives. Nor do the Graecisms of 3Q15 seem to provide a decisive argument in this respect, if we pay closer attention to certain phonetic phenomena found in the Qumran texts, such as the weakening of guttural consonants, most probably under the influence of Greek.

In view of the fact that the radiocarbon dates established recently for some of the Dead Sea Scrolls at the University of Arizona[36] have generally confirmed the correctness of palaeographic dating, I presume that also in the case of the Copper Scroll the results of palaeographic studies should be used as a starting point for drawing conclusions. I am also of the opinion that, of the two alternative expert judgments, the one expressed by F.M. Cross (assigning the scroll a date not later than 75 CE) should be accepted. There are at least two reasons for such a preference. First, the text mentions objects (perhaps, among other things, high priests' garments) associated with temple worship, which came to an end in 70 CE. I also wish to emphasize that the formal aspects of the text, most importantly its careless manner of writing, phonetically motivated mistakes and irregular composition should be considered to indicate that the document was written quickly and hastily, most probably during a period of warfare and looming danger rather than peace and security. Second, some of the deposits are said to contain consecrated objects of the *ḥerem* type, forbidden after the fall of the Temple. Notwithstanding M.R. Lehmann's analysis of this term, I do not think it refers in this case to the money obtained from the redemption of objects pledged against the official prohibition, which could be legally demonetized, after defacing, by means of water, not necessarily the waters of the Dead Sea. In my opinion, this is doubtful, first of all because the intent of the relevant regulation was to annihilate the pledge, not just to conceal it; further, because it is not certain that all the three caches containing *ḥerem* objects were located in places connected with water.

As for the question of topographical identifications, which seems to be of great importance for explaining the origin of the text, it ought to be

36. A.J.T. Jull, D.J. Donahue, M. Broshi and E. Tov, 'Radiocarbon Dating of Scrolls and Linen Fragments from the Judean Desert', *Atiqot* 28 (1986), pp. 85-91.

stressed very emphatically that the location of a clear majority of the places is insecure. It also seems that the identifications offered by B. Pixner have not significantly changed this state of things. Despite frequent doubts as to the precise location of numerous toponyms, it is generally accepted that most of the places mentioned in the text were located within Jerusalem and in the area south-east of the city. Assuming the correctness of such a localization, and taking into account the cultic character of some of the articles and the enormous value of the deposits, the claim that the Copper Scroll treasure belonged to the Jerusalem Temple seems convincing to me. It cannot be ruled out, however, that some of the hoards, for example those located (according to Milik and Pixner) outside the ethnically Jewish area, contained deposits dedicated to the Temple but not removed from it.

I believe that Mount Gerizim is particularly important among the toponyms occurring in the text. If we agree that the name refers to a mountain in Samaritan territory, I think there are two ways of explaining the fact that 60 talents of silver were buried there. First, a Jewish, possibly Essene, community may have existed in the area, and we might regard them as the custodians or even owners of the deposit; there is, however, no mention of such a group anywhere. Second, it is possible that the deposit was brought from Jerusalem and buried at Mount Gerizim in some dramatic, extreme circumstances. In the latter case the concealment would supposedly have taken place before the Roman capture of that territory, probably during 67 CE. The evacuation of that, and also of other deposits from the Temple, could have been prompted by the increasing importance of the Zealot party and carried out by the weakening priestly/Sadducean faction. It seems that some support for such a conjecture is provided by the Greek letters in 3Q15, which, according to Pixner, represent the initial syllables of Greek names. The bearers of those names might have been the people responsible for the operation, who were members of that milieu, prone to Hellenistic influence. Interestingly enough, one of the names in question (Θεβουτι) is identical with the patronymic of the priest who, according to Josephus, surrendered to Titus part of the hidden valuables belonging to the Temple (Jesus, son of Θεβουτι, cf. *War* 6.387).

In the light of the above argument I think that among the hypotheses posited so far the most plausible ones are those that associate the origin of the Copper Scroll with the events of the First Revolt against Rome, and that consider the text to be a register of Temple treasure. At the same time I do not exclude the possibility that the scroll is of Essene origin. J.-B.

Humbert's suggestions as to the possibility that there was an Essene temple at Qumran,[37] if accepted, would provide an important argument in favour of such a proposal. To conclude, I wish to emphasize that in my opinion the question of the origin of the scroll remains open, and that the data at our disposal are not sufficient to decide the issue at present.

37. J.-B. Humbert, 'L'espace sacré a Qumrân: Proposition pour l'archéologie', *RB* 101 (1994), pp. 161-211.

18

The Copper Scroll: Novel Approaches

Brenda Lesley Segal

I would like to begin by sharing something I have recently become acutely aware of. In addition to being the author of three novels, one of which deals with the Jewish War or First Revolt[1] and another that fictionalizes the Bar Kokhba uprising or Second Revolt,[2] I have been the editor of a Jewish community newspaper for the last eight years, serving a readership that stretches from Princeton, New Jersey, across the Delaware River to Bucks County, Pennsylvania. It is an area that mirrors to a large degree the concerns and activities of most large, affluent Jewish communities in the major metropolises of the late twentieth century.

Every year, before the advent of the Jewish New Year, our newspaper lists the synagogue services at the local temples with a 'key' to each house of worship's particular brand of Judaism: 'O' for Orthodox, 'C' for Conservative, 'R' for Reform. The first year I became the editor, we had to add a fourth identifying code: 'Rc' for Reconstructionist. That was in 1988. Two weeks ago, as I prepared the list for the High Holy Days ushering in the Jewish year 5757, I noted that in addition to the four denominations cited above, we were publishing the following as requested: 'MO' (Modern Orthodox/Young Israel), 'L' (Lubavitch), 'LR' (Liberal Reform), 'JR' (Jewish Renewal), 'TE' (Traditional/Egalitarian) and 'H' (Havurah). The only congregations not acknowledged were a lesbian/gay group (who haven't decided what they are) and a group of Messianic Jews who would love to have been included but were felt not to represent legitimate Judaism, and so constituted the quintessential oxymoron.

I share this because I believe it would be a fallacy to consider the Intertestamental period, the time generally assigned to the writing of the

1. *The Tenth Measure* (New York: St Martin's Press, 1980).
2. *If I Forget Thee* (New York: St Martin's Press, 1983).

Dead Sea Scrolls, as being any less pluralistic—politically as well as religiously—than that of the modern Jewish community.

In his Appendix to the edition of the MMT fragments by Elisha Qimron and John Strugnell, Professor Ya'acov Sussmann of the Hebrew University writes:

> The end of the Second Temple period was a dynamic and effervescent era as far as religious thought and observance were concerned. The Hasmonean victories brought in their wake not only a great national awakening and devotion to Jews' ancestral land, but also (and perhaps especially) a great religious awakening and revival of devotion to the ancestral traditions.[3]

Substitute 'Twentieth Century' for 'Second Temple' and 'Israeli' for 'Hasmonean' and Sussmann's statement still rings true.

Now to the Copper Scroll. It is, quite simply, the stuff of a novelist's best dreams; for what are fiction writers, after all, but daydreamers taking notes? One of the scholars at the Manchester Symposium has told me he finds the text of the Copper Scroll 'quite boring'. It is—if one is looking for elegance of style, profundity of thought, historical allusions or any kind of theological revelation. It isn't—if some of your happiest moments were spent following Tom and Becky into a dark cave, searching for the Grail with Arthur's knights, or sailing the seven seas with Blackbeard.

In the most perfunctory manner, written in a bald, tense style whose abruptness may have been occasioned by real circumstance or by the deficiency of its scribe, the Copper Scroll touches the most basic, elemental part of us: the child within, who longs to solve a mystery and find a treasure.

Boring? I think not. Between the lines of artless script pounded into three sheets of beaten copper found in a cave near Khirbet Qumran in 1952, a series of tantalizing scenarios rises up like the clouds of dust left swirling in the wake of an explorer's jeep. Our imagination is stirred as much as our curiosity; because the Copper Scroll poses so many questions and provides so few answers.

Who wrote this so-called 'laundry list' of buried coins, priestly items and fantastic amounts of gold and silver—and are those amounts perhaps too fantastic to be real? Who buried this treasure, and why? Where did it

3. Y. Sussmann, 'The History of the Halakha and the Dead Sea Scrolls: Preliminary Talmudic Observations on *Miqṣat Ma'aśe Ha-Torah* (4QMMT)', in E. Qimron and J. Strugnell, *Qumran Cave 4.V: Miqṣat Ma'aśe ha-Torah* (DJD X; Oxford: Clarendon Press, 1994), p. 196.

come from? And the most tantalizing question of all: Does the Copper Scroll's treasure yet await discovery? Are the silver bowls, the coins, the gold bars still in their secret deposits, still hidden after all these centuries?

We have enough material here for a dozen books. Indeed, one wonders why, of all the many novels inspired by the Dead Sea Scrolls, only two, to my knowledge, speak of the Copper Scroll: *The Copper Scrolls* by N.N. Weinreb and *Earthly Remains* by Peter Hernon.[4] *Earthly Remains* does not focus exclusively on the Copper Scroll, but is a vehicle for what I have come to call the 'Jesus connection'. By that, I mean that, while scholars continue to debate whether or not there is a Christian content or parallels to Christianity in the sectarian writings, and/or their relative significance for New Testament ideas, nearly all the authors of these novels focusing on the finds in the Judaean desert are convinced the message of the scrolls has little or nothing to do with Jews and everything to do with Christian theology.

In *Earthly Remains*, for example, the Copper Scroll gives direction for finding what is presumably the body of Jesus and the head of John the Baptist. The author makes clever use of the cemetery at Qumran. However, his account of the heroine's discovery and reading of the scroll would undoubtedly make John Allegro roll over in his grave with laughter. Not only can our fictional archaeologist, Brooklyn-born Israeli Sara Garner, decipher ancient script with a flick of her cleaning brush, but also she unrolls the Copper Scroll in the field by means of a piece of wire cut from a jeep's radio antenna and cuts it apart with a 'pair of snippers'! It is tempting to add here that the method described above is only slightly less preposterous than the text revealed by her, which of course is a description of a treasure unlike anything in the actual Copper Scroll. What is interesting in Hernon's novel is the patina of authenticity that coats the fictional tale. Hernon is well acquainted with the 1947 discovery by the Bedouin, Sukenik's acquisition of the first scrolls, the general topography, and the scrolls themselves. His description of the climate of the time, the Bethlehem dealer who is also a cobbler (obviously modelled on Kando), his knowledge of the *Rule of the Community*, the *Nash Papyrus*, the Copper

4. N.N. Weinreb, *The Copper Scrolls* (New York: G.P. Putnam, 1958); Peter Hernon, *Earthly Remains* (New York: Birch Lane Press, 1989). Weinreb's *The Copper Scrolls* was described by J. Reumann as a historical novel which 'mixes sex and ascetic sanctity': 'The Dead Sea Scrolls in America: A Survey of Five Years of Popular Literature', *LQ* 12 (1960), pp. 91-110. I am grateful to Al Wolters for informing me about Weinreb's novel.

Scroll and the cemetery at Qumran, are all to be admired. His adherence to the Essene theory, along with identifying the Teacher of Righteousness as Jesus, places this novelist in the same class as several others who have investigated the scrolls.

My own efforts to write a novel inspired by the Copper Scroll are a somewhat similar combination of authenticity and imaginative recreation. *The Jerusalem Syndrome*, a work still in progress, is a thriller set in the modern Jewish state in the year following the Arafat–Rabin signing of the Declaration of Principles in Washington DC, which are commonly, if mistakenly, called the 'Peace Accord'. Urged by my friend of many years, Professor Emanuel Tov of the Hebrew University in Jerusalem, to write a novel about the Dead Sea Scrolls in the vein of my other historical works, about a decade ago, I found myself drawn to the Copper Scroll. Pragmatism added to its allure. No chance of stepping on any ecclesiastical toes, if I stuck to the script provided by the real scroll. And the very fact that the Copper Scroll is an anomaly within the body of the Dead Sea Scrolls, difficult to place within the pluralism of late Second Temple period Judaism as described above, bestows a certain and unique license that no fiction writer would not appreciate.

The fact that this novel is so long in the making rests with the ongoing, evolving flow of information from the scholars in the field whose work is a constant inspiration to me and whose ideas and methods I find it impossible to ignore. What a loss to the reader it would be to omit a description of the exciting space-age technology used by Marilyn Lundberg and Bruce Zuckerman to read hitherto 'unreadable' scroll fragments, or the fascinating high-tech methods of the Electricité de France team. Whether or not one agrees with his theory, Israel Knohl's dramatic presentation of a meticulously thought-out scenario stirs the imagination. Al Wolters's new reading of the text clarifies so much. And Meir Bar-Ilan's discussion of the process of list-making has not only set off a light bulb above this writer's head, it had me sketching out a chapter that very afternoon!

And there are the scholars themselves, all of whom, singly or in composite fashion must find their way into the pages of my book—from cool assured 'youngsters' like Hanan and Esti Eshel, to the sweetly grave 'authority figure' of Émile Puech. Images—all welcome—flood my mind: the constantly precise but approachable John Lübbe; petite brilliant Ruti Fidler; Florentino García Martínez, following each and every presentation with a finger tracing the text of his personal copy of the Copper Scroll; Judah Lefkovits, who, if there is such a thing as 'past lives', was surely a talmudic scholar in all of them. I shall not forget the enthusiasm and generous spirit of Lawrence Schiffman, the twinkle in the eye of Barbara Thiering, the courtliness of Hartmut Stegemann, the intense focus of Vendyl Jones directed at each presentation.

This, too, is the stuff that fuels a novelist. And for this opportunity to observe and learn I shall always be grateful to George Brooke of the Manchester–Sheffield Centre for Dead Sea Scrolls Research. My thanks to him and to Professor Tov, Editor of the Dead Sea Scrolls Project, for their generous acceptance of a non-academic's efforts to give dramatic scope and perhaps contemporary relevance to the ancient world.

As a novelist my task is not to decipher definitively the Copper Scroll (although that would be lovely), but to induce in the reader that 'willing suspension of disbelief' that is at the core of all good fiction. At the same time, I must confess that I am cheered by the thought that the theories and concepts I have espoused in my published novels as well as in *The Jerusalem Syndrome* are not incompatible with many of the ideas presented at this Symposium. In fact, I am not at all sure that my 'writer's intuition' has produced anything more or less improbable regarding the Copper Scroll than what I have heard thus far.

Lest you judge me too harshly for this, I beg the reader to consider the words of the English poet John Keats. In a letter to one Benjamin Bailey, dated 22 November 1817, Keats writes: 'I am certain of nothing but the holiness of the heart's affections and the truth of the imagination…'

19

The Copper Scroll: King Herod's Bank Account?

Barbara Thiering

Introductory Conjectures

It has come to be accepted that the Copper Scroll was a list of real treasure, not a work of fantasy as Milik initially thought,[1] the problems being to account for the enormous sums involved, to deal with the extremely difficult text and to identify the locations.

The deposits mostly name talents, some silver, a few gold, most with the metal unspecified. There could be at least 5000 talents. In another Qumran document, 4Q159, the talent is defined as 6000 half-shekels, in a context relating it to the annual temple tax. Taking a half-shekel to be an amount affordable by all, as the rule of the temple tax laid down (Exod. 30.15), say the equivalent of $100, then some 5000 talents would be the equivalent of US$3,000,000,000 (3000 million, or in USA, 3 billion). Then there were the gold and silver bars.

The first place to turn to for relevant information would be within the scrolls themselves, and especially the above-mentioned document, 4Q159, in the Ordinances group, the first fragment of which deals in detail with a system of taxation. The system is based on the temple tax, which is mentioned also in 11QT[a] 39.8, but in this document with significant differences from the biblical rule.

4Q159 gives a total of money coming from a group called the Six Hundred Thousand, paying a half-shekel each, as well as some further groups. The Six Hundred Thousand yield 100 talents, each one paying a half-shekel. The half-shekel is said to be an 'atonement for his life'

1. J.T. Milik, 'Le rouleau de cuivre provenant de la grotte 3Q (3Q15)', in M. Baillet, J.T. Milik and R. de Vaux, *Les 'petites grottes' de Qumrân* (DJDJ III; Oxford: Clarendon Press, 1962), pp. 281-82.

(כפר נפשו), as is the temple tax in Exod. 30.12, but then a new point is added: 'Only once shall he give it in all his days.' After this, as F. Weinert has shown and F. García Martínez agrees,[2] lines 10-12 give a further list, also concerning a half-shekel payment, and they have supplied the word 'peace offering' in the lacuna. This further list is naturally read as an additional payment, not another version of the previous tax.

Who were the Six Hundred Thousand? The term indicates an Israel of men, as this was the number of men said to have come out of Egypt at the Exodus (Exod. 12.37). If it were a real figure, as the calculations of income indicate that it was, then it points to the Diaspora, where, as Josephus reports, 'myriads of our race' lived (*Apion* 1.194). The population of Jerusalem itself, on an early estimate, was 120,000 (*Apion* 1.198). Diaspora Jews had for a long time been contributing enormous wealth to the Jerusalem temple (*Ant.* 14.110).

The initial half-shekel of the Ordinances list, to be paid only once in a lifetime, as a 'ransom' or 'atonement', suggests a system of initiation for Diaspora Jews, from which they received benefits understood as religious salvation, paying at the same time a half-shekel, which was understood in terms of the temple tax. It was a once-and-for-all initiation and atonement. The number indicates that they formed a New Israel, seeing themselves not simply as exiles from the homeland, but as part of a larger Israel, with teaching suitable to Diaspora conditions. The requirement of an act of initiation would be an innovation. At the same time they were willing for their money to be used for a temple in the homeland.

The once-and-for-all payment would bring in only 100 talents in total. But the additional payment of a half-shekel, called a peace offering, would be annual, connected with an annual feast, as the temple tax was (Exod. 30.1-16). Ongoing fees, reflecting the Levitical system of annual sacrifices of animals or grain for the removal of sin (Lev. 23.19), would have been seen as a suitable way of substituting for sacrifices, by money payments from those who could not attend the Jerusalem temple. These fees would ensure continuing membership, and would have been accompanied by some kind of declaration of forgiveness of sin. A link with the practice of annual promotions for virtue, described in 1QS 5.24, is suggested at this point. It would be these additional fees that would ensure an enormous

2. F.D. Weinert, '4Q159: Legislation for an Essene Community outside of Qumran?', *JSJ* 5 (1974), pp. 179-207; F. García Martínez, *The Dead Sea Scrolls Translated* (Leiden: E.J. Brill, 1994), p. 86. 'Peace offering' is omitted in the Study Edition (*The Dead Sea Scrolls: A Study Edition* [Leiden: E.J. Brill, 1997]).

income of the type described in the Copper Scroll. Over 50 years, 100 talents annually would bring in 5000 talents.

In a different context,[3] I have argued that the final form of the Temple Scroll is best understood, on its own data, as a plan offered by the Qumran ascetics to Herod the Great at the time he announced his intention to renovate the Jerusalem temple, in the twenties BCE. It was at this time also that, according to Josephus, he showed favour to the Essenes, represented by Menahem (*Ant.* 15.378-80). As may be shown,[4] the Essenes had particular reason, based on their chronological theories, for believing and hoping that God was directing Herod to rebuild the temple at this time, and they, with their associated ascetic Sadducees and Pharisees,[5] offered their architectural plan, with the obvious intention of taking control in the new temple, their priesthood officiating, now restored to their rightful place. So confident were they that God was overruling, because the date coincided with their prophecy of a restoration, that they were prepared to include criticisms of Herod and his polygamous ways, a point not unnoticed by Herod when he turned down their plan.

Herod did rebuild the temple, although on his own magnificent plan, and undertook also massive building works at Masada and in the harbour at Caesarea. Where did he get the money from? On the precedent of previous large donations to the temple from the Diaspora, he would certainly have got it from the Diaspora. But the new point suggested by the present sources is that it was done in a highly organized, systematic way, with benefits received by the Diaspora members, one of their conditions being the formalization of an updated kind of Judaism that they were practising under Hellenistic influence, thinking of it as a New Israel. The term New Covenant would also have arisen in such circumstances (1QpHab 2.3-4; CD 6.19; 8.21; 19.34; 20.12).

Following the earthquake of 31 BCE, Qumran lay deserted for some years, unable to be occupied because the water system was not function-

3. 'The Date of Composition of the Temple Scroll', in G. Brooke (ed.), *Temple Scroll Studies* (JSPSup, 7; Sheffield: JSOT Press, 1989), pp. 99-120.

4. B.E. Thiering, *Jesus the Man* (Sydney: Transworld Doubleday 1992); in USA *Jesus and the Riddle of the Dead Sea Scrolls* (San Francisco: Harper Collins, 1992), Appendix 1; *idem, Jesus of the Apocalypse* (Sydney: Transworld Doubleday, 1995), part II, ch. 6.

5. A coalition that I have long argued for: *Redating the Teacher of Righteousness* (Sydney: Theological Explorations, 1979), p. 147.

ing.[6] Between 31 and 21 BCE the ascetics, now received back in Jerusalem because of Herod's favour for the Essenes, might have agreed to influence their own Diaspora members to support his temple project (a Diaspora form of the ascetic life is, of course, evidenced in the accounts of the Therapeutae of Egypt), hoping to have their plan for the temple accepted. At the same time, they might have offered him the deserted buildings at Qumran as a suitable place for storing the money that was expected to flow in. It could be guarded by men who were stationed at the building at Ain Feshkha, two miles further down the shore of the Dead Sea, which had not been affected by the earthquake and where there was a spring.

All of this is, so far, merely a series of conjectures from relevant scrolls and from the proposed date of the Temple Scroll.[7]

Detail of Locations

In the second part of this paper, I would like to deal with points about the actual locations of the deposits, in support of the suggestion that after the earthquake Qumran was the place where the Diaspora money intended for Herod's building projects was stored.

The first step is the observation that the Copper Scroll was made of three strips of metal, each containing four columns, with each successive strip riveted to the previous one. The first strip contained, in all, 22 items (using the divisions that G. Vermes retains,[8] although there may be doubt about the points of division). Of these, the last (at 4.13) introduces the

6. R. de Vaux, *Archaeology and the Dead Sea Scrolls* (London: The British Academy; Oxford University Press, 1973), pp. 23-24.

7. But it may be stated briefly here that there is a very great deal of evidence to support the foregoing conjectures, when a much wider field of data, the New Testament, is taken into account. It would, however, be necessary to argue step by step why this field of data is relevant. For the moment, one may simply add another conjecture, that the Christian use of the terms New Covenant and the concept of the New Israel, together with the remarkable emphasis in the gospels on money (parables about the increase of pounds, that is 100 half-shekels, and of talents; emphasis on rejection of money; Jesus overturning the tables of the money changers; even the little story about getting the shekel out of the mouth of the fish) could be used in a hypothesis that the ultimate form of the Diaspora New Covenant indicated in the scrolls was the Christian Church, but only after the practice of charging fees for religious salvation, and paying money for forgiveness of sins, was abolished.

8. G. Vermes, *The Complete Dead Sea Scrolls* (London: Penguin Books, 1997), pp. 585-89.

name Sekakah, and it appears again in items 23 (5.2), 24 (5.5), and 26 (5.13) at the beginning of the next strip, not appearing again after that.

There can be little doubt that Sekakah was a name for the Qumran vicinity, the Sekakah of Josh. 15.61. This has been sufficiently agreed to give the name Sekakah, shown in the official survey map, to the wadi beginning in the vicinity of Jebel El Muntar, flowing past Khirbet Mird, and about two miles inland above Qumran meeting its tributary, the wadi Qumran, which flows down the cliff at the south end of the plateau. In 3Q15 5.1-2 'the beginning of the water conduit…Sekakah from the north' (ברוש אמת המים...סככא מן הצפון) would mean the beginning of the aqueduct that starts from the north side of the wadi and runs along the neck of land towards the buildings. 3Q15 5.13 includes the phrase 'from Jericho to Sekakah', a further indication that Sekakah was Qumran, eight miles south of Jericho.

It may be argued that the 21 items in the first strip prior to the introduction of Sekakah refer to places within the Qumran grounds, and those after it refer to places outside, going further and further away, the last group probably in Jerusalem and Samaria. The first strip was 82 cm or 32 ins. long, a reasonably manageable length, and on this view the strip would have been used alone for some time, while it was thought that Qumran, deserted from 31 BCE, was sufficient to hold the deposits. When the site was reoccupied about the turn of the era, money continued to come in, but was no longer stored within the grounds where people lived, but in a series of places outside. The subsequent strips recording these were fastened to the original one, the second strip beginning with Sekakah, the wadi area just south of the plateau, and placing its first item, 3Q15 4.13-14, at the end of the first strip in what may have been an empty space.

The reasons for believing that items 1–21 all refer to the Qumran grounds are as follows. Six of the items speak of a 'cistern' (בור) (1.6; 2.1, 6, 7, 10; 4.1). Within the Qumran complex there are six large rectangular cisterns (Fig. 19.1, loci 71, 48, 58, 91, 117, 118). Another one at the far north-west corner (loc. 138) is smaller and square, and a smaller one near the south-east (loc. 68) is also square, but the six major ones attached to the buildings are all much larger, and rectangular. It is to these, it is suggested, that the word 'cistern' applies. When the meaning of some terms to be discussed below is understood, then two of these fit the description in the items speaking of cisterns.

Moreover, the detail in 3Q15 1.1-4 (item 1) points satisfactorily to a particular vault, still to be seen at Qumran, at the same time supplying some of the meanings of terms that explain the others. Item 1 has been translated by Milik, followed for the most part by Vermes: 'At Chorebbeh, which is in the valley of Achor, under the steps going to the east, (dig) forty cubits, a casket of silver, in all a weight of 17 talents.'[9] F. García Martínez translated: 'In the ruin which is in the valley, pass under the steps leading to the East, forty cubits',[10] treating as a common noun and a verb both words translated by the others as names. Both Vermes and García Martínez omit the word 'dig', which is not in the text but supplied by Milik, and they are surely right, for a depth of 40 cubits is 60 ft, or 18 m. Vermes's 'stairs which go eastwards forty cubits'[11] is also difficult, for the same reason, that it would be a very large flight of steps.

At many points Milik, the first translator, saw difficult words as names, and most of these have to be reconsidered. García Martínez has good reason for translating חריבה as 'ruin', but had less so for treating עכור as a verb, for the latter word follows 'valley' and, since 4.6 contains the phrase 'valley of Achon', 1.1 surely means the valley of Achor, the biblical name for the area just west of the Jordan, in the Jericho vicinity (Josh. 7.24-26). It was a boundary point for the territory of Judah (Josh. 15.7), and in poetic use (Hos. 2.15) was the first place to which the migrants from Egypt came. The fragment 4Q522 contains this name. 'The ruin in the valley of Achor' would be an appropriate description of Qumran after the earthquake.

The deposit was at 'steps going to the east'. According to the original archaeological description and photographs, now made more fully available by J.-B. Humbert and A. Chambon,[12] there was a set of seven steps running from just below the round well at Qumran up to a platform above the room in which the large furnace was located (Fig. 19.2, loc. 101). The steps have now been taken away, but their support remains, and they are clearly visible in the photographs published early on. However, they are not on the east but the west side of the complex, and they go up in a southerly direction. Just beside them is a large niche, some 70 cm wide and more than a metre deep, formed by the space between them and the

9. Milik, DJDJ III, p. 212.

10. García Martínez, *Dead Sea Scrolls Translated* (1994), p. 461. The 1997 edition has 'valley of Achor'.

11. Vermes, *Complete Dead Sea Scrolls*, p. 585.

12. J.-B. Humbert and A. Chambon, *Fouilles de Khirbet Qumrân et de Ain Feshkha* (Freiburg: Universitätsverlag; Göttingen: Vandenhoeck & Ruprecht, 1994), I; plates 231 and 236 show the steps.

further wall, in a shape that at once suggests use as a vault, needing only a covering at the top at the same level as the top of the steps. The constructions in this corner were built in a second phase, taking the place of an original door communicating from loc. 101 to the south end of the long courtyard (loc. 111), which lay west of the large well.

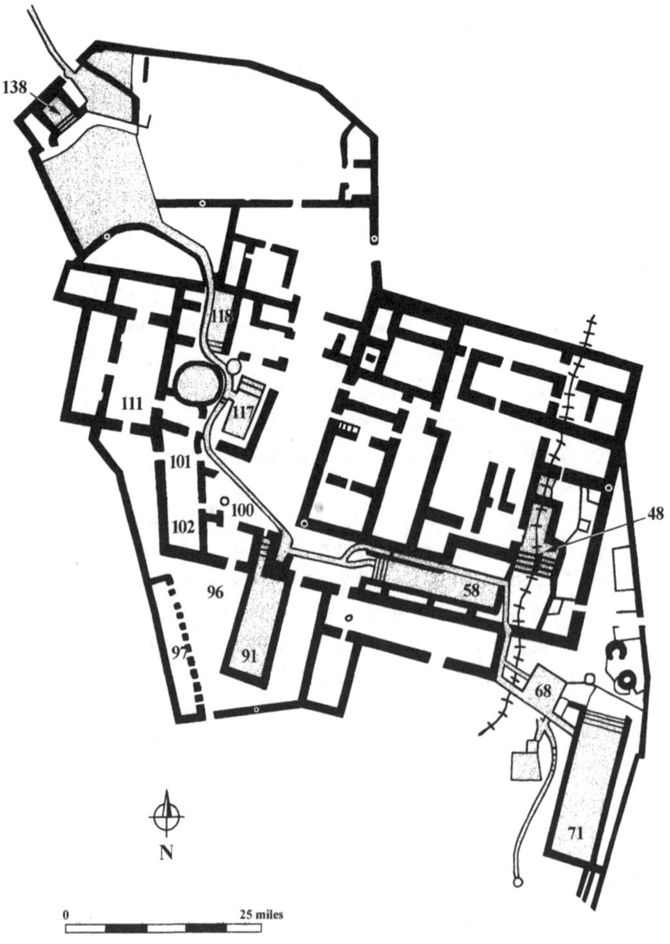

Fig. 19.1. *Period 1b: c. 103–31 BCE* (adapted from P.R. Davies, *Qumran* [Cities of the Biblical World; Guildford: Lutterworth Press, 1982])

An interpretation may be offered[13] about the uses of these rooms, the courtyard and loci 101-102. Far from being in an unimportant workshop area, the long north–south courtyard to the west of the well was the substitute sanctuary of the original Qumran priests who were exiled there

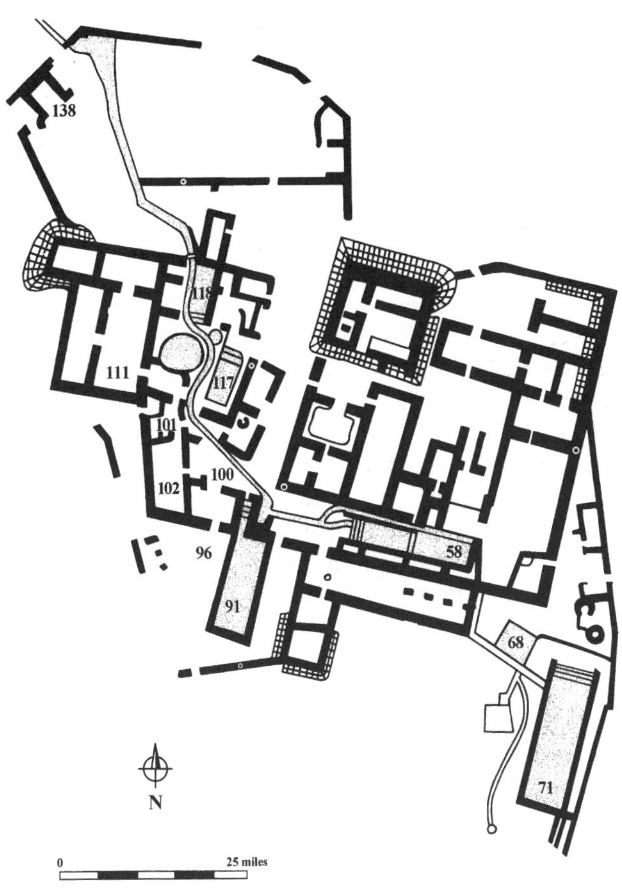

Fig. 19.2. *Period II* (adapted from Davies, *Qumran*)

13. Cf. Thiering, *Jesus the Man*, Appendix II: Locations.

in the late second century BCE. Measured from below the northern chamber and including its south wall, the courtyard is 30 cubits long and 10 cubits wide inside the walls, 12 cubits wide including the side walls.[14] A line of stones runs across the northern part of the courtyard, dividing it into an upper third and a lower two-thirds. This division, and the dimensions of 30 × 10 cubits, make it a half-scale reproduction of Solomon's temple, which was 60 × 20 cubits, with the upper third the Holy of Holies and the lower two-thirds the Holy House. Counting the side walls, it has the same dimensions as the wilderness tabernacle, which was 30 cubits long and 12 cubits wide (1 Kgs 6.2, 16, 17; Exod. 36.20-30).

Rooms corresponding to the holy chambers of the temple surrounded this courtyard, and from those beside the upper third large windows looked into it, as if to guard this part especially. When the 10 cubit width of the northern chamber is added to the 30 cubits of the courtyard, there are 40 cubits to the south end. On this interpretation, a spot 'at 40 cubits', that is, at the lower end of the wall of the sanctuary including the northern holy chamber, would be a significant location. This is the point at which the niche suspected to be the vault of 3Q15 1.1-4 is placed.[15]

Just north of the niche is an inlet with a semicircle of stones, then the door in the lower eastern wall of the courtyard. If the courtyard were a substitute temple, one running north–south rather than east–west in order to avoid its being treated as an actual temple, it still needed an eastern door, for it was here, according to Ezek. 46.1-3, that the king sat at new moons, when the villagers came up to the temple. The inlet looks like a place for a person to stand. On this interpretation, the term 'east' would have an absolute, not a relative meaning, the area around the revered east door of the sanctuary. The communicating room running south, adjoining the corner of the sanctuary (loc. 101) would be part of this fixed East, and the steps going up to its roof, for the men to stand on while guarding the treasure, would be 'steps coming in at the East'.

The same meaning of the term 'East' would then apply throughout, the fixed area on the east side of another place, defined as having a lesser level of holiness, being a threshold to the other place. In the temple itself it was a porch, but when the sanctuary was placed north–south it was simply an

14. Using an 18 ins. cubit, which is the exact size of the tops of the carved pillar bases found in the same area.

15. 3Q15 4.4, in which the phrase '40 cubits' may appear, would have a similar significance. The word 'one', making it 41, is not necessarily to be supplied in the lacuna.

eastern approach. The less holy place was suitable for deposits of money.

In 2.7 a cistern is described: 'In the cistern which is before the eastern gate, distant 15 cubits from it…' This fits exactly the large rectangular cistern, loc. 117, which is 15 cubits from the eastern door of the courtyard. The Eastern Gate would have been the name for this door.

Moreover, 2.10-12 speak of 'the cistern under the wall from the east, at the tooth of rock' (שן הסלע). A rectangular cistern north of the well, loc. 118, is a little closer than the one mentioned above to the eastern wall of the sanctuary, and at the entry to the aqueduct just beside it is a free-standing pointed stone that readily fits the description 'tooth of rock'.[16]

Thus a vault and two cisterns, as well as the agreement of the number of cisterns, fit details of the text in the first strip of the Copper Scroll, once the meaning of the courtyard is understood.

Koḥlit

Three more items in this strip (at 1.9; 2.13; 4.11), use the word *koḥlit* (כחלת), which has been taken by all to be a name. It appears only in this strip and in the final item of the whole work, where it is said that a second copy of the Copper Scroll is located in this place. Two of the descriptions of *koḥlit* (2.13; 4.11) contain the word 'east'.

There is reason for seeing this term as applying to the southern one of the two rooms that were originally connected by doors with the south-east corner of the courtyard (loc. 102). If the courtyard were a sanctuary, then a place was needed where the rule of Ezek. 44.19, for Zadokite priests, could be kept. They had to exchange their loose white linen sanctuary robes for outside garments, that is, they needed a vestry.

According to 1QM 7.9-11 (repeated in 4Q491) priests while on the battlefield had special battle garments that must not be taken into the sanctuary—linen tunic and breeches, a turban, and a girdle embroidered in blue, purple and scarlet thread. The colours of the Levitical priests, which had been used in the tabernacle (Exod. 26.1; 28.5-6), had gone down in status and now belonged in unholy places.

The only known derivation for *koḥlit* is 'blue', used once in the Bible (Ezek. 23.40), and in modern Hebrew 'to paint blue'. It is not the same word as תכלת, the violet-blue of the tabernacle colours. Another location in the Copper Scroll, in Vermes's item 41 (3Q15 9.4), is called בתכלת

16. Humbert and Chambon, *Fouilles de Khirbet Qumrân*, pls. 216, 218. It would be a small-scale version of the 'tooth of the crag' of 1 Sam. 14.4 and Isa. 22.16.

השני, and these are the words for the Levitical violet-blue and scarlet. Vermes has seen this, and translated 'At "Violet-scarlet"',[17] while Milik made it a proper name. On this analogy, it is to be suggested that *koḥlit* means 'the Blue'.

Since colours were worn in the outside world, the vestry would be the place where the priests changed into the colours, and the northern room of the two (loc. 101), part of the East, might well have been where they changed into scarlet, purple and violet-blue, at a particular spot that became known by these names. Below the level of violet-blue may have been a lesser level, where a different shade of blue, *koḥlit*, was worn by men lower in status than the priests, using the southern room, which was further away from the sanctuary. Such gradations would reflect the hierarchical thinking that is well evidenced in the Qumran literature.

There was a third class of men, ranked under the priests and Levites, called 'the sons of Israel', and in the ceremony described in 1QS 1-2 'those entering the Covenant' were required to say 'Amen, Amen' after the priests and Levites (CD 14.3-6; 1QS 1.20; 2.18). In 4Q164, the pesher on Isa. 54.11, the phrase 'I will lay your foundations with sapphires' is taken to mean 'the congregation of his elect...like a sapphire among stones', showing an association of a congregation with blue. The southern one of the two vestry rooms, separated by a dais from the northern one, would be suitable to seat a congregation in the later sense of the word, laymen looking northwards towards the priests and Levites, and saying 'Amen' when required. It may be further noted in this connection that a blue thread was used to embroider the rectangular shapes on the scroll wrappers in Cave 1, and that scroll wrappers were said in the Mishnah to be susceptible to uncleanness.[18]

This southern room had an eastern door, and outside it was a marked-off area, loc. 100, bounded by the aqueduct, where several structures stood, including two carved circular pillar bases, these being in marked contrast to the rough stones of the rest of the building. If laymen used the southern room, calling it the 'Blue', then came outside into the open, this would be their East, a step further into the outside world. Col. 2 line 13 gives directions 'east of *koḥlit*', and 4.11 speaks of an 'eastern שית (foundation? seat?) in the north of *koḥlit*'. Col. 1 lines 9-12, describing *koḥlit*, speaks of an 'opening in the skirts [שולי] of the aqueduct from the north, six

17. Vermes, *Complete Dead Sea Scrolls*, p. 587.

18. D. Barthélemy and J.T. Milik, *Qumran Cave 1* (DJD I; Oxford: Clarendon Press, 1955), pp. 20, 24-26; *m. Kel.* 28.4.

cubits to the dipping hole [ניקרת הטבילה]'. The well-defined triangular area of the pillar bases had the aqueduct as its hypotenuse, running down from the north. There would be several possible candidates for a 'dipping hole' six cubits away, one of them being part of the aqueduct itself.

In the final item, 12.10-11, concerning *koḥlit* as the hiding place of the second scroll, it is said that 'graves' were at its mouth. The southern wall of the south room, now collapsed, adjoined the north of the long esplanade, loc. 96, and according to 3.11 there was a grave in the north-east corner of the מלה, a word that Milik and Vermes have read as *millah*, from 'to fill', and translated 'esplanade'. Other readings also indicate the esplanade. This grave would correspond to the graves of 12.11, outside the southern wall of the south vestry, in the open space of the esplanade. The room called 'the Blue' would have been a suitable place for storing a copy of the scroll.

The familiar names of the areas that had been in use prior to the earthquake would still have been known to the former inhabitants, who could use them as a means of partial concealment, to give directions to those who understood them, while an outsider, even if in possession of the Copper Scroll, would not understand.

The Greek Letters

One of the main mysteries of the Copper Scroll concerns the Greek letters, which appear only in the section in question, the first strip. Although no proof can be offered, a suggestion would be that they are used as numerals and refer to deposits of Greek coins kept separate in the hiding places, and to distinguish between the coins as to whether they are copper, gold or silver, the order, from left to right, being that determined by their conventions, in which the more important was placed in the centre, the next to the right, and the next to the left. Thus Chi–Alpha–Gamma at the end of 1.12 would mean 600 copper coins, 1 gold coin and 3 silver coins. Tau–Rho at the end of 3.7 would be 300 copper, 100 silver, with no gold.

The difficulties of deciphering and translating the Copper Scroll mean that continuing teamwork is needed at the present stage. The foregoing is offered as a way of opening up further directions that would have the effect of integrating the Copper Scroll into the overall history of Qumran.

Some Palaeographical Observations Regarding the Cover Art

Lika Tov

Why would I, an artist specialized in print-making, feel the need to write about the Copper Scroll? I started to be interested in the background of the writing of the Copper Scroll after I was commissioned to design an artistic view of this scroll, which resulted in the collagraph presented as the frontispiece in this volume.

While studying the Hebrew and Greek characters incised in the sheets of copper as preparation for my print, I gained what I believe to be significant insights into the different forms of handwriting and the nature of this scroll. These insights have enabled me to develop a theory on how this scroll was created and why it has such an unusual shape.

I submit the following observations on the background of the writing.

Multiple Scribes

I suggest that the scroll was not written by one scribe, as is generally assumed by scholars, but by 25 different ones. The differences between these scribes are visible in their handwriting and the different shapes and sizes of the letters. Also, some scribes erred more than others.

Scribe H (Col. 3.1-7) wrote in a neat and stylized fashion. The next one, scribe I (3.8-13), apparently imitated the script of his predecessor, but, after one line, he lapsed into sloppiness (see especially 3.11-13). Again another one, scribe M (4.12-14), wrote letters in different sizes and shapes and with large spacing between them and between the words.

Almost all the sections of the scroll were written by different individuals, while some scribes wrote more than one section in adjacent columns. See below on scribes P, Q and W.

After each section of writing, a different person filled in the value of the treasure in square characters as well as his own initials in Greek. In 1.4 this is visible because the added words KEN שבעשרה are written 2 mm below the writing surface of the preceding words. Also, elsewhere, the secondary character of the words indicating value (1.8; 9.13; 12.1) and the numbers themselves are clearly visible (cf. the shape of the numbers in 3.7 with 6.6 and 7.13).

The Greek initials do not refer to the scribes, but to the persons who filled in the monetary value of the treasure (1.4, 12; 2.2, 4, 9; 3.7; 4.2). However, only a few treasures were initialized in this way. See further below.

I recognize the handwriting of the following scribes:

Scribe A: 1.1-4. Being the first, he tried out the shapes more than those who followed him. Some examples are shown below:

ב 1.1	ב ב ב	1.2	ב		
ה 1.1	ה	1.2	ה ה	1.3	ה ה
ח 1.1	ח	1.2	ח		
כ 1.1	כ	1.3	כ כ		
מ 1.1	מ	1.2	מ מ מ	1.4	מ
ק 1.1	ק	1.4	ק		
ר 1.1	ר	1.2	ר	1.3	ר ר

List of Sections of the Text where the Next Scribes Took Over

Scribe B: 1.5-8
Scribe C: 1.9-12
Scribe D: 1.13–2.2
Scribe E: 2.3-4
Scribe F: 2.5-9
Scribe G: 2.10-15
Scribe H: 3.1-7
Scribe I: 3.8-13
Scribe J: 4.1-2
Scribe K: 4.3-5
Scribe L: 4.6-11
Scribe M: 4.12-14
Scribe N: 5.1-4

Scribe O: 5.5-6
Scribe P: 5.7-14
Scribe Q: 6.1-10
Scribe P (again): 6.11–7.3
Scribe Q (again): 7.4-10
Scribe R: 7.11-16
Scribe S: 8.1-13
Scribe T: 8.14–9.6
Scribe U: 9.7-13
Scribe V: 9.14-17
Scribe W: 10.1-6
Scribe X: 10.8-17
Scribe W (again): 11.1-11
Scribe X (again): 11.12–12.3
Scribe Y: 12.4-13 [end of the scroll]

Purpose of the Scroll

I noticed that in the first sheet of copper there is a hole in the middle of the margin to the right of the first column. I suggest that this hole was inserted in the sheet before the writing was begun. The purpose of this hole was to tie the scroll with a string to a certain fixed place, such as on a wall, either to facilitate the writing or to enable easy handling.

When combining this information with my suggestion that the scroll was written by a large number of scribes, we can speculate further on the background of the writing. I imagine that the different scribes came from the areas mentioned in the scroll. Each of them described the location of the treasure(s) known to him and sometimes other experts filled in the value. Probably all the persons who wrote the sections of the Copper Scroll gathered at one place and wrote one after another, in small groups, in the location where the copper sheet was kept.

At the outset the text of what is now the Copper Scroll was written on three connected copper sheets. Only at a later stage was the scroll rolled up in order to be stored away. At that time it broke into two parts. The mentioning of the copy of this scroll in 12.11, at the end of the scroll, may imply that a copy was prepared, possibly by a single scribe, at the same occasion when the first one was composed.

21

David J. Wilmot and the Copper Scroll

Michael O. Wise

Introduction

In late 1986, after a long and debilitating illness, David J. Wilmot passed away. He was only 43 years old. David left behind many friends and admiring former students. I am one of them. He also left behind a nearly completed doctoral dissertation on which he had labored, on and off, for fully a decade.

This dissertation, which he titled 'The Copper Scroll: An Economic Document of First Century Palestine', had its genesis in a University of Chicago seminar devoted to the Copper Scroll that Norman Golb had convened in the academic year 1973–74. David brought to the seminar an excellent knowledge of Greek—he was a student of Robert Grant's in the Ancient Christian Literature program—as well as of economic history and rabbinic Hebrew. The seminar became a parade example of the proverb, 'As iron sharpens iron, so does a man sharpen the countenance of his friend.' Golb, David and the other students (one was Dennis Pardee, now a distinguished professor of Semitic languages) struggled to work, as much as was possible, only from the inadequate photographs of 3Q15 then available. Their approach was to put no implicit faith in the published decipherments of this difficult Hebrew text. During the course of the year David came to believe that the Copper Scroll had all the earmarks of an economic document of autograph character emanating from Jewish circles in Roman Palestine. It was only a matter of time before he concluded that this text should serve as the subject of his dissertation, both for its own sake and for conclusions that might be drawn from it concerning the economy of Jewish Palestine in the Roman period.

I propose in the following pages to present a summary of salient aspects of David's research. In composing this summary I have drawn on all the materials David left behind; those materials comprise not only the dissertation proper, but also a long and detailed outline of the dissertation that includes ideas David never had a chance to develop within the dissertation itself. I have also consulted an unpublished paper that David gave at the 1984 SBL meetings, entitled 'The Copper Scroll of Qumran (3Q15) and the Graeco-Roman Temple Inventories'. Often I have used David's own wording.

Because David's dissertation was never truly completed, some of his ideas have come to me better developed than others. Accordingly, a balanced presentation of his theses is not possible, and space would not permit one if it were. Nevertheless, I think it valuable here to list those theses, both to credit David's ideas and to stimulate further scholarly discussion and research:

- The Copper Scroll was engraved by four scribes, each having his own set of letterforms and distinctive pattern of scribal habits. The error-making process of the third scribe (scribe C) demonstrates that 3Q15 was copied and abridged from a cursive *Vorlage.*
- The economic terminology of the Copper Scroll distinguishes between gold and silver in bullion and gold and silver specie in coin, using language consonant with the conventions known from late Phoenician, Hebrew, Aramaic, Greek and Latin texts of the Greco-Roman period. The treasures listed as cached in 3Q15 are of a size reasonable for a large institution of the first century CE in light of the coin hoards retrieved in the modern period, and on the basis of the report of the will of Gaius Caecilius Isodorus and other references.
- The sacral terminology of the Copper Scroll indicates that its makers were associated with the גזברין, 'treasurers', of the Jersualem Temple.
- The genre of the Copper Scroll is that of a summarizing inventory list. This fact can be ascertained by form criticism, guided by the study of analogous formularies. 3Q15 is an inventory of caches in space, just as the *Megillat Ta'anit* is an inventory of days in time. The actual process of drafting this summarizing inventory occurred during the engraving of the Copper Scroll itself. In this sense, the Copper Scroll is an autograph of an occasional economic document.

Some of the substance of these theses will become apparent in the pages that follow. At points, what David left behind was so sketchy that I have felt compelled to carry his points a bit farther than he did himself. In so doing, however, I have endeavored always to travel along the paths of research that he had mapped out. It has been my intention that in this way David might receive the fullest hearing for his ideas, and that these pages, like the dissertation itself, might be, in some small way, both a tribute to David's life and a testament to what might have been.

The Genre of the Copper Scroll

In March of 1952 the Copper Scroll was found *in situ* by an archaeological survey crew searching the caves of the Qumran region for manuscript deposits. In the winter of 1955–56, the two copper rolls were successfully cut open in Manchester, England. On 1 June 1956, the official report of the decipherment of the text of the Copper Scroll was released simultaneously to the general press in England, France, Jordan and the USA. It was front-page news that day in the *New York Times.* Among other things, the official communiqué stated that the Copper Scroll was 'the first document of its kind—a guide to treasure trove—ever to be found'.

This statement was an identification of the genre of the Copper Scroll, and represented the view of J.T. Milik, the text's official editor. In his publication of the Copper Scroll in DJDJ III, Milik included a detailed discussion of the problem of genre. He recognized that the Copper Scroll is a list of more than 60 repeating entries that can be schematized into a formulaic pattern. Milik accurately characterized the structure of the repeating formulary:

> The elements comprising the description of the cache are: (1) the location, with one or more indications, of increasing specificity; (2) measurements: approximate or exact distances, depth of the cache, explicit or implied (on the surface?); (3) the nature and quantity of the treasures, in general terms.[1]

Milik went on to note:

> In his composition, which is no more than a plain list of topographical information and numerical data, the author of 3Q15 gives us not a word about the character of the treasure, nor the reason for his laborious efforts. It is through analysing his work and comparing it with accounts *and similar lists* that we must determine the nature of this catalogue and the motives that prompted its author (pp. 279-80; Wilmot's emphasis).

1. J.T. Milik, 'Le rouleau de cuivre provenant de la grotte 3Q (3Q15)', in M. Baillet, J.T. Milik and R. de Vaux, *Les 'petites grottes' de Qumrân* (DJDJ III; Oxford: Clarendon Press, 1962), pp. 201-302 (235).

The foundation of the discipline of form criticism is, of course, the identification of the form. In a document as formulaic as the Copper Scroll, it is crucial to isolate the structure of the form and to identify its *Sitz im Leben*, the social context that led to the form's creation. Milik believed that he had succeeded in doing so. He found the fundamental clue in a story narrated by the church historian Sozomen (*fl.* 439–50 CE), a continuator of Eusebius. In a decisive passage of this story[2] Milik discovered the three components characteristic of the formulary of 3Q15: (1) the indication of locale, 'a certain garden'; (2) a distance measurement giving an azimuth and an indication of depth ('Dig down two cubits, after measuring off from the stone wall at the garden, on the side of the road that goes down to the town Bittherbin');[3] and (3) a detailed description of the deposit ('a double coffin, wood outside and lead inside, a glass vessel full of water and two snakes'), and so on.

This formulary is a structural element in a folkloristic story describing the recovery of a sacred treasure, the body of the prophet Zechariah. This was the key that opened Milik's interpretation of the genre. The tale in Sozomen originates in a milieu of the fourth and fifth centuries CE, when Christians in Palestine were 'rediscovering' relics and holy places associated with biblical events, initiated by St Helena's 'retrieval' of the True Cross. Since the items inventoried in the Copper Scroll are gold and silver, for Milik the text was self-evidently one of folkloristic treasure trove.[4] The connection with the temple was clear from the appearance of the term חרם, describing items cached, of אפודת (a form of ephod, the priestly garment), and of types of gold and silver vessels itemized in 3.1-4 of the Copper Scroll. Consequently, Milik thought it obvious that the Copper Scroll stood in that stream of Jewish folklore that describes the concealment of sacred objects and treasures by Jeremiah and others at the time when the Babylonians destroyed the First Temple. Hints of this Jewish folklore may be found in 2 Macc. 2.4-8, Josephus, *Ant.* 8.89-94, and elsewhere. Nevertheless, Milik observed:

2. The decisive passage may be conveniently located in Migne, *PG* 67, col. 1628 line 36 through col. 1629 line 1.

3. Cf. 3Q15 9 1-2, where the phrases משח אמות, 'measure off cubits *x*', and חפור אמות, 'dig down cubits *y*', occur jointly.

4. Milik, DJDJ III, p. 280: 'doubtless the majority of the caches described in 3Q15 are the treasures of the Temple'.

> This list of treasures, rendered on leather or papyrus and subsequently recopied on bronze plates, offers us a unique example of this genre bequeathed to us from antiquity.[5]

Indeed, this genre of literature was so unusual that Milik could cite only two later examples, both medieval in date, one from the Jewish world, *Massechet Kelim*, 'the Tractate of Vessels', and one of Arabic origin, *Kitab al-durr al-maknuz wa'l-sirr al-ma'zuz*, 'the Book of Buried Pearls and Precious Mysteries'.[6] Milik did not defend his association of all three works as a unit constituting a distinctive genre, but he did provide a re-edition of the text of the *Massechet Kelim*, utilizing a new date furnished by the two marble 'plaques of Beirut' made available to him by Jean Starcky,[7] and he gave a generous sample of quotations from the Arabic work.

Milik's argument for the alignment of these works as a folkloristic literary genre of treasure trove apparently rested upon three considerations. First, all three texts are characterized by an extensive and detailed listing of places and the enumeration of large treasures found in the itemized locales. Second, the size of the treasures recorded in all three documents is prodigious. And third, both the Copper Scroll and the *Massechet Kelim* share the rare toponym כחלת.[8]

Yet Milik's identification of 3Q15 with this putative genre was not at all convincing. Both of the medieval texts possess striking features in addition to their listing of hiding places and treasures cached. The Arabic work contains formularies and 'Ephesian' symbols associated with the magical papyri of Greco-Roman antiquity. *Massechet Kelim*, on the other hand, has

5. Milik, DJDJ III, p. 279.

6. Editions of *Massechet Kelim* are available in A. Jellinek, *Bet ha-Midrasch, Sammlung kleiner Midraschim und vermischler Abhandlungen aus der ältern Jüdischen Literatur* (I–IV Leipzig: 1853–57; V–VI Vienna 1873–77; repr. Jerusalem: Wahrmann Books, 1967); J.E. Eisenstein, *Ozar Midrashim: A Library of Two Hundred Minor Midrashim* (New York: n.p., 1915; repr. in Israel, n.p. and n.d.), pp. 260-62. For the Arabic work see Ahmed Bey Kamal (ed.), *Livre des perles enfouies et du mystère précieux* (2 vols.; Cairo: L'institut Français d'archéologie orientale, 1907).

7. J.T. Milik, 'Notes d'epigraphie et de topographie palestiniennes: vii Traite des vases (מסכת כלים)', *RB* 66 (1959), pp. 567-75. L.H. Silberman, 'A Note on the Copper Scroll', *VT* 10 (1960), pp. 77-79, was the first person to call attention to the *Massechet Kelim*, a vital step on the road to the recognition that the Beirut plaques were a witness to this midrash.

8. Milik, DJDJ III, pp. 274-75, 281; *idem*, 'Le rouleau du cuivre de Qumrân (3Q15): Traduction et commentaire topographique', *RB* 66 (1959), pp. 321-57 (355-57).

a narrative framework connecting the treasure with the destruction of the First Temple. The final section of the Hebrew midrash closes with messianic language, predicting the treasure's recovery when 'a righteous king will arise for Israel', when 'David, the son of David, shall arise' at the ingathering of Israel from the four corners of the earth.[9] This narrative feature likens the *Massechet Kelim* to the apocrypha of the Hebrew Bible.

In contrast, 3Q15 lacks any narrative framework, and contains neither explicit statement identifying the treasure's owner nor any explanation for the treasure's being concealed. The Copper Scroll contains no formularies or 'Ephesian' letters derivable from the realm of Greco-Roman magic, as does the *Kitab al-durr al-maknuz wa'l-sirr al-ma'zuz*. From the perspective of literary genre it is simply an unlabeled inventory list. Milik, too, acknowledged this fundamental fact:

> a list of an administrative type, where information is given in disconnected phrases and where the thought or rationale of the document remain implicit and have to be painfully sought among the virtually unordered collection of presumably real data... The author of 3Q15 succeeds fairly well in arranging the material in his work by grouping the hiding places geographically, though within each group he rarely follows an order. This reminds one of deeds and administrative lists of the time, which are often arranged in order...[10]

Milik evidently regarded the author's method as a sort of stylistic trick, providing a well-turned folkloristic document of treasure trove with an air of reality. What is most arresting in Milik's analysis of the formulary of 3Q15 is what is not there. One searches in vain for any comparison of component phrases to contemporary Jewish lists or, more broadly, Greco-Roman inventory lists. Milik saw the formulary as a mere stylistic device. He seems never to have asked the question whether the same type of formulary might characterize other inventory lists of the Greco-Roman world.

Unlike Milik, John Allegro did not consider the Copper Scroll a fictitious fairy tale. He was impressed by the realistic nature of the text and the absence of those features that might align it with haggadic stories about the destruction of the First Temple in 586 BCE.[11] The title of Allegro's book, *The Treasure of the Copper Scroll*, reveals his approach to inter-

9. *Massechet Kelim*, Mishnah 12.

10. Milik, 'Le rouleau du cuivre', p. 355.

11. J. Allegro, *The Treasure of the Copper Scroll* (London: Routledge & Kegan Paul, 1960), pp. 56-58, and *idem*, *The Treasure of the Copper Scroll* (Garden City, NY: Doubleday, 2nd rev. edn, 1964), pp. 39-42.

preting 3Q15. He believed the treasure to be real, and the text to be an inventory of its caches. Yet Allegro did not really provide sound scholarly reasons for his understanding. He gave no discussion of the formulary of the work, nor did he define or explain (a) why the text falls within the documentary genre of inventory, or (b) how it correlates with other known Jewish lists, such as the *Megillat Ta'anit* or the Bethphage ossuary lid, emanating from the late Second Commonwealth period.

Allegro's apprehension of the Copper Scroll was essentially intuitive. The pivotal moment for his understanding of the Copper Scroll came one evening as he discussed it with his wife, Joan, over the supper table. As he talked of his day's work in deciphering the newly opened document, he handed her a tentative translation of the text. As Allegro told the story:

> 'Let's have a look,' she said, and scanned my translation for a moment. Then, she handed it back with that infuriating look of intuitively acquired knowledge characteristic of her sex. 'Yes, well, of course,' she said, 'it's a list of buried treasure.'[12]

His wife Joan had matter-of-factly stated the obvious. Allegro instantly grasped the implication of her comment. To demonstrate that a map to buried treasure is authentic, one naturally goes there and digs it up again. Allegro attempted to do just that. He mounted two treasure-hunting expeditions, one in December 1959–January 1960, and another in March–April 1960. Nothing was ever found, and the activities were halted by government authorities just as the team was about to begin 'leurs depradations à l'ésplanade de la Mosquée de Omar'.[13]

In the quarter century 1962–84 (the last year covered by Wilmot's research), scholars who wrote on the Copper Scroll were about evenly divided, some siding with Milik in assigning its genre to the sphere of folklore, and others aligning with Allegro in regarding the scroll as a genuine, ancient administrative document of the Second Temple. Of these only Chaim Rabin suggested a new identification of the genre: he called it a 'witnesses' deposition'.[14] But Rabin offered neither analysis nor discussion of the point, so his suggestion is not open to critical review.

12. Allegro, *Treasure of the Copper Scroll* (1964), p. 14.

13. So R. de Vaux, 'Manuscripts de Qumrân', *RB* 68 (1961), p. 147.

14. C. Rabin, 'Hebrew and Aramaic in the First Century', in M. de Jonge and S. Safrai (eds.), *Compendia Rerum Iudaicarum ad Novum Testamentum, Section 1: The Jewish People in the First Century: Historical Geography, Political History, Social, Cultural and Religious Life and Institutions* (2 vols.; Philadelphia: Fortress Press, 1974–), II, pp. 1007-1039 (1018).

One other scholar wrote extensively on the Copper Scroll in this period, and he in fact subjected the scroll to the most thorough review and reconsideration that it received. This man was Bargil Pixner, a Benedictine archaeologist and a member of the Theological Faculty of the Dormition Abbey, Mount Zion, Jerusalem.[15] Pixner focused mainly on topography, but he did render an opinion on the problem of genre. For Pixner, the Copper Scroll was the product of one man inexpert in scribal skills. His supralinear corrections show that 'he did his work in a hurry', and his fear of running out of writing material accounts for the cramped and crowded lines in the last columns of the document. Pixner further considered the Copper Scroll to be a copy of a longer text that was probably drafted on leather. The genre he characterized as a 'personal aide-memoire', by which he meant a text prepared 'for people already familiar with the whereabouts of most of the hiding places', written in 'telegram style'.[16]

Pixner had borrowed the phrase 'aide-memoire' from Milik, who himself clearly never intended it as an identification of genre, and Pixner failed to discuss the characteristics of the putative genre 'personal aide-memoire'. Neither did he offer ancient examples to support his notion. In fact, Pixner analyzed neither the formulary of the Copper Scroll nor its structure. Despite the value of his work otherwise, then, it is impossible to guess what Pixner meant by his characterization, and it did not advance discussion of the genre of the Copper Scroll.

Written materials that have been retrieved from antiquity may be divided into two basic and distinct categories: literary and non-literary texts. Literary texts are the products of human imagination; they are a mimesis of human reality, assuming their own genres and fictional forms: epic poetry, tragedy and comedy, philosophic dialogues, and so on. These works circulated in particular formats in Greco-Roman antiquity. They were characterized by formal scripts, or carefully drafted bookhands, and by distinctive layouts in the form of a scroll or codex.

In contrast, non-literary writings, or documents, are the products of daily activities and human affairs. They originate not in the creative impulse of human imagination, but in the need to record daily work, business records and contracts. Documents include receipts of payment, ledgers of various kinds, bills of sale and leases. For the historian they are the primary evidence of historical fact and event. In the Greco-Roman

15. B. Pixner, 'Unravelling the Copper Scroll Code: A Study on the Topography of 3Q15', *RevQ* 11 (1983), pp. 323-61.

16. Pixner, 'Unravelling the Copper Scroll Code', pp. 326, 359.

period, documents were characterized by a business hand (generally a fluent, cursive script); a distinctive format (usually determined by the way in which the document was filed for reference and safe-keeping); genres of precise and repeating formularies, and contents of concrete numbers, personal names and toponyms.

Among the Dead Sea Scrolls are found both literary and non-literary texts. The vast bulk of the deposits of the Qumran caves are literary works, displaying formal bookhands and inscribed on leather. On the other hand, the majority of the Bar-Kokhba finds are documentary texts, drafted in cursive or semi-cursive scripts, written on single papyrus sheets, folded and stored in accordance with record-keeping procedures.

Milik argued that the Copper Scroll is a product of human imagination, a work of literature. Yet if so, why does it lack the format, layout and content of literary productions? Indeed, Milik's analysis really treated none of these aspects in any detail. And Milik discovered no true literary parallels to the mere repeating pattern of listing that characterizes 3Q15. The parallels he did suggest insert the inventory list in some narrative framework. Further, the numbers these parallels contain are not only incredibly large, but are always round numbers. They never have the specificity and concrete feel of those attested in the Copper Scroll.

Interestingly, both Milik and Joan Allegro referred to the Copper Scroll as a 'list'. They used the term offhandedly, but this is actually a sound starting point for the analysis of its genre. Greek and Latin papyrologists and epigraphers have long recognized 'list' as a classification of documentary and administrative texts. Among the finds of Wadi Murabba'at are preserved several examples of this form in Greek, lists of grain (*p. Mur.* 94-97). A single Hebrew example also survived among these deposits, *p. Mur*. 8. An even clearer example is the Bethphage ossuary lid, for it is better preserved.[17]

The genre 'list' possesses a distinctive format. It is arranged in two columns, and set in a line entry pattern. The first column of each entry comprises a written or verbal notation, while the second column contains an abbreviation of the contents itemized and a numerical count given in ciphers. Milik recognized that the line entry format was the outstanding scribal feature of 3Q15:

17. For the lid see most conveniently Jean-Baptiste Frey, *CII* 2.1285. Note that 1286 is not considered. W.F. Albright, 'A Biblical Fragment from the Maccabaean Age: The Nash Papyrus', *JBL* 56 (1937), pp. 145-76 (161 n. 46), demonstrated that this lid is a modern forgery.

> Despite his care for economy, the scribe of 3Q15 in principle began the description of each new hiding place on a new line but without indenting, with one exception, xi 11 (and xi 15: sort of heading). If the end of the preceding description did not fill a line, it was usually written in the middle of the column. For these latter details the author of the catalogue was inspired by administrative lists, epitaphs and monumental inscriptions.[18]

In the Bethphage lid the feeling for line entry is so strong that it is even marked by a *paragraphos* line, familiar from the Greek papyri of Egypt. But here an additional question must be put: is there in 3Q15 the genre list's requisite concept of two columns in each cache entry? The answer is both yes and no. As to yes—the two-column layout in an entry is clearly apparent in 3Q15 4.12; 7.13; 8.16; 9.9, 13; 10.7, 14 and perhaps elsewhere. What falls in the second column, the 'contents' column of the list, is usually the abbreviation for talents (ככ for ככרין), followed by a number rendered in ciphers. Here we have precisely the pattern for lists found in Greek and Latin inscriptions and papyri, and also attested in the Bethphage lid and *p. Mur.* 8. With two exceptions (the book [ספר] of 8.3 and the document [כתב] of 12.11), the items indexed in the contents column are of four types:

1. gold and silver in bullion
2. gold and silver coin
3. votive vessels
4. priestly garments.

Shortly we shall have a good deal more to say about the Greek inscriptions of the Isle of Delos. These provide many examples of the annual reports, filed mainly in the period 180–90 BCE, of the men elected as temple treasurers (ἐπὶ τὴν φυλακὴν τῶν ἱερῷ χρημάτων). Here let it be noted that these inventory lists that the treasurers submitted itemize *precisely the same four categories of goods* as the Copper Scroll.

Yet we had said that there was also a 'no' to the question of whether the Copper Scroll evidences the concept of two columns in line entry required by the genre 'list'. The fact is that the formulary of the Copper Scroll, while at times bipartite, is, more often, as Milik correctly analyzed it, tripartite. The formulary usually comprises (1) a phrase indicating site location, (2) a specification of measurement, and then (3) a listing of contents cached. Does this tripartite structure disprove the suggestion that the Copper Scroll is, by genre, a list? Not at all, for the Copper Scroll is

18. Milik, DJDJ III, pp. 215-16.

not unique in its structure. Another work, clearly a list but likewise possessing a tripartite structure, has survived from the Jewish world of the Second Commonwealth: the *Megillat Ta'anit.*

Written in Aramaic, the *Megillat Ta'anit* is a summarizing inventory list of the days when fasting and mourning were prohibited.[19] The first entry of the month of Elul, *Megillat Ta'anit* §6, clearly illustrates the three components of its formulary:

1. date mark: בארבעה באלול
2. the name of the festival: חנכת שור ירושלם
3. an instruction clause, using an imperatival syntax: ודי לא למספד

In the light of *Megillat Ta'anit*, a closer look at the structure of the Copper Scroll is instructive. 3Q15 6.11-13 may be taken as an example:

1. site component: (a) במשכן המלכא (b) בצד חמערבי
2. instruction and direction: (a) חפור (b) אמות (c) שתים
3. contents: (a) ככ (b) 25

This structure may be generalized into the following schema, which applies to the entire scroll:

1. *locale:* (a) ב-landmark (b) ב-architectural detail
2. *instruction:* (a) חפור (imperative) (b) **אמות**
3. *contents:* (a) ככ (abbrev. for ככרין) (b) ciphers

It is at once obvious that the components of the Copper Scroll's formulary are analogous to those of the *Megillat Ta'anit.* The locale clause of 3Q15 corresponds to the date mark clause of the *Megillat Ta'anit*; the scroll's instruction clause, with its syntax of command or compulsion, corresponds to the instruction clause of *Megillat Ta'anit*, and the contents clause equates with *Megillat Ta'anit*'s festival name.

The similarity extends yet farther. Both the locale clause of 3Q15, and the corresponding date clause of *Megillat Ta'anit*, make use of what might be called the 'double *beth* formula'. In the example from the Copper Scroll, a *beth* precedes both the landmark itemized and the architectural detail that narrows the locale: במשכן המלכא בצד המערבי. For *Megillat*

19. For the text, see most conveniently J.A. Fitzmyer and D.J. Harrington, *A Manual of Palestinian Aramaic Texts* (Rome: Biblical Institute Press, 1978), pp. 184-85. Actually, Wilmot's argument from the structure of *Megillat Ta'anit* might just as well be made today using the Qumran calendar texts—for example, 4Q317—which likewise exhibit the structure of 'list'.

Ta'anit, a *beth* precedes both the number of the day in the month and the month name: בארבעה באלול. In fact, this 'double *beth* formula' is a regular idiom in biblical and postbiblical Hebrew and Aramaic. It has as well several variations according to the linguistic situation. For example, in the Copper Scroll the preposition תחת, 'under', substitutes for the second *beth* if the architectural detail demands it. That is to say, a given cache may have been concealed 'under' rather than 'at' something. Likewise for the *Megillat Ta'anit*, where the preposition *lamedh*, in this environment a semantic equivalent, sometimes does duty for the second *beth.* Also, because some festivals extend over several days, a מן...עד construction ('from...until') sometimes occupies the place of the second *beth.*

Comparison of the *Megillat Ta'anit* and Copper Scroll suggests that the instruction clause in both lists is a secondary element, an addition to the essentially bicolumnar structure that characterizes both texts as lists. The contents of their respective instruction clauses differ, naturally, because of the differences in what is being inventoried.

What is perhaps most remarkable about the locale and instruction clauses of the formulary of the Copper Scroll is that they find precise parallels in the aforementioned temple inventories from the Isle of Delos.[20] Posted in 180 BCE, inscription 588 may serve as a model of the typical temple inventory document there. Line 1 of the text reads, 'We have received in the Temple of Apollo [ἐν τῷ ναῷ τοῦ Ἀπόλλωνος] from the priestly workers'; line 156 reads, 'And thus we received in the House of the Brave' (ἐν τῷ Ἀνδρίων οἴκ ῳ); line 177 says, 'And thus we received in the Temple of Artemis' (ἐν τῷ ναῷ τῆς Ἀρτέμιδος). These three ἐν clauses function exactly like the first *beth*, the *beth* of landmark, in the double *beth* formula. This is the locale clause or site indicator of the Copper Scroll.

Lines 3-20 of the inscription index a large number of votive objects, including crowns, jugs, rings and earrings, and coins (line 6). All of these items are said to be located 'on the first shelf' (ἐν τῷ πρωτῷ ῥυμῷ) in lines 20-21. Lines 21-25 then go on to specify the number and weight of votives placed on the second shelf, on the third shelf, and so on, until the fifteenth shelf. The ἐν clauses that specify these shelves are the functional equivalent of the second *beth* of the locale formula of 3Q15, the *beth* of architectural detail. In the same manner, the inscription lists another set of shelves as a storage place for sacred vessels in the Temple of Artemis (lines 204-11).

20. W. Dittenberger, *Sylloge Inscriptionum Graecarum* (2 vols.; Leipzig: S. Hirzel, 2nd edn, 1900).

Moreover, in the immediate vicinity of this last itemizing appears a parallel to the direction clause of 3Q15: 'These things are on the right when people enter, (those things) are on the left when they enter' (lines 211-12). The direction clauses 'on entering on the right/left' (δεξίας/ ἀριστερᾶς εἰσίοντι/ἐισιόντων) also appear in the description of the inventory stored in the Temple of Apollo (lines 36, 39, 61, 109). This wording and function is, of course, a precise match for the instruction clause of 3Q15, ביאתך לסמולו, 'on the left when you enter' (10.5-6; cf. 2.12; 3.9; 4.3; 5.13; 12.1).

Thus, all three components that comprise the formulary of the Copper Scroll—locale clause, instruction clause and contents clause—characterize also the formulary of the Delos temple inventories, the reports filed by the sacred treasurers of the city. The contents clauses itemize the same things: gold and silver in bullion and coin, votive objects and priestly garments. The detailed correspondences between the Copper Scroll and lists from ancient times—the Delos inventories, the Bethphage ossuary lid and *Megillat Ta'anit*—support the proposal that 3Q15 is likewise, by genre, no work of literature or folklore. It is a genuine business document. It is a list.[21]

What type of list is the Copper Scroll? It is a temple inventory list. This judgment emerges not only from the comparisons with the Delos inventories, but from a consideration of the material upon which the work was inscribed. The Copper Scroll was, of course, written on copper. Why? Because the use of copper was an archival method of permanent record-keeping. Numerous examples from the Greco-Roman world establish that fact. Copper was used for non-literary texts—documents—as shown, for instance, by the *lex Coloniae Genetivae Juliae*, inscribed in the year 710 of the Roman era.[22]

21. Further support for this identification may come from the phenomena of the Copper Scroll's numbers. These numbers or ciphers always follow, rather than precede, the item counted—precisely in the manner of extant lists, but contrary to both tannaitic and biblical usage generally. For both types of Hebrew, cardinal numbers (except for אחד, אחת) precede the noun they modify. The one notable exception to this rule is stated in GKC §134c: 'In the absolute state… [the numeral appears] *after* the object numbered…especially in long lists, since in these the substantives naturally come first, e.g., Gn 32[15], Nu 7[17], 28[19].' See also M.H. Segal, *A Grammar of Mishnaic Hebrew* (Oxford: Clarendon Press, 1927), §394.

22. *CIL* II, suppl., 5439. See J. Mallon, 'Los bronces de Ossuna', *Archivo Español de Arqueologia* 17 (1944), pp. 213-37.

This same method characterized the *lex Cornelia de XX quaestoribus.*[23] This bronze tablet, inscribed in 673 of the Roman era and *in scroll format*, was 'found at Rome in the ruins of the Temple of Saturn, which was the regular place of deposit of state archives'.[24] Pliny also testified to the use of copper for archival records:

> The employment of bronze was a long time ago applied to securing the perpetuity of monuments, by means of bronze tablets on which records of official enactments are made.[25]

Copper was used for the safe-keeping of non-literary records, Roman public laws, and even the private discharge papers of Roman veterans, the so-called *diplomata militaria* of the imperial period. Roman period temples in Egypt further testify to the use of copper for temple inventories and archives.[26]

In fact, one temple inventory from Roman period Egypt, inscribed on copper, has actually survived to our day. The Demotic text, CG 30691, originated in Medinet Habu and possesses the bicolumnar layout of a list.[27] It has two columns on one copper plate and is inscribed front and back—clear testimony that its function was for record-keeping rather than public posting and display. This text is a striking parallel to the Copper Scroll: a temple inventory list, laid out in two columns, inscribed on copper for permanence.

The Copper Scroll clearly falls into the category of non-literary text, of document. Its characteristics indicate that it is a business record produced for a specific purpose at a particular moment in time. An analysis of the contents listed in the Copper Scroll, with their rubrics, argues that the text is a document of the גזברין of the Second Jerusalem Temple. (The crucial

23. *CIL* I, 202.

24. F.D. Allen, *Remnants of Early Latin* (Boston: Ginn & Co., 1893), p. 49.

25. *Natural History* 34.21.99.

26. See W. Helck and E. Otto, *Lexicon der Ägyptologie* (1984), s.v. 'Schreibtafel'. Regarding one such text, BM 57371 and 57372, the remarks of A.F. Shore, 'Votive Objects from Dendera of the Greco-Roman Period', in J. Ruffle, G.A. Gaballa and K.A. Kitchen (eds.), *Glimpses of Ancient Egypt: Studies in Honor of H.W. Fairman* (Warminster: Aris & Phillips, 1979), p. 158, are pertinent: 'Since the two tablets are inscribed on both sides they can hardly have been intended for display in the temple of Dendera. Though these plates are not ritual objects…the most likely place for them to have been kept would have been in a temple treasury or magazine…'

27. See W. Spiegelberg, *Die Demotischen Inschriften* (Heidelberg: C. Winters, 1921), 1.80-81.

passage is *t. Šeq* 2.15.)[28] The instruction clause of the scroll, 'dig down *x* cubits', implies that the business operation recorded was the concealment of the temple treasure. That such a concealment occurred is explicitly stated by Josephus. The Copper Scroll was the 'final' administrative document of the treasures of the Second Jerusalem Temple, inscribed in the waning years of the First Revolt, sometime in 68–70 CE.[29]

Aspects of the Copper Scroll's Terminology

משקל

The problem of the 'fabulous amounts of the treasures' of 3Q15 quickly evaporates if the document is treated in an economic light. The early Roman empire was a thoroughly moneyed economy. It is a well-known fact that in Greek and Latin the same terms are used both for weights and for denominations of money. There is the unit of account *mina* and the

28. 'The three treasurers (גיזברין)—what did they used to do with them (i.e., the shekel payments)? They would redeem (things dedicated to the temple): valuations (of people and animals dedicated; ערכין), property set apart for temple use (חרמין), things dedicated for sacred use (הקדשות), and the tithe (מעשר); all cultic tasks (מלאכת קודש) were financed with them (the shekels; נעשית בהן).'

This passage says, then, that the treasurers would take money in lieu of people, animals or things dedicated to the temple. These monies would then be referenced by the appropriate technical terms, and presumably kept separate for book-keeping purposes. Since several of these technical terms appear in the Copper Scroll, the implication is that the treasurers must have been involved with the hiding of the treasure. This tannaitic passage is remarkably consonant with Josephus, *War* 6.390-91, according to which one Phineas, a treasurer of the temple, delivered up to the Romans various treasures and sacred garments. The treasurers had evidently hidden at least some of the temple treasures, precisely as the very existence of the Copper Scroll argues; Phineas, under torture, then divulged the location of some of what had been secreted.

29. An observation made by Saul Lieberman in his *Hellenism in Jewish Palestine* (New York: Jewish Theological Society of America, 2nd edn, 1962) lends support, however tentatively, to the notion that the Copper Scroll originated in Jerusalem. He commented of the Copper Scroll: 'That our Scroll is of the Jerusalem type is confirmed by the fact that the medial מ occurs in it frequently instead of the ם.' He went on to appeal to a passage in *j. Meg.* I, 9, 71d: ' "The people of Jerusalem used to write [in their scrolls] ירושלים and ירושלימ(ה) indiscriminately"—i.e., they used the final ם and the medial מ promiscuously' (p. 23). When F.M. Cross discussed the palaeography of the *mem* in the Copper Scroll, he noted: 'The scribe of 3Q15 does not distinguish between medial and final *mem*. This practice is not usual but it is by no means uncommon among the late semiformal scripts' (DJDJ III, p. 220). Perhaps we should say 'among the late semiformal *Jerusalem* scripts'?

weight *mina*; there is the unit of account *talent*, and the weight *talent*. The same is true for both the *denarius* and the *drachma*. Hebrew had the weight זוז and the coin זוז, the weight שקל and the coin שקל. They did not necessarily amount to the same thing in terms of precious metal; inflation was common in the ancient world as in the modern.

When the ancients wished to distinquish the weight of a *mina* of silver—found, for instance, in a tableware service—from a *mina* paid in silver cash or coin, they employed the term 'weight'. Thus, ὁλκὴ is used in the Delos temple inventories in this way. Neither Milik nor Allegro realized that, when the Copper Scroll employed the phrase משקל ככרין, '*talents* by weight', this convention, by linguistic borrowing, was operative in the Hebrew document as well. The distinction is also attested in late Phoenician and tannaitic texts.

Twice the Copper Scroll employs the term in this sense, at 1.4 and 12.9. Otherwise, whenever the terms כסף and זהב are independent items in the list and are modified by no more than the term '*talents*', they are to be understood as referring to silver coins and gold coins, as is common in tannaitic usage. In the same vein, the word '*talents*' is everywhere, apart from the two exceptions noted, to be understood as *talents* of account, of reckoning, that is, 3000 coined *shekels* to the *talent*, or 6000 *denarii* to the *talent*. In the cases where the idiom שקל ככרין appears, the *talent* is a measure of weight, by biblical standards approximately 33 kg.

Attention to the precision with which the Copper Scroll uses its economic terminology leads to a different view of the dimensions of the treasure concealed. If one counts the face value of coins retrieved from hoards originating in Roman times, the amounts of cash recorded in the small caches of 3Q15 are actually matched by hoards recovered in modern times. The sum total of money listed in 3Q15 is approximately equal to the sum total of coin or cash on hand bequeathed by the Roman freedman Gaius Caecilius Isodorus (died 8 BCE) to his heirs: '60 million *sesterces* in cash'.[30] Thus it is clear that the quantity of treasure inventoried in the Copper Scroll is of a reasonable size for a large, viable institution of the first century CE such as the Jerusalem Temple.

כלי דמע

The phrase כלי דמע, which occurs in the contents column of 3Q15, has not been rightly understood, and should be translated 'votive vessels'. דמע alone can denote any votive object. The reasoning is as follows.

30. Pliny, *Natural History* 33.135.

H.M.Y. Gevaryahu was the first to demonstrate that the word דמע of the Copper Scroll is attested in tannaitic Hebrew as a synonym for תרומה, the priestly tithe or heave offering. Consequently, Gevaryahu—and Ben-Zion Lurie and Manfred Lehmann after him—interpreted the phrase כלי דמע to mean different types of containers holding tithed agricultural produce.[31] Yet this notion is contradicted by the internal evidence of the Copper Scroll. The decisive passage is 3.2-4. Here the phrase כלי כסף וזהב של דמע occurs, and immediately thereafter follows the specification: 'sprinkling basins, cups, bowls, pitchers: in all, six hundred and nine'.

That דמע is a synonym of תרומה is indisputable; yet that fact can and should lead not only to tannaitic materials, but also in directions that Gevaryahu and subsequent scholars have left unexplored. One such avenue is Late Biblical Hebrew usage, for a direct parallel to the Copper Scroll's phrase and usage appears in Ezra 8.25-30. Verses 26-30 of this passage comprise an inventory list of gold, silver and vessels delivered to the priests and Levites of the early Second Temple for deposit in the temple treasury (לשכות בית יהוה). The vessels are said to be 'holy' (קדש), and the gold and silver are described as a 'free-will offering' (נדבה) to the Lord (Ezra 8.28). All the precious items are characterized as תרומת בית אלהינו. Here תרומה clearly does not mean agricultural tithes of wheat, barley and so on, paid to the priests. It refers to gold, silver and vessels placed in the Second Temple storehouses—items that in the case of Greek temples are called ἀναθήματα, 'votive offerings'.

An identical usage of תרומה in Exod. 25.2, 3; 35.5, 21, 24 and 36.6 confirms this meaning. Exod. 36.3 in particular makes it clear that תרומה can refer to votive objects generally: 'So they took from Moses all of the votive offerings [תרומה] that the children of Israel had brought to maintain the rites of the holy service; and each morning they would bring to him additional free-willing offerings [נדבה]'.

Tannaitic evidence is also significant: 'What did they do with the surplus of the *Terumah* [מותר התרומה]?... The surplus of the *Terumah* was devoted to vessels of ministry [כלי שרת]' (*m. Šeq.* 4.4); 'The [Red] Heifer and the scapegoat and the crimson thread were bought with the

31. H.M.Y. Gevaryahu, 'Observations on the List of Treasures in the Copper Scroll in the Light of Talmudic Sources', *Third World Congress of Jewish Studies: Jerusalem, 25 July–1 August 1961, Report* (Jerusalem: World Union of Jewish Studies, 1965), pp. 94-95 (Hebrew); M. Lehmann, 'Identification of the Copper Scroll Based on its Technical Terms', *RevQ* 5 (1964), pp. 97-105; B.-Z. Lurie, מגלת הנחשת ממדבר יהודה (Jerusalem: Kiryath Sepher, 1963), *passim.*

Terumah from the Shekel-chamber [תרומת הלשכה]' (*m. Šeq.* 4.2).[32] In the first instance, the 'surplus of the *Terumah*' was apparently forged into vessels to be used in the temple services; thus the *Terumah* must have been votive precious metals. In the second instance, various items were purchased with the *Terumah*, so again, here the reference must have been to precious metals, not agricultural produce.

The logic is simple. Since תרומה and דמע are synonyms in tannaitic diction, and since תרומה can clearly refer to votive objects—both in tannaitic Hebrew and in earlier Late Biblical Hebrew—דמע, also, may have had this meaning. The internal evidence of 3Q15 3.2-4 argues that in fact it did. The phrase כלי דמע ought therefore to be translated 'votive vessels' throughout the Copper Scroll, and דמע alone may mean simply 'votive object' (a priestly garment, אפודה, is so described in 1.9-10).

Suggested Readings for the Copper Scroll

In attempting to solve the puzzles of the Copper Scroll, Milik and Allegro —and subsequent scholars in the first quarter-century after its publication in DJDJ—generally neglected a methodology of identifying (and attempting to reverse) scribal error. Instead, they preferred to appeal to comparative Semitic etymology, and particularly exploited the Arabic lexicon in their search for the meanings of obscure graphemes. In this way, for example, Milik ended up with a whole list of spices and aromatics that 3Q15 supposedly listed among the caches.

But this approach was at best mildly successful, and many Semitists were unconvinced that Milik had unlocked the scroll's meaning by this appeal to comparative Semitic evidence. Jonas Greenfield, in the one major review of DJDJ III to appear,[33] leveled what can only be described as devastating criticism of Milik's approach. He observed that 'when examining the commentary grave doubts are raised as to the method of compiling the information used in it and the method used in establishing the meaning of many words'.[34] In fact, Greenfield felt compelled to take 'strong exception' to fully 28 of Milik's definitions and etymological explanations. Considering that Milik had listed only 212 different words in the text, this amounted to the rejection of fully 13 per cent of Milik's

32. Translations follow H. Danby, *The Mishnah* (Oxford: Oxford University Press, 1933).

33. J.C. Greenfield, 'The Small Caves of Qumran', *JAOS* 89 (1969), pp. 128-41.

34. This quotation appeared on p. 138 of the review.

vocabulary—and a much higher percentage, of course, of the less obvious words. So dissatisfied was Greenfield that he ended by calling for a new edition of the Copper Scroll, stating that 'the Copper Scroll has yet to reveal its text and its meaning'.[35]

Many of the problematic words and phrases in the scroll become transparent or at least less difficult, however, if one postulates a process of scribal error. This postulate can, of course, lead to substantially subjective interpretations of what remains, and so it must be constrained by form criticism of the scroll and balanced judgment. Yet the postulate cannot be avoided or denied if it is true, as Frank Moore Cross argued, that the scroll was copied from a cursive *Vorlage*.[36] Significant numbers of errors could occur in the process of transcription because of the multivalence of many cursive letterforms. The scribes of the Copper Scroll clearly did not always comprehend what they were inscribing on the metal, and they may have been (particularly in the case of scribe C, who copied 8.16–11.14) more metalsmith than scribe.

The following are some suggested readings that emerge from the postulate of systematic scribal error. Comparisons are with the readings suggested by Milik in the *editio princeps*.

1.7 for הפרסטלון בירך קרקעו read הפרסטלון {בור} בקרקעו.
2.14-15 for [כ]סף ארבעין [כ]כר read 20 [כ]סף {ארבעין} [כ]כר<ין>
2.3 for במערת בית המרה הישן read במערת בית תמר {ה} הישן.
3.11 for בקבר שבמלה ממזרחו read בקבר שבמלחם <ה>מזרחי, and restore בקבר <ה>מזרחי שבמלחם.
3.12-13 for אמות תחת המדף שלוש read אמות תחת המת שלוש, and restore <חפר> אמות שלוש תחת המת.
4.14 for אמת כסף read אמת <שלוש??> כספ.
5.13 for מירחו read most probably מזרחי and restore lines 12-13 perhaps thus: בקבר <ה>מזרחי בנחל הכפא בביאה לסככא.
6.9-10 for חפר בפתח אמות תשע restore בפתח חפר אמות תשע.
7.8 for במערא שאצלה בקר[ב]ו ל read and restore במערא שאצל המקר[א] של. Wilmot translated lines 8-9 as 'At the burial cave which is next to the cold-chamber of Bet HaQotz'.
9.2-3 for חפור וגב שעת שבע בדין read <כ>כרין חפור{ר} אמ{ש} ות שבע.
9.4 for בתכלת השני גב צריח read בחבלת השניא בצריח.

35. Greenfield, 'Small Caves', p. 138.

36. Cross, DJDJ III, p. 217.

9.15 for בצחיאת גר פלע read ב<י> צ{ה} יאת גי פלע.
10.5 for באשיח שיבית הכרם read באשוח של בית הכרם.
10.6 for רגמות read אמות.
10.9-10 for אבן שהזדוגא בעזת שתין הו הפתח read and restore
מעתו אבן שחור{ר}א הי הפתח אמו{ו}ת שתין.
10.13 for רגמות read אמות.
10.15-16 for בית המים שלוחי לתחת השקת read and restore
בית המים של רחיל תחת השוקת.
11.4 for כלי דמע סוח דמע סנה ותכן אצלם read and restore
כלי דמע <ע>סרה {דמע <ע>סרה} ו<כ>תבן אצלם.
11.10 for כלי דמע א<ר>ז דמע סוח read and restore
כלי דמע א{ר}רב<ע> עסרה.
11.14 for כלי דמ<ע> לאה דמע סירא read and restore
כלי דמ<ע> {ל} אחד {מ} עסר{ר}א.
12.2 for בידן read כוזין.
12.6 for שמ restore <ש>שמ?
12.8 for הברך כלבית הברך read and restore
הבור {כל}<ב>בית הבור.[37]
12.10 for בשית שבצח בצפון read and restore בשית {שבצח} שבצפון.

David's dissertation contains many other incisive insights into the problems of the Copper Scroll. The hope is that it shall shortly appear in its entirety.

37. I cannot resist here suggesting a somewhat different tack from Wilmot's. Read instead מלבית הבור, and understand the entire clause as 'in the big pipe of the cistern, at the point where it joins the cistern'. The syntagm מלבית ה- is then the equivalent of the more usual Hebrew מבית ל-.

22

Palaeography and Literary Structure as Guides to Reading the Copper Scroll

Al Wolters

Introduction

It has been said that the Copper Scroll is the most difficult of the Dead Sea Scrolls,[1] and there is much to justify this claim. Among the reasons for the difficulty of reading 3Q15 have been the inadequacy of the published reproductions of its text (the photographs in DJDJ III are virtually illegible, while the hand-drawn facsimiles prepared by Allegro, Baker and Milik often disagree among themselves), and the failure of the Copper Scroll's script to distinguish between such look-alike letters as *beth* and *kaph*, *daleth* and *resh*, *waw* and *yod*. The result is that a given sequence of letters may allow for a whole series of different readings. For example, the last four letters of 2.3 are usually read as רובד, that is, *rōbed*, 'landing' or 'ledge', but Milik reads them as דיבר, that is, *diber*, a putative variant of *dĕbîr*, translated 'recess' or 'réduit'.[2] In fact, this four-letter sequence of characters could in principle represent 16 permutations—quite a number of which spell possible Hebrew words.[3]

1. Klaus Beyer, *Die aramäischen Texte vom Toten Meer. Ergänzungsband* (Göttingen: Vandenhoeck & Ruprecht, 1994), p. 224. See also Y. Thorion, 'Beiträge zur Erforschung der Sprache der Kupfer-Rolle', *RevQ* 12 (1985–87), pp. 163-76 (174-75).

2. See J.T. Milik, 'The Copper Document from Cave III of Qumran: Translation and Commentary', *ADAJ* 3–4 (1960), pp. 137-55 (139), and *idem*, 'Le rouleau de cuivre provenant de la grotte 3Q (3Q15)', in M. Baillet, J.T. Milik and R. de Vaux, *Les 'petites grottes' de Qumrân* (DJDJ III; Oxford: Clarendon Press, 1962), pp. 200-302 (286); cf. 228 (sub B 5c) and 239 (sub C 6). The latter work will henceforth be referred to as Milik, DJDJ III.

3. The possible permutations are: דובד, דובר, דוכר, דוכד, דיבד, דיבר, דיכר, דיכד, רובד, רובר, רוכר, רוכד, ריבד, ריבר, ריכר and ריכד.

While the choice of רובד over דיבר can in this case be fairly easily justified,[4] there are many other cases where it is difficult to decide which of a number of palaeographically possible readings is to be preferred. The choice between competing readings often seems to be completely arbitrary. Furthermore, this apparent arbitrariness also extends to other aspects of the interpretation of the Copper Scroll. How can we decide, for example, whether the recurring phrase כתבן אצלם and its variants are the conclusion of one section (so Allegro and Lurie) or the beginning of another (so Milik and Pixner)?

It is the thesis of the present paper that it is possible, by paying closer attention than heretofore to the palaeography and literary structure of the Copper Scroll, to reduce (though by no means to eliminate altogether) the element of arbitrary choice that is involved in deciding between such competing readings. I shall first deal with some examples where palaeographical considerations favour one reading over another, and then turn to an examination of how the overall literary structure of the Copper Scroll can help us in selecting a more probable interpretation.

Palaeographical Considerations

Very little work has been done on the palaeography of the Copper Scroll since 1962, when the brief essay by Frank M. Cross Jr entitled 'Excursus on the Palaeographical Dating of the Copper Document' was incorporated into Milik's edition in DJDJ III.[5] Cross identified the script as a late Herodian substyle of the 'vulgar semiformal' hand, which he placed chronologically 'in the second half of the Herodian era, within the broad limits AD 25–75'.[6] Cross has reaffirmed this dating in other publications.[7]

4. A Hebrew noun דיבר is not attested elsewhere, whereas רובד is well-attested in Mishnaic Hebrew, and also occurs elsewhere in the Dead Sea Scrolls (11QT^{a} 46.5-8; see the discussion by Y. Yadin, *The Temple Scroll* [3 vols.; Jerusalem: Israel Exploration Society, Hebrew University, Shrine of the Book, 1983], I, p. 273). Accordingly, this is the reading which I have adopted in my edition of the text. See A. Wolters, *The Copper Scroll: Overview, Text and Translation* (Sheffield: Sheffield Academic Press, 1996), p. 55.

5. Frank M. Cross Jr, 'Excursus on the Palaeographical Dating of the Copper Document', in DJDJ III, pp. 217-21. There is, for example, no separate section on the palaeography of the Copper Scroll in the detailed treatment of the scroll by Judah K. Lefkovits, *The Copper Scroll—3Q15: A Reevaluation: A New Reading, Translation and Commentary* (STDJ, 25; Leiden: E.J. Brill, 2000).

6. Cross, 'Excursus', p. 217.

In the light of subsequent developments, his discussion needs to be supplemented and corrected on a number of points. In the present context I will restrict myself to three observations.

First of all, it should be noted that Cross's 1962 palaeographical dating of the Copper Scroll has been influential in some quarters, but ignored in others. On the one hand, it has served as a palaeographical benchmark against which the scripts of other documents have been measured. This is how it was used, for example, in Eric M. Meyers's Harvard dissertation in 1969,[8] and more recently in the official edition of 4QMMT by Elisha Qimron and John Strugnell.[9] In these publications, the script of the Copper Scroll is considered 'late Herodian', and thus to be dated no later than the 70s CE. On the other hand, Milik and others have preferred a later date, appealing to the authority of William F. Albright, who wrote in 1960 that the script of the Copper Scroll could be dated anywhere between 70 and 135 CE.[10] It is this later dating that made possible the overall interpretations of the Copper Scroll defended by Milik, M. Lehmann, E.-M. Laperrousaz and Ben-Zion Lurie, though it meant setting aside Cross's palaeographical dating.

My second observation has to do with the confusion of look-alike letters in the Copper Scroll. Cross fails to point out that not only *waw*/*yod*, but also *beth*/*kaph* and *daleth*/*resh* are consistently written without any discriminating characteristics. These pairs of letters are palaeographically indistinguishable in the Copper Scroll. This point is significant in two ways. First, it supports the hypothesis that the scribe or scribes of the Copper Scroll were illiterate (at least in Hebrew), since anyone who had

7. See Frank M. Cross Jr, *The Ancient Library of Qumran and Modern Biblical Studies* (New York: Anchor Books, rev. edn, 1961), p. 24; *idem*, 'The Scrolls from the Judaean Desert', in *Archaeological Discoveries in the Holy Land* (New York: Bonanza, 1967), pp. 156-67 (158); and *idem, Scrolls from the Wilderness of the Dead Sea* (San Francisco: American Schools of Oriental Research, 1969), p. 28.

8. Eric M. Meyers, *Jewish Ossuaries: Reburial and Rebirth* (BibOr, 24; Rome: Biblical Institute Press, 1971), pp. 50, 57, 63-64 (n. 69).

9. Elisha Qimron and John Strugnell, *Qumran Cave 4.V: Miqṣat Ma'aśe ha-torah* (DJD X; Oxford: Clarendon Press, 1994), pp. 3-5.

10. William F. Albright, 'Reports on Excavations in the Near and Middle East (Continued)', *BASOR* 159 (1960), pp. 37-39. It is one of the curiosities of Copper Scroll scholarship that this passing remark by Albright (it was made as an aside in a review of another work) has had such influence. Note that Albright had stated four years earlier that 'the Copper Scrolls were written between 1 and 68 AD' (*New York Times*, 1 June 1956, p. 21).

learned to read and write Hebrew would have been taught to observe the small but significant differences that usually distinguish a *beth* from a *kaph* and a *daleth* from a *resh*. Secondly, it means that the interpreter of the Copper Scroll must always consider alternative readings for the words that contain these look-alike letters.

Our third observation is that Cross did not sufficiently distinguish between the scripts of different columns of the Copper Scroll. It is true that he notes a greater proportion of cursive forms in the later columns,[11] and the occurrence of the 'box-headed' *daleth* especially in the early columns,[12] but he does not systematically inquire whether certain forms are characteristic of certain columns or stretches of text.

It is not possible, within the compass of this paper, to give a comprehensive and systematic reconsideration of the palaeography of the Copper Scroll. For an extensive discussion that goes beyond Cross we will have to await the publication of the University of Chicago dissertation by David J. Wilmot, who reportedly distinguishes four different hands in the Copper Scroll.[13] For present purposes, I propose to analyze the changes undergone by a small selection of letters, and to show how such an analysis can help resolve ambiguities in the reading of the text.

The relationship of the *zayin* to the *waw*/*yod* is particularly instructive. Although the *waw*/*yod* sometimes (especially in the first two columns) consists of a single vertical line, it is usually marked by a *keraia* or 'flag' extending to the left from the top of the vertical stroke. (Sometimes this *keraia* is little more than a slight bulge, but it regularly occurs at the top left of the vertical.) The *zayin* is also once or twice written as a simple vertical line (and is then indistinguishable from the simple *waw*/*yod*; see 2.9 מזקא and 2.10 מזרח), but it usually differs from the *waw*/*yod* by the fact that it has a *keraia* extending to the right from the top of the vertical stroke. (Again, the *keraia* may be little more than a bulge, but it regularly occurs at the top right.) This general pattern is consistent, and provides a reliable guide for reading the Copper Scroll, until we get to the last four columns. Suddenly, we find the flag-to-the-right form used not only for the *zayin*, but also for the *waw*/*yod*. For example, the *waw* of צופא in 9.4 and 9.7, and the *yod* of מים in 9.11 clearly have the *keraia* pointing to the right, and there are at least five further examples in col. 10, and another

11. Cross, 'Excursus', p. 217.

12. Cross, 'Excursus', p. 219.

13. See Michael O. Wise, 'David J. Wilmot and the Copper Scroll', in the present volume.

five in col. 11.[14] Conversely, there are two examples in the last four columns of the flag-to-the-right form used for *zayin* (see הזדוגא in 10.9 and זהב in 12.1).

Awareness of the breakdown of the pattern that distinguishes *zayin* from *waw/yod* in the rest of the Copper Scroll allows me to suggest some new readings in these last four columns. For example, it enables us to recognize the word בירך, 'in a recess', in 9.8. The second letter here is not *zayin* (as Allegro and Milik assumed), but *yod*. We find the same word in 1.7 and 2.6, where it is also spelled, as here, with a medial *kaph*. The reading is further confirmed by the fact that in both 2.6 and 9.8 בירך is the last word of a treasure description beginning with בצירח(י), 'vault(s)'. Consequently, we need not take refuge in an otherwise unattested noun זרב, as Milik and others have done.[15]

We find a similar example in 10.9. The recognition that the flag-to-the-right form can represent a *waw/yod* in this column enables us to discern the word מעות, the plural of מעה, a small coin. מעות is in fact the same word, in plene spelling, as the מעת of the previous line.

As a third example we mention the beginning of 10.6, which Milik reads as לסמול רגמות. What he takes to be a cursive *resh*, the first letter of an otherwise unattested noun, is in fact the flag-to-the-right form of the *waw*, and represents the pronominal suffix on the preceding word. We therefore read לסמולו גמות, 'notches to the left of it'.

Of course the recognition of the palaeographical confusion of *zayin* and *waw/yod* in these columns is not an unmixed blessing. Occasionally we may be tempted to read an apparent *waw/yod* as a *zayin* when this is in fact not warranted. We find an interesting example of this in 11.1, where Milik reads זהב,[16] but which should probably be read as והב, the obscure Moabite toponym 'Waheb' mentioned in Numbers 21. This might seem

14. See 10.6 (second *waw* of לסמולו); 10.7 (*waw* of ושנין); 10.12 (יד); 10.13 (second *waw* of חפו[ו]ר); 10.15 (בית); 11.4 (סוח; cf. סוח in 11.10); 11.7 (both *waws* in שבשילוחו); and 11.13 (both *waw* and *yod* in מימות). See also 12.8 (the first הכוך).

15. Milik, DJDJ III, pp. 293-94; cf. 245-46 (sub C 81). The reading זרב at 9.8 is also found in J.M. Allegro, *The Treasure of the Copper Scroll* (London: Routledge & Kegan Paul, 1960), p. 49; B.-Z. Lurie, *The Copper Scroll from the Desert of Judah* (Jerusalem: Kiryath Sepher, 1963), p. 108 [in Hebrew]; and Lefkovits, *3Q15: A Reevaluation*, p. 288. On the other hand, the reading בירך in 9.8 is also adopted by Beyer (*Die aramäischen Texte*, p. 229).

16. Milik, DJDJ III, p. 296. Note, however, that in his Addenda he changes this reading to the suffix יהם- (p. 302). Lefkovits, *3Q15: A Reevaluation*, p. 358, reads מקצועותיה בכלי.

like a particularly farfetched reading, if it were not for the fact that each of the two preceding columns also contain an obscure Moabite toponym mentioned in Numbers 21, namely Oboth (9.17) and Zered (10.8). This remarkable pattern justifies our taking the apparent *waw/yod* here at face value.

Another pair of graphically similar letters is *he/ḥeth*. In the standard Jewish script of the Herodian era (as indeed in the familiar square script of printed Hebrew today) the *he* was distinguished from the *ḥeth* by a gap between the top of the left leg and the horizontal crossbar. We could speak of the 'open' form of the *he* as compared to the 'closed' form of the *ḥeth*. In the Copper Scroll—insofar as we can rely on the sometimes contradictory published facsimiles—this distinction is often not observed, although there are other patterns that do emerge. In the first two columns all examples of *he* and *ḥeth* are closed, so that they are indistinguishable. In cols. 3 to 10, the standard distinction is generally observed, with two or three exceptions in every column, almost always cases of *he* written with a closed form. These exceptions suddenly become much more frequent in the last two columns, with a total of 28 cases of closed *he*'s, as opposed to one doubtful example of an open *ḥeth* (חרם in 11.7). This overall pattern in the palaeography of the scroll means that it is generally a safe bet to read a closed form as a *he* in the first two and the last two columns, but a much riskier proposition in the intervening columns. On the other hand, an open form is much more likely to be a *he* than a *ḥeth*; in my edition of the text I recognize only eight exceptions to this general trend.[17] Note that half of these occur in col. 9. These statistics are based on taking Milik's facsimile as most authoritative; it would be lower if I were to go by Allegro's facsimile.

The palaeographical pattern discerned in the forms of *he* and *ḥeth* does not provide clear-cut criteria for identifying a given letter, but it does give some guidance in interpreting ambiguous forms. For example, it helps to pin down the correct reading of an important but as yet unidentified place name that occurs four times in the Copper Scroll. I am referring to the four-letter sequence that Milik and Allegro originally read as בחלה,[18] but

17. These exceptions are מזרח (3.5), חפור (5.14), חטוף (7.15), ומחצא (9.6), צריחי (9.7), חרם (9.10), בקילה (9.11) and חרם (11.7).

18. J.T. Milik, 'Le travail d'édition des manuscrits du désert de Juda', *Volume du Congrès, Strasbourg 1956* (VTSup, 4; Leiden: E.J. Brill, 1957), pp. 17-26 (22), and Allegro, *Treasure of the Copper Scroll*, pp. 33, 35, 39, 55.

which Allegro subsequently read as כהלת,[19] and Milik as כחלת.[20] It occurs at 1.9; 2.13; 4.11-12; and 12.10—in each case as the name of a place near which treasure was hidden. Although it is still uncertain whether the first letter should be read as a *beth* or a *kaph*, we can be fairly certain that the last two letters must be read as a *lamedh* and a *taw*. But what about the second letter—is it a *he* or a *ḥeth*? In the light of the above-mentioned palaeographical pattern, it is almost certainly a *ḥeth*, since in all four cases it is written as a closed form.

The example of *he*/*ḥeth* illustrates another general point about the palaeography of the Copper Scroll that has heuristic value. It has been noticed that four of the eight exceptions to the way *ḥeth* is normally written are found in col. 9—in fact they are all found within six lines of each other (in lines 6, 7, 10 and 11). In other words, we can feel much more confident about reading an apparent *he* as a *ḥeth* in this column than in others. It turns out that something similar is true of other letters; certain palaeographical confusions seem to be concentrated in certain delimited parts of the text.

Take, for example, the confusion of *mem* and *beth*/*kaph*, which is also concentrated in col. 9. Although the *mem* is usually distinguished from the *beth*/*kaph* by the fact that its top crossbar extends leftwards beyond the *keraia* that normally rides on it, this feature is absent in the *mem* of אמות (9.8) and חרם (9.10—my reading). This provides a clue to deciphering the desperately difficult series of characters in line 2 of this column. Where Milik reads וגב, and assumes that *gab* here has the meaning normally reserved for the phrase על גב, 'on top of',[21] I read וגם, 'and also', which is not nearly as awkward.

Another example is the rare occurrence, once again in col. 9, of an unusual form of the *waw*, in which the characteristic leftward-pointing flag is elongated to the point of making the letter look like a *daleth*/*resh*. As Milik and others have recognized, an apparent *daleth*/*resh* is in fact to be read as a *waw* in בשולי and משולו (first *waw*) in the first line of this column. Recognition of this peculiarity helps to decipher the beginning of

19. J.M. Allegro, *The Treasure of the Copper Scroll* (Garden City, NY: Doubleday, 2nd rev. edn, 1964), pp. 21-23.

20. Milik, DJDJ III, pp. 284, 286, 288, 298. See his discussion of the word on pp. 274-75 (sub D 71). Milik's reading of *ḥeth* has been followed most recently by Lefkovits, *3Q15: A Reevaluation*, p. 73.

21. Milik, DJDJ III, pp. 293-94; cf. pp. 255-56 (sub C 182). For other proposals see Lefkovits, *3Q15: A Reevaluation*, pp. 279-81.

line 6, where Milik has been forced to supply an *'ayin* in order to make sense of the text. Instead of Milik's דמ<ע> הצא, in which the second word is unattested, I read with Allegro and others[22] ומחצא, 'and a half', which makes perfect sense after the preceding שמונא, 'eight'. In this case the correct reading depends on recognizing that col. 9 has unusual forms, not only of *waw*, but also (as noted above) of *ḥeth*.

A final illustration of the concentration of unusual forms is the cursive *resh*, which occurs only in the last three columns. Examples are found in כברין and רחיל (10.7), הדרומית (11.2) and גריזין (12.4). The possibility of a cursive *resh* in this environment helps us to recognize that 10.8 contains a reference to זרד, one of the three Moabite toponyms that I mentioned earlier.

The foregoing discussion has dealt with what we may call 'localized deviations' from the regular pattern of the script of the Copper Scroll. The findings would seem to lend support to Wilmot's hypothesis of a number of different scribes or engravers for the scroll, although of course it is theoretically possible that the script of the metal scroll faithfully reflects a variety of hands in the leather or papyrus *Vorlage* from which the engraver worked. Whatever the case may be, it is clear that the interpretation of ambiguous forms in the Copper Scroll must take into consideration the palaeographical variety of the text as we have it. On the basis of this undeniable variety, I have sought to adhere to the following rule in my edition of the Copper Scroll: do not accept an unusual form of a letter unless there are one or more parallels of this form in the surrounding context, preferably in the same column. However tempting it may be, I have not read a *mem* as a *beth*, or a *waw* as a *resh*, unless there are other examples of the same confusion nearby.

I turn now to a number of examples where this rule has not been followed, with the consequence not only that an unnecessary degree of arbitrariness has been introduced into the interpretation of the Copper Scroll, but also that some significant probable readings have been overlooked. It is my thesis that it is palaeographically unwarranted to assume *isolated* cases of letter confusion.

In 8.3, for example, the sixth letter from the end is read by Milik as *nun*, the final letter of the word ספרין, 'scrolls'.[23] But this letter is written with

22. Allegro, *Treasure of the Copper Scroll*, p. 49. See also Lurie, *The Copper Scroll*, p. 10, Beyer, *Die aramäischen Texte,* p. 229, and Lefkovits, *3Q15: A Reevaluation*, p. 284.

23. Milik, DJDJ III, p. 292; also Lefkovits, *3Q15: A Reevaluation*, p. 245.

a leftward-pointing *keraia* at the top, a feature that *nun* does not have in any other place in the scroll. Instead, as we have seen, this is a normal feature of the *waw/yod* throughout, and an occasional feature of *zayin* in cols. 10 and 12. I have therefore read the letter in question as a *waw*, introducing the phrase ואלת כס<ף>, 'and a bar of silver', which fits the context very well. This example is of more than passing interest, because if the letter in question is not a *nun* at the end of the previous word, but a *waw* at the beginning of the next one, then the word before it is ספרי, with a first person singular suffix. If I am right, this is one of three treasure descriptions in the Copper Scroll that have this feature: 'my garments' in 8.3 (לבושי), 'my scrolls' here in 8.3 (ספרי), and 'my pure things' in 11.9 (טהורתי). The implications of these readings for the authorship of the scroll are potentially quite significant.[24]

Another potentially significant example of the point I am making is found in 12.10, where Milik and Pixner read a *ṣade* in the second word of the line. However, not only does this cause them to postulate an otherwise unattested noun (צח in the case of Milik,[25] and the toponym צהב in the case of Pixner[26]), but it makes them assume a shape of the *ṣade* that occurs nowhere else in the Copper Scroll. The 'branch' at the upper right of the *ṣade* elsewhere consists either of two roughly equal strokes, one vertical and one horizontal, or of a curved diagonal line. The form interpreted as a *ṣade* by Milik and Pixner in 12.10 has neither of these features: there is only a short vertical line very close and parallel to the main downstroke, with only a hint of a horizontal line connecting the two verticals. If Milik's facsimile can be trusted, then the apparent *ṣade* is really a double letter: *waw/yod* plus *nun*. My own examination of the original in Amman in 1991 confirms that there is no horizontal cross-stroke—in fact, it looks as though even the short vertical line is not really part of the engraved script at all; it may be an accidental scratch or discoloration. The letter in question is certainly not a *ṣade*; it may be either a *nun* alone (so my edition), or a *nun* preceded by a *waw* or *yod*. In fact, the first of these options was

24. See A. Wolters, 'History and the Copper Scroll', in M.O. Wise *et al.* (eds.), *Methods of Investigation of the Dead Sea Scrolls and the Khirbet Qumran Site: Present Realities and Future Prospects* (Annals of the New York Academy of Sciences, 722; New York: New York Academy of Sciences, 1994), pp. 285-95 (292-93).

25. Milik, DJDJ III, p. 298.

26. B. Pixner, 'Unravelling the Copper Scroll Code: A Study on the Topography of 3Q15', *RevQ* 11 (1983), pp. 323-65 (358).

originally chosen by Milik (שכנה),[27] and the second by Allegro (שכינה).[28]

The reason why this restored reading is potentially significant is that the word which now emerges in 12.10 may well be *šᵉkīnâ*, the Shekinah or divine presence. This possibility seems to have been overlooked by previous interpreters, even those who correctly saw that the disputed letter was not a *ṣade*. Allegro and Milik interpret the word שכ(י)נה to be a feminine adjective meaning 'nearby', but this is unlikely. The word *šĕkēnâ* is not attested as an adjective elsewhere, but is found in Mishnaic Hebrew as the feminine equivalent of the noun *šākēn*, 'neighbour', and thus means 'neighbour's wife' or 'neighbouress'.[29] In my judgment it is less likely that the final hiding place of the Copper Scroll, identified as שית שכנה, is 'the cavern of a neighbour's wife' than 'the cavern of the Presence'.[30] If this judgment is correct, then the Copper Scroll contains what is probably the earliest attestation of 'Shekinah' as a designation of the divine presence.

Let me mention one further example of how an interesting reading has been obscured by assuming an unparalleled letter form. In 12.2 we find a sequence of characters that Milik interprets as בידן, that is, *bĕyādān*, which he translates 'près de là' or 'nearby'.[31] However, the *daleth* on this reading is very peculiar. Not only does it have a *keraia* at the upper right-hand corner (found elsewhere only in cols. 5 and 8), but there is a small downstroke suspended from the upper left-hand corner. This is sufficient to arouse suspicions about the correctness of this reading, especially when we note that the top crossbar is missing altogether in the facsimiles prepared by Baker and Allegro. As it turns out, these suspicions are amply justified: my own examination of the original in Amman confirms that there is no crossbar joining the two verticals, and that Allegro was right to read two letters (*waw* and *zayin*) instead of one. It is a mystery why Milik added the crossbar when he revised Wright Baker's facsimile in 1959.

27. Milik, 'Le travail d'édition', p. 22.

28. Allegro, *Treasure of the Copper Scroll*, p. 55. Lefkovits (*3Q15: A Reevaluation*, p. 427) opts for שבינח, which he understands as a defective spelling to be rendered as 'which is in Janoah'.

29. See M. Jastrow, *A Dictionary of the Targumim, the Talmud Babli and Yerushalmi, and the Midrashic Literature* (repr.; New York: Judaica Press, 1989), s.v. שָׁכֵן.

30. This is the translation that I have adopted in my edition of the text (see n. 4). Note that *šĕkînâ* as divine designation is commonly used without the article, as here.

31. Milik, DJDJ III, p. 298 (cf. his discussion of the term on p. 239 sub C 9), and 'The Copper Document', p. 142.

The correction of Milik's misreading (which was also improbable from a philological point of view)[32] has an important consequence. It means that Allegro and Lurie were right to read here the word כוזין (taking the first letter to be a *kaph* rather than the indistinguishable *beth*), and that the treasure being described consists of *juglets*. At first glance it may seem odd that a treasure should consist of juglets, but the oddity disappears in the light of the discovery in 1988, in a cave near 3Q where the Copper Scroll was found, of a juglet of expensive oil.[33] Since a *kuz* in Mishnaic Hebrew referred to '*an oil vessel*, used in the Temple',[34] it may well be that the newly discovered juglet, which was found buried about a metre under the cave floor, is a remnant of the cache of oil vessels from the temple which is here recorded in the Copper Scroll.[35]

The foregoing concludes my discussion of the palaeographical considerations that can help to decide how to read the letter forms that are visible on the Copper Scroll. However, there is one more palaeographical point that needs to be made about letter forms which are *not* currently visible on the surviving segments of the scroll. What I have in mind are not the letters that have been lost as a result of corrosion or other accidental damage to the text, but letters that may have been destroyed as a result of the process by which the Copper Scroll was cut open 40 years ago. Are there any cases where the vertical line of cut coincided with a vertical line engraved in the copper? In other words, is it possible that a *waw*/*yod* or final *nun*, which are often written as a single vertical downstroke, were destroyed because Wright Baker's circular saw passed exactly along the groove of such a letter?

Wright Baker was aware of the problem, and he tells us in his account of the opening of the scroll that he was careful to position the line of the cut in such a way that no letter would be destroyed.[36] Although he acknowledged that it was possible that a single stroke of the text might

32. There is virtually no evidence that Hebrew ביד can mean 'à côté' (Milik, DJDJ III, p. 239 sub C 9), let alone that this phrase plus pronominal suffix (here בידן) can mean 'près de là' (p. 298).

33. See J. Patrich and B. Arubas, 'A Juglet of Balsam Oil (?)', *IEJ* 39 (1989), pp. 43-59.

34. See Jastrow, *Dictionary of the Targumim*, s.v. כוז.

35. Wolters, 'History and the Copper Scroll', pp. 293-95. כוזין is also the preferred reading of Lefkovits, *3Q15: A Reevaluation*, p. 399.

36. H. Wright Baker, 'Notes on the Opening of the Copper Scrolls from Qumrân', in DJDJ III, pp. 203-10 (206).

have been destroyed,[37] he was apparently confident that no letter of the text was eliminated by the cutting open of the scroll.[38] Allegro, on the other hand, who advised Wright Baker during part of the cutting operation, and who realized that there are some Hebrew letters that consist of nothing but a single vertical line, was not so confident, and in his notes on the Copper Scroll hypothesized on a number of occasions that *waw*/*yod* or a final *nun* should be read 'on the cut'.[39] Such a hypothesis is of course always highly speculative, but the possibility cannot be entirely discounted. As a matter of fact, it is possible to show that there is at least one case where a *waw* was destroyed by being on the cutting path of Wright Baker's saw.

The *waw* I have in mind is found in the word חפור in 7.9. The line of cut runs directly between the *pe* and the *resh*, and there is no trace of a *waw* between these letters on the surviving copper segments. However, we know that a *waw* was originally there on the basis of the small bits of text that showed through on the outside of the scroll before it was opened, and that were transcribed and published by K.G. Kuhn in 1954.[40] By a curious chance, these bits of text included the word חפור (spelt with a *waw*) in 7.9.[41] It was in fact partially on the basis of this reading that Kuhn made his brilliant guess, long before the Copper Scroll was opened in Manchester, that it contained a list of buried treasure.[42]

There are two bits of corroborative evidence that support the original presence of a *waw* in this occurrence of חפור. The first is the fact that the word חפור (the imperative or infinitive absolute of the verb חפר) is a standard element in the stereotypical phraseology of the Copper Scroll, and that in 17 out of 20 occurrences elsewhere it is spelt plene, that is,

37. Wright Baker, 'Notes', p. 206.

38. Wright Baker, 'Notes', p. 206.

39. See the 'Notes to the Translation' in Allegro, *Treasure of the Copper Scroll*, nn. 8, 18, 24, 36, 49, 72, 144, 195, 300.

40. K.G. Kuhn, 'Les rouleaux de cuivre de Qumrân', *RB* 61 (1954), pp. 193-205 (199).

41. Kuhn, 'Les rouleaux', p. 199. 'Ligne 9' of the fragment 'A 1' corresponds with 7.9.

42. Kuhn, 'Les rouleaux', p. 204.

43. The word is usually understood as an imperative (see, e.g., Milik, DJDJ III, p. 235 [sub B 22b]), but as possibly an infinitive absolute in J. Carmignac, 'L'infinitif absolu chez Ben Sira et à Qumrân', *RevQ* 12 (1985–87), pp. 251-61 (256-57).

with a *waw* as *mater lectionis*.[44] In other words, the usual spelling of the word would lead us to expect a *waw* as penultimate letter. The other bit of evidence is the fact that although the *waw* is usually written with a *keraia* at the top (a feature which would probably not have been completely eliminated by the saw), the simple form of the *waw* is found on two other occasions in col. 7, including an example in the line preceding the חפור in question. Taking all of this into account, it is safe to assume that an original *waw* was in this case 'on the cut', and to include it in the printed edition of the text, as I have done.

Now of course the fact that a *waw/yod* or final *nun* (or even, at a stretch, a *zayin*) may theoretically have belonged to the text before the saw passed through it, does not mean that we can assume the presence of one of these letters 'on the cut' whenever it would be convenient. In my opinion, Allegro was far too free in making use of this hypothesis in order to explain a difficulty in the surviving text (he does so at least nine times).[45] However, I believe there is one place where the hypothesis may be reasonably invoked.

The case in question is found in 12.8, where Lurie reads כל בית, and Milik (followed by Pixner) reads כלבית. Allegro, however, suggests that a *yod* belongs right after כל, so that the original reading was כלי (as in line 6 of the same column). This makes good sense in the context, yielding the reading (in my edition) כל<י> בית הכוך, 'vessels of the crypt chamber'. It is quite possible that in this case (as distinct from כל<י> in line 6) the *yod* was lost because it was on the line of cut. Wright Baker's saw did in fact pass through the metal exactly between the *lamedh* and the *beth*, and a small straight-line *waw/yod* does occur several times in this column. Ironically, this is a place where Allegro did *not* appeal to the line of cut as a justification for his emendation, although such an appeal would in this case have been thoroughly warranted.

The Relevance of Literary Structure

We turn now to the second major part of this paper: the relevance of literary structure to the reading of the Copper Scroll. It has been recognized since the first decipherment of the entire Copper Scroll in 1956 that

44. The *plene* spelling is found at 2.14; 4.13; 5.3, 10, 14; 6.3; 7.1, 12, 15; 8.5, 9, 12, 14; 9.5, 8, 13; 10.13. The defective spelling is found only at 3.6; 6.9 and 12.

45. See the nine numbered notes listed above in n. 39.

it represents an inventory of hidden treasure composed according to a definite plan. It clearly consists of 60 or more parallel sections, each of which has at least two parts: one describing a hiding place and the other describing the treasure hidden there. Milik especially, in his edition of the scroll in DJDJ III, recognized the stereotypical nature of the scroll's literary form.[46] However, he did not push his analysis very far, and there are a number of aspects of the scroll's parallelism that he failed to observe.

As I have argued elsewhere,[47] an analysis of the content of the text reveals that it contains seven clearly distinguishable types of material, which may be described as follows:

A. *Place*: a designation of a hiding place.
B. *Specification*: a further specification of the hiding place.
C. *Command*: a command to dig or measure.
D. *Distance*: a distance, expressed in a specific number of cubits (or, in two cases, גמות).
E. *Treasure*: a treasure description.
F. *Comments*: additional comments on the hiding place or treasure.
G. *Greek*: a pair or trio of cryptic Greek letters.

Although no single section of the scroll contains all seven types of material, there is nothing in the scroll which is not readily classifiable under one of these seven categories. Accordingly, each of the 64 sections can be analyzed into identifiable components representing six or fewer of the seven categories. These components are clearly recognizable by the presence of characteristic catchwords or other stereotypical phraseology. It is as though the author of the Copper Scroll had only seven slots at his disposal, and had very limited freedom in choosing and filling those slots.

This impression of limited freedom is reinforced when we notice that the same slot is never filled twice within a given section, and that the slots are invariably filled in a fixed order. Although no section incorporates all seven components, those which *are* incorporated invariably follow the sequence of the list given above. For example, the 'Command' component does not occur in every section, but if it does occur, it never comes *before* the 'Place' or 'Specification' component, or *after* the 'Distance' or 'Treasure' component. Similarly, the 'Greek' component is always last in a

46. Milik, DJDJ III, p. 278. See also pp. 235 (sub B 22c) and 256 (sub C 196-97).

47. A. Wolters, 'Literary Analysis and the Copper Scroll', in Z.J. Kapera (ed.), *Intertestamental Essays in Honour of Józef Tadeusz Milik* (Kraków: Enigma Press, 1992), pp. 239-52.

section. In other words, the author was apparently bound, not only to seven slots, but to a fixed order in which these slots could be filled. In composing his inventory, he appears to have been filling a mental grid that allowed for no structural variation.

The mental grid or pattern underlying the Copper Scroll can be most easily made clear by arranging the scroll's contents into seven parallel columns.[48] By organizing the material in this way it is easy to show how the individual section components that belong to the same column share a number of recognizable features.[49] This proves to be a great help in settling certain disputed questions of interpretation, since the standard phraseology and fixed sequence of the columns establish limits on possible or plausible readings and interpretations. The overall pattern tends to rule out certain readings and interpretations, while favouring or suggesting others.

To begin with, I shall deal with two instances in which a recognition of the pattern allows us to choose between competing interpretations in previous scholarship on the Copper Scroll. My first example is found in the very first line of the scroll, which begins with these words: 'In the ruins which are in the Valley', followed by a word that can be read as either עכור or עבור, and then by the words 'under the steps which go eastward'. On the first reading, which is that of Allegro, Milik, Lurie and others, including Lefkovits, the first line should be translated: 'In the ruins which are in the Valley *of Achor*, under the steps...' This puts the hiding place of the first treasure in the biblically attested 'Valley of Achor', near Jericho (see Josh. 7.24, 26; 15.7; Isa. 65.10; Hos. 2.15). On the second reading, which is that of Pixner and García Martínez, the opening line is rendered: 'At the ruin which is in the Valley, *go past* below the steps...'[50] This puts the hiding place in 'the Valley', without specifying its name. According to the former interpretation of the word, reading its second letter as a *kaph*, we have a geographical proper noun; according to the latter interpretation, reading the second letter as *beth*, we have the imperative (or infinitive absolute) of the verb עבר, 'pass over', 'go past'. Palaeographically, both readings are possible, since *kaph* and *beth* are not distinguished in the script of the Copper Scroll.

48. See Wolters, 'Literary Analysis', pp. 248-52. Lefkovits (*3Q15: A Reevaluation*, pp. 17-18 and n. 70) promises further analysis along these lines.

49. Wolters, 'Literary Analysis', pp. 244-46.

50. See Pixner, 'Unravelling the Copper Scroll Code', p. 342, and Florentino García Martínez, *The Dead Sea Scrolls Translated: The Qumran Texts in English* (trans. Wilfred G.E. Watson; Leiden: E.J. Brill, 1994), p. 461.

However, a brief consideration of the scroll's compositional pattern will make clear that Pixner's reading must be rejected. It should be observed first of all that section 1 has regular components under six columns. If Pixner's reading עבור were correct, then we would have a component under the one remaining column as well, namely col. C. However, this would break the pattern on two counts: it would be the only instance of the verb עבר in col. C, which elsewhere has only חפר (21 times) or משח (two times), and it would be the only case where the command does not precede the word אמות (or גמות) of col. D, but precedes instead one of the serial prepositional phrases characteristic of col. B. On the other hand, if we read the proper noun עכור, the regular pattern is maintained, with עכור forming part of a standard component under col. B. Furthermore, the phrase 'Valley of Achor' is a familiar geographical term that designates a location in the same general area as most of the other hiding places in the Copper Scroll. Pixner's objection that the place in question is called the 'Valley of Achon' elsewhere in the scroll (4.8),[51] carries little weight, since the valley in question had strong biblical associations with a man variously called עכן and עכר.[52] It is therefore safe to conclude that the correct reading in the initial line of the Copper Scroll must be עכור, and not עבור.

This conclusion is of more than incidental exegetical interest, because it affects the major interpretative proposal put forward by Pixner in his 1983 article. In this article Pixner argues that the sections of the Copper Scroll are grouped according to the different geographical areas in which the hiding places are located. Specifically, he contends that the first 18 sections all refer to the area in or near the 'Essene Quarter' in Jerusalem.[53] But this claim cannot be maintained if the first hiding place is in the Valley of Achor, near Jericho. It seems, therefore, that Pixner has tailored his reading of the text to fit his overall theory. As my analysis shows, however, this means that he is forced to do violence to the regular pattern of 3Q15.

My second example is the phrase כתבן אצלם and its variants, which I mentioned at the beginning of this essay. It occurs four times: once in 5.7 and three times in col. 11 (11.1, 11 and 15)—one more time if we emend

51. Pixner, 'Unravelling the Copper Scroll Code', p. 342 n. 2.

52. See Milik, DJDJ III, p. 257 (sub C 200); see also the discussion in Lefkovits, *3Q15: A Reevaluation*, pp. 33-34. It is also possible that the final *nun* of עכון in 4.6 is to be read as a cursive *resh* (so Allegro).

53. Pixner, 'Unravelling the Copper Scroll Code', pp. 341-47.

11.4 to conform to the others. It is a matter of dispute whether the phrase should be interpreted as the end of one section, or the beginning of another. Most students of the Copper Scroll have chosen the first option, but Milik and Pixner choose the second.[54] However, a consideration of the literary pattern of the scroll soon makes abundantly clear that the phrase in question, variously read as (ו)בתכן אצלם (אצלן) or (ו)כתבן אצלם (אצלן), does not belong at the beginning of a section. That would break the pattern of col. A, which everywhere else begins with a preposition (usually ב) followed by a hiding place, which is then specified by the col. B component. As it happens, each case of our phrase is immediately *followed* by a typical col. A and col. B component, so that the overall pattern is maintained intact if the phrase is in each case placed at the end of the previous section, that is, in col. F. This placement also comports well with the pattern of col. F, since this column allows for a variety of additional comments that do not fit elsewhere.

My conclusion with respect to the placing of the words כתבן אצלם is supported by a number of other considerations, such as the fact that these words consistently follow mention of 'vessels of tribute' (כלי דמע or כאלין של דמע), and are also consistently situated in the scroll's layout in such a way that the following col. A component begins a new line, even if this means leaving a gap between אצלם and that component (so clearly in 11.15).

If the pattern of the scroll leads us to consider the words in question as a stock phrase at the *end* of a section, then this conclusion also has implications for the choice between the readings בתכן or כתבן. Since the script of the Copper Scroll does not make a distinction between *beth* and *kaph*, both readings are palaeographically possible. However, the former reading can be made to yield sense only with the greatest difficulty, resulting in wildly divergent and highly speculative renderings for the phrase בתכן אצלם. Milik has 'tout près de là',[55] Allegro first gave the translation

54. Milik, DJDJ III, pp. 290, 297, and Pixner, 'Unravelling the Copper Scroll Code', pp. 348, 355-57. They are followed by Vermes, García Martínez and Lefkovits, *3Q15: A Reevaluation*, p. 190. For a detailed but somewhat inconclusive discussion of the various alternatives for this phrase see Lefkovits, *3Q15: A Reevaluation*, pp. 546-53.

55. Milik, DJDJ III, pp. 290, 297. His English rendering is 'just nearby' ('The Copper Document', p. 142). See his discussion of the phrase in DJDJ III, pp. 254 (sub C 155) and 256 (sub C 183).

'and inside them figured coins',[56] but later abandoned this in favour of 'arranged side by side', with his remaining uncertainty indicated by a question mark.[57] Lurie took תכן to represent the noun *token*, 'contents', in which 'image-bearing coins' were found.[58] A more plausible reading was suggested by Sarfatti in 1972, who read כתבן אצלם, meaning 'their dockets with them', and restored this reading also at 11.4.[59] In his view, the 'dockets' refer to inscribed sherds, which, according to rabbinic literature were put inside tithe vessels, that is, the 'vessels of tribute' with which this phrase is always associated in the Copper Scroll. Since the pronominal suffixes in the phrase come at the conclusion of a section, they naturally refer to the vessels mentioned earlier in the section.[60] The same reading was later proposed by Golb, although he interpreted the כתבן as possibly referring to hidden scrolls.[61] I follow Sarfatti and Golb's reading, but interpret כתבן to mean 'their document', since the masculine plural ending is regularly written ין- in the Copper Scroll. The reading כתבן אצלם yields a simple and straightforward meaning, which requires no lexicographical gymnastics. As a result, we have a satisfactory interpretation of the disputed phrase that fits nicely with the overall pattern of the scroll.

To this point I have used the pattern of the scroll to choose between existing interpretations, but there are also new interpretations that it suggests. In what follows I shall offer a brief sampling of these, necessarily limited by the constraints of space.

56. Allegro, *Treasure of the Copper Scroll*, p. 148 n. 109. Cf. also Manfred R. Lehmann, 'Identification of the Copper Scroll Based on its Technical Terms', *RevQ* 5 (1964), pp. 97-105 (104), who translates אצלם as 'defaced coins'.

57. Allegro, *Treasure of the Copper Scroll* (1964), p. 23.

58. Lurie, *The Copper Scroll*, p. 87.

59. G.B.A. Sarfatti, 'כתבן אצלם: A Riddle from the Riddles of the Copper Scroll', *Leš* 36 (1971–72), pp. 106-11 (in Hebrew, with English summary).

60. The variation of *mem* and *nun* is explained by the fact that these phonemes in final position had come to be pronounced in the same way in Second Temple times; see E. Qimron, *The Hebrew of the Dead Sea Scrolls* (Harvard Semitic Studies, 29; Atlanta: Scholars Press, 1986), p. 27 (§200.142).

61. Norman Golb, 'The Problem of Origin and Identification of the Dead Sea Scrolls', *Proceedings of the American Philosophical Society* 124 (1980), pp. 1-24 (20). Golb writes there (n. 51): '[A]t times the editors have read a meaningless *btkn 'ṣln* instead of *ktbn 'ṣln* = *ketābīn eṣlān* ("writings are near it") or *ketābān eṣlān* ("their writing is near it").'

As we saw in the last example, the literary pattern of the Copper Scroll is particularly helpful in defining the limits of the various sections. A striking example is found in 11.16–12.3, where a recognition of regularity can bring order into apparent confusion. These five lines (the first two of which are badly damaged) were taken to constitute a single section by Allegro,[62] but correctly subdivided into three different ones by Milik (his sections 58-60). But Milik divided them in such a way that section 59 began with 'sixty talents', continued with the words ביאתו מן המ<ע>רב, which he translated 'en y entrant du côté ouest', and concluded with the prepositional phrase 'sous la pierre noire'.[63] In other words, he marked off a section consisting of components from col. E, col. F and col. B—in that order. He was apparently not troubled by the fact that no other section of the Copper Scroll has this sequence of components. Awareness of the scroll's seven-column structure soon makes clear that 'sixty talents' belongs with the treasure description of the foregoing section 58, that ביאתו מן המ<ע>רב—on the analogy of parallel constructions in col. F in sections 4 (1.11), 11 (2.12) and 15 (3.9-10)—means 'its entrance is on the west', and that section 59 begins with 'under the black stone', just as sections 10 (2.9), 14 (3.5) and 43 (9.10) begin with the 'Specification' component. This has the further implication that the following word, which should be read as בוזין (as we have seen), represents the 'Treasure' component of section 59. Such a cultic item has many parallels in the treasure descriptions of other sections, such as the 'vessels of tribute' of sections 4 (1.9), 15 (3.9), 24 (5.6-7), 35 (8.3), and so on, and the 'basins, cups, bowls, flagons' of section 13 (3.3-4). Since the following component in the text is again a col. B item, I conclude that section 59, like section 43, has only the two components B and E, and thus ends with בוזין. Once this has been established, it turns out that the subsequent section also consists of these two components, yielding the translation, 'Under the threshold of the crypt: 42 talents.' The result of applying our knowledge of the overall structure of the scroll to these lines is therefore that Milik's delimitation of sections 59 and 60 has to be corrected, and that the reading בוזין commends itself.

62. Allegro, *Treasure of the Copper Scroll*, pp. 53-55 (his Item 57). Similarly Beyer, *Die aramäischen Texte*, p. 232 (his §54), and Lefkovits, *3Q15: A Reevaluation*, p. 399 (his §56).

63. Milik, DJDJ III, p. 298. Milik's English translation has 'on circling around from the west side, beneath the black rock' ('The Copper Document', p. 142).

Another deviation from the regular pattern of the scroll is found in Milik's interpretation of 7.14-15, which he translates as follows: 'Au débouché de la sortie d'eau à ha-Koziba, (en allant) vers le mur de soutènement, creuse trois coudées: 60 talents (d'argent) d'or.'[64] As it stands, this looks like a standard section, comprising successively the components A, B, C, D and E. However, the translation obscures the fact that in the original the phrase עד הטור, translated '(en allant) vers le mur de soutènement', comes *after* the command 'dig' (חפור) and the distance 'three cubits' (אמות שלוש), which is highly unusual. In every other section, the 'Distance' component is followed directly by the 'Treasure' component, never by a preposition plus noun. Furthermore, the position of עד הטור is often occupied, in other sections, by a description of the *kind* of treasure involved, for example, silver (so in 3.6; 4.4, 10, 12, 14, etc.). In other words, the apparent anomaly in the pattern would disappear if עד הטור were not a prepositional phrase, but a description of treasure.

If we examine the relevant letters of the facsimile with this in mind, we discover that another possible reading is עד חטוף. Note that the final letter is read as a *pe* also by Allegro and Lurie,[65] and that *he* and *ḥeth* (as we have noted) are often written alike in the Copper Scroll.[66] This new reading can be translated 'plundered loot', taking *'ad* as the noun for 'booty', and חטוף as the passive participle of the verb חטף, 'seize' or 'rob'.[67] This reading would give us the treasure description that the scroll's pattern would lead us to expect. Consequently, I read the 'Treasure' component of section 34 (7.15-16) as follows: '60 talents of plundered loot, two talents of gold.' It is now evident that זהב finds its counterpart in עד חטוף, and that the regular structure of the scroll is not disturbed.

64. Milik, DJDJ III, p. 292. Milik's English translation reads as follows: 'By the outlet of the water channel, at ha-Koziba, (proceeding) towards the retaining wall, dig three cubits: 60 talents (of silver), two talents of gold' ('The Copper Document', p. 141).

65. See Allegro, *Treasure of the Copper Scroll*, p. 45, and Lurie, *The Copper Scroll*, p. 97.

66. See n. 17 above, where חטוף in 7.15 is listed as one of the eight (admittedly exceptional) examples of *ḥeth* written with an 'open' form.

67. See Gustaf H. Dalman, *Aramäisch–Neuhebräisches Wörterbuch zu Targum, Talmud und Midrasch* (Frankfurt: J. Kauffmann, 1897–1901), s.vv. I am grateful to John Elwolde for pointing out the similar collocation of עד and חטף in *t. Šeb.* 7.12 on Gen. 49.27; see n. 40 of his essay '3Q15: Its Linguistic Affiliation, with Lexicographical Comments', in the present volume.

My final two examples are of special interest, because they are related to two of the places where a first person singular pronominal suffix can be discerned. The first is found in 3.9-10, where Milik's translation speaks of 'vase de résine de pin d'Alep, (caché) à son entrée, sous l'angle occidental (du Parvis)'.[68] As I have argued elsewhere, this translation is very implausible, and a more probable interpretation would yield the translation 'vessels of tribute, my garments. Its entrance is under the western corner.'[69] It is important to remember that the expression 'its entrance [ביאתא] is under the western corner' is one variant of a standard component of col. F, as we saw above in connection with 12.1 (ביאתו מן המ<ע>רב). The word לבושי that precedes ביאתא cannot be interpreted as a construct plural, since ביאתא and its analogues in col. F consistently mark the beginning of a new sentence. It is therefore confirmed that one of the treasure descriptions of the Copper Scroll ends with the first person singular pronominal suffix, namely לבושי, '*my* garment(s)', perhaps better rendered 'my vestment(s)'.[70] The author of the Copper Scroll was apparently the owner of valuable vestments that were hidden along with the other treasures.

There is a somewhat similar case in 8.3, where the 'Treasure' component begins with the familiar כלי דמע, 'vessels of tribute', followed by the reading ספרי, 'my scrolls', which I discussed above. There then follow six more letters, which have been variously interpreted. Milik, reading the first of these as a final *nun* (see the palaeographical discussion above), construes the remaining five letters as אל תבם, and translates 'Ne (te) les *approprie* pas!'[71] He acknowledges, however, in the relevant 'note de lecture' in DJDJ III, that the reading is uncertain, and that this kind of warning is unprecedented in the rest of the scroll.[72] This point is only reinforced when we look at his interpretation in the light of the scroll's seven-column pattern, since verbal forms (apart from participles) occur

68. Milik, DJDJ III, p. 288. Milik's English translation reflects a somewhat different understanding: 'vase(s) with resin from the Aleppo pine; (the pit) whose entrance is under the western corner (of the Court)' ('The Copper Document', p. 139).

69. See Wolters, 'Notes on the Copper Scroll (3Q15)', *RevQ* 12 (1985–87), pp. 589-96 (593-94).

70. It is, of course, also possible to read the suffix as a *waw*, and thus to represent a *third* person singular pronoun, but this seems less probable, since there is no obvious antecedent to which it could refer.

71. Milik, DJDJ III, p. 293. Milik's English version has 'Do not *appropriate* (*them*)!' ('The Copper Document', p. 141).

72. Milik, DJDJ III, p. 293.

elsewhere only in col. C, and even there are restricted to the forms חפור and משח. What the scroll's pattern would lead us to expect at this point is simply the completion of the treasure description, since section 36 begins on the next line, and there is not enough room left for a col. F component.

Another solution to the problem of the last six letters of 8.3 is offered by Beyer. Like Milik, he reads the first of the six as a final *nun*, followed by אלתכל, which he interprets as a proper noun, and translates 'Eltūkal (weiss Bescheid)', that is, 'Eltūkal (has the information)'.[73] But this again introduces a completely unprecedented element into the literary structure of the Copper Scroll.

We therefore have reason to re-examine the six letters in question. The first four are quite clearly *waw*/*yod* plus אלת, which I interpret to mean the copula plus the construct of the noun אלה (*'allâ*), here in its Mishnaic Hebrew sense of 'spear' or 'bar'.[74] The two remaining characters in the line are a *beth*/*kaph* and an incomplete letter that looks like half of either *samekh* or *lamedh*. The engraver appears to have been interrupted in mid-letter, and to have forgotten, when he returned to his work, that he had not completed the line. The most plausible interpretation of his unfinished last word is probably כס<ף> (a very frequent word in the scroll), so that the third item of the treasure description is ואלת כסף, 'and a bar of silver'. This treasure is thus comparable to the 'ingots of gold' (עשתות זהב) of 1.5-6 and 2.4.

Once again, the guidance provided by the underlying pattern of the Copper Scroll allows us to find a plausible alternative to other interpretations. The 'Treasure' component of section 35 (8.3) may therefore be translated as 'vessels of tribute, and my scrolls, and a bar of silver'. On this reading there is nothing that breaks the pattern which is so religiously followed elsewhere in the Copper Scroll.

Conclusion

Many readings and translations of parts of the Copper Scroll will probably always remain uncertain. In a good number of cases, we can do no more than choose one of a number of possible ways of construing the text. In

73. Beyer, *Die aramäischen Texte*, p. 229.

74. See A. Wolters, 'The Copper Scroll and the Vocabulary of Mishnaic Hebrew', *RevQ* 14 (1990), pp. 483-95 (490). The reading אלת כס<ף> has been accepted by Geza Vermes (see his *The Dead Sea Scrolls in English* [London: Penguin Books, 4th edn, 1995], p. 376) and García Martínez (*Dead Sea Scrolls Translated*, p. 462).

this paper I have argued that careful attention to the palaeographical and literary features of the text yields criteria for recognizing some possible readings as more plausible than others. In many cases where the various editions and translations of the Copper Scroll disagree we are dealing with degrees of relatively low probability. If we are to advance in our understanding of this very difficult text, it is best to refrain from overconfident assertions, and to look instead for ways in which the probability quotient of possible readings can be lowered or raised. This paper seeks to be a contribution toward that end.

Select Bibliography

Copper Scroll References

Allegro, J.M., *The Treasure of the Copper Scroll* (Garden City, NY: Doubleday, 2nd rev. edn, 1964 [1960]).

Baillet, M., J.T. Milik and R. de Vaux, *Les 'petites grottes' de Qumrân* (DJDJ III; Oxford: Clarendon Press, 1962).

Baker, H.W., 'Notes on the Opening of the "Bronze" Scrolls from Qumran', *BJRL* 39 (1956), pp. 45-56.

Beyer, K., *Die aramäischen Texte vom Toten Meer. Ergänzungsband* (Göttingen: Vandenhoeck & Ruprecht, 1994).

García Martínez, F., *The Dead Sea Scrolls Translated: The Qumran Texts in English* (trans. W.G.E. Watson; Leiden: E.J. Brill, 1994). Study Edition, 1997.

Goranson, S., 'Sectarianism, Geography and the Copper Scroll', *JJS* 43 (1992), pp. 282-87.

Kuhn, K.G., 'Les rouleaux de cuivre de Qumrân', *RB* 61 (1954), pp. 193-205.

Lefkovits, J.K., *The Copper Scroll—3Q15: A New Reading, Translation and Commentary* (2 vols.; PhD dissertation, New York University, 1993; printed by UMI Dissertation Services, Ann Arbor, MI, 1994).

— *The Copper Scroll—3Q15: A Reevaluation: A New Reading, Translation and Commentary* (STDJ, 25; Leiden: E.J. Brill, 2000).

Lehmann, M.R., 'Identification of the Copper Scroll Based on its Technical Terms', *RevQ* 5 (1964), pp. 97-105.

— 'Where the Temple Tax Was Buried: The Key to Understanding the Copper Scroll', *BAR* 19 (1993), pp. 38-43.

Lurie, B.-Z., *The Copper Scroll from the Desert of Judah* (Jerusalem: Kiryath Sepher, 1963) (Hebrew).

McCarter, P.K., 'The Mysterious Copper Scroll: Clues to Hidden Temple Treasure?', *BR* 8 (1992), pp. 34-41, 63-64.

— 'Copper Scroll Treasure as an Accumulation of Religious Offerings', in M.O. Wise *et al.* (eds.), *Methods of Investigation of the Dead Sea Scrolls and the Khirbet Qumran Site: Present Realities and Future Prospects* (Annals of the New York Academy of Sciences, 722; New York: New York Academy of Sciences, 1994), pp. 133-48.

Morawiecki, L., 'The Copper Scroll Treasure: A Fantasy or Stock Inventory?', *Qumran Chronicle* 4.3-4 (1994), pp. 169-74.

Muchowski, P., *Zwój miedziany (3Q15): Implikacje spornych kwestii lingwistycznych* (Copper Scroll 3Q15: Implications of the controversial linguistic problems) (International Institute of Ethnolinguistic and Oriental Studies, Monograph Series 4; Poznan, 1993).

Pixner, B. 'Unravelling the Copper Scroll Code: A Study on the Topography of 3Q15', *RevQ* 11 (1983), pp. 323-65 and Plans i-iv.

Puech, É., 'Quelques résultats d'un nouvel examen du Rouleau de Cuivre (3Q15)', *RevQ* 70 (1997), pp. 163-90.

Puech, É., and N. Lacoudre, 'The Mysteries of the "Copper Scroll"', *NEA* 63 (2000), pp. 152-63.

Sarfati, G., '*btkn 'ṣlm*—A Riddle of the Copper Scroll', *Lešonenu* 36 (1971–72), pp. 106-11.

Wise, M.O., 'The Copper Scroll', *Parabola* 19 (1994), pp. 44-52.

Wolters, A., 'The Last Treasure of the Copper Scroll', *JBL* 107 (1988), pp. 419-29.

— 'The Copper Scroll and the Vocabulary of Mishnaic Hebrew', *RevQ* 14 (1990), pp. 483-95.

— 'Literary Analysis and the Copper Scroll', in Z.J. Kapera (ed.), *Intertestamental Essays in Honour of Jósef Tadeusz Milik* (Qumranica Mogilanensia, 6; Kraków: Enigma Press, 1992), pp. 239-52.

— 'History and the Copper Scroll', in M.O. Wise *et al.* (eds.), *Methods of Investigation of the Dead Sea Scrolls and the Khirbet Qumran Site: Present Realities and Future Prospects* (Annals of the New York Academy of Sciences, 722; New York: New York Academy of Sciences, 1994), pp. 285-98.

— *The Copper Scroll: Overview, Text and Translation* (Sheffield: Sheffield Academic Press, 1996).

— 'The Shekinah in the Copper Scroll: A New Reading of 3Q15 12.10', in S.E. Porter and C.A. Evans (eds.), *The Scrolls and the Scriptures: Qumran Fifty Years After* (JSPSup, 26; Roehampton Institute London Papers, 3; Sheffield: Sheffield Academic Press, 1997), pp. 382-91.

— 'The Copper Scroll', in P.W. Flint and J.C. Collins (eds.), *The Dead Sea Scrolls after Fifty Years: A Comprehensive Assessment* (2 vols.; Leiden: E.J. Brill, 1998–99), I, pp. 302-23.

— 'Copper Scroll', in L.H. Schiffman and J.C. VanderKam (eds.), *Encyclopedia of the Dead Sea Scrolls* (2 vols.; Oxford: Oxford University Press, 2000), I, pp. 144-48.

Other Useful References

Brooke, G. (ed.), *Temple Scroll Studies* (JSPSup, 7; Sheffield: JSOT Press, 1989).

Cross, F.M., *The Ancient Library of Qumran and Modern Biblical Studies* (Grand Rapids, MI: Baker Book House, 1980).

Schiffman, L.H. (ed.), *Archaeology and History in the Temple Scroll: The New York University Conference in Memory of Yigael Yadin* (JSPSup, 8; Sheffield: JSOT Press, 1990).

Stegemann, H., *The Library of Qumran: On the Essenes, Qumran, John the Baptist and Jesus* (Grand Rapids: Eerdmans, 1998).

Vaux, R. de, *Archaeology and the Dead Sea Scrolls* (London: The British Academy; Oxford University Press, 1973).

Vermes, G., *The Complete Dead Sea Scrolls* (London: Penguin Books, 1997).

Wise, M., M. Abegg Jr and E. Cook, *The Dead Sea Scrolls: A New Translation* (San Francisco: HarperSanFrancisco, 1996).

INDEX OF COPPER SCROLL REFERENCES

Index of Authors